BOICHI

Dr. Stone received the Shogakukan Manga Award in the Shonen category. Thank you, Inagaki Sensei. My other series, *Origin*, won the Grand Prize in the Manga division at the Japan Media Arts Festival. Thank you everyone, truly. I'll keep doing all I can to live up to these honors.

(Meaning, I'll keep on drawing!)

RIICHIRO INAGAKI

For research purposes, I took a ride in a hot-air balloon! In the lower left of the picture above, you can see a rope tying the balloon down, but during the actual flight, we were unanchored and soaring really high.

The basket was much shorter than I expected, so you really feel like it's just your body that's up in the clouds. It's a bizarre sensation. I recommend it.

Boichi is a Korean-born artist currently living and working in Japan. His previous works include *Sun-Ken Rock* and *Terra Formars Asimov*.

Riichiro Inagaki is a Japanese manga writer from Tokyo. He is the writer for the sports manga series *Eyeshield 21*, which was serialized in *Weekly Shonen Jump*.

Dr. STONE

10

SHONEN JUMP Manga Edition

Story **RIICHIRO INAGAKI**
Art **BOICHI**

Science Consultant/**KURARE** **(with Yakuri Classroom of Doom)**
Translation/**CALEB COOK**
Touch-Up Art & Lettering/**STEPHEN DUTRO**
Design/**JULIAN [JR] ROBINSON**
Editor/**JOHN BAE**

First published in Japan in 2017 by SHUEISHA Inc., Tokyo.
English translation rights arranged by SHUEISHA Inc.

Printed in the U.S.A.

Published by VIZ Media, LLC
P.O. Box 77010
San Francisco, CA 94107

10 9 8 7 6 5 4 3 2 1
First printing, March 2020

Consulted Works:

- Asari, Yoshito, *Uchu e Ikitakute Ekitainenryo Rocket wo DIY Shite Mita (Gakken Rigaku Sensho)*, Gakken Plus, 2013
- Dartnell, Lewis, *The Knowledge: How to Rebuild Civilization in the Aftermath of a Cataclysm*, translated by Erika Togo, Kawade Shobo Shinsha, 2015
- Davies, Barry, *The Complete SAS Survival Manual*, translated by Yoshito Takigawa, Toyo Shorin, 2001
- Jackson, Donald Dale, *The Aeronauts: The Epic of Flight*, translated by Asajiro Nishiyama and Kazuo Oyauchi, Time-Life Books, 1981
- Kazama, Rinpei, *Shinboken Techo (Definitive Edition)*, Shufu to Seikatsusha, 2016
- *Mechanism Encyclopedia*, Edited by Shigeru Ito, Ohmsha, 2013
- McNab, Chris, *Special Forces Survival Guide*, translated by Atsuko Sumi, Hara Shobo, 2016
- Olsen, Larry Dean, *Outdoor Survival Skills*, translated by Katsuji Tani, A&F, 2014
- *Sagara Oil Field: History and Mysterious Origin*, Haibara Public High School Hometown History Research Club, 2018
- Weisman, Alan, *The World Without Us*, Translated by Shinobu Onizawa, Hayakawa Publishing, 2009
- Wiseman, John, *SAS Survival Handbook, Revised Edition*, Translated by Kazuhiro Takahashi and Hitoshi Tomokiyo, Namiki Shobo, 2009

VIZ MEDIA
viz.com

SHONEN JUMP
shonenjump.com

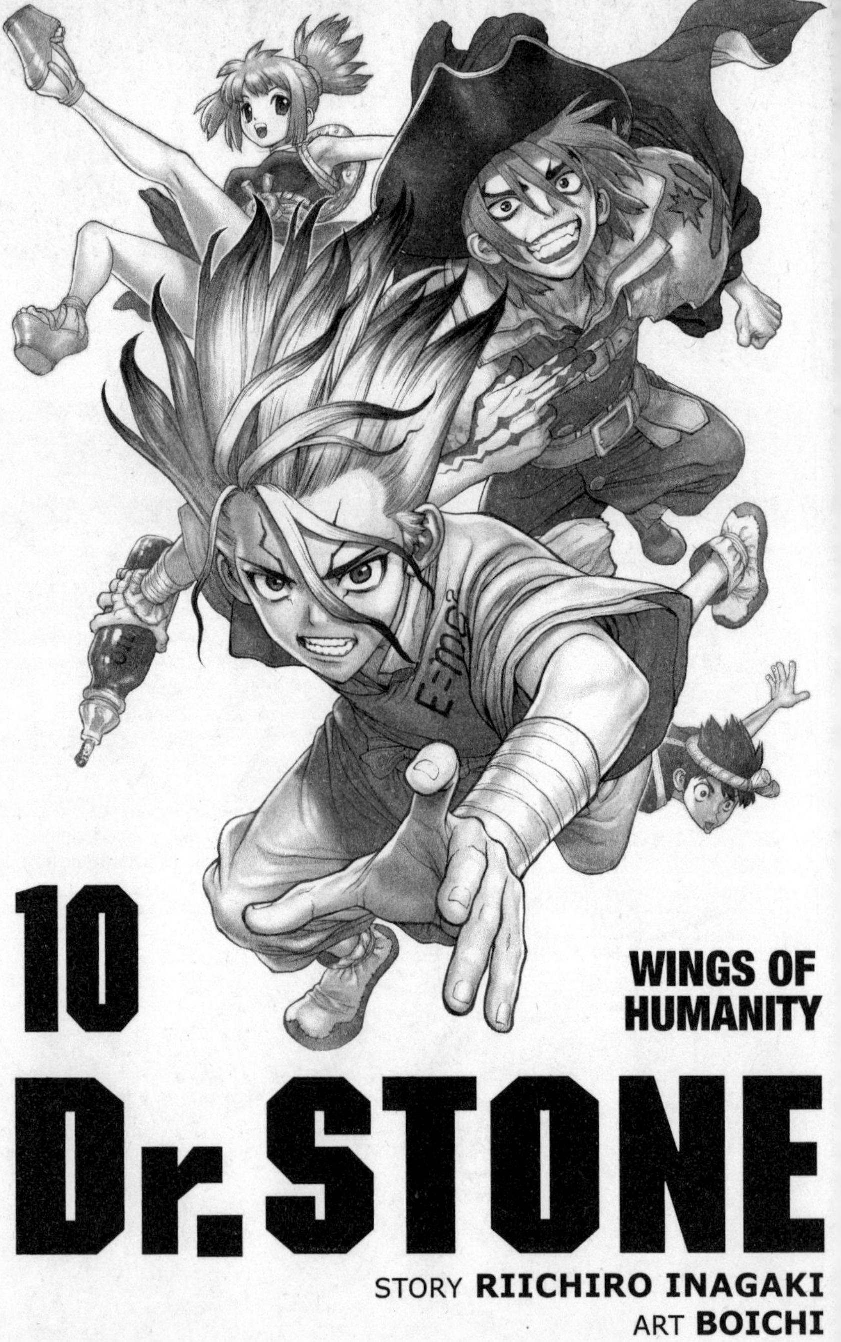
$E=mc^2$

10

WINGS OF HUMANITY

Dr.STONE

STORY **RIICHIRO INAGAKI**
ART **BOICHI**

CHARACTERS

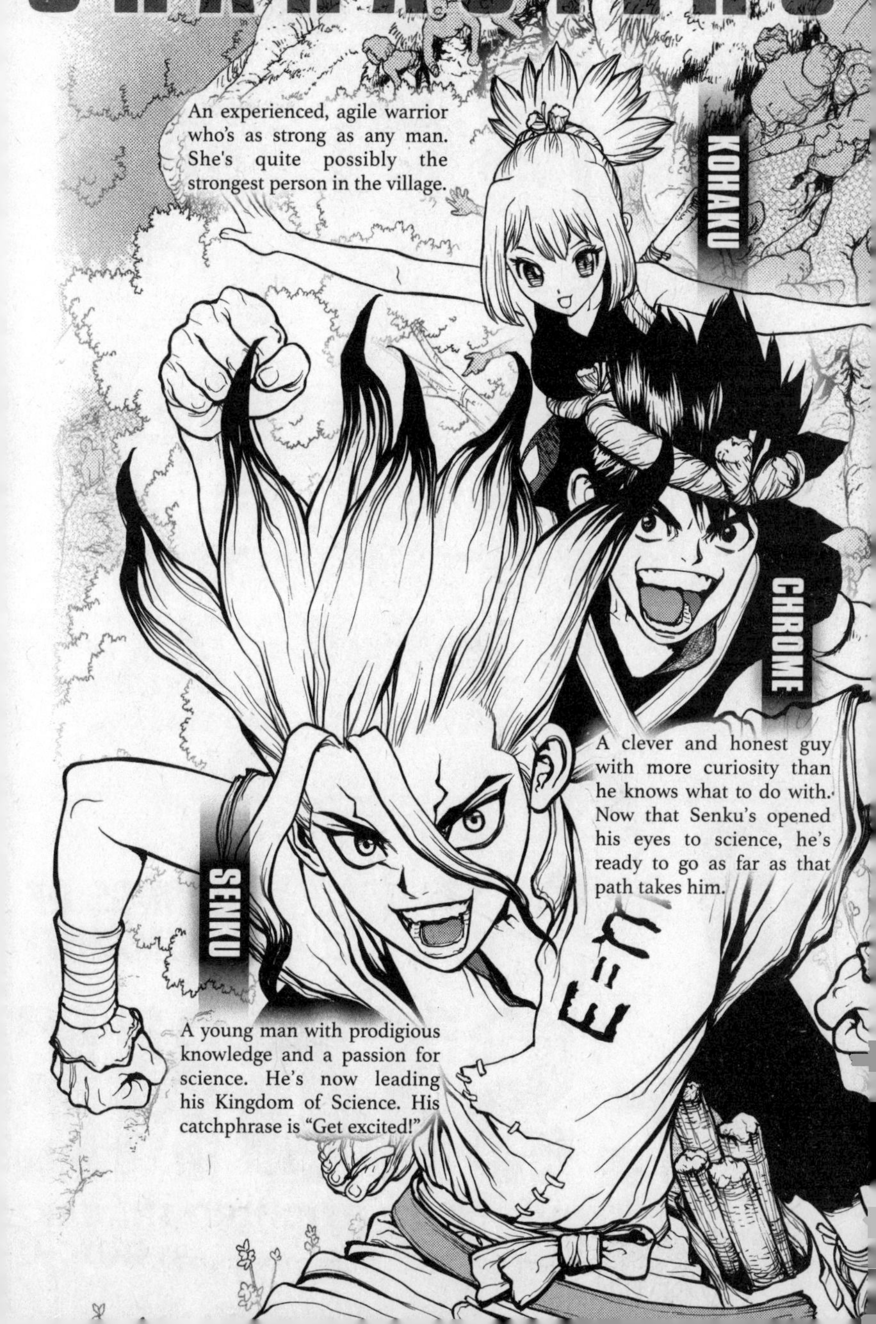

KOHAKU

An experienced, agile warrior who's as strong as any man. She's quite possibly the strongest person in the village.

CHROME

A clever and honest guy with more curiosity than he knows what to do with. Now that Senku's opened his eyes to science, he's ready to go as far as that path takes him.

SENKU

A young man with prodigious knowledge and a passion for science. He's now leading his Kingdom of Science. His catchphrase is "Get excited!"

Dr.STONE

STORY

Every human on earth is turned to stone by a mysterious phenomenon, including high school student Taiju. Nearly 3,700 years later, Taiju awakens and finds his friend Senku, who revived a bit earlier. Together, they vow to restore civilization, but Tsukasa, once considered the strongest high schooler alive, nearly kills Senku in order to put a stop to his scientific plans.

After being secretly revived by his friends, Senku arrives at a village and wins the villagers' trust thanks to his scientific knowledge. But when word of Senku's survival gets back to Tsukasa, the war between the two forces begins!

The Kingdom of Science is now in the final battle against the Tsukasa Empire for the miracle cave! The kingdom's tank gives them an edge, which they parlay into a ceasefire deal with Tsukasa and Hyoga. As part of the agreement, Senku promises to revive Tsukasa's little sister Mirai. However, Tsukasa is stabbed through the chest by the traitorous Hyoga.

YUZURIHA

HYOGA

TSUKASA

UKYO

MIRAI

TAIJU

GEN ASAGIRI

CONTENTS

10
WINGS OF
HUMANITY

Z=80: Humanity's Strongest Tag Team

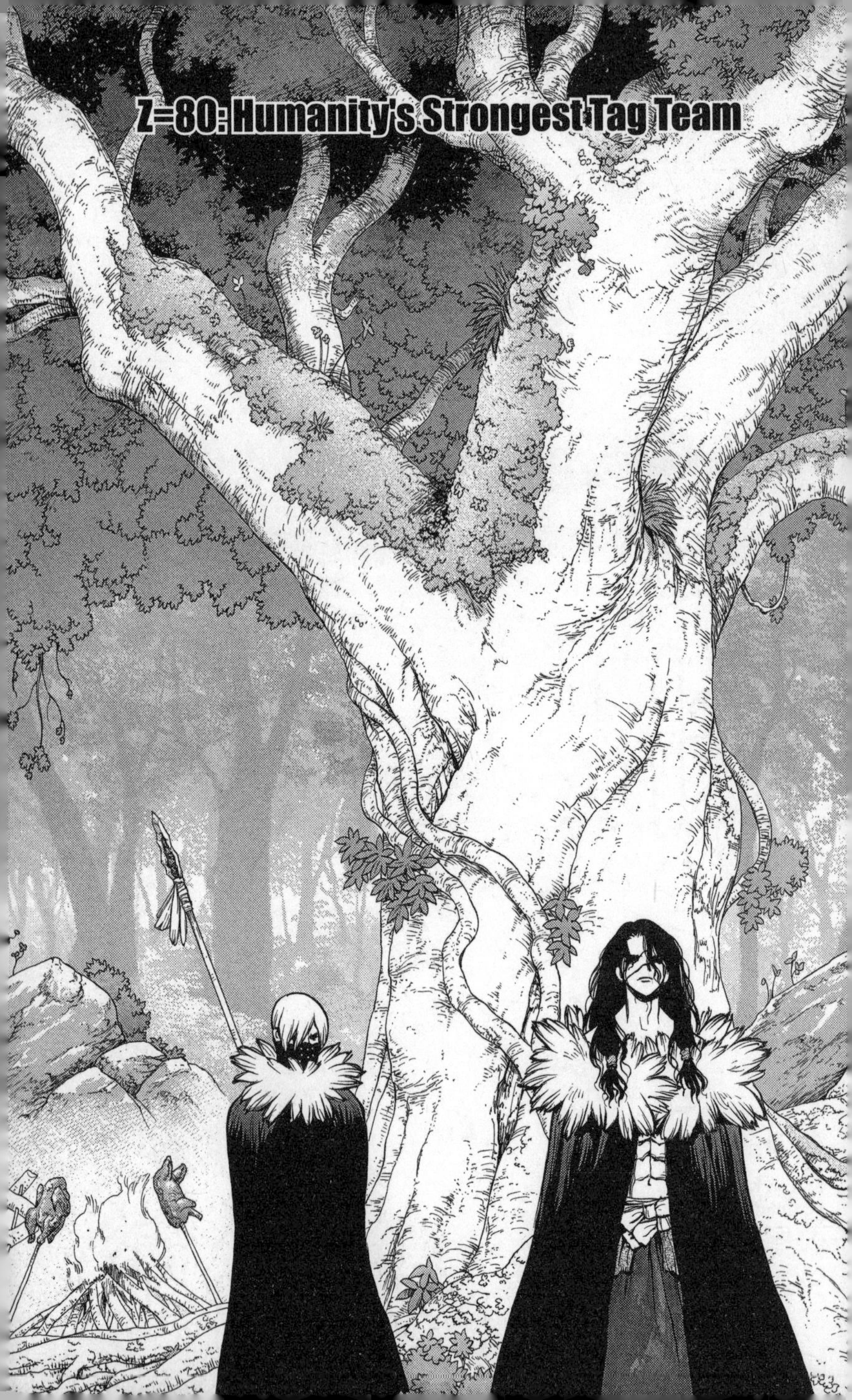

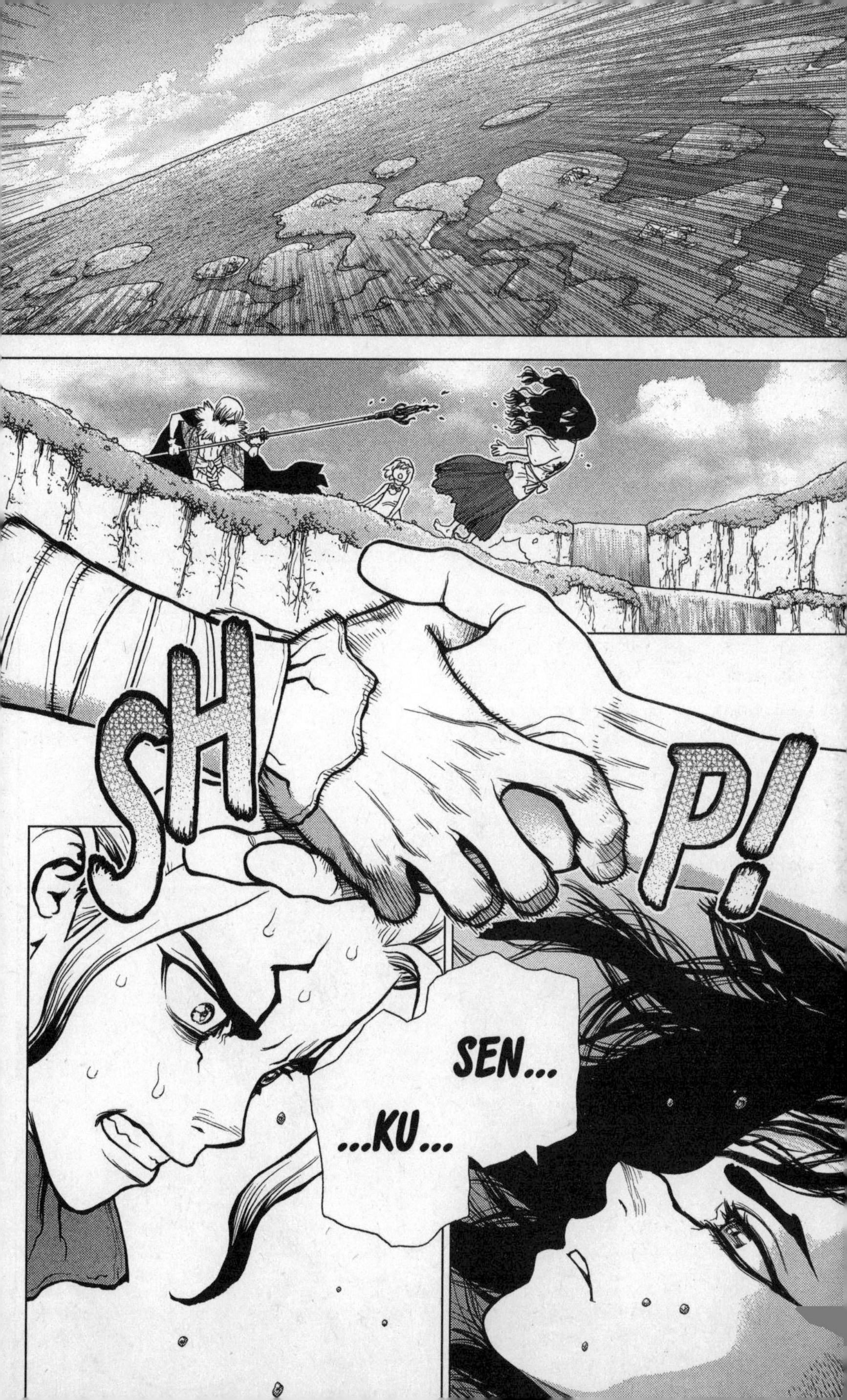
SH...P!
SEN...
...KU...

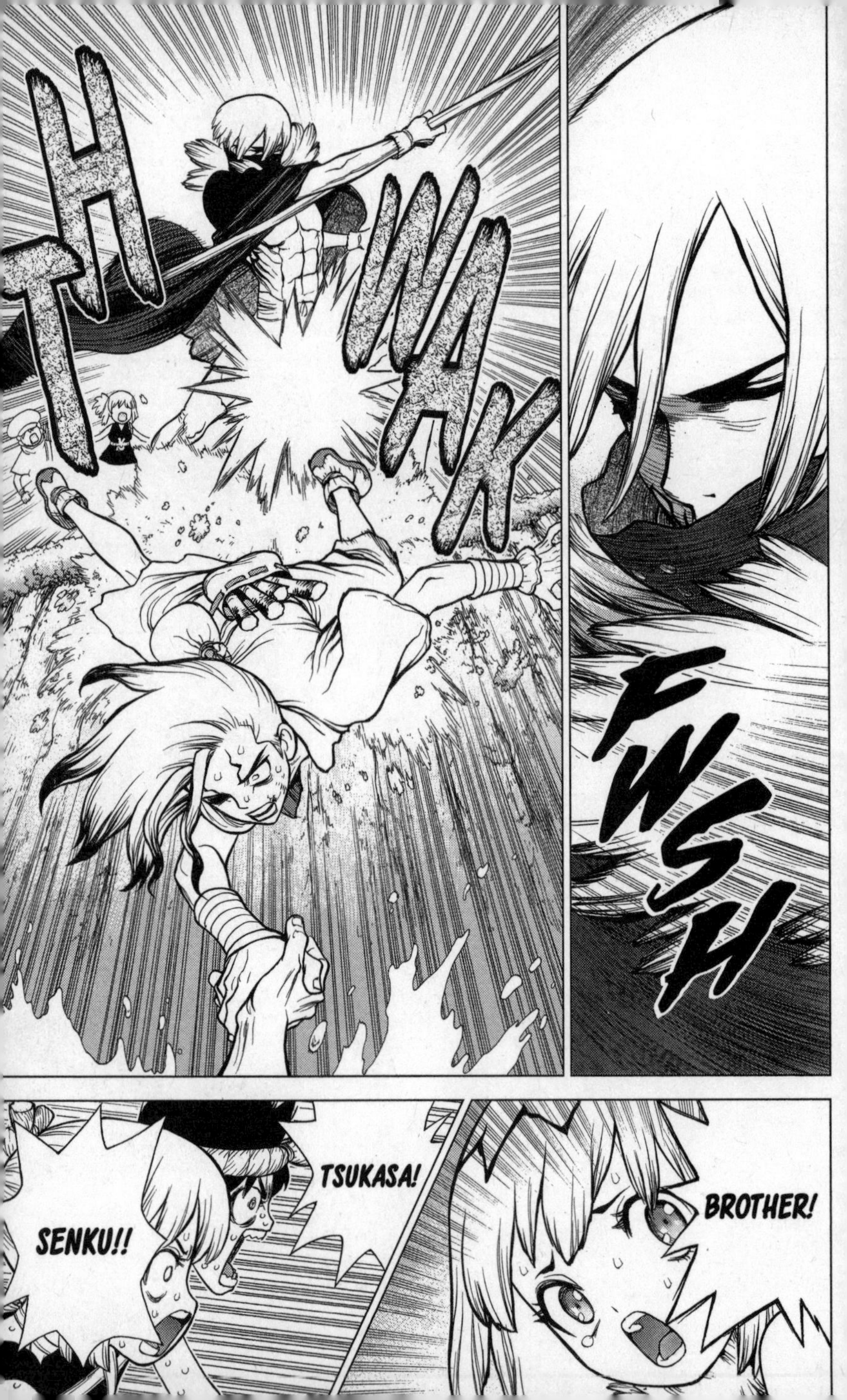
FWSH
THWAK
BROTHER!
TSUKASA!
SENKU!!

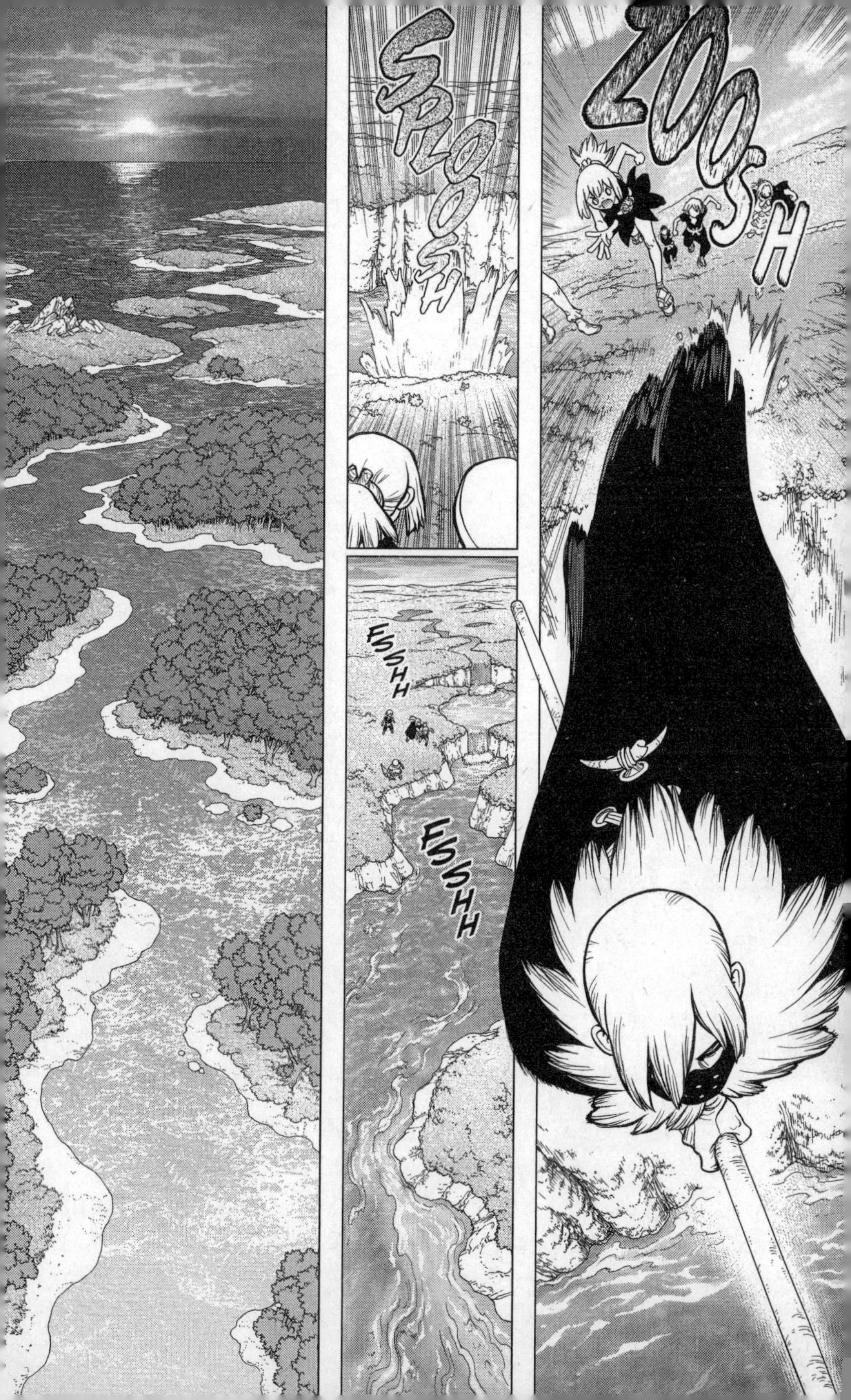
ZOOOSH
SPLOOSH
FSSHH
FSSHH

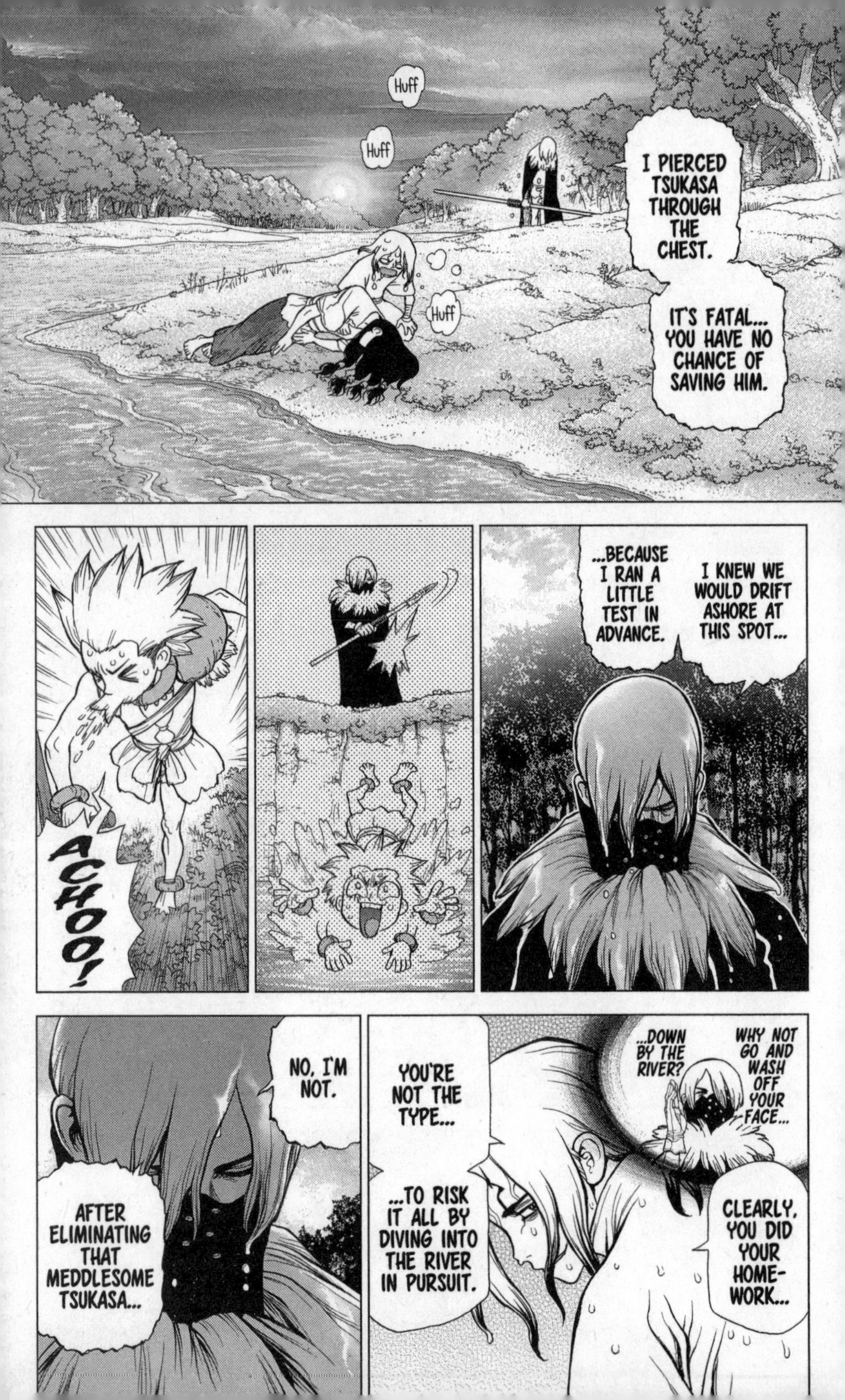

I PIERCED TSUKASA THROUGH THE CHEST.
IT'S FATAL... YOU HAVE NO CHANCE OF SAVING HIM.
Huff
Huff
Huff
I KNEW WE WOULD DRIFT ASHORE AT THIS SPOT...
...BECAUSE I RAN A LITTLE TEST IN ADVANCE.
ACHOO!
WHY NOT GO AND WASH OFF YOUR FACE...
...DOWN BY THE RIVER?
CLEARLY. YOU DID YOUR HOME-WORK...
YOU'RE NOT THE TYPE...
...TO RISK IT ALL BY DIVING INTO THE RIVER IN PURSUIT.
NO, I'M NOT.
AFTER ELIMINATING THAT MEDDLESOME TSUKASA...

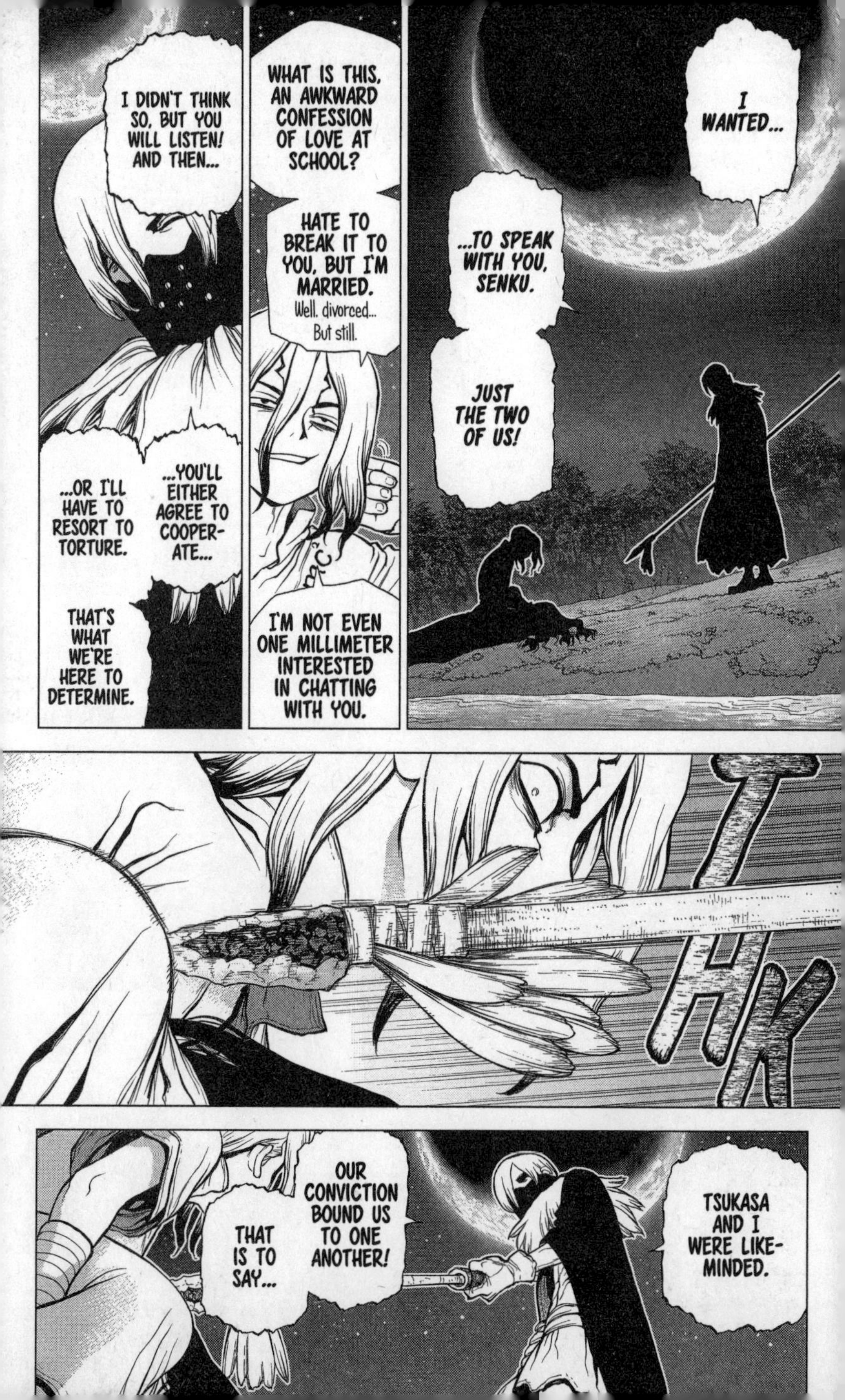
I WANTED...
...TO SPEAK WITH YOU, SENKU.
JUST THE TWO OF US!
WHAT IS THIS, AN AWKWARD CONFESSION OF LOVE AT SCHOOL?
HATE TO BREAK IT TO YOU, BUT I'M MARRIED. Well, divorced... But still.
I'M NOT EVEN ONE MILLIMETER INTERESTED IN CHATTING WITH YOU.
I DIDN'T THINK SO, BUT YOU WILL LISTEN! AND THEN...
...YOU'LL EITHER AGREE TO COOPER-ATE...
...OR I'LL HAVE TO RESORT TO TORTURE.
THAT'S WHAT WE'RE HERE TO DETERMINE.
THK
TSUKASA AND I WERE LIKE-MINDED.
OUR CONVICTION BOUND US TO ONE ANOTHER!
THAT IS TO SAY...

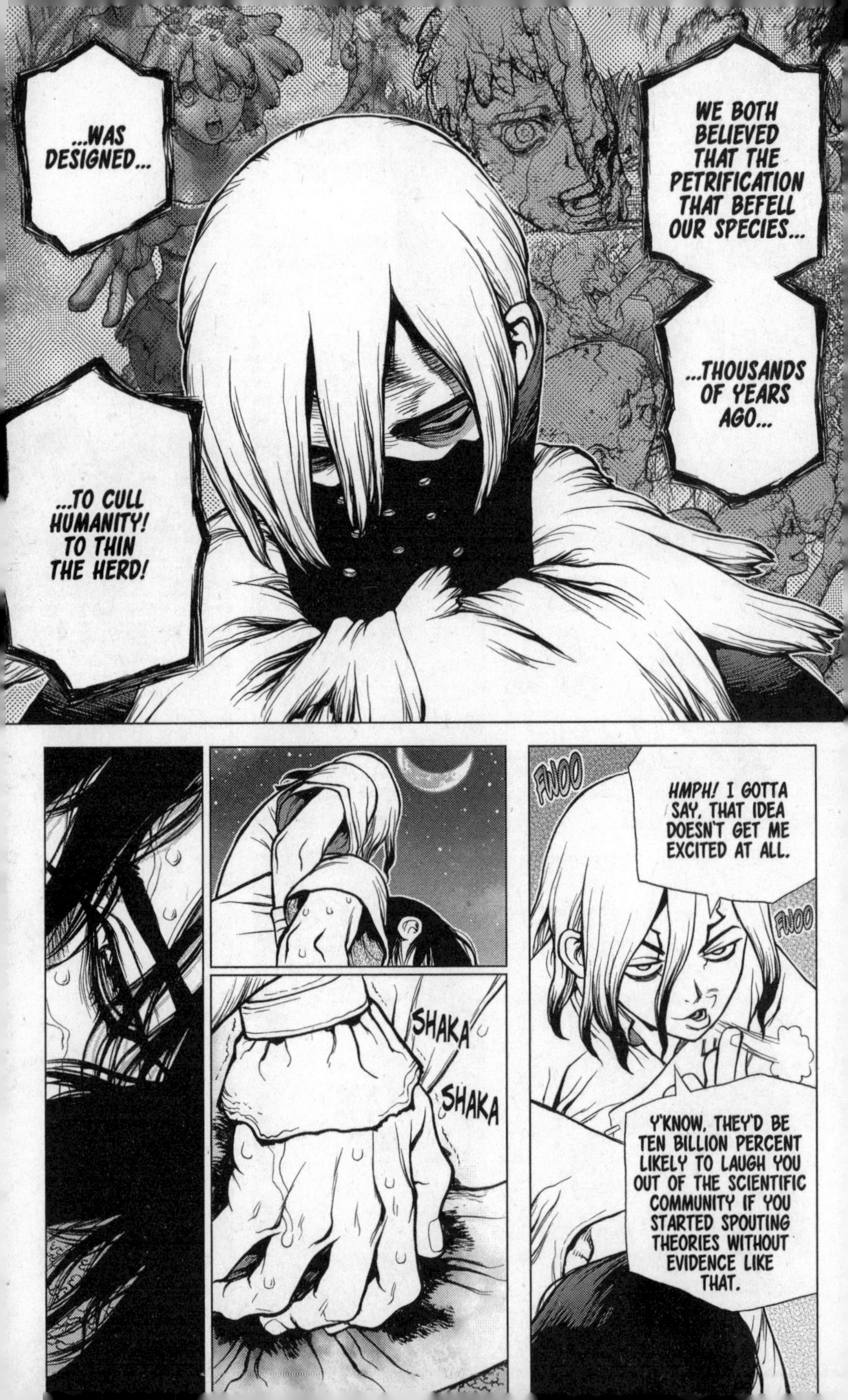
WE BOTH BELIEVED THAT THE PETRIFICATION THAT BEFELL OUR SPECIES...
...THOUSANDS OF YEARS AGO...
...WAS DESIGNED...
...TO CULL HUMANITY! TO THIN THE HERD!
FWOO
HMPH! I GOTTA SAY, THAT IDEA DOESN'T GET ME EXCITED AT ALL.
FWOO
Y'KNOW, THEY'D BE TEN BILLION PERCENT LIKELY TO LAUGH YOU OUT OF THE SCIENTIFIC COMMUNITY IF YOU STARTED SPOUTING THEORIES WITHOUT EVIDENCE LIKE THAT.
SHAKA
SHAKA

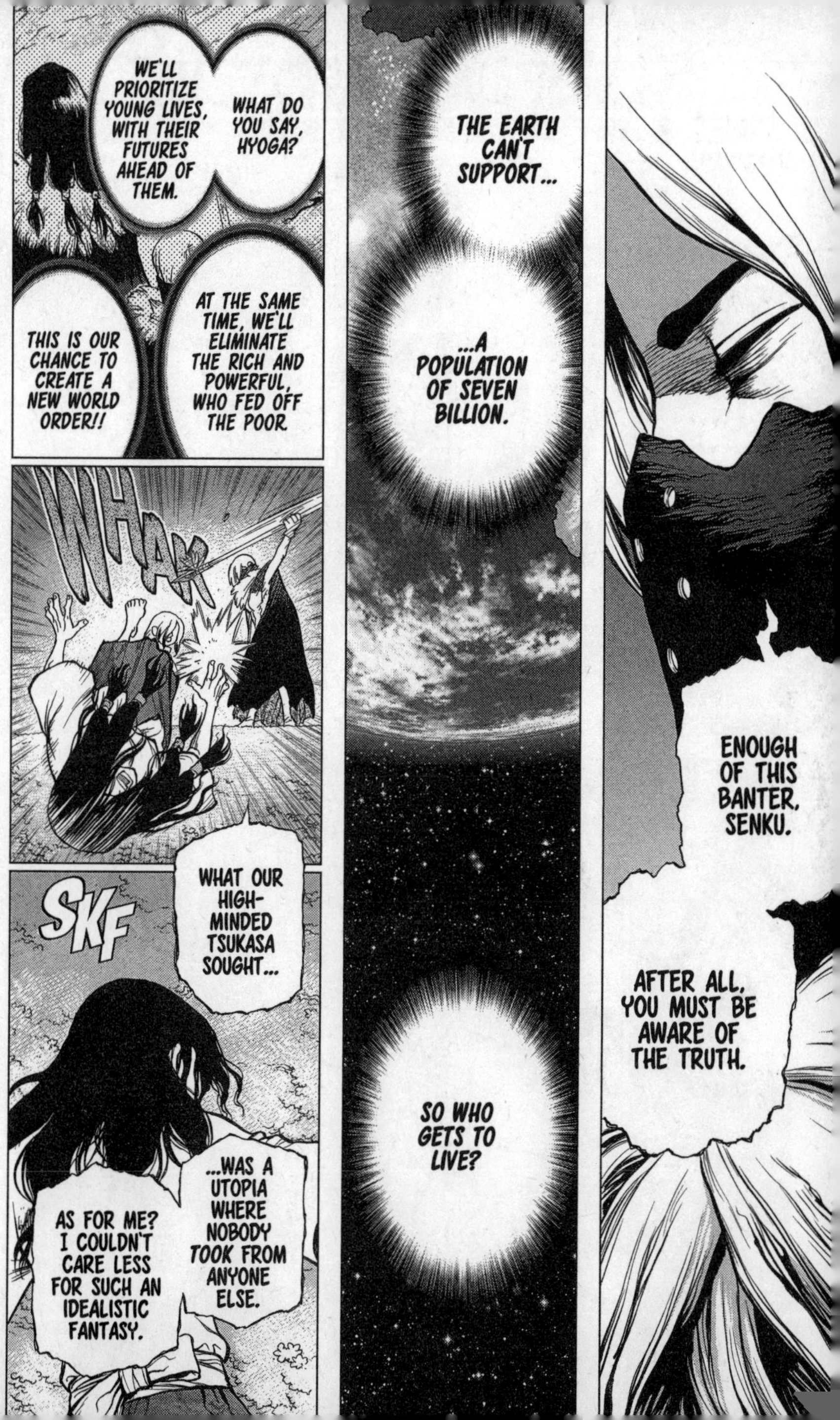
ENOUGH OF THIS BANTER, SENKU.
AFTER ALL, YOU MUST BE AWARE OF THE TRUTH.
THE EARTH CAN'T SUPPORT...
...A POPULATION OF SEVEN BILLION.
SO WHO GETS TO LIVE?
WHAT DO YOU SAY, HYOGA?
WE'LL PRIORITIZE YOUNG LIVES, WITH THEIR FUTURES AHEAD OF THEM.
AT THE SAME TIME, WE'LL ELIMINATE THE RICH AND POWERFUL, WHO FED OFF THE POOR.
THIS IS OUR CHANCE TO CREATE A NEW WORLD ORDER!!
WHAK
SKF
WHAT OUR HIGH-MINDED TSUKASA SOUGHT...
...WAS A UTOPIA WHERE NOBODY TOOK FROM ANYONE ELSE.
AS FOR ME? I COULDN'T CARE LESS FOR SUCH AN IDEALISTIC FANTASY.

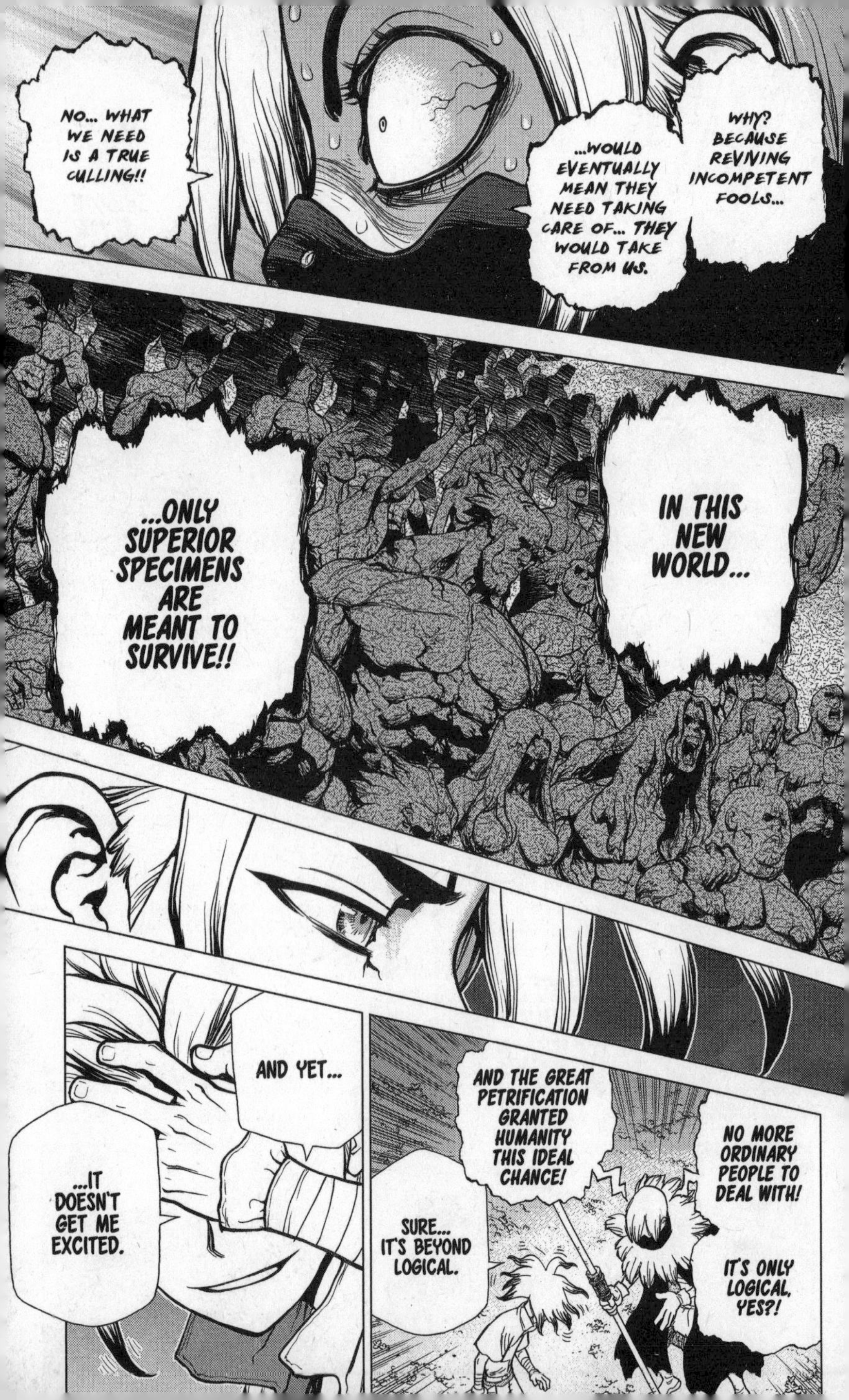
WHY? BECAUSE REVIVING INCOMPETENT FOOLS...
...WOULD EVENTUALLY MEAN THEY NEED TAKING CARE OF... THEY WOULD TAKE FROM US.
NO... WHAT WE NEED IS A TRUE CULLING!!
IN THIS NEW WORLD...
...ONLY SUPERIOR SPECIMENS ARE MEANT TO SURVIVE!!
NO MORE ORDINARY PEOPLE TO DEAL WITH!
AND THE GREAT PETRIFICATION GRANTED HUMANITY THIS IDEAL CHANCE!
IT'S ONLY LOGICAL, YES?!
SURE... IT'S BEYOND LOGICAL.
AND YET...
...IT DOESN'T GET ME EXCITED.

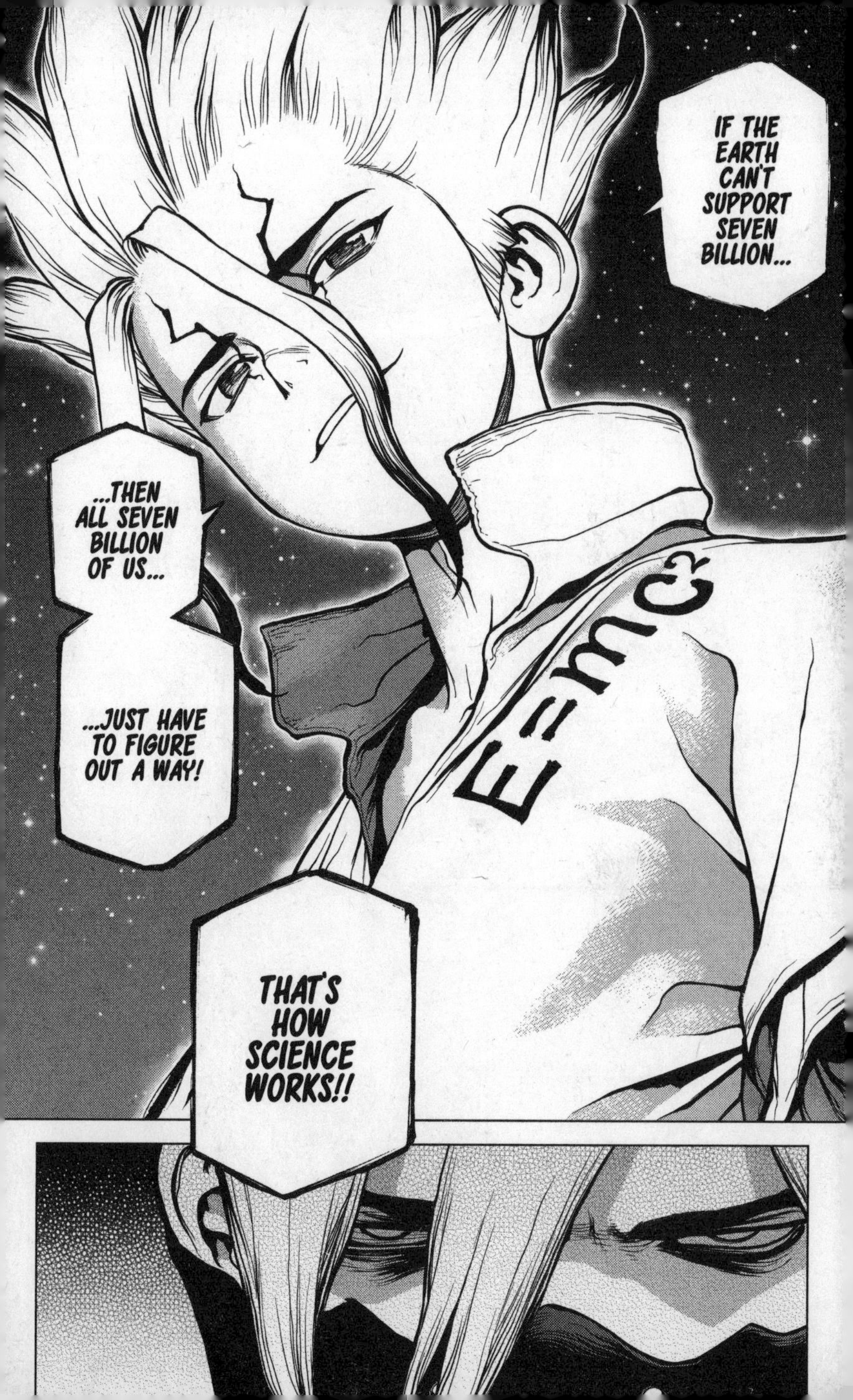
IF THE EARTH CAN'T SUPPORT SEVEN BILLION...
$E=mc^2$
...THEN ALL SEVEN BILLION OF US...
...JUST HAVE TO FIGURE OUT A WAY!
THAT'S HOW SCIENCE WORKS!!

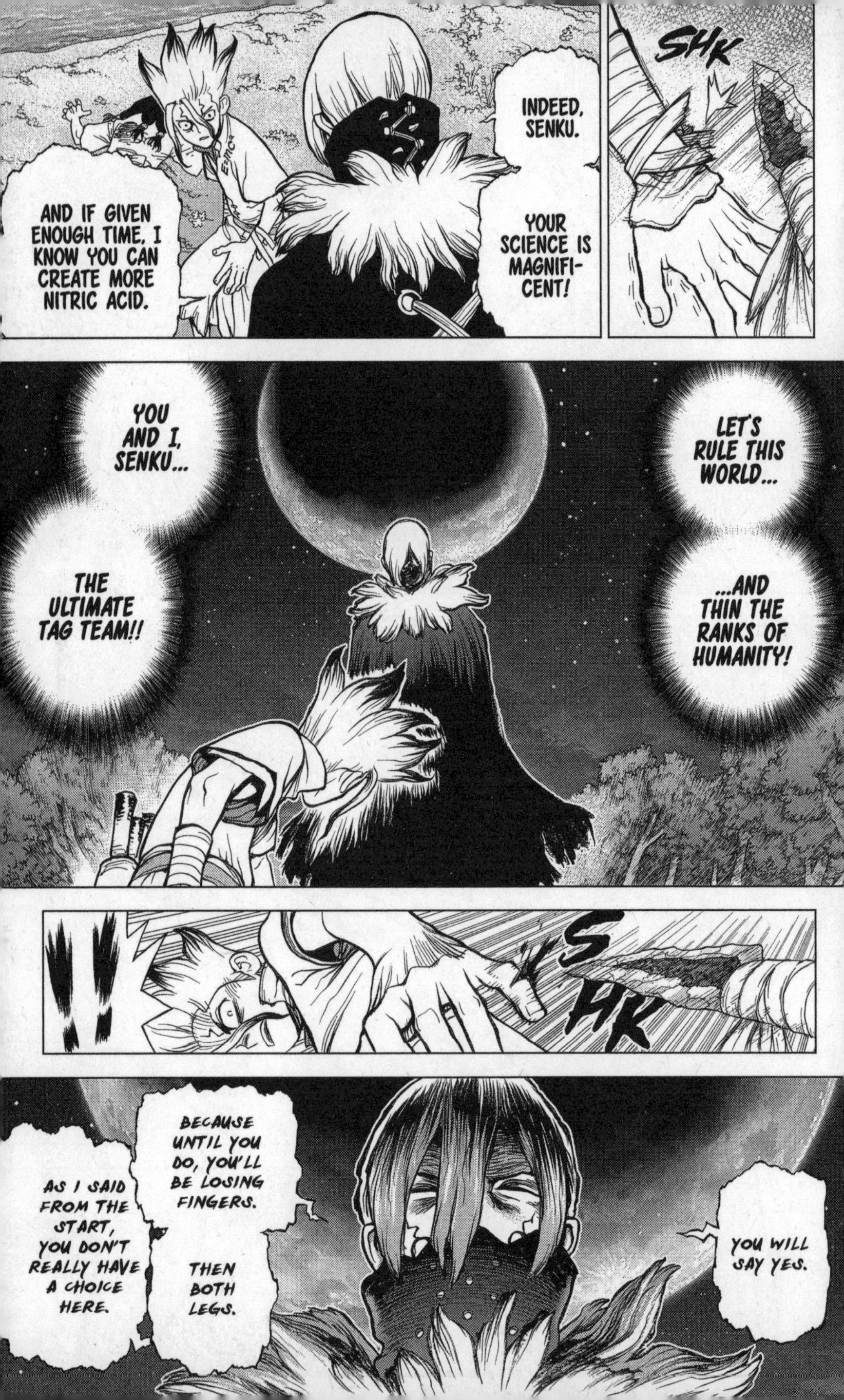

SHK
INDEED, SENKU.
YOUR SCIENCE IS MAGNIFICENT!
AND IF GIVEN ENOUGH TIME, I KNOW YOU CAN CREATE MORE NITRIC ACID.
LET'S RULE THIS WORLD...
...AND THIN THE RANKS OF HUMANITY!
YOU AND I, SENKU...
THE ULTIMATE TAG TEAM!!
SHK
!!
YOU WILL SAY YES.
BECAUSE UNTIL YOU DO, YOU'LL BE LOSING FINGERS.
THEN BOTH LEGS.
AS I SAID FROM THE START, YOU DON'T REALLY HAVE A CHOICE HERE.

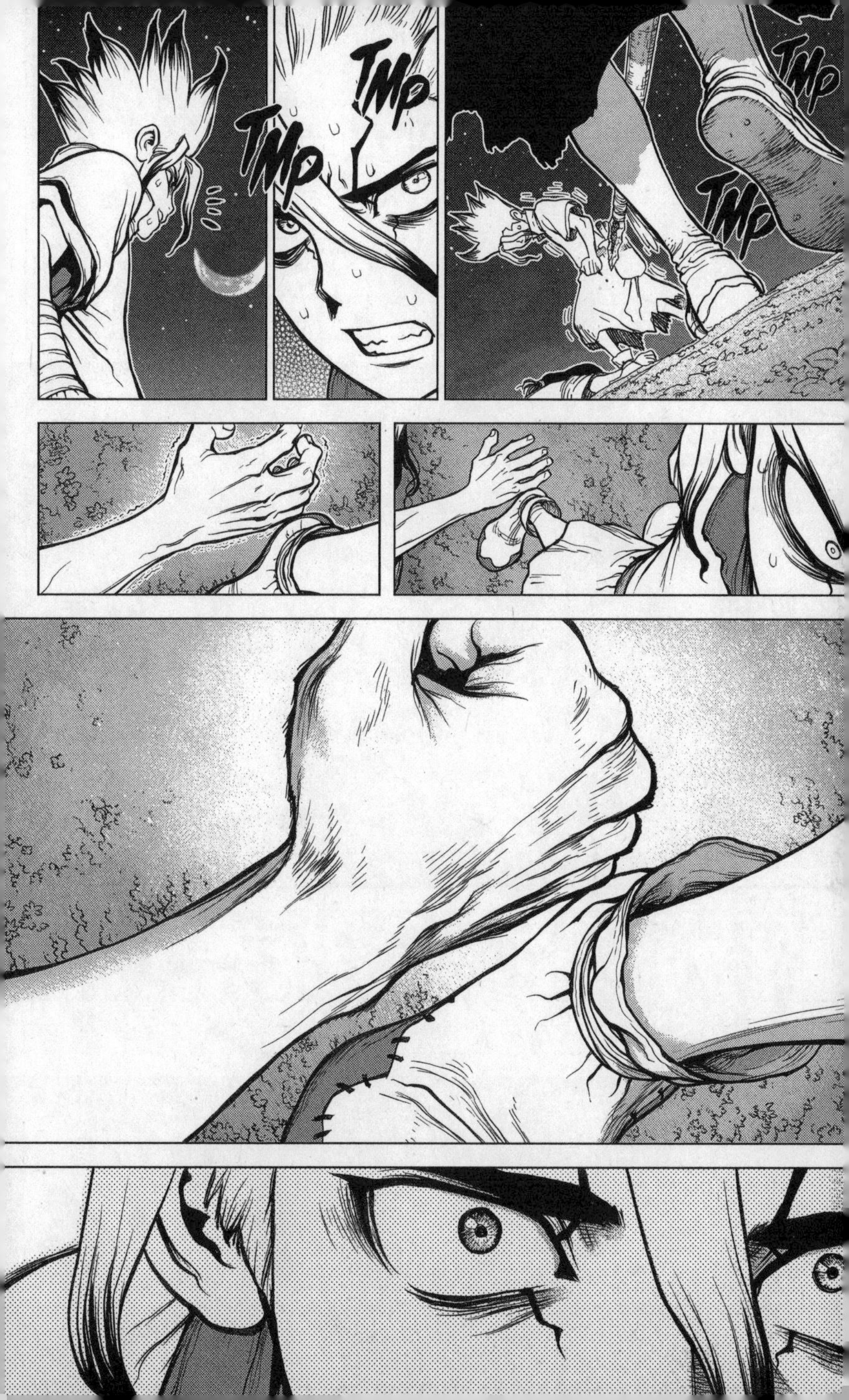
TMP
TMP
TMP
TMP

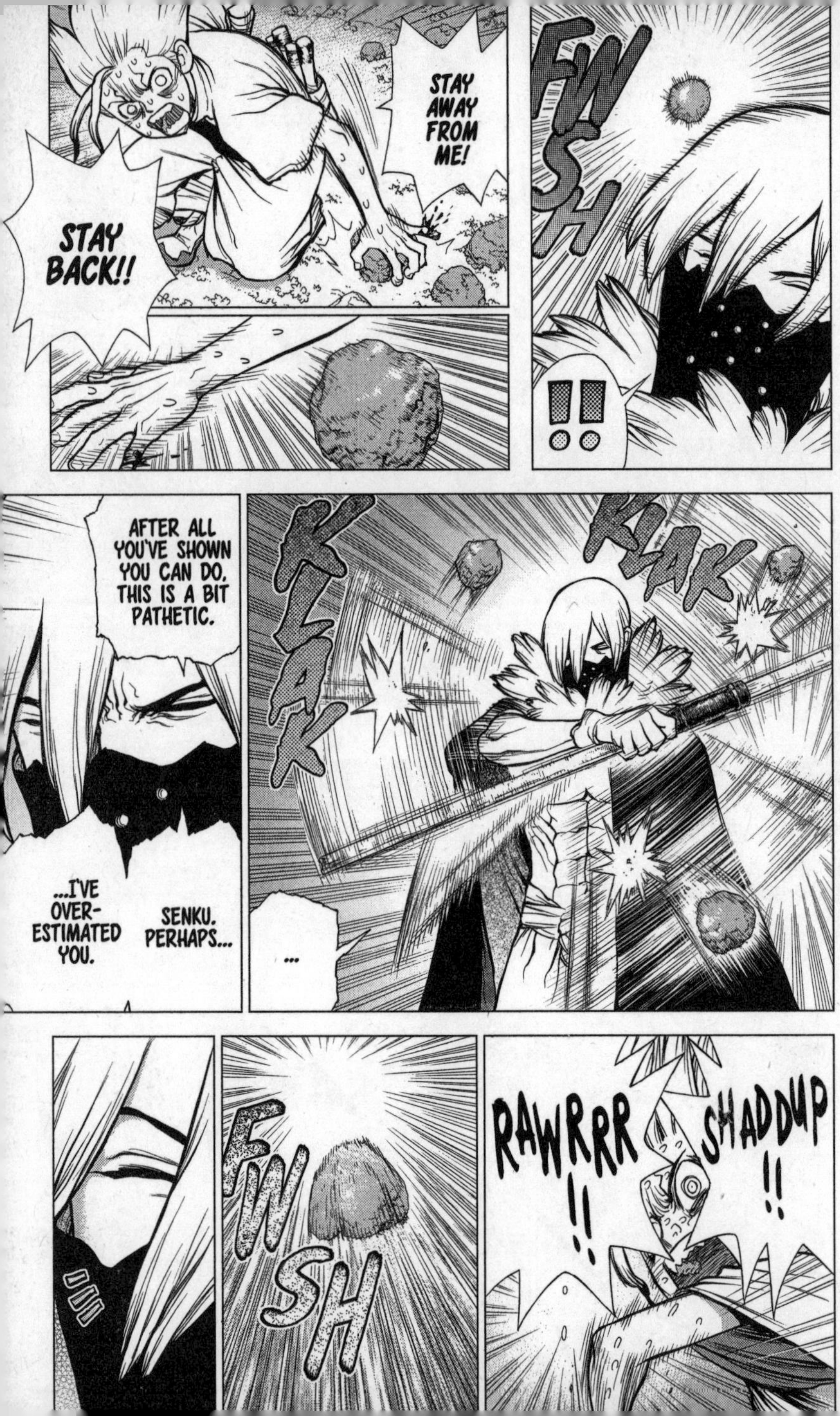

FWSH
!!
STAY AWAY FROM ME!
STAY BACK!!
KLAK
KLAK
...
AFTER ALL YOU'VE SHOWN YOU CAN DO, THIS IS A BIT PATHETIC.
SENKU. PERHAPS...
...I'VE OVER-ESTIMATED YOU.
SHADDUP!!
RAWRRR!!
FWSH

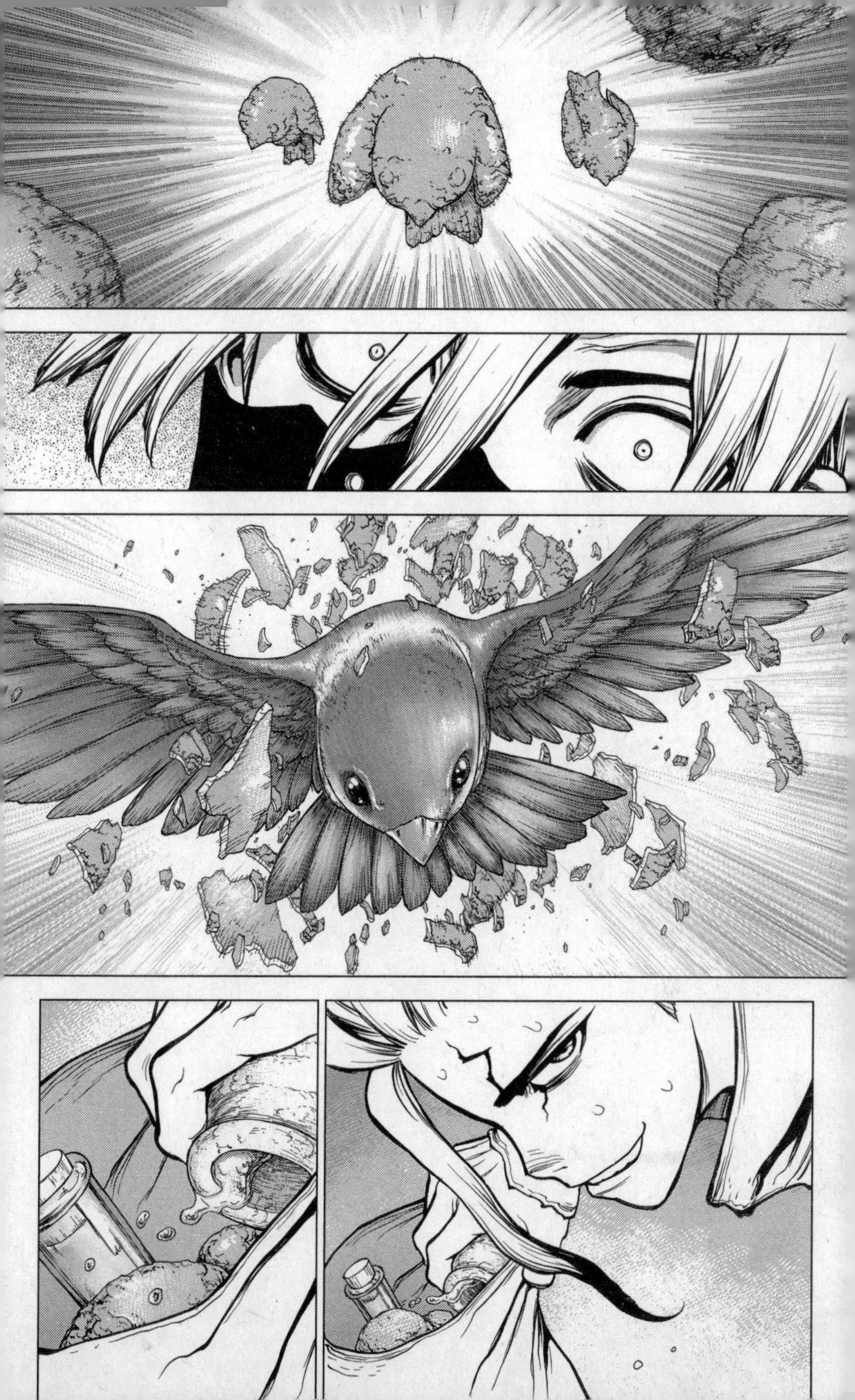

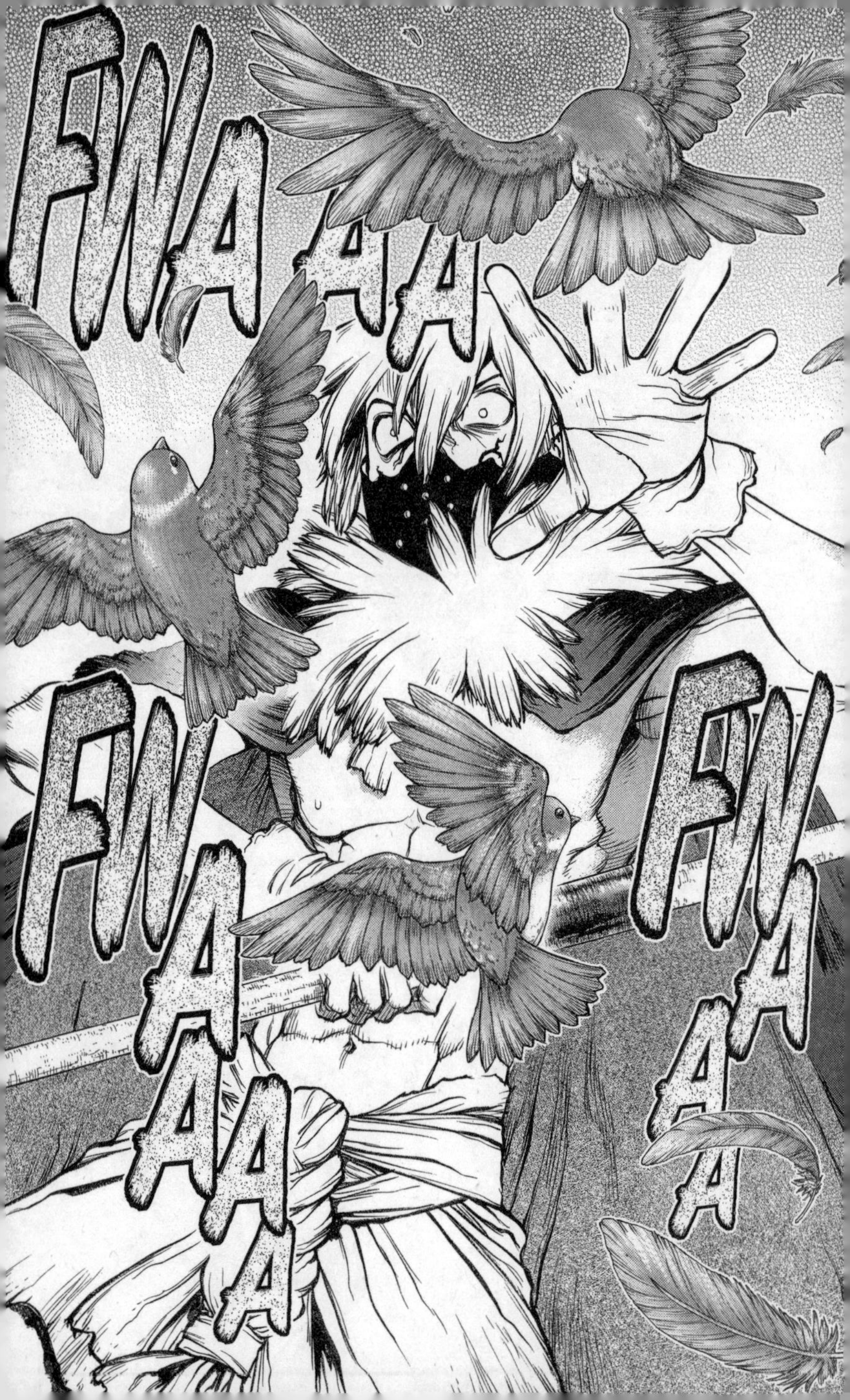
FWAAA
FWAAAA
FWAAAAA

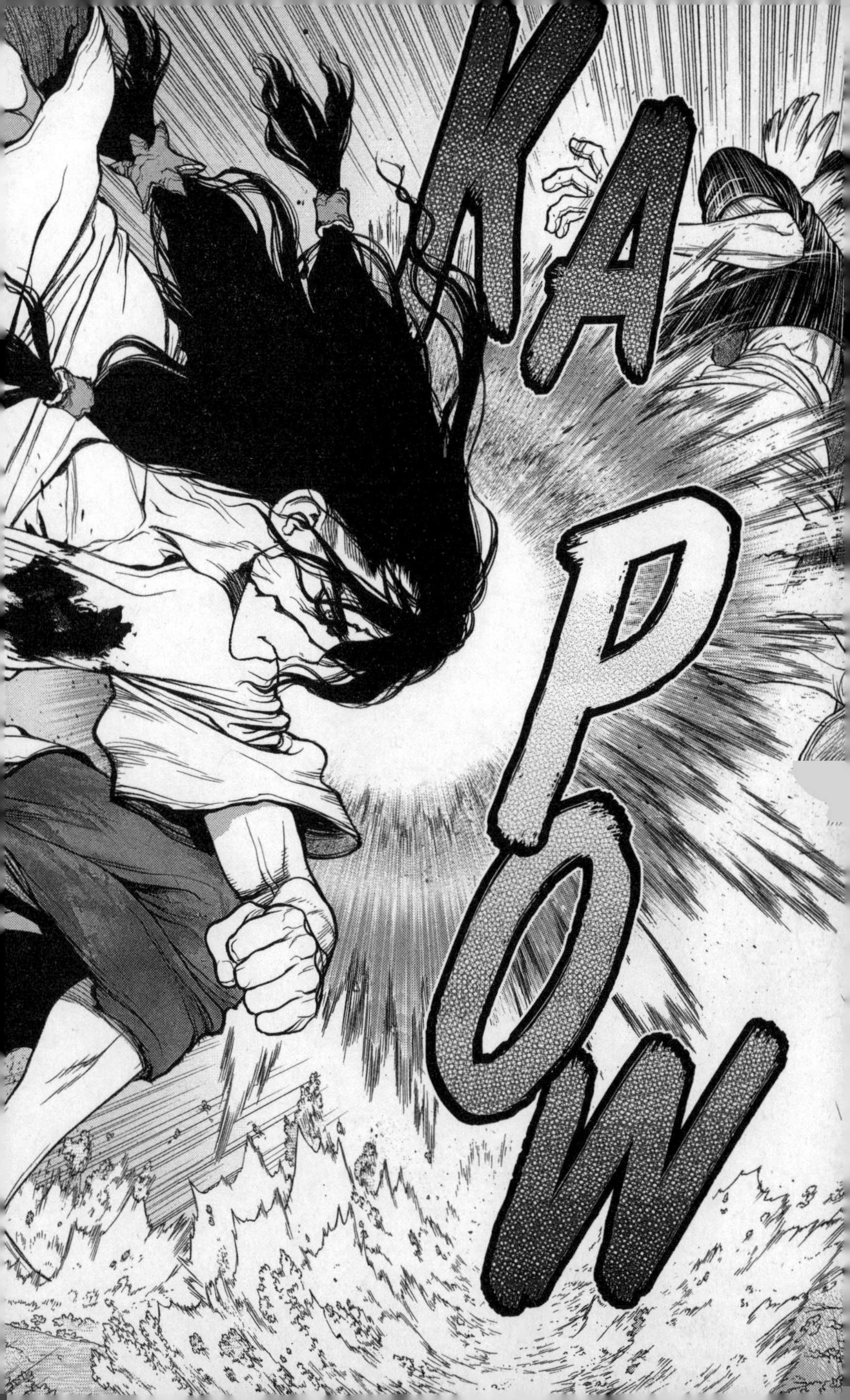
KAPOW

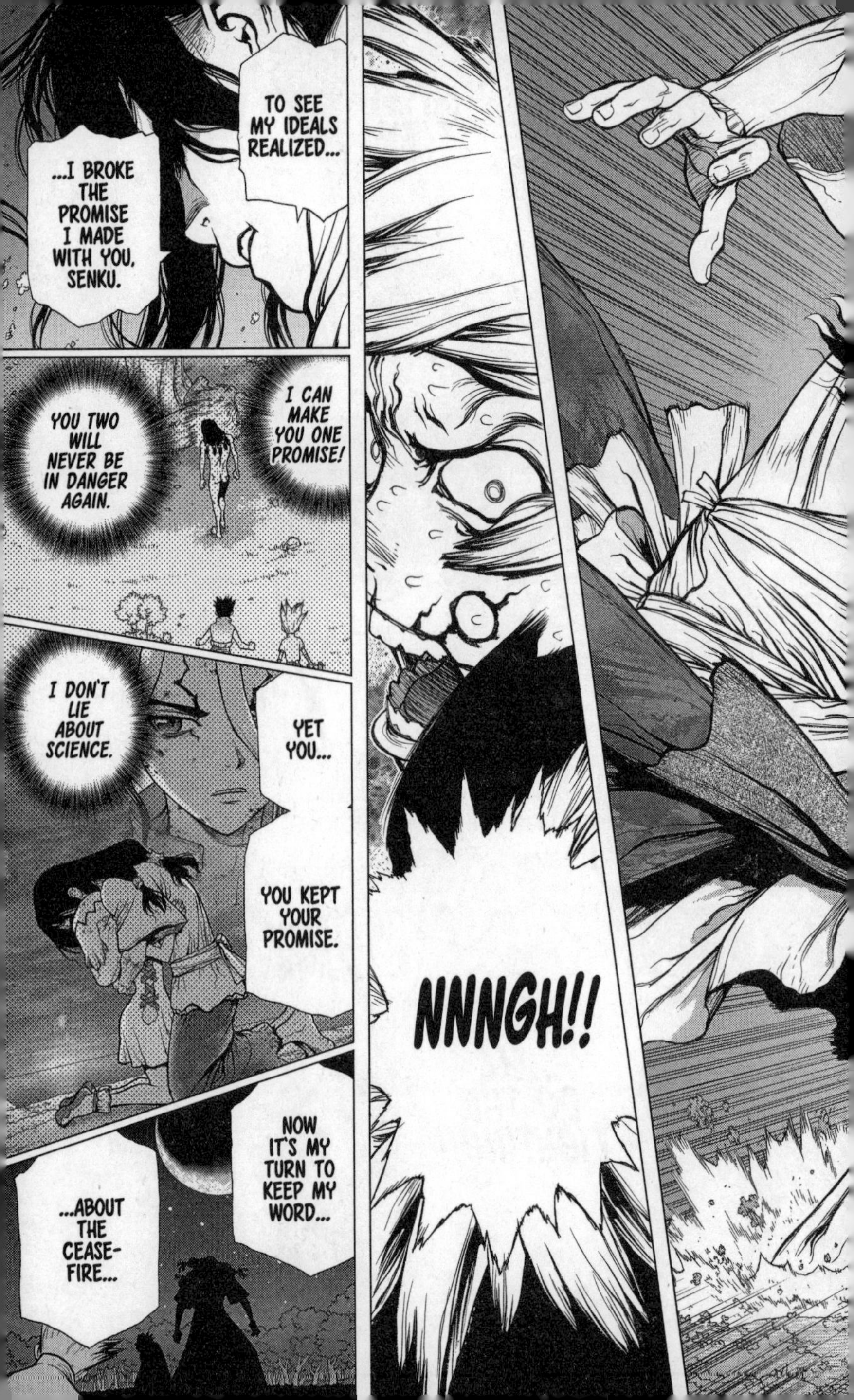
NNNGH!!
TO SEE MY IDEALS REALIZED...
...I BROKE THE PROMISE I MADE WITH YOU, SENKU.
I CAN MAKE YOU ONE PROMISE!
YOU TWO WILL NEVER BE IN DANGER AGAIN.
I DON'T LIE ABOUT SCIENCE.
YET YOU...
YOU KEPT YOUR PROMISE.
NOW IT'S MY TURN TO KEEP MY WORD...
...ABOUT THE CEASE-FIRE...

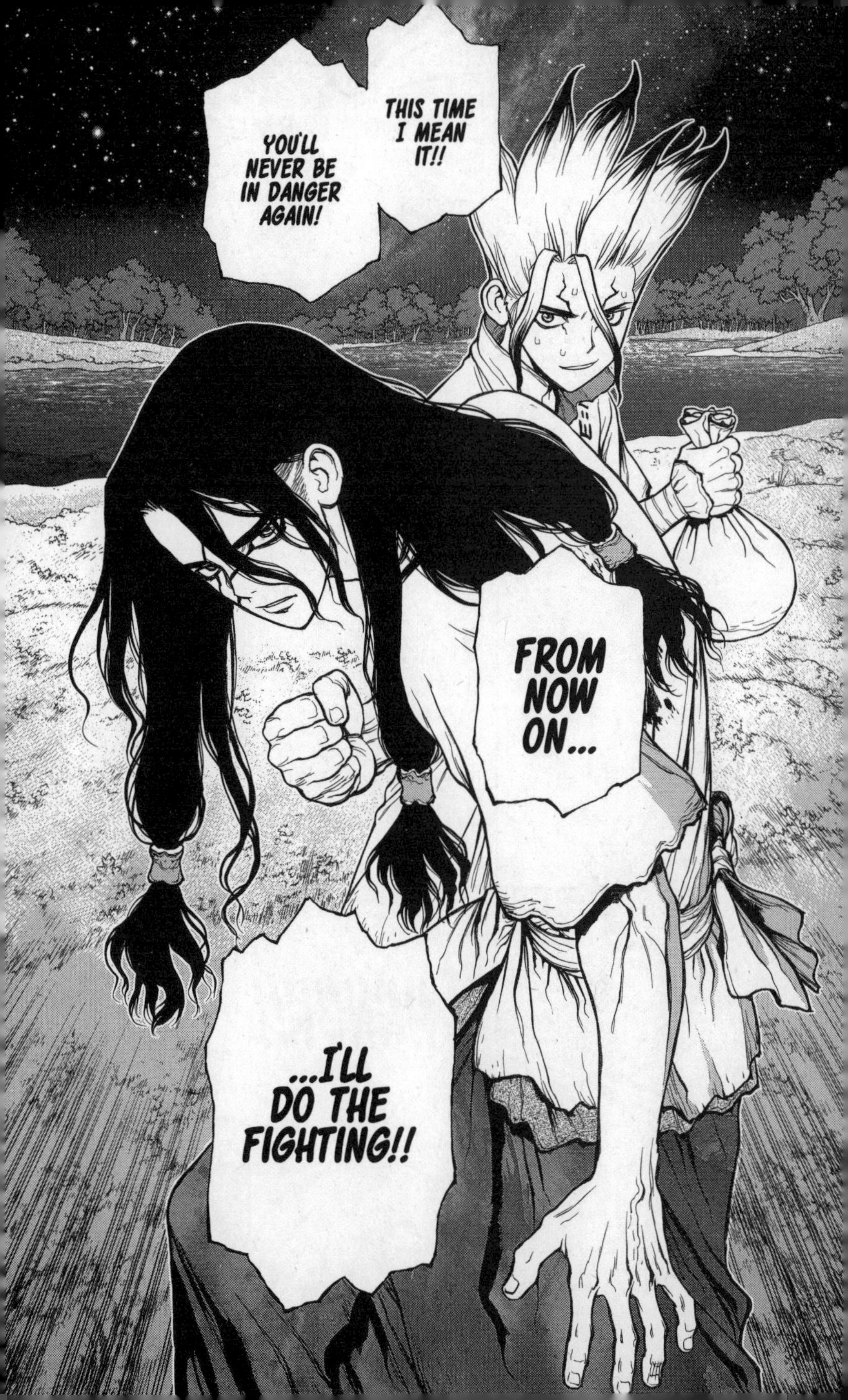
THIS TIME I MEAN IT!!
YOU'LL NEVER BE IN DANGER AGAIN!
FROM NOW ON...
...I'LL DO THE FIGHTING!!

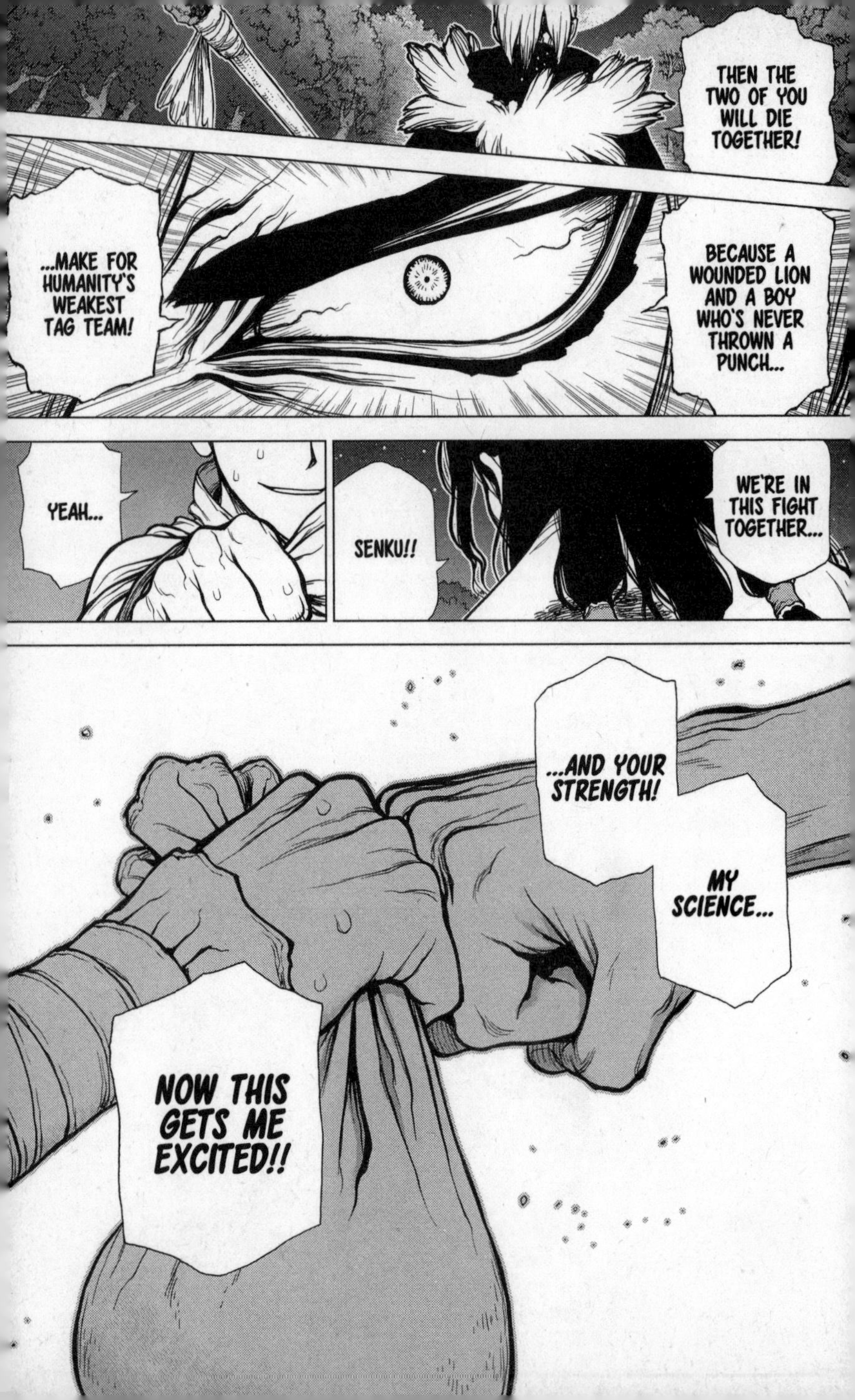
THEN THE TWO OF YOU WILL DIE TOGETHER!
BECAUSE A WOUNDED LION AND A BOY WHO'S NEVER THROWN A PUNCH...
...MAKE FOR HUMANITY'S WEAKEST TAG TEAM!
WE'RE IN THIS FIGHT TOGETHER...
SENKU!!
YEAH...
MY SCIENCE...
...AND YOUR STRENGTH!
NOW THIS GETS ME EXCITED!!

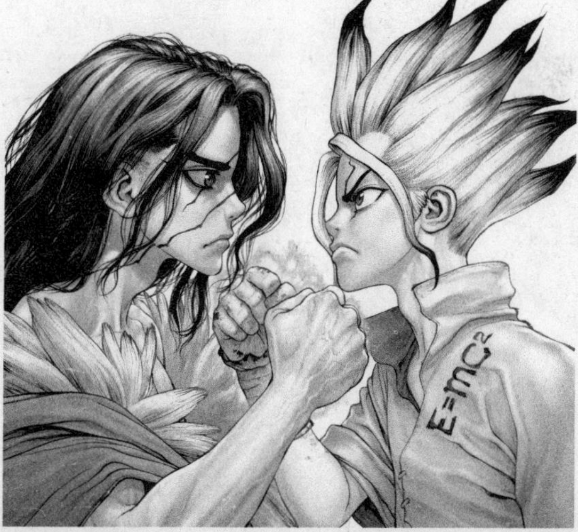
E=MC²

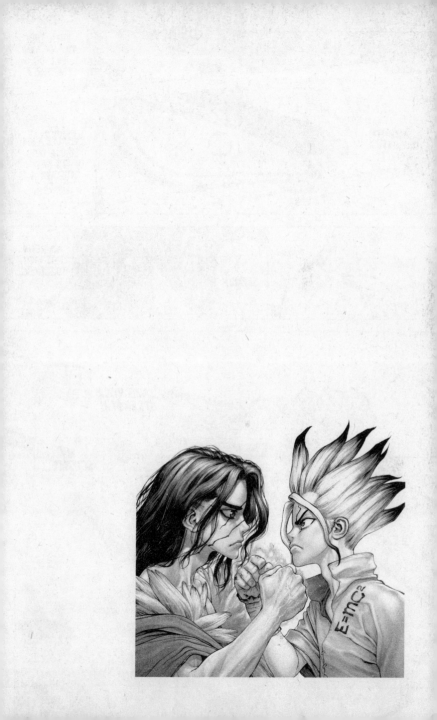

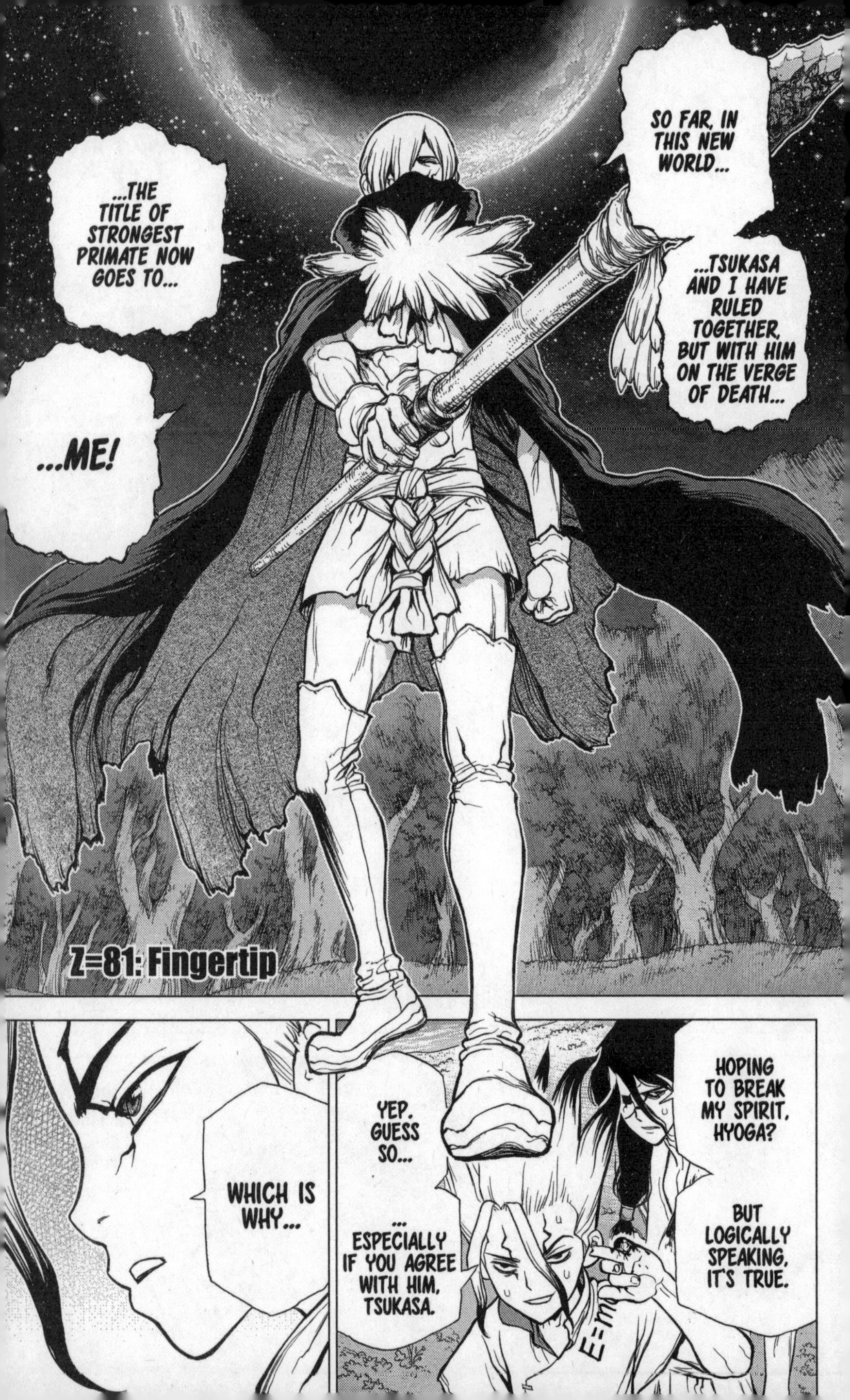
SO FAR, IN THIS NEW WORLD...
...TSUKASA AND I HAVE RULED TOGETHER, BUT WITH HIM ON THE VERGE OF DEATH...
...THE TITLE OF STRONGEST PRIMATE NOW GOES TO...
...ME!
Z=81: Fingertip
HOPING TO BREAK MY SPIRIT, HYOGA?
BUT LOGICALLY SPEAKING, IT'S TRUE.
YEP. GUESS SO...
...ESPECIALLY IF YOU AGREE WITH HIM, TSUKASA.
WHICH IS WHY...

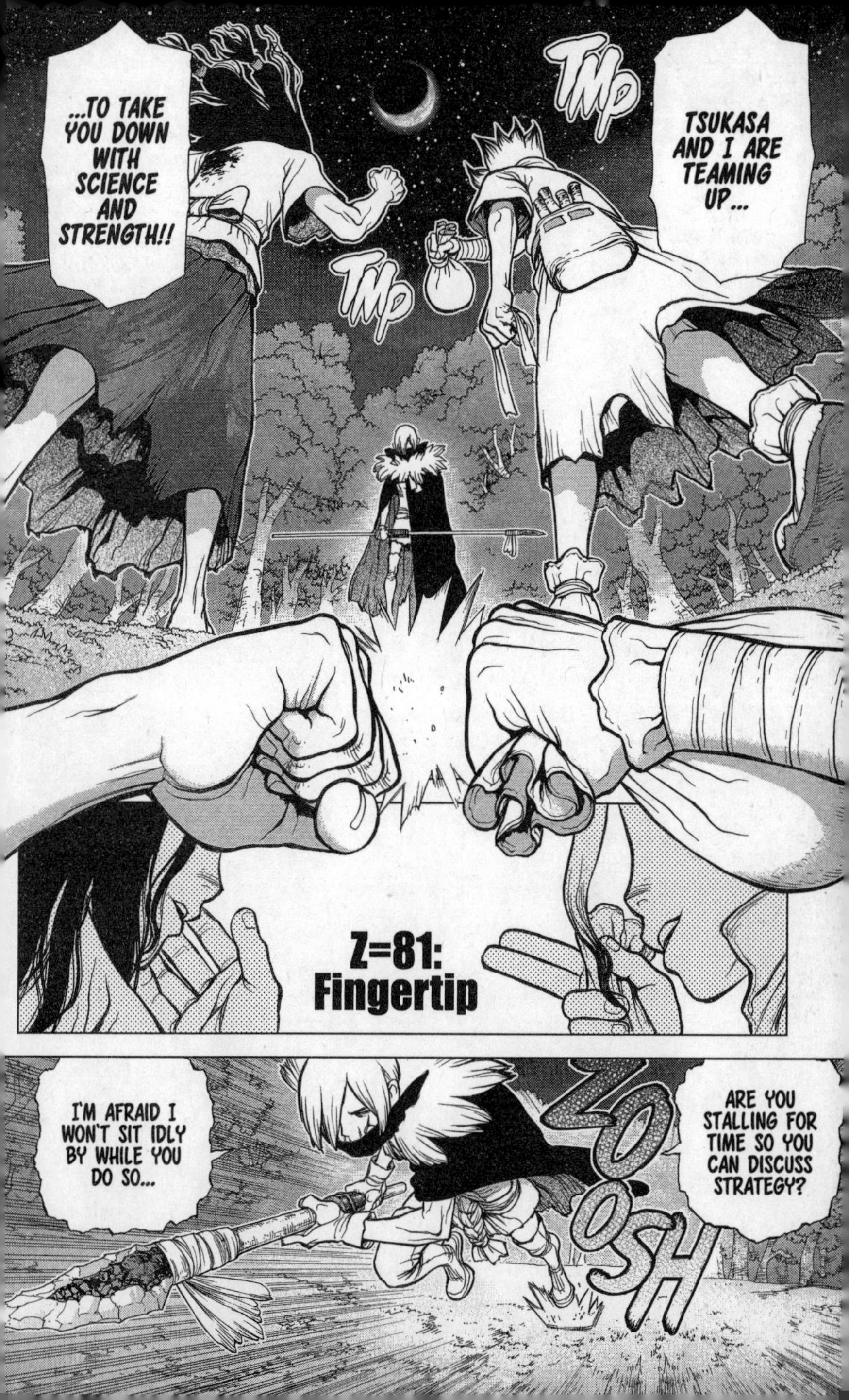
TSUKASA AND I ARE TEAMING UP...
TMP
TMP
...TO TAKE YOU DOWN WITH SCIENCE AND STRENGTH!!
Z=81: Fingertip
ARE YOU STALLING FOR TIME SO YOU CAN DISCUSS STRATEGY?
ZOOSH
I'M AFRAID I WON'T SIT IDLY BY WHILE YOU DO SO...

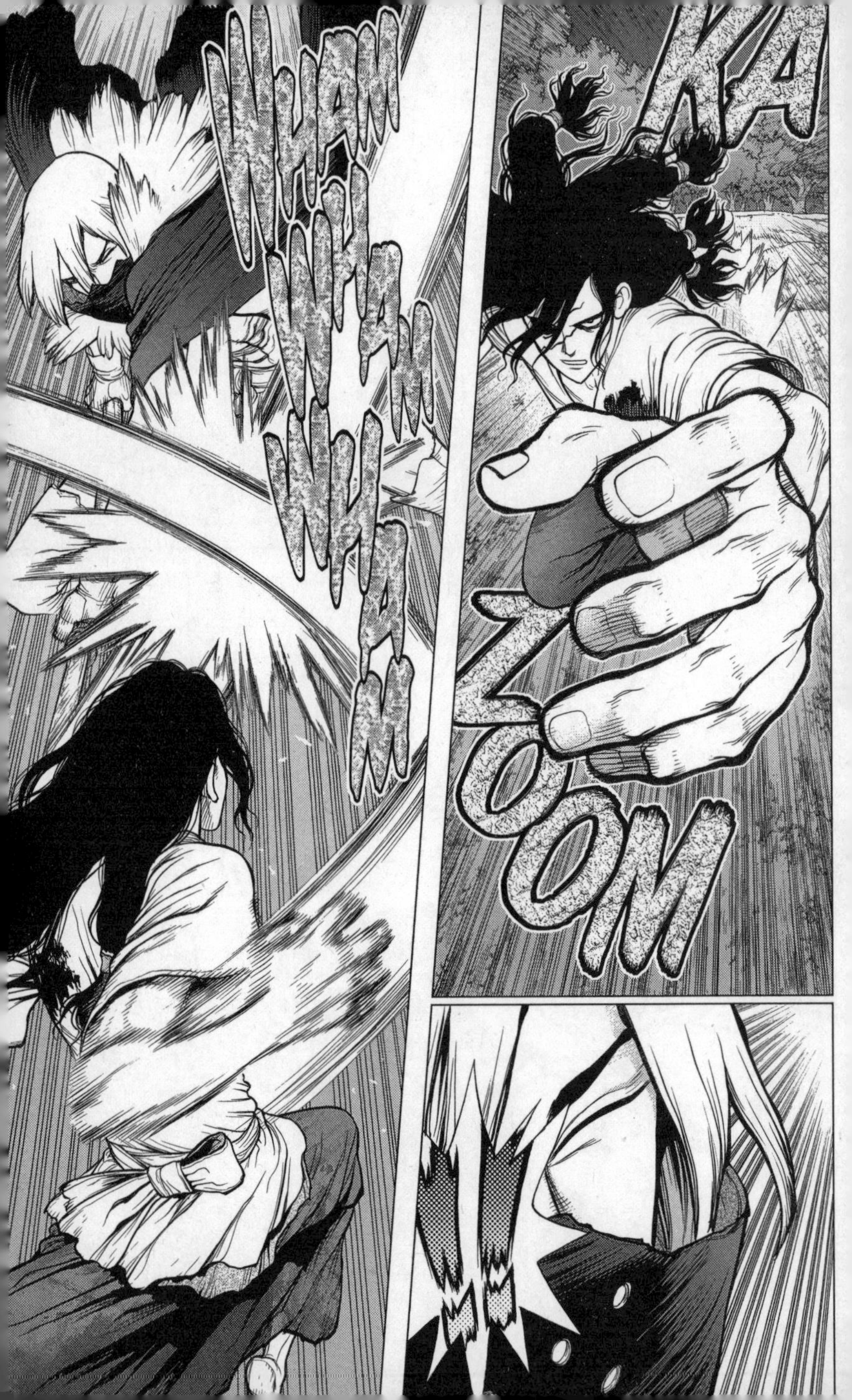
KA
ZOOM
WHAM WHAM WHAM

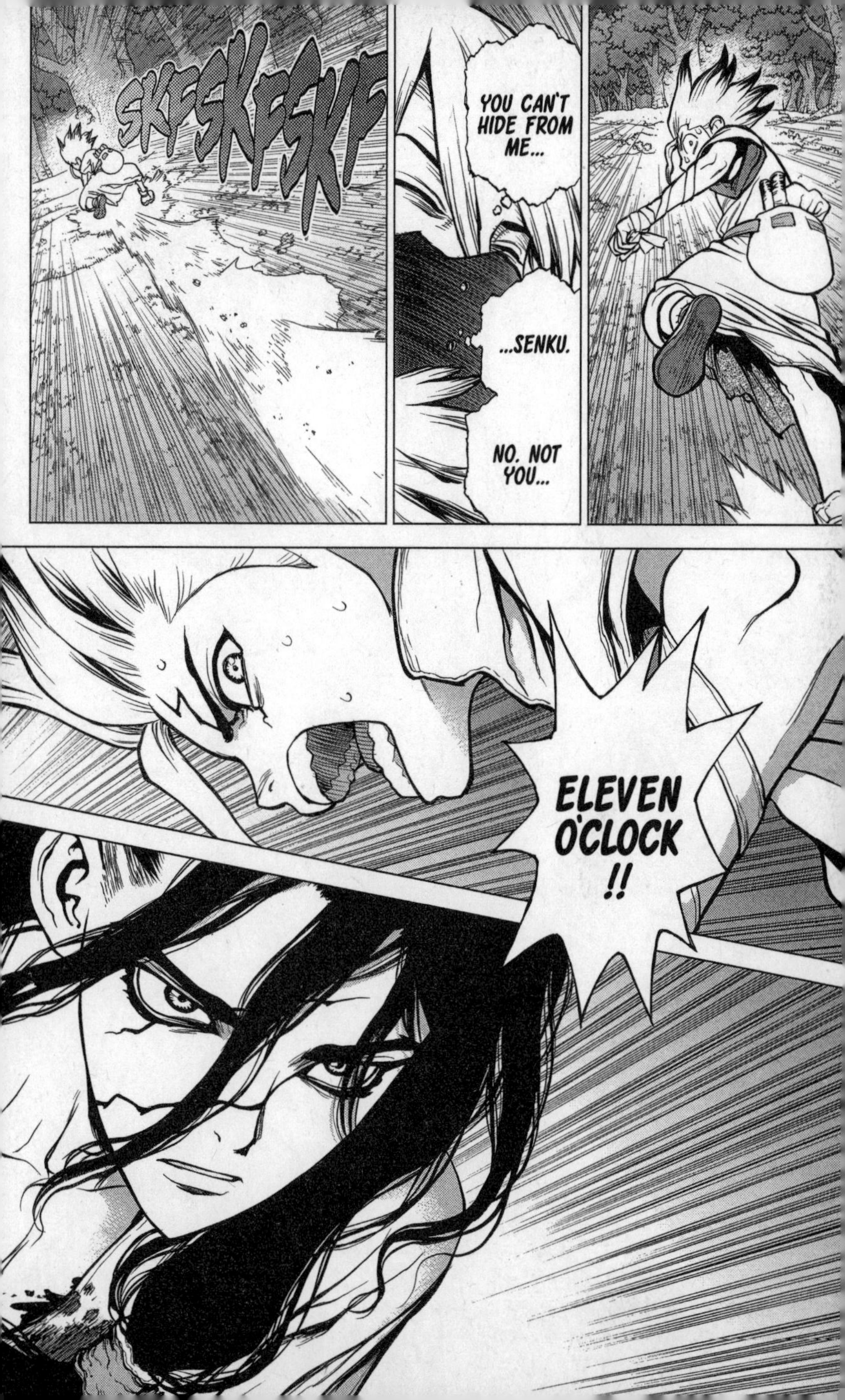
YOU CAN'T HIDE FROM ME...
...SENKU.
NO. NOT YOU...
SKFSKFSKF
ELEVEN O'CLOCK !!

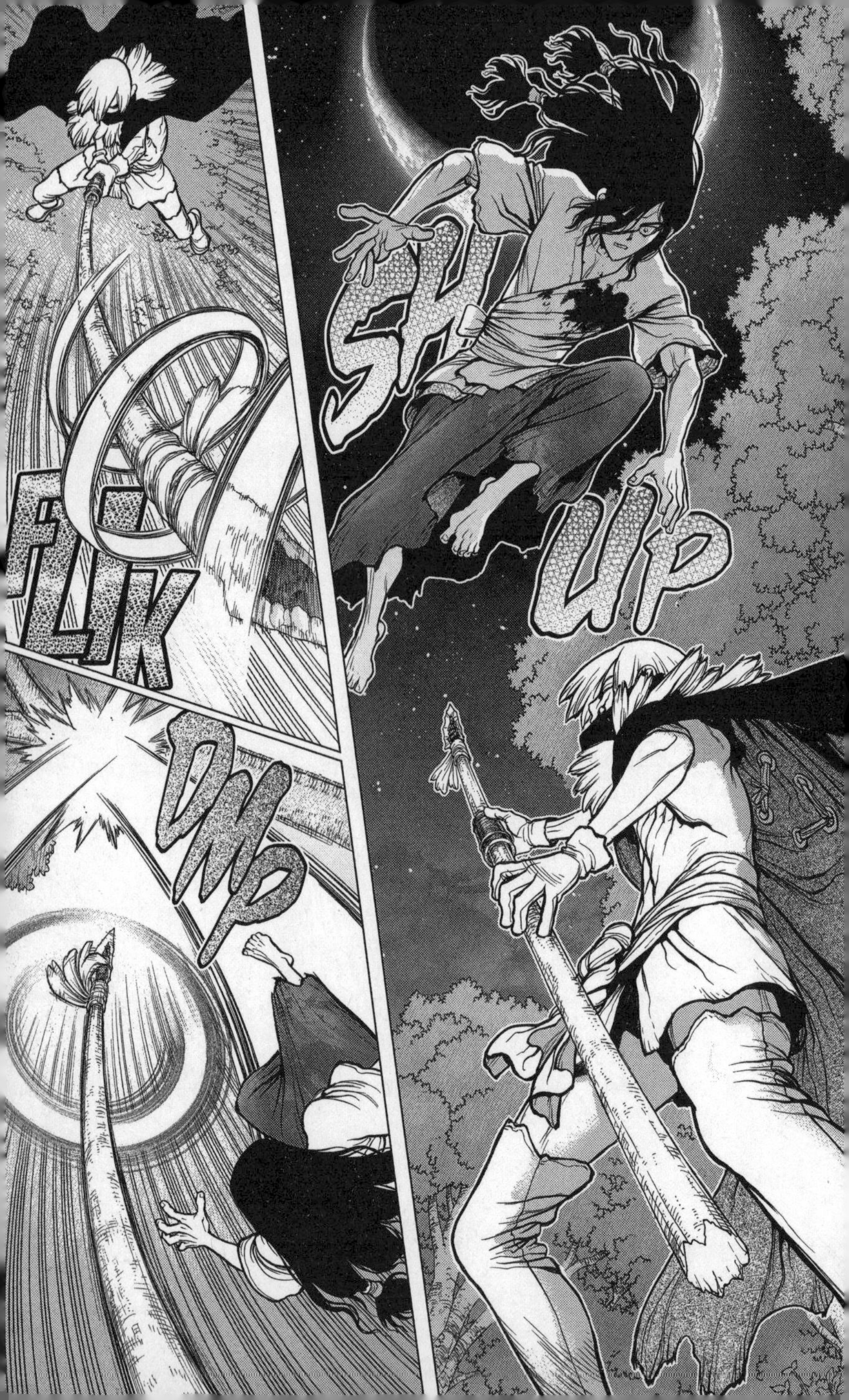
SH
UP
FLIK
DMP

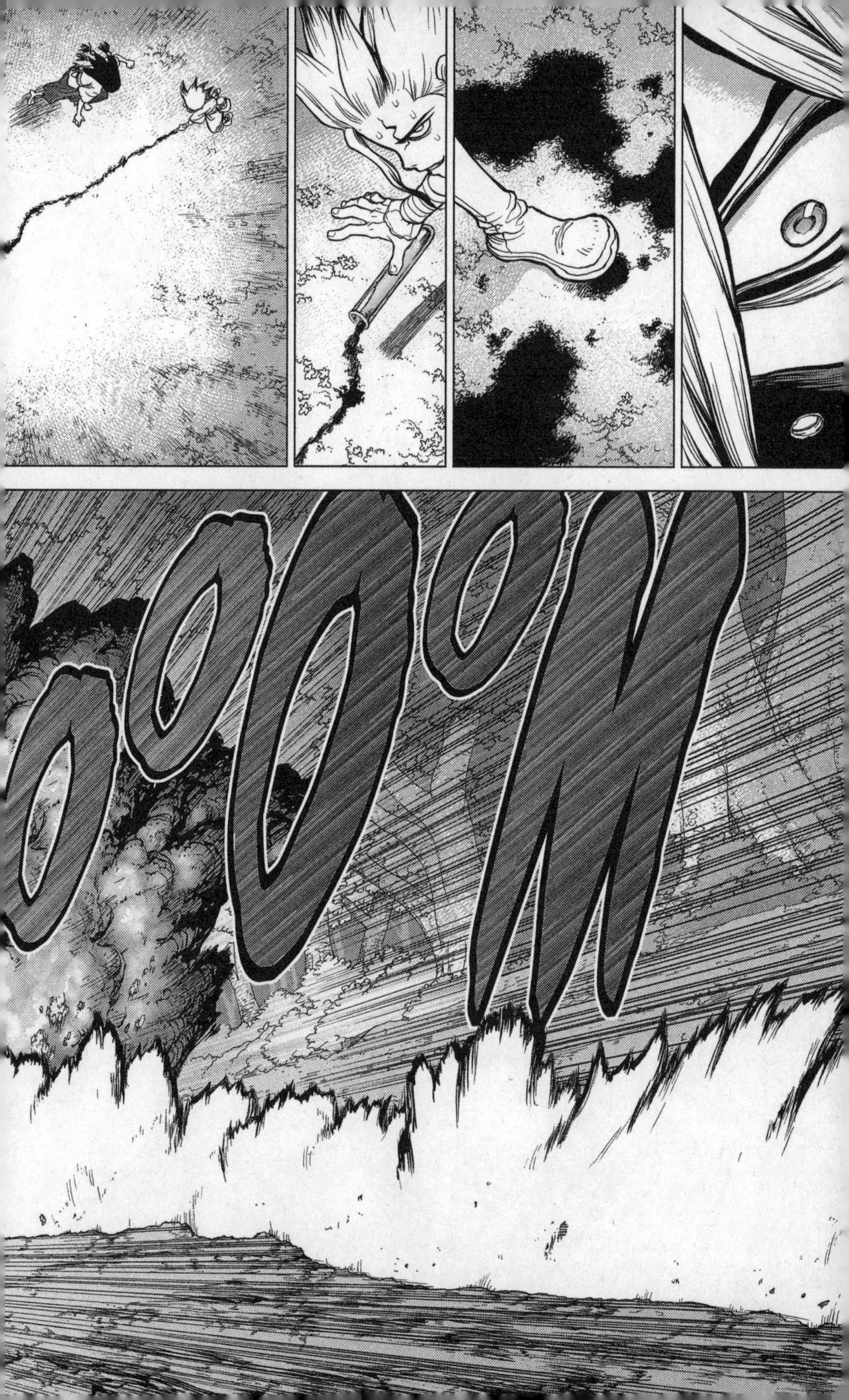

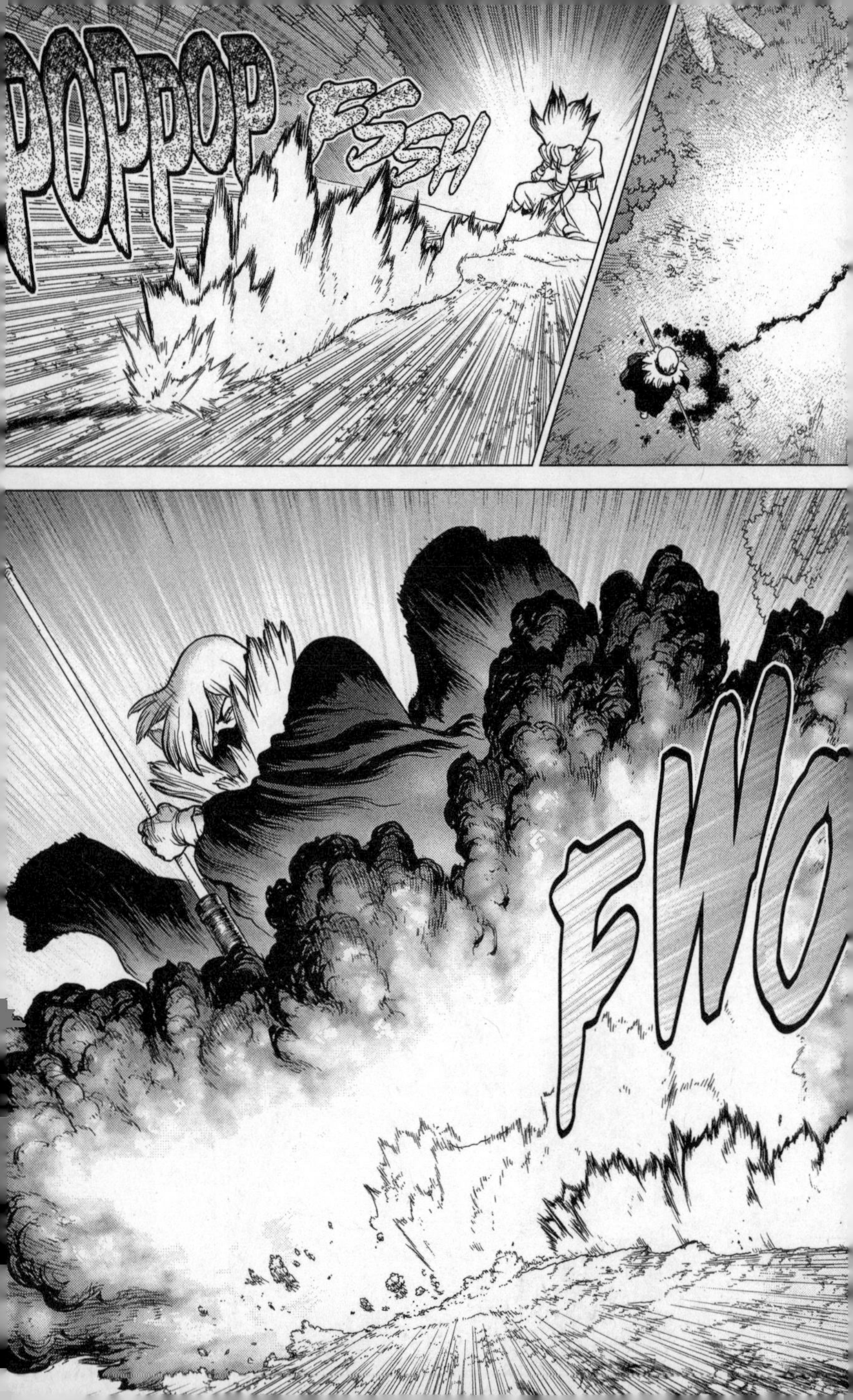
FSSH
POPPOP
FWO

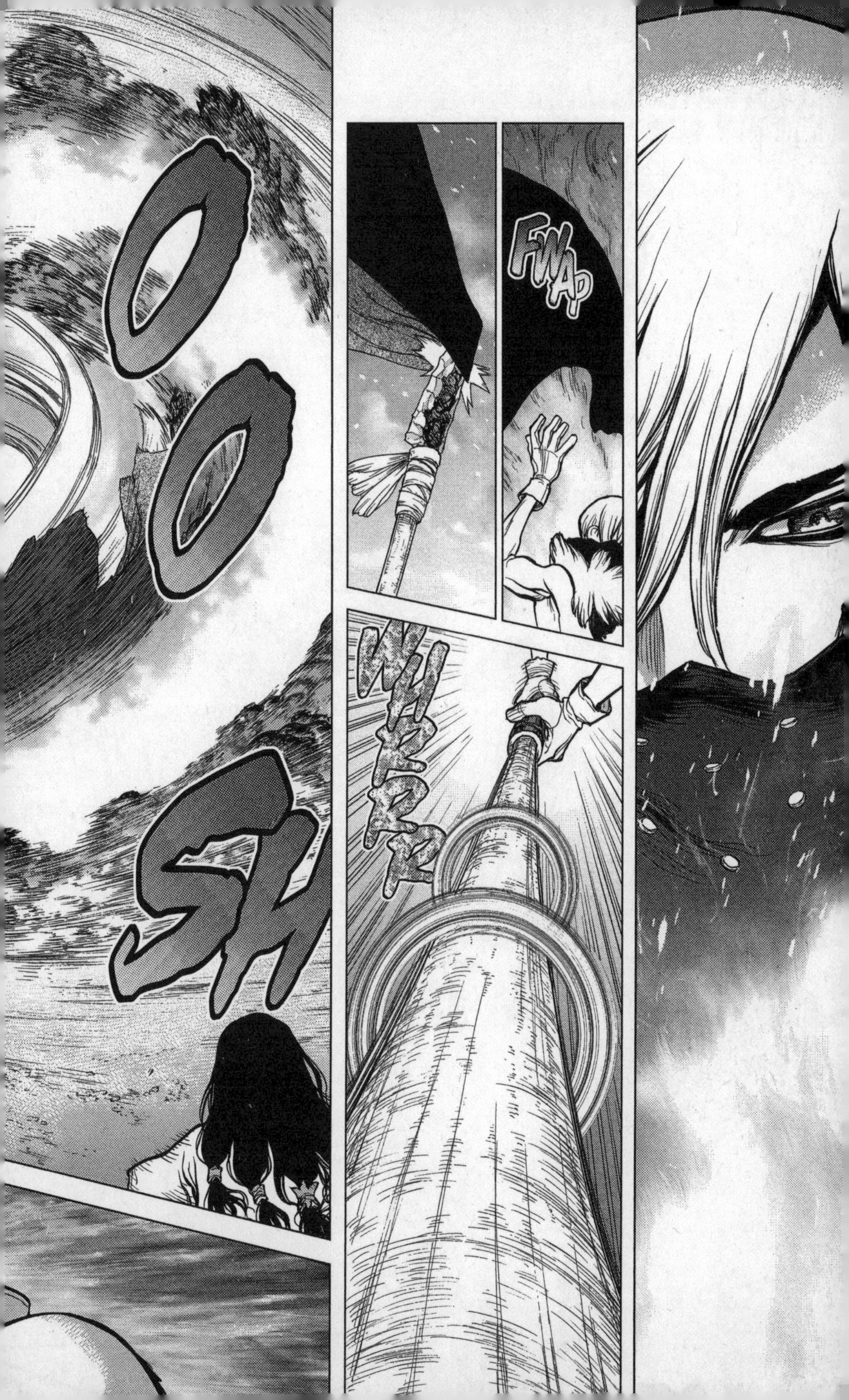
FWAP
WHRRR
OO
SH

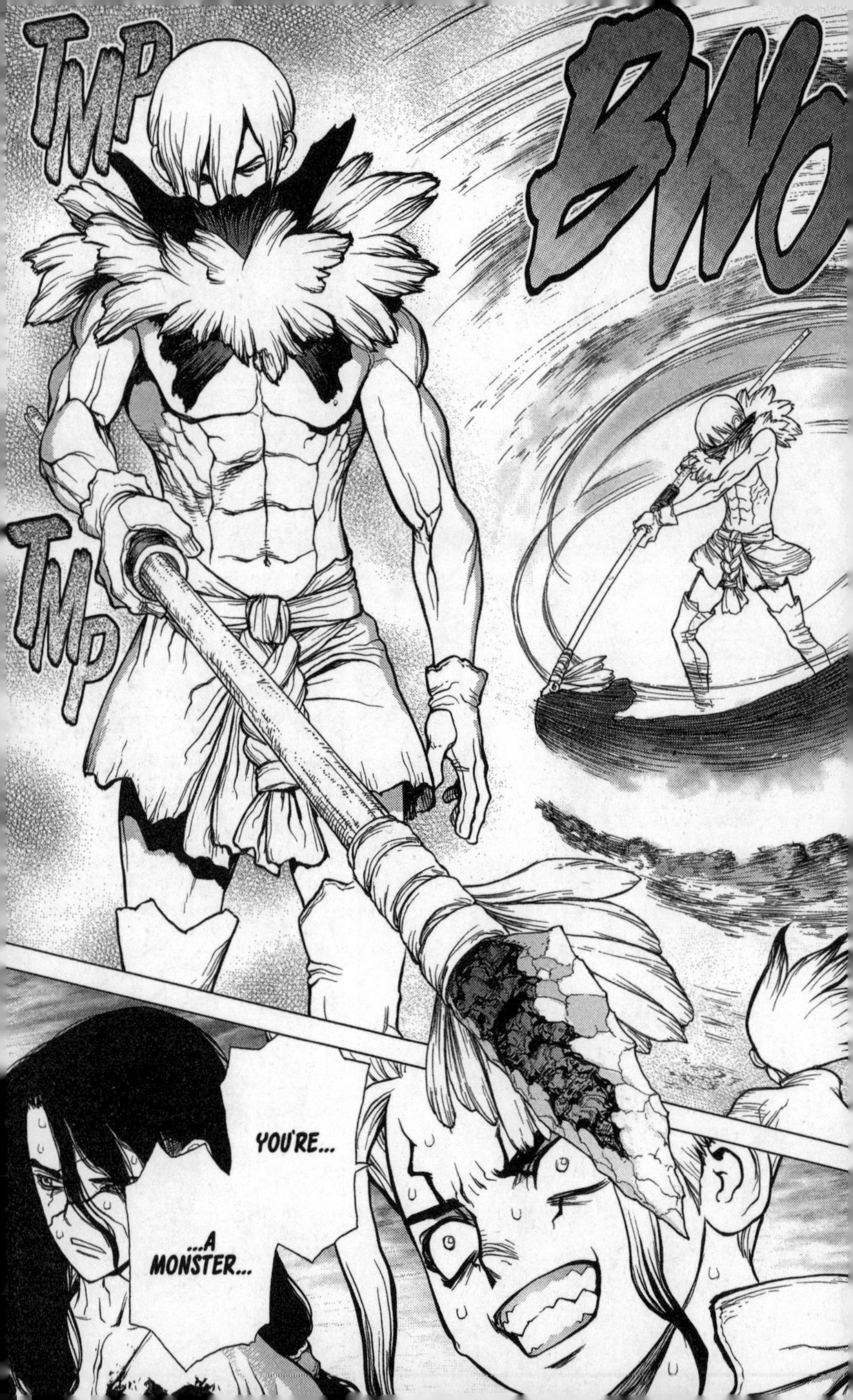
BWO
TMP
TMP
YOU'RE...
...A MONSTER...

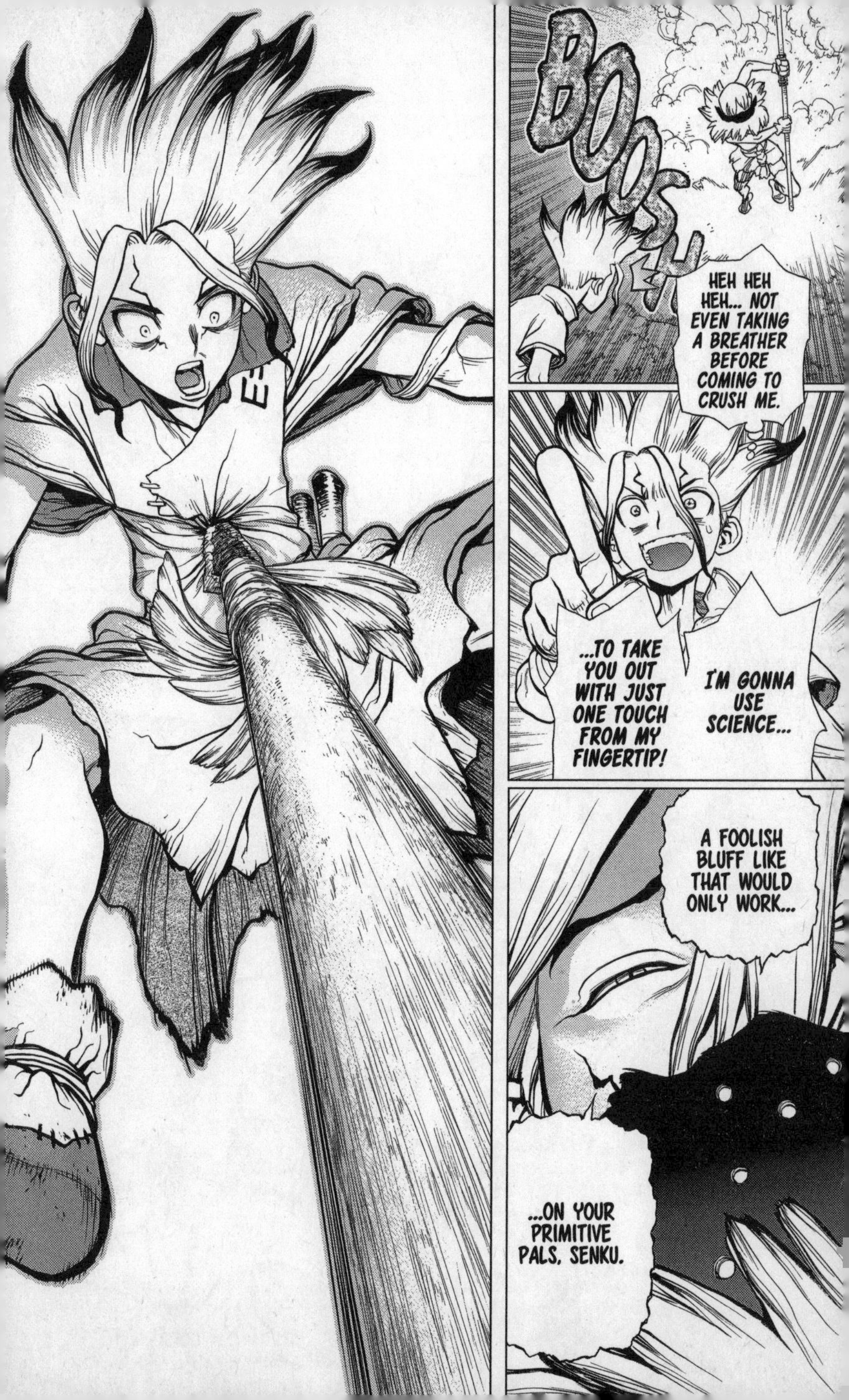
BOOOSH
HEH HEH HEH... NOT EVEN TAKING A BREATHER BEFORE COMING TO CRUSH ME.
I'M GONNA USE SCIENCE...
...TO TAKE YOU OUT WITH JUST ONE TOUCH FROM MY FINGERTIP!
A FOOLISH BLUFF LIKE THAT WOULD ONLY WORK...
...ON YOUR PRIMITIVE PALS, SENKU.

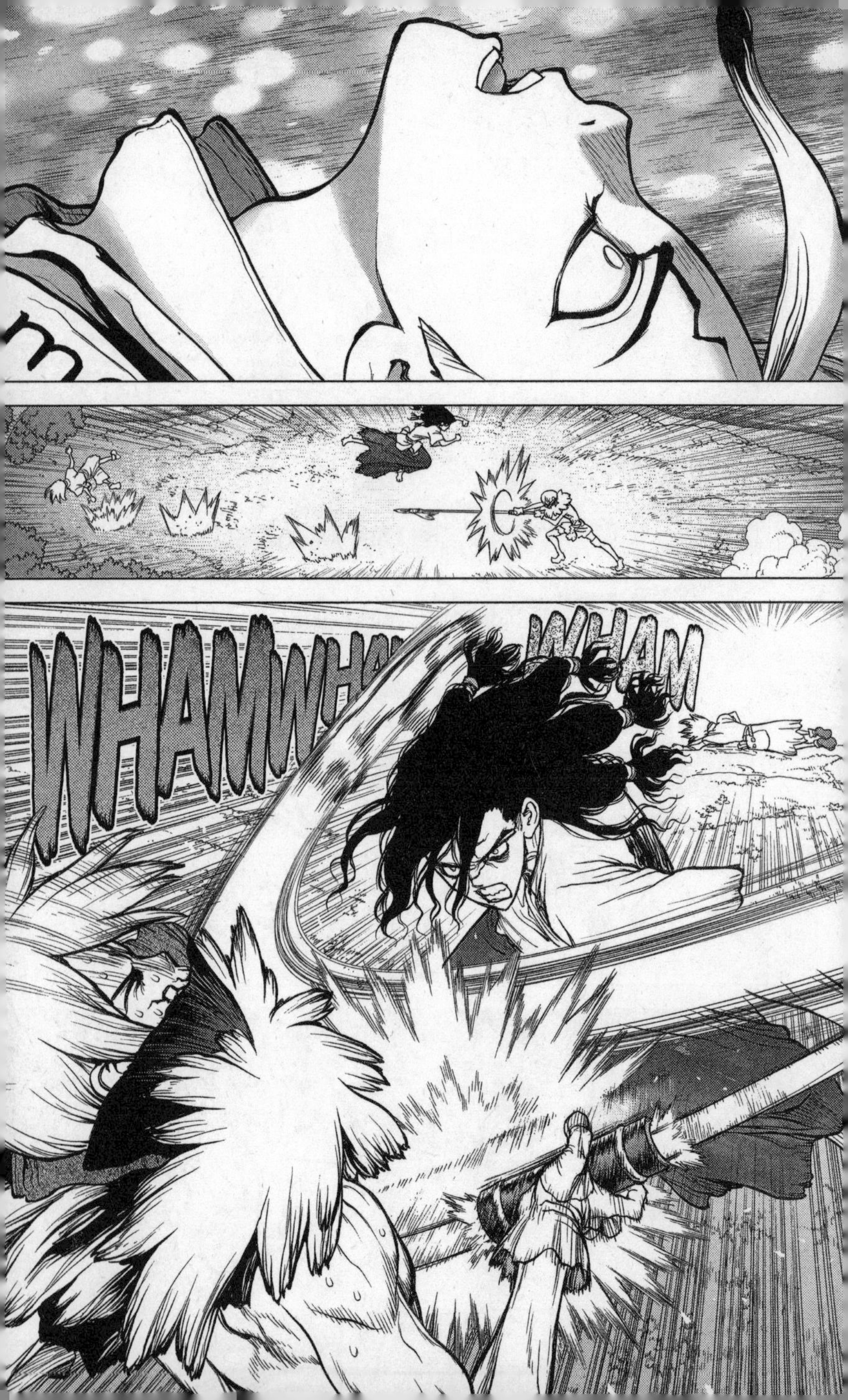
WHAM
WHAMWHAM

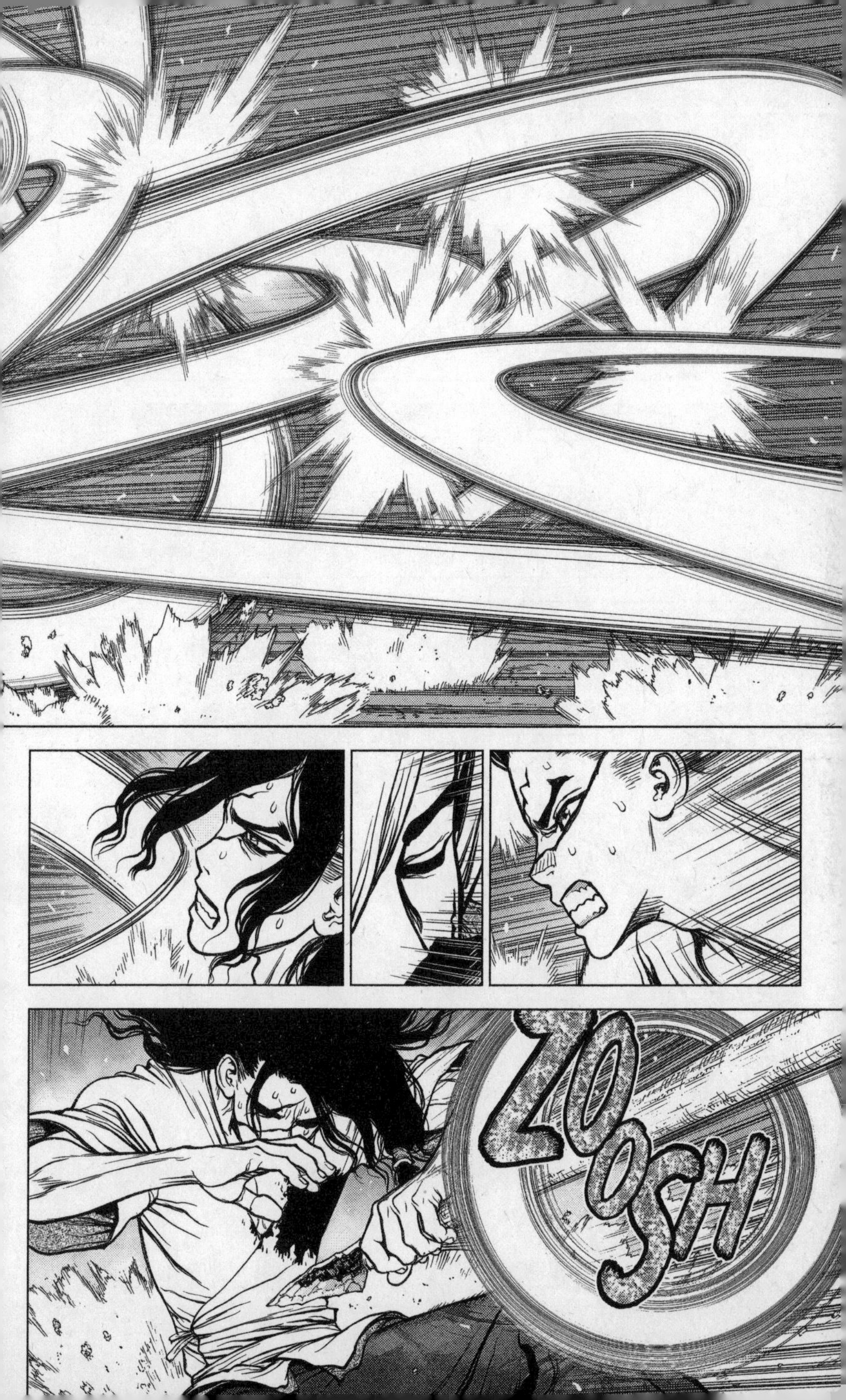
ZOOSH

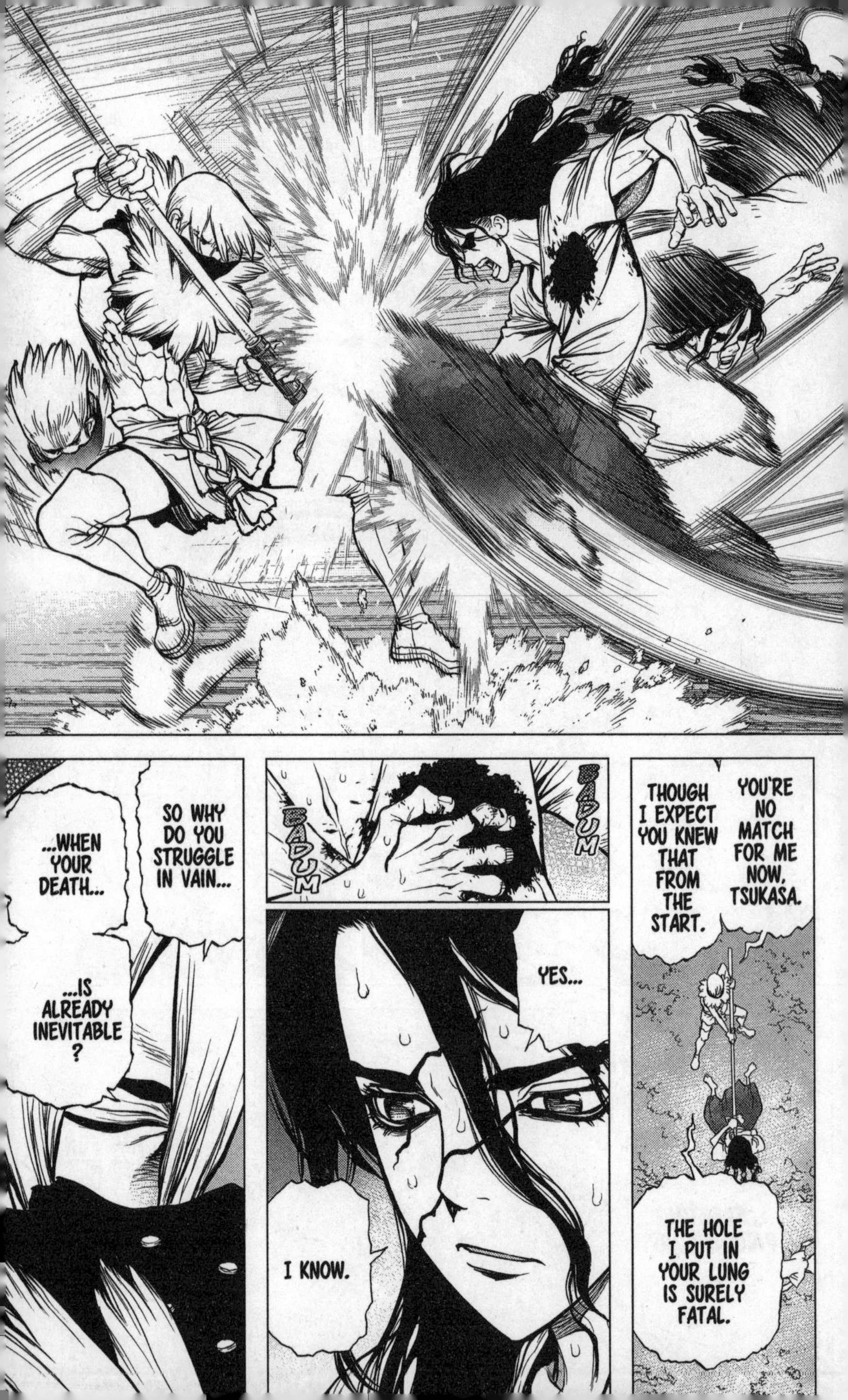
YOU'RE NO MATCH FOR ME NOW, TSUKASA.
THOUGH I EXPECT YOU KNEW THAT FROM THE START.
THE HOLE I PUT IN YOUR LUNG IS SURELY FATAL.
BADUM
BADUM
YES...
I KNOW.
SO WHY DO YOU STRUGGLE IN VAIN...
...WHEN YOUR DEATH...
...IS ALREADY INEVITABLE?

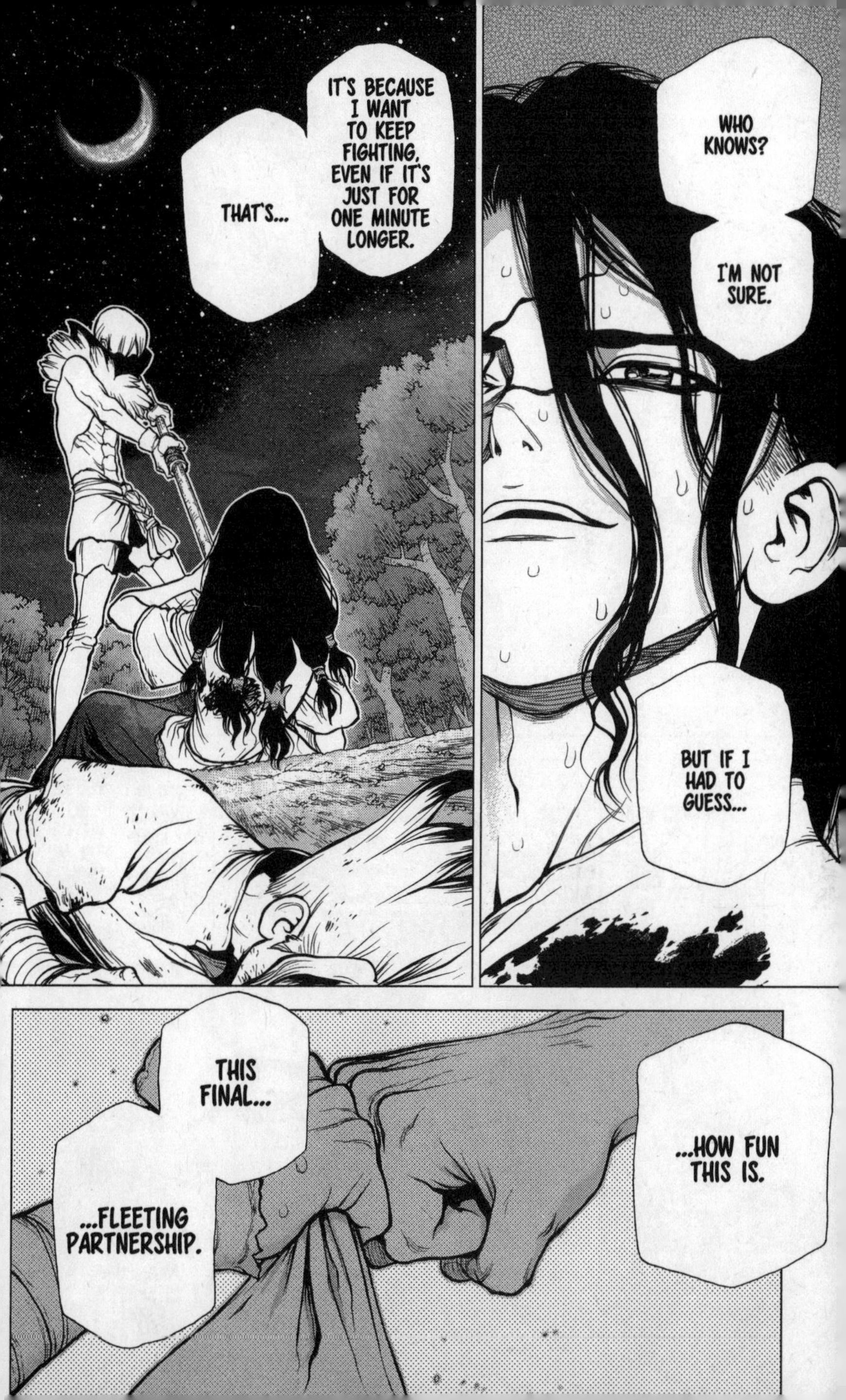
WHO KNOWS?
I'M NOT SURE.
BUT IF I HAD TO GUESS...
THAT'S...
IT'S BECAUSE I WANT TO KEEP FIGHTING, EVEN IF IT'S JUST FOR ONE MINUTE LONGER.
...HOW FUN THIS IS.
THIS FINAL...
...FLEETING PARTNERSHIP.

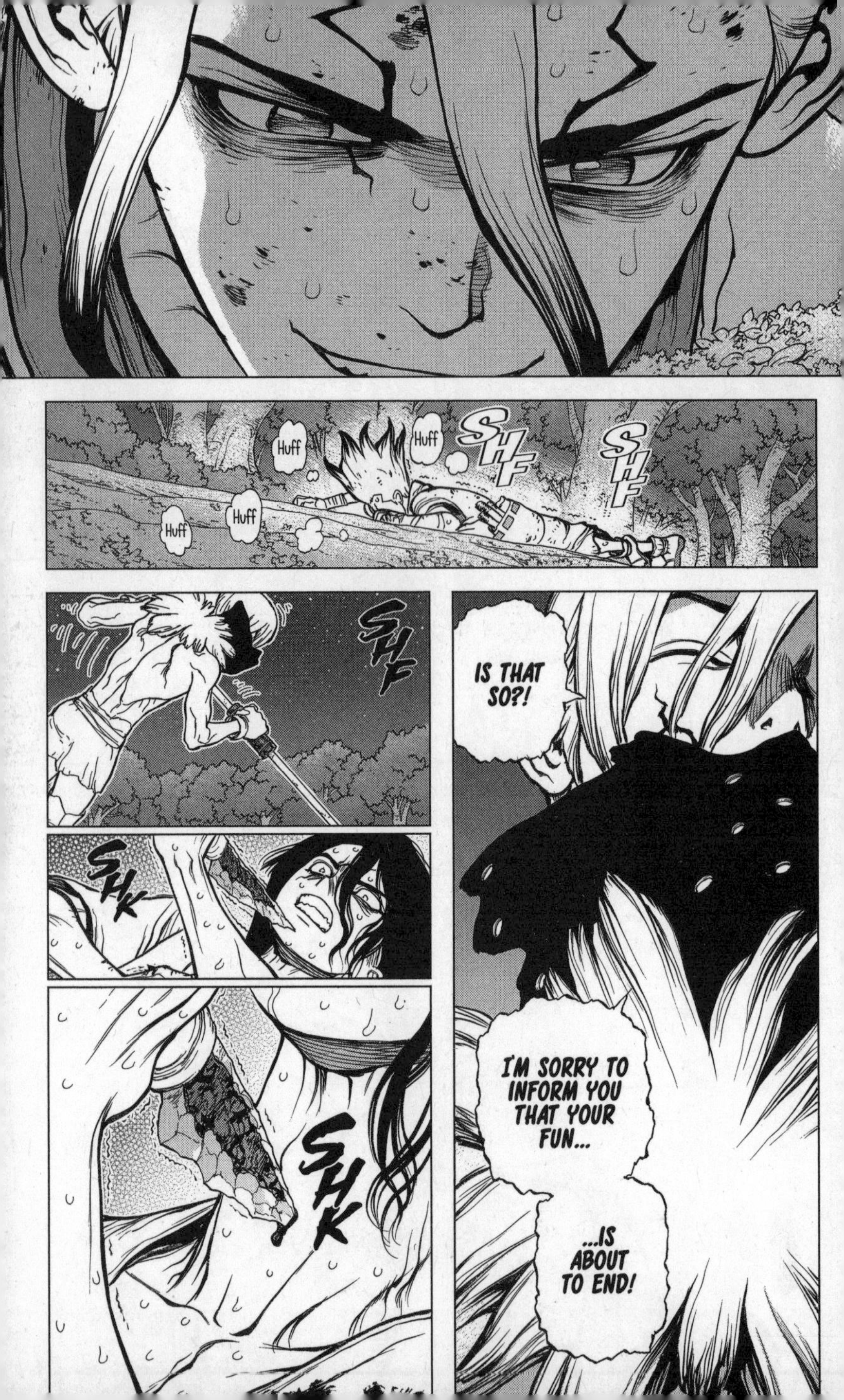
SHF
SHF
Huff
Huff
Huff
Huff
IS THAT SO?!
I'M SORRY TO INFORM YOU THAT YOUR FUN...
...IS ABOUT TO END!
SHF
SHK
SHK

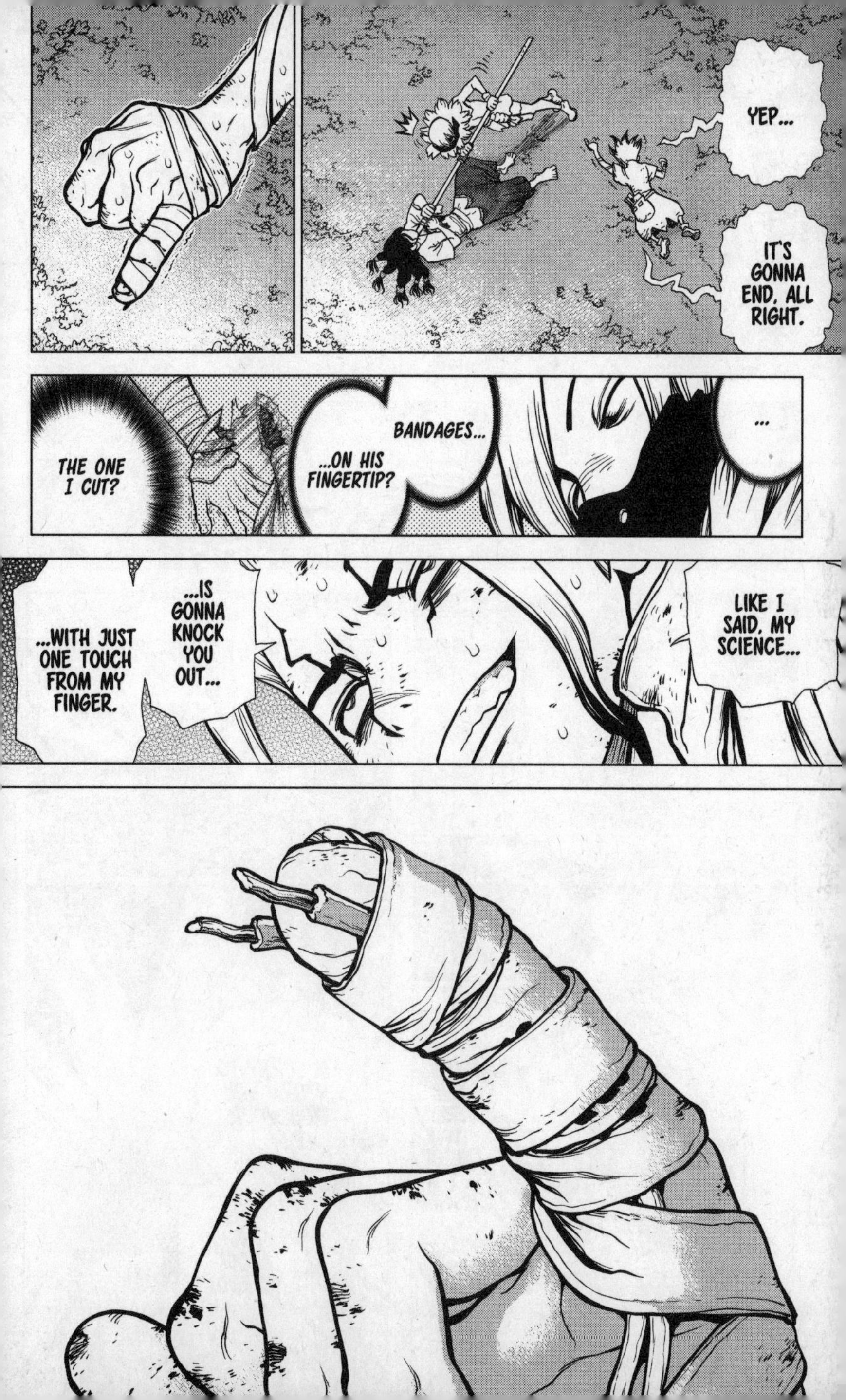
YEP...
IT'S GONNA END, ALL RIGHT.
...
BANDAGES...
...ON HIS FINGERTIP?
THE ONE I CUT?
LIKE I SAID, MY SCIENCE...
...IS GONNA KNOCK YOU OUT...
...WITH JUST ONE TOUCH FROM MY FINGER.

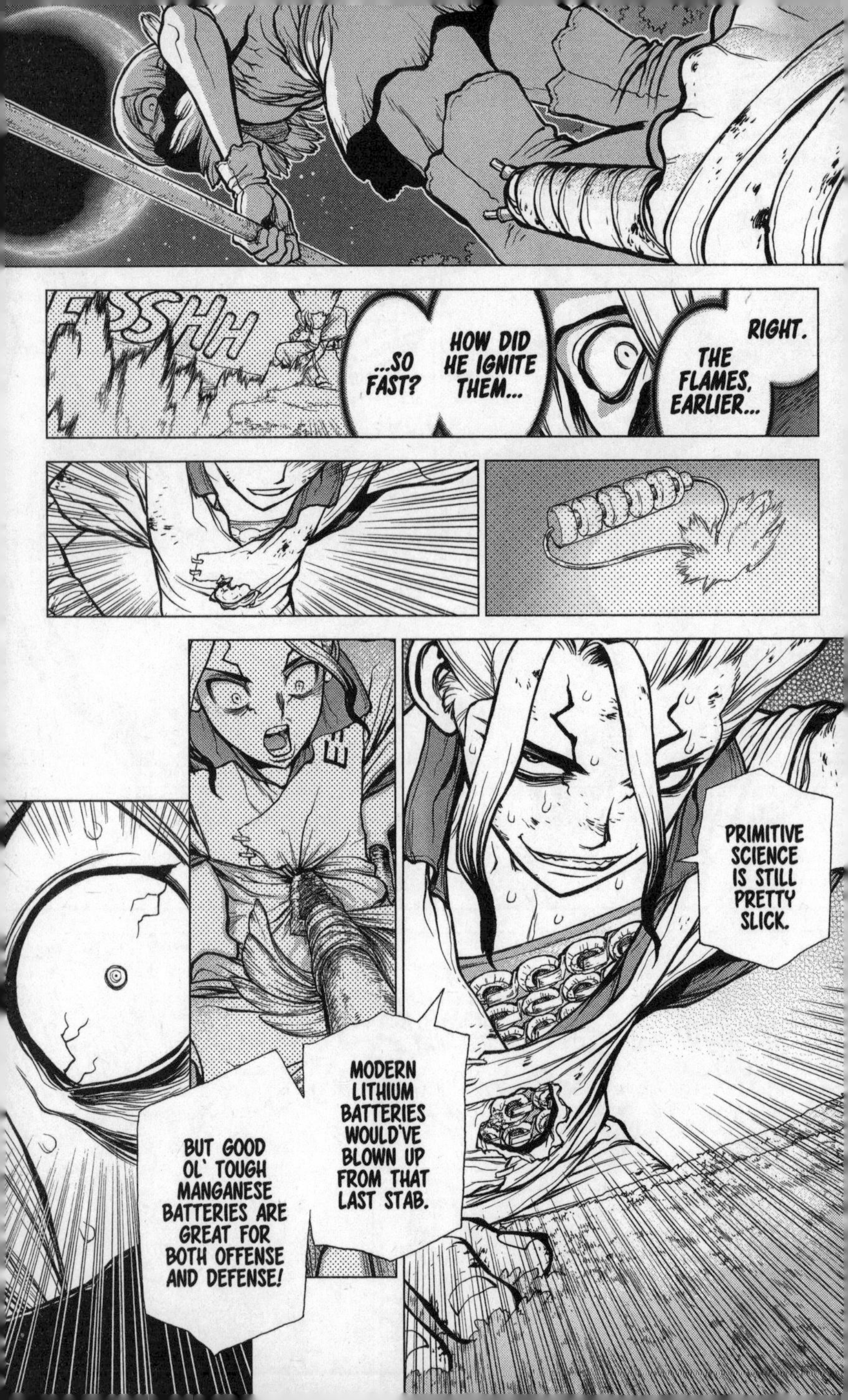
RIGHT. THE FLAMES, EARLIER...
HOW DID HE IGNITE THEM...
...SO FAST?
FSSHH
PRIMITIVE SCIENCE IS STILL PRETTY SLICK.
MODERN LITHIUM BATTERIES WOULD'VE BLOWN UP FROM THAT LAST STAB.
BUT GOOD OL' TOUGH MANGANESE BATTERIES ARE GREAT FOR BOTH OFFENSE AND DEFENSE!

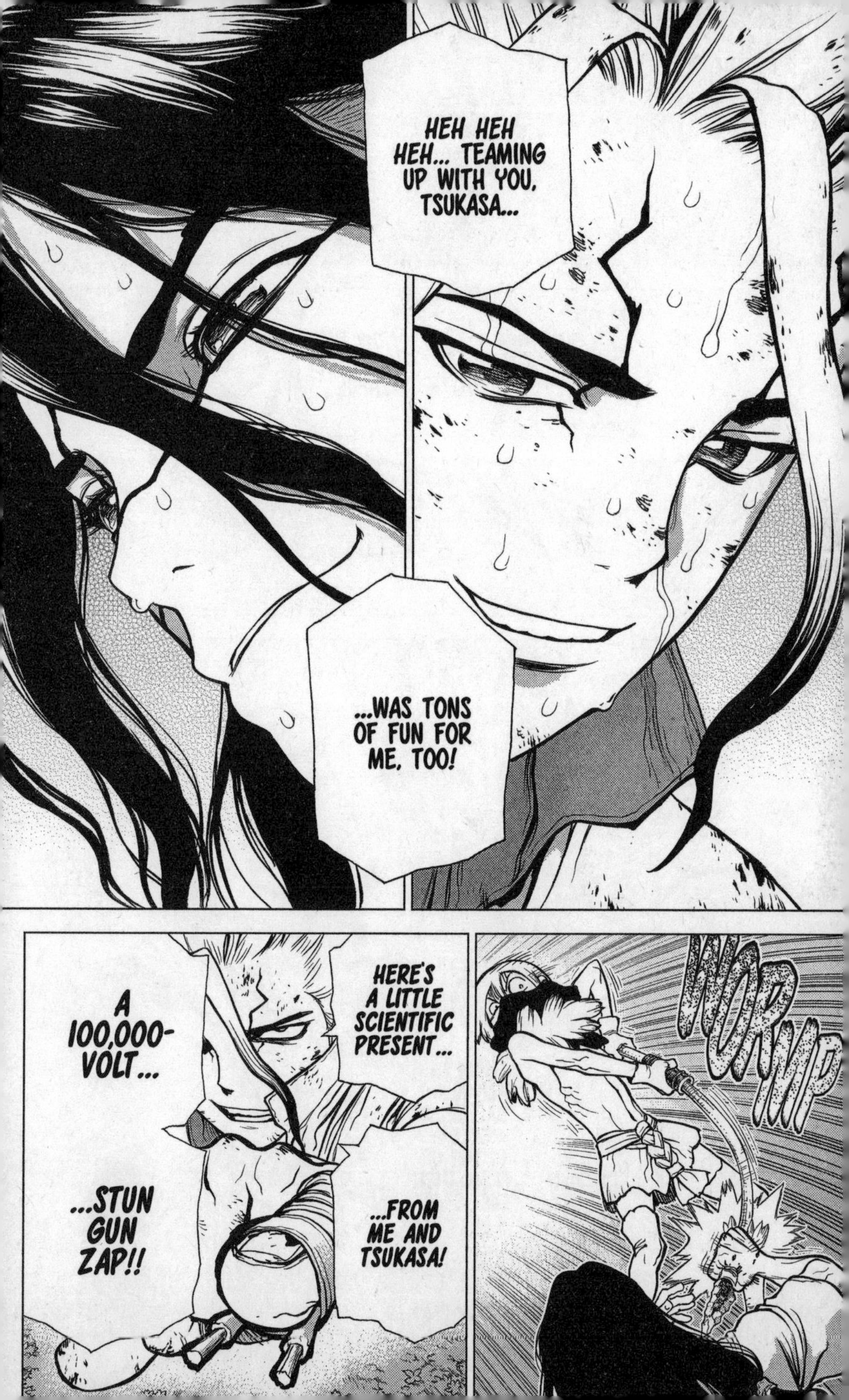
HEH HEH HEH... TEAMING UP WITH YOU, TSUKASA...
...WAS TONS OF FUN FOR ME, TOO!
WORMP
HERE'S A LITTLE SCIENTIFIC PRESENT...
A 100,000-VOLT...
...FROM ME AND TSUKASA!
...STUN GUN ZAP!!

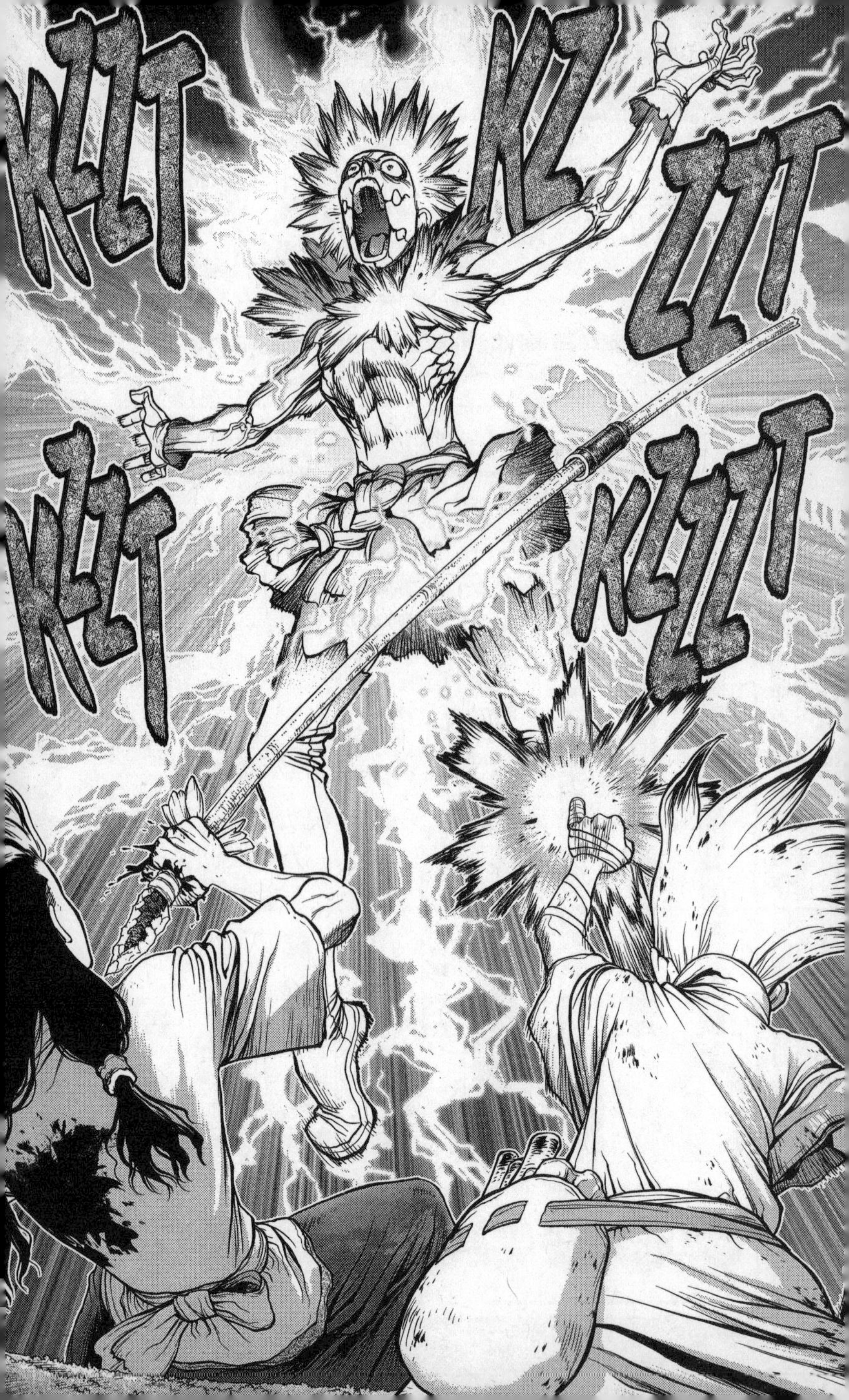
KZZ
ZZZT
KZZT
KZZZT
KZZT

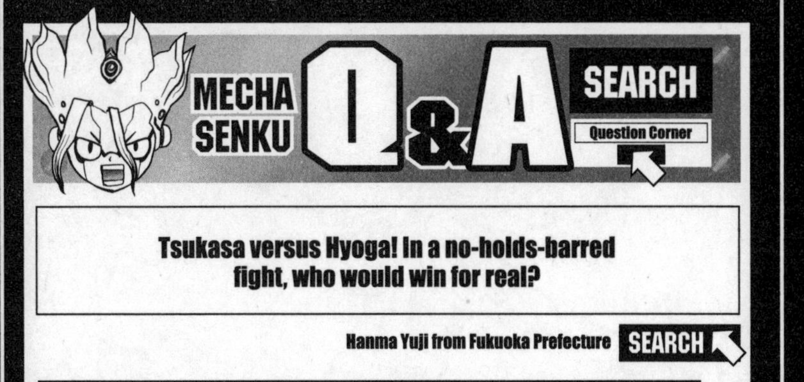
MECHA SENKU
Q&A
SEARCH
Question Corner

Tsukasa versus Hyoga! In a no-holds-barred fight, who would win for real?

Hanma Yuji from Fukuoka Prefecture

SEARCH

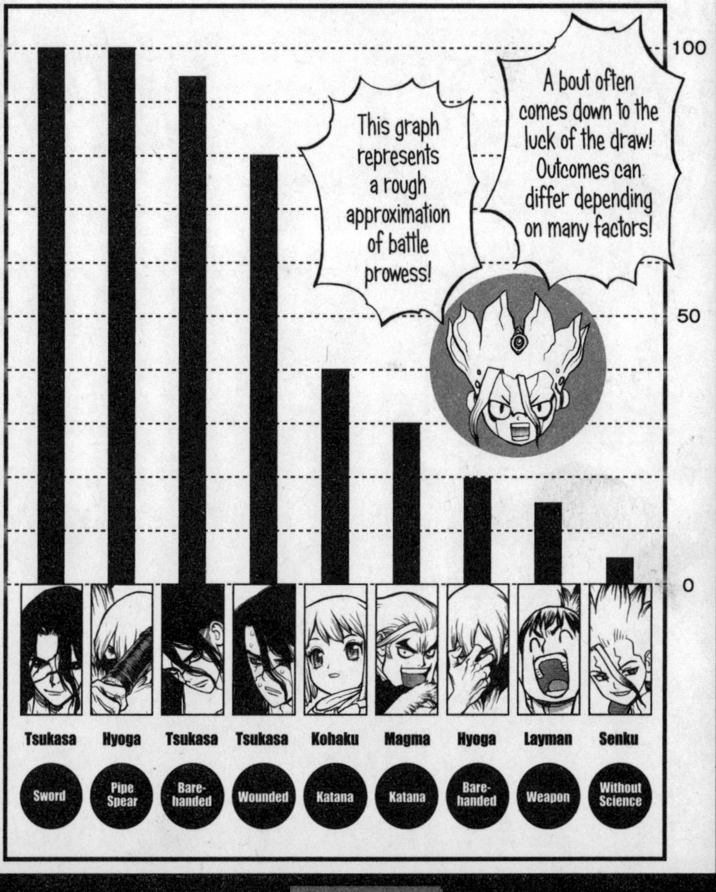
This graph represents a rough approximation of battle prowess!
A bout often comes down to the luck of the draw! Outcomes can differ depending on many factors!
100
50
0
Tsukasa
Sword
Hyoga
Pipe Spear
Tsukasa
Bare-handed
Tsukasa
Wounded
Kohaku
Katana
Magma
Katana
Hyoga
Bare-handed
Layman
Weapon
Senku
Without Science

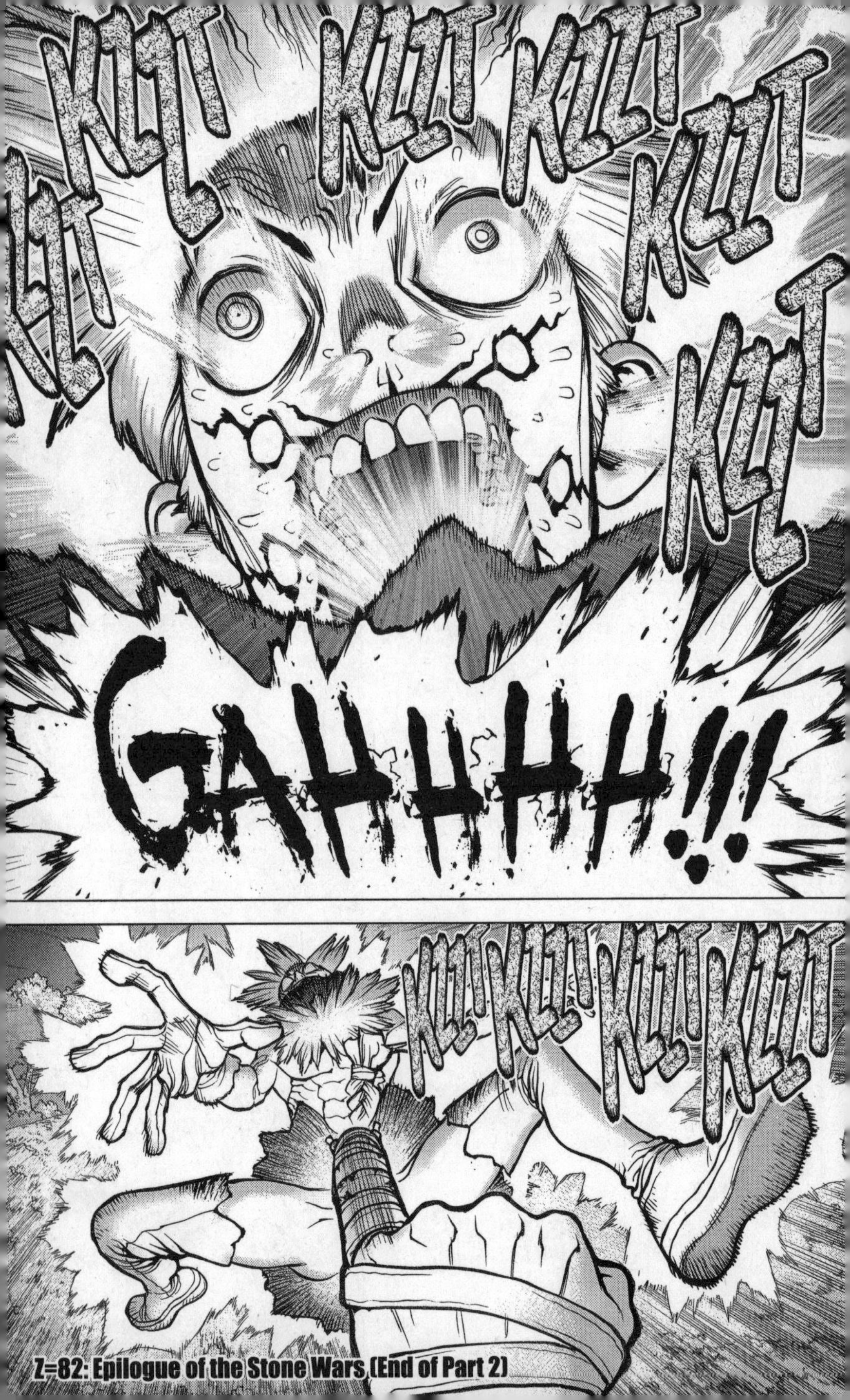
KZZT KZZT KZZT KZZT KZZT KZZT
GAHHHHH!!!
KZZT KZZT KZZT KZZT
Z=82: Epilogue of the Stone Wars (End of Part 2)

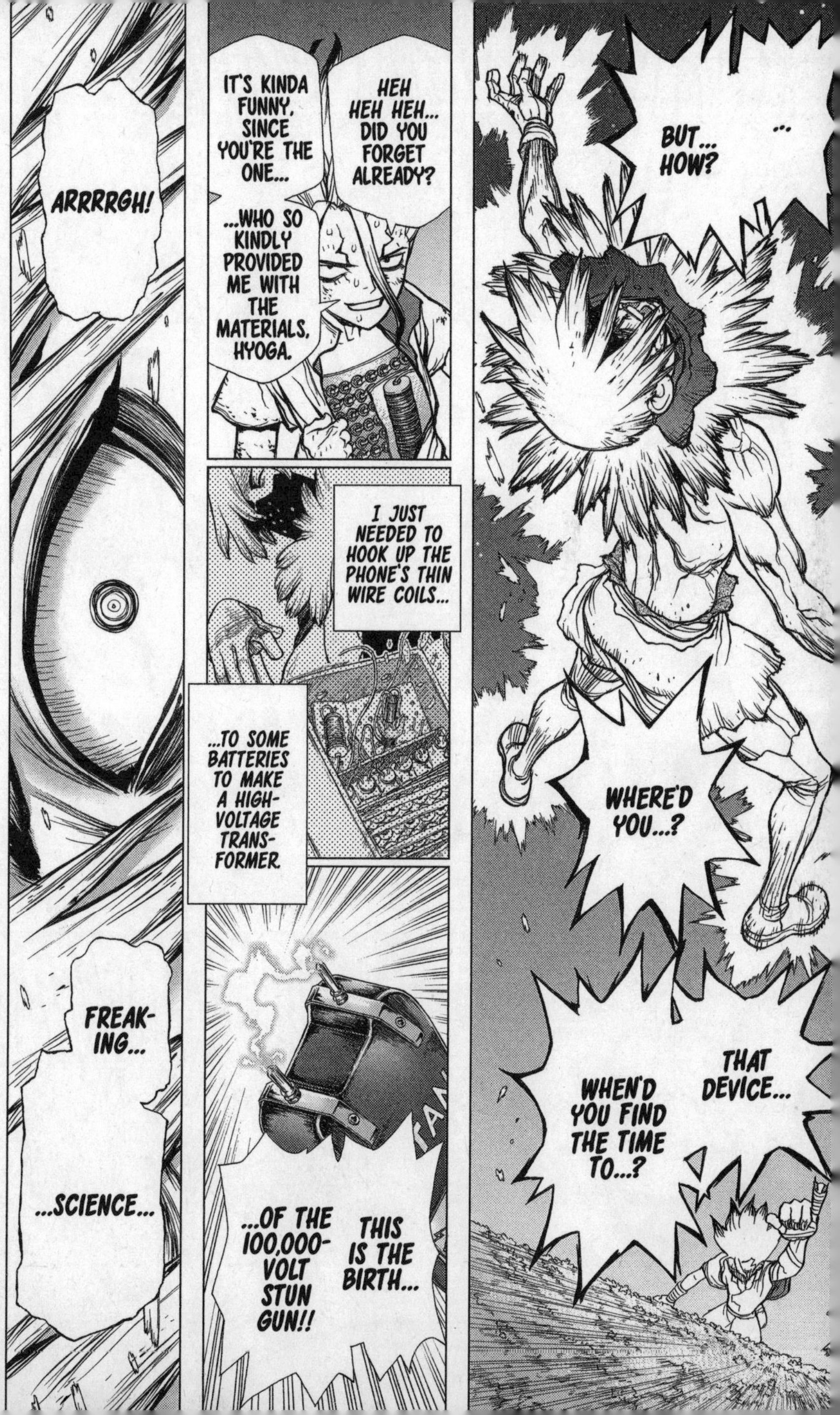
...
BUT... HOW?
WHERE'D YOU...?
THAT DEVICE...
WHEN'D YOU FIND THE TIME TO...?
HEH HEH HEH... DID YOU FORGET ALREADY?
IT'S KINDA FUNNY, SINCE YOU'RE THE ONE...
...WHO SO KINDLY PROVIDED ME WITH THE MATERIALS, HYOGA.
I JUST NEEDED TO HOOK UP THE PHONE'S THIN WIRE COILS...
...TO SOME BATTERIES TO MAKE A HIGH-VOLTAGE TRANS-FORMER.
THIS IS THE BIRTH...
...OF THE 100,000-VOLT STUN GUN!!
ARRRRGH!
FREAK-ING...
...SCIENCE...

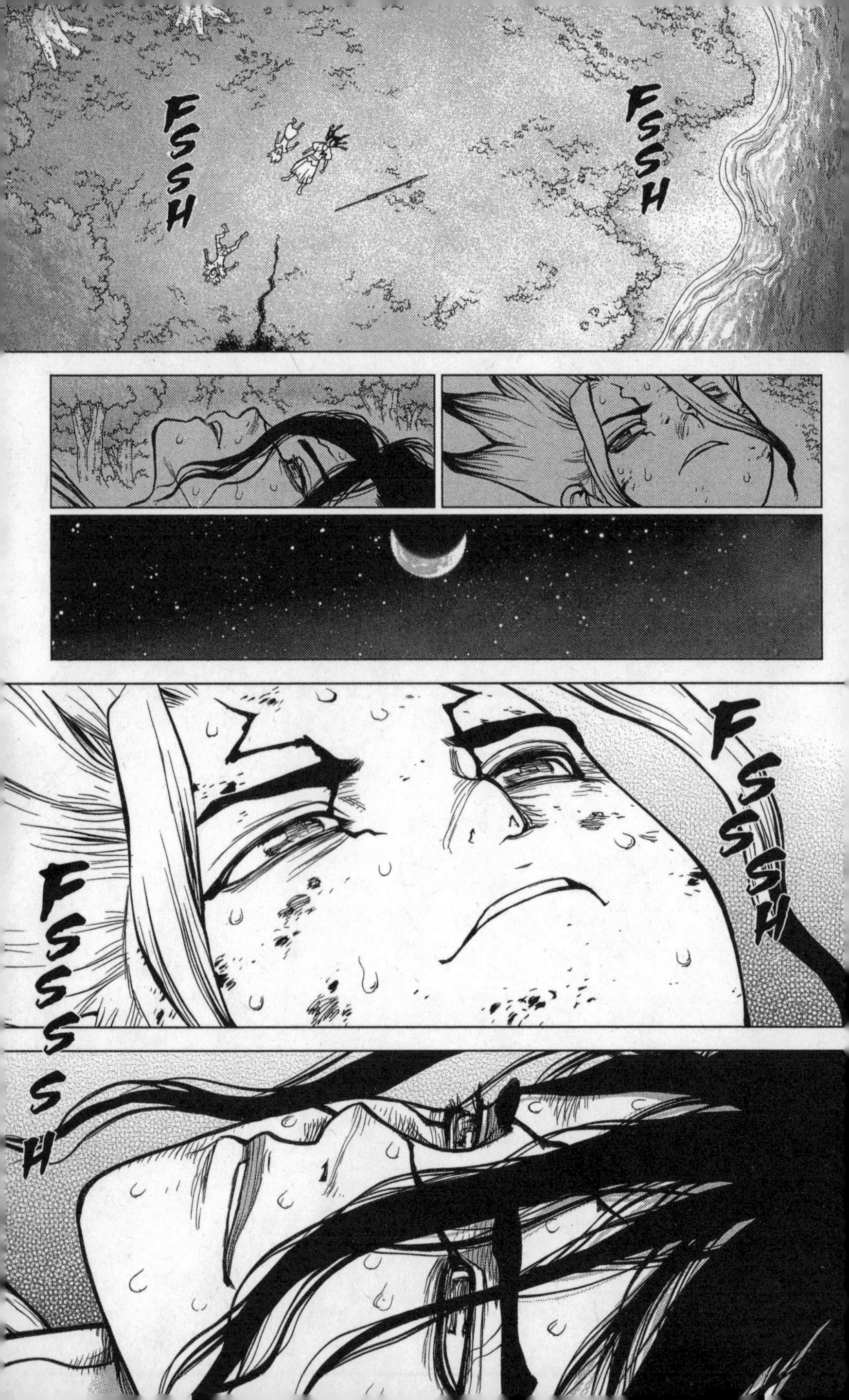
FSSH
FSSH
FSSSH
FSSSSH

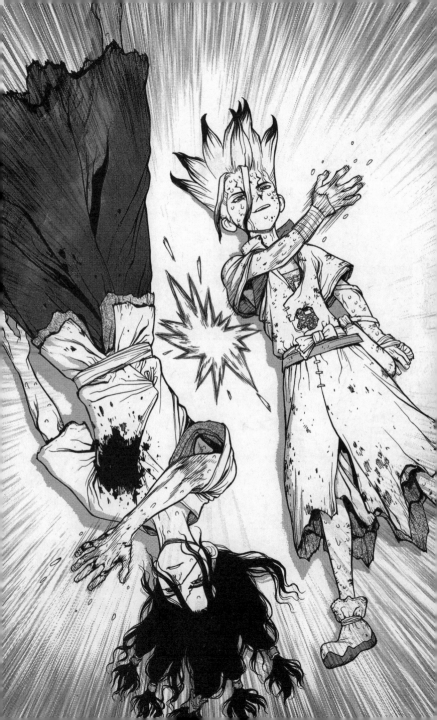

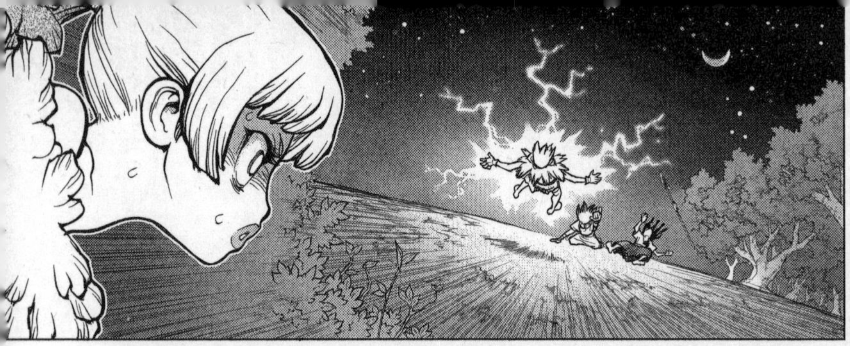

Z=82: Epilogue of the Stone Wars (End of Part 2)

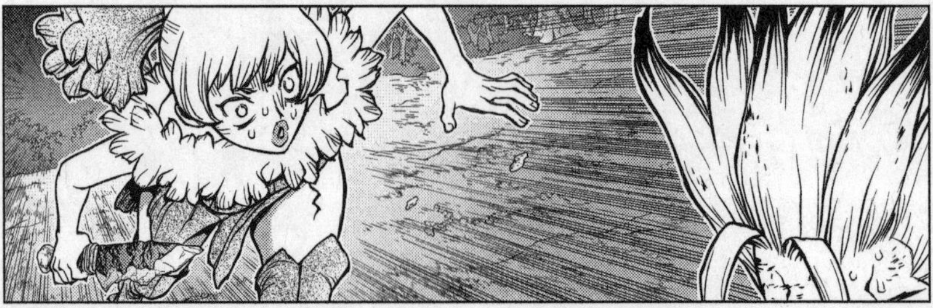

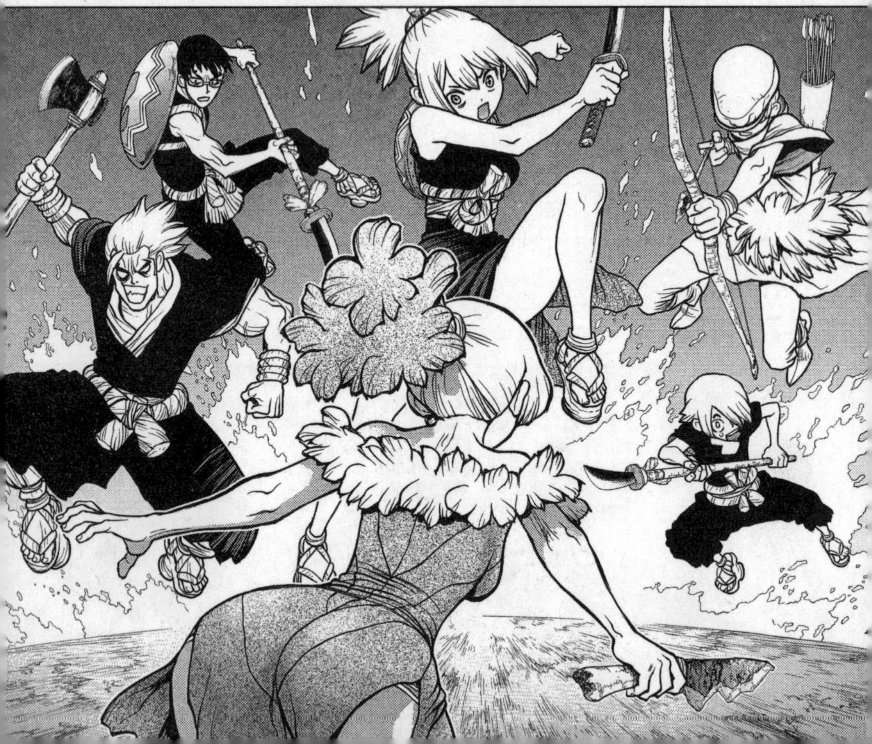

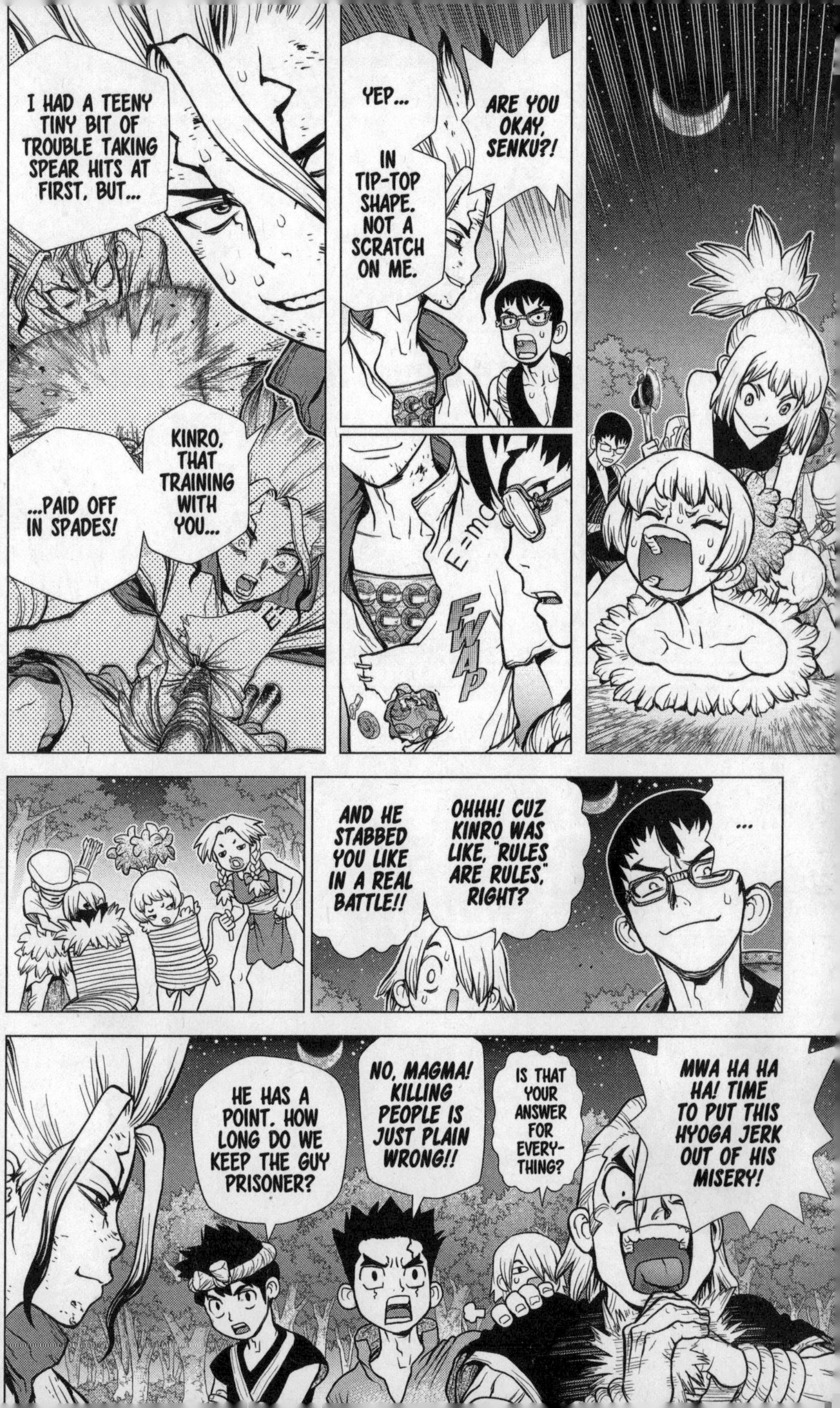
ARE YOU OKAY, SENKU?!
YEP...
IN TIP-TOP SHAPE. NOT A SCRATCH ON ME.
E=mc
FWAP
I HAD A TEENY TINY BIT OF TROUBLE TAKING SPEAR HITS AT FIRST, BUT...
KINRO, THAT TRAINING WITH YOU...
...PAID OFF IN SPADES!
...
OHHH! CUZ KINRO WAS LIKE, "RULES ARE RULES," RIGHT?
AND HE STABBED YOU LIKE IN A REAL BATTLE!!
MWA HA HA HA! TIME TO PUT THIS HYOGA JERK OUT OF HIS MISERY!
IS THAT YOUR ANSWER FOR EVERYTHING?
NO, MAGMA! KILLING PEOPLE IS JUST PLAIN WRONG!!
HE HAS A POINT. HOW LONG DO WE KEEP THE GUY PRISONER?

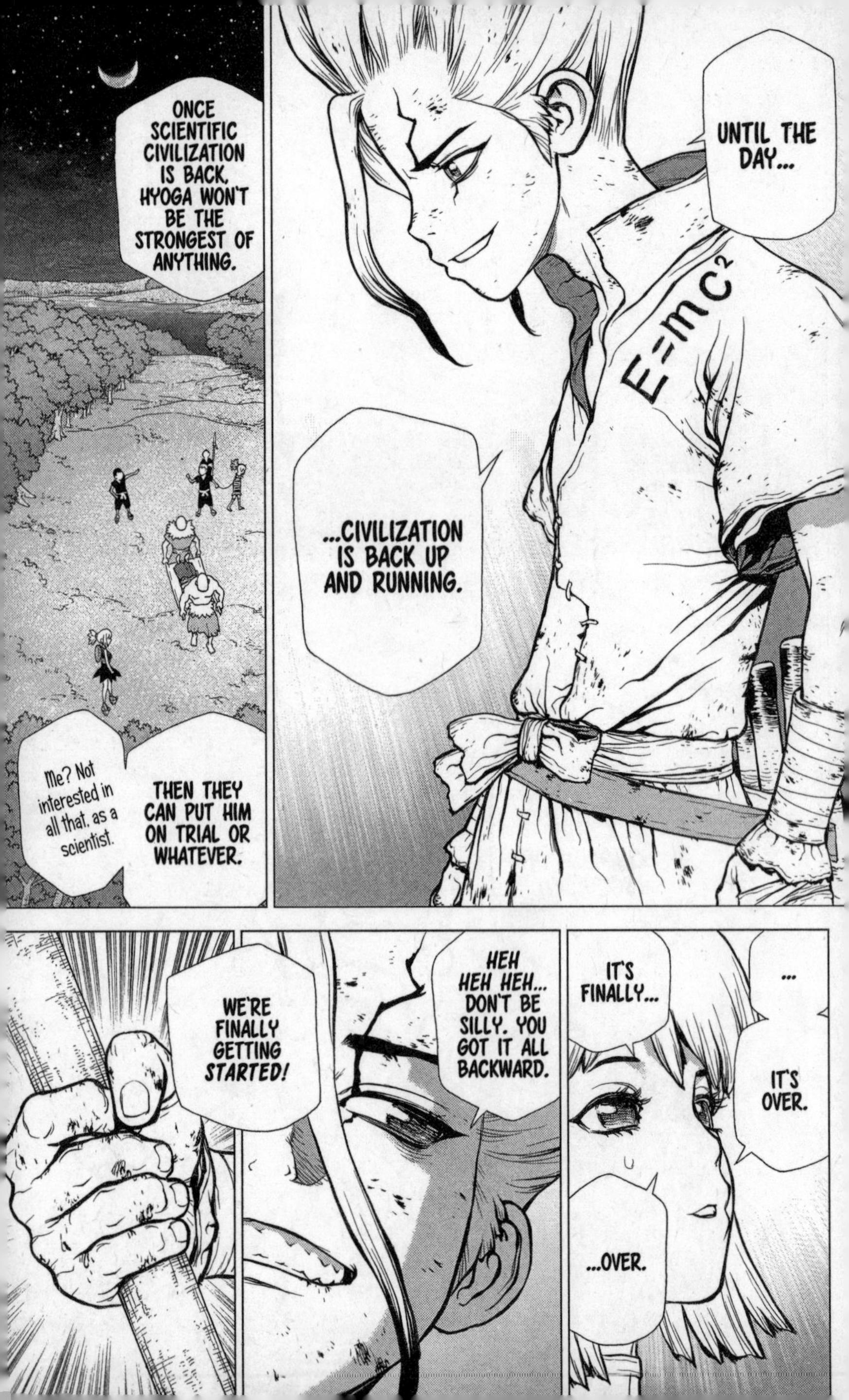
UNTIL THE DAY...
E=mc²
...CIVILIZATION IS BACK UP AND RUNNING.
ONCE SCIENTIFIC CIVILIZATION IS BACK, HYOGA WON'T BE THE STRONGEST OF ANYTHING.
THEN THEY CAN PUT HIM ON TRIAL OR WHATEVER.
Me? Not interested in all that, as a scientist.
...
IT'S OVER.
IT'S FINALLY...
...OVER.
HEH HEH HEH... DON'T BE SILLY. YOU GOT IT ALL BACKWARD.
WE'RE FINALLY GETTING STARTED!

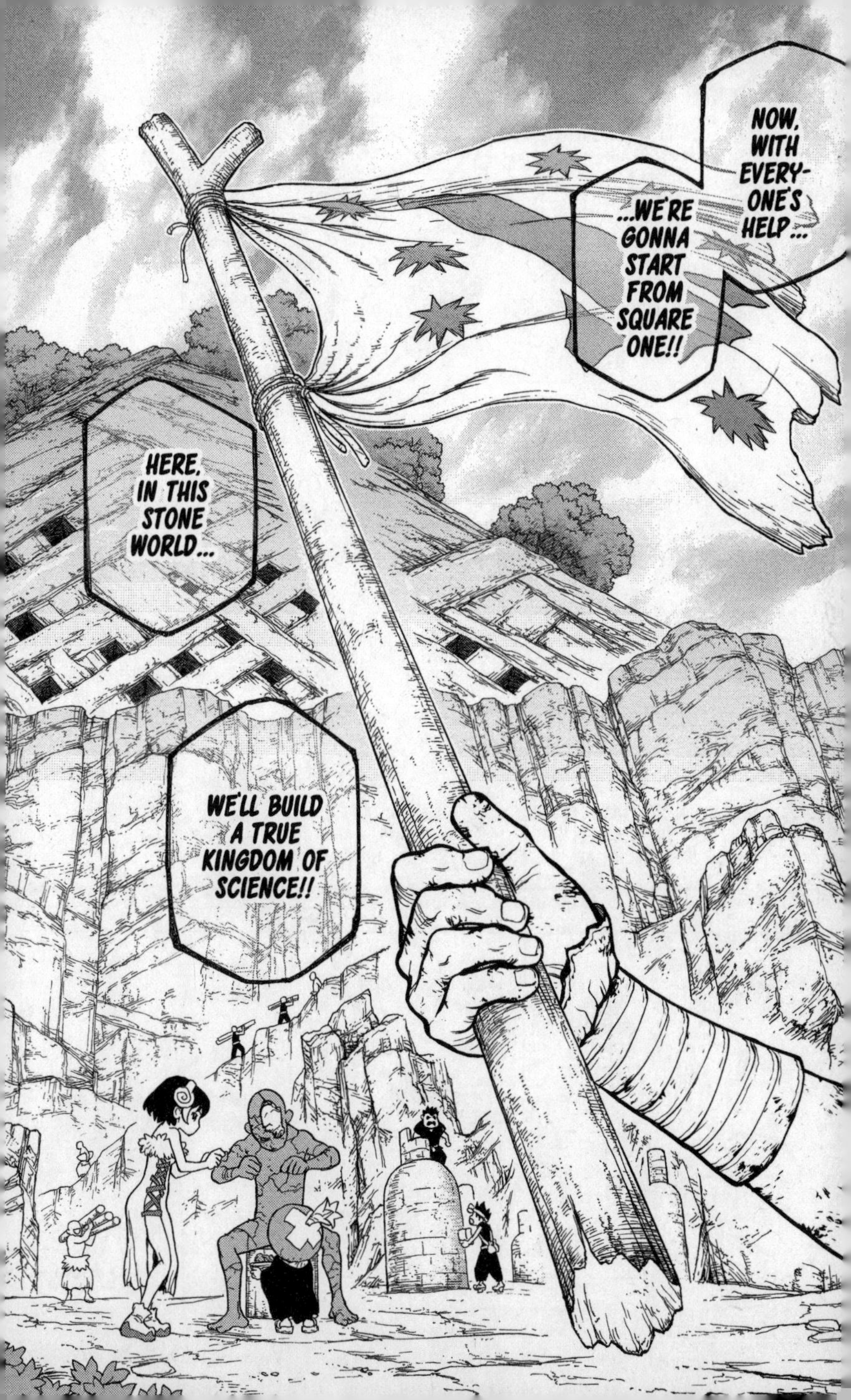
NOW, WITH EVERYONE'S HELP...
...WE'RE GONNA START FROM SQUARE ONE!!
HERE, IN THIS STONE WORLD...
WE'LL BUILD A TRUE KINGDOM OF SCIENCE!!

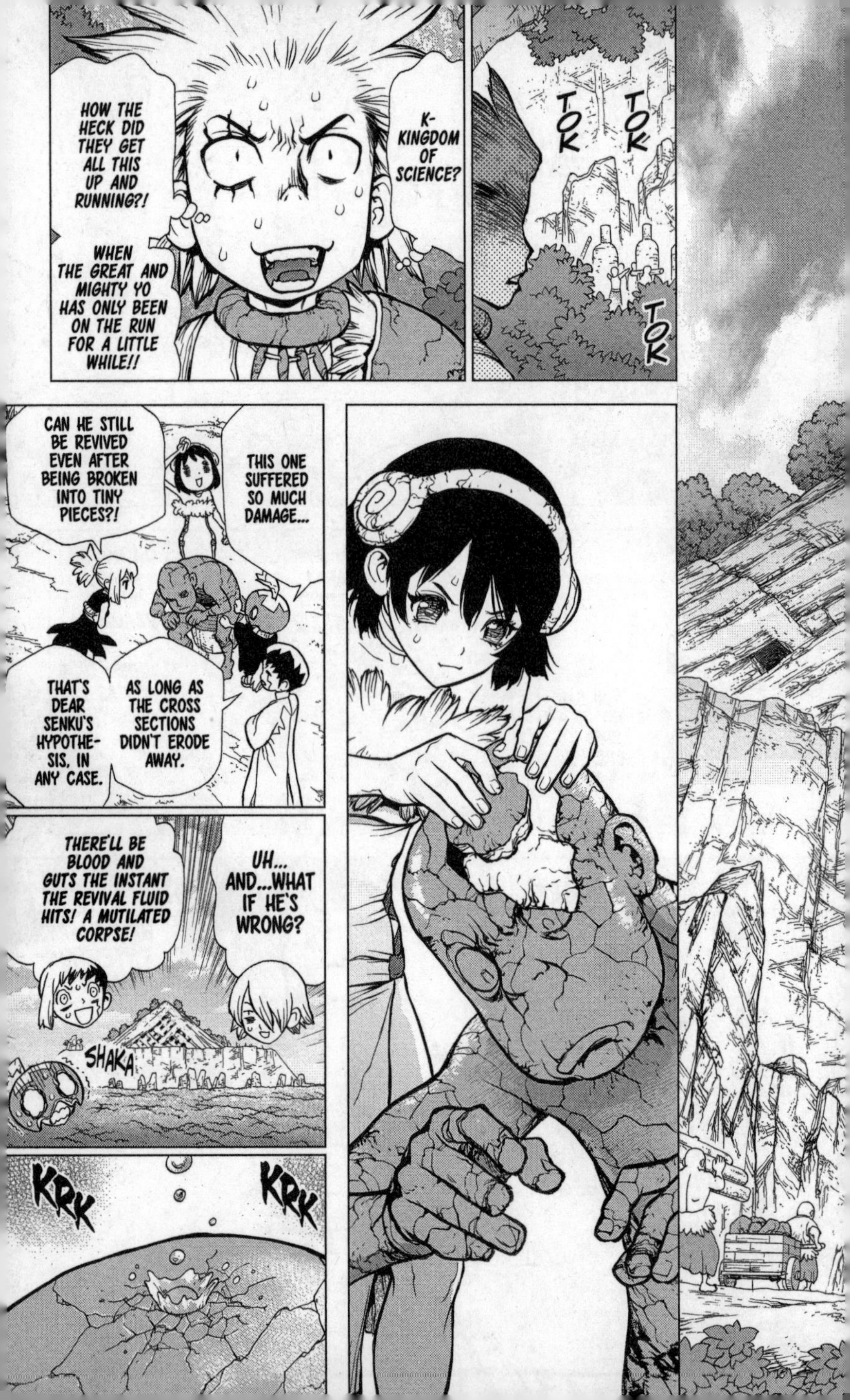
TOK TOK
K-KINGDOM OF SCIENCE?
TOK
HOW THE HECK DID THEY GET ALL THIS UP AND RUNNING?!
WHEN THE GREAT AND MIGHTY YO HAS ONLY BEEN ON THE RUN FOR A LITTLE WHILE!!
THIS ONE SUFFERED SO MUCH DAMAGE...
CAN HE STILL BE REVIVED EVEN AFTER BEING BROKEN INTO TINY PIECES?!
AS LONG AS THE CROSS SECTIONS DIDN'T ERODE AWAY.
THAT'S DEAR SENKU'S HYPOTHESIS, IN ANY CASE.
UH... AND...WHAT IF HE'S WRONG?
THERE'LL BE BLOOD AND GUTS THE INSTANT THE REVIVAL FLUID HITS! A MUTILATED CORPSE!
SHAKA
KRK
KRK

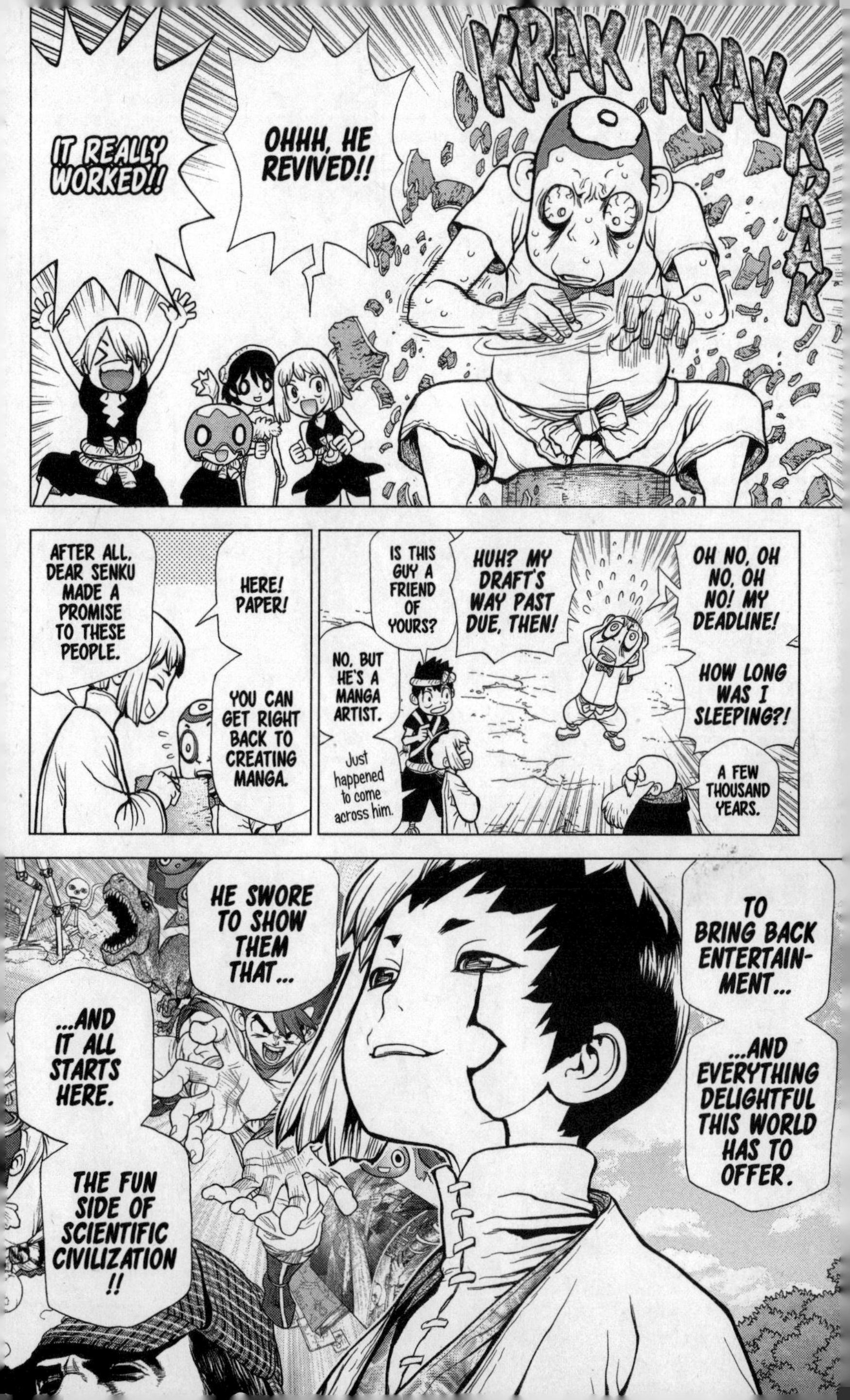
KRAK KRAK KRAK
OHHH, HE REVIVED!!
IT REALLY WORKED!!
OH NO, OH NO, OH NO! MY DEADLINE!
HOW LONG WAS I SLEEPING?!
A FEW THOUSAND YEARS.
HUH? MY DRAFT'S WAY PAST DUE, THEN!
IS THIS GUY A FRIEND OF YOURS?
NO, BUT HE'S A MANGA ARTIST.
Just happened to come across him.
HERE! PAPER!
YOU CAN GET RIGHT BACK TO CREATING MANGA.
AFTER ALL, DEAR SENKU MADE A PROMISE TO THESE PEOPLE.
TO BRING BACK ENTERTAINMENT...
...AND EVERYTHING DELIGHTFUL THIS WORLD HAS TO OFFER.
HE SWORE TO SHOW THEM THAT...
THE FUN SIDE OF SCIENTIFIC CIVILIZATION!!
...AND IT ALL STARTS HERE.

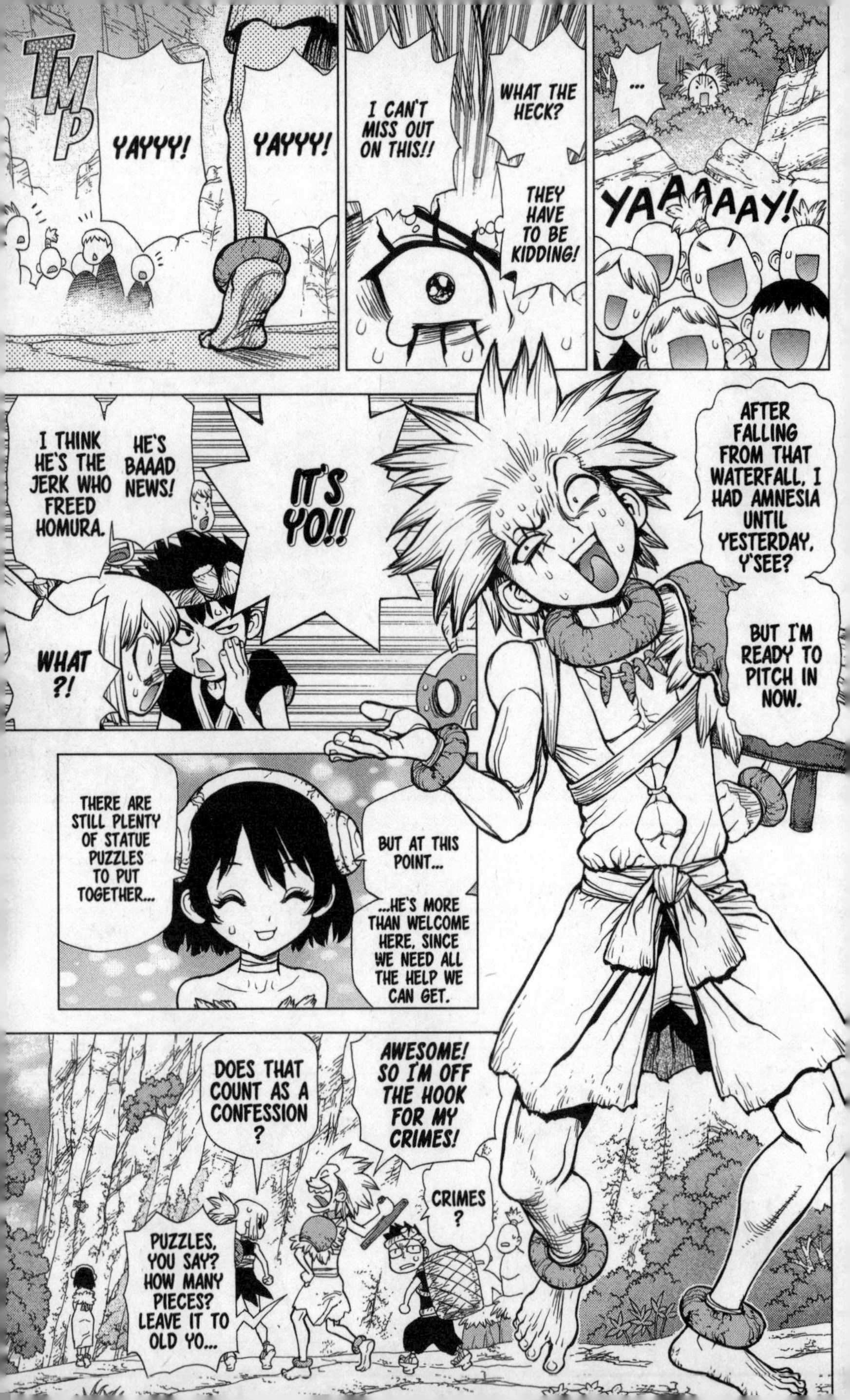
...
YAAAAAY!
WHAT THE HECK?
I CAN'T MISS OUT ON THIS!!
THEY HAVE TO BE KIDDING!
TMP
YAYYY!
YAYYY!
AFTER FALLING FROM THAT WATERFALL, I HAD AMNESIA UNTIL YESTERDAY, Y'SEE?
BUT I'M READY TO PITCH IN NOW.
IT'S YO!!
HE'S BAAAD NEWS!
I THINK HE'S THE JERK WHO FREED HOMURA.
WHAT ?!
THERE ARE STILL PLENTY OF STATUE PUZZLES TO PUT TOGETHER...
BUT AT THIS POINT...
...HE'S MORE THAN WELCOME HERE, SINCE WE NEED ALL THE HELP WE CAN GET.
AWESOME! SO I'M OFF THE HOOK FOR MY CRIMES!
DOES THAT COUNT AS A CONFESSION ?
CRIMES ?
PUZZLES, YOU SAY? HOW MANY PIECES? LEAVE IT TO OLD YO...

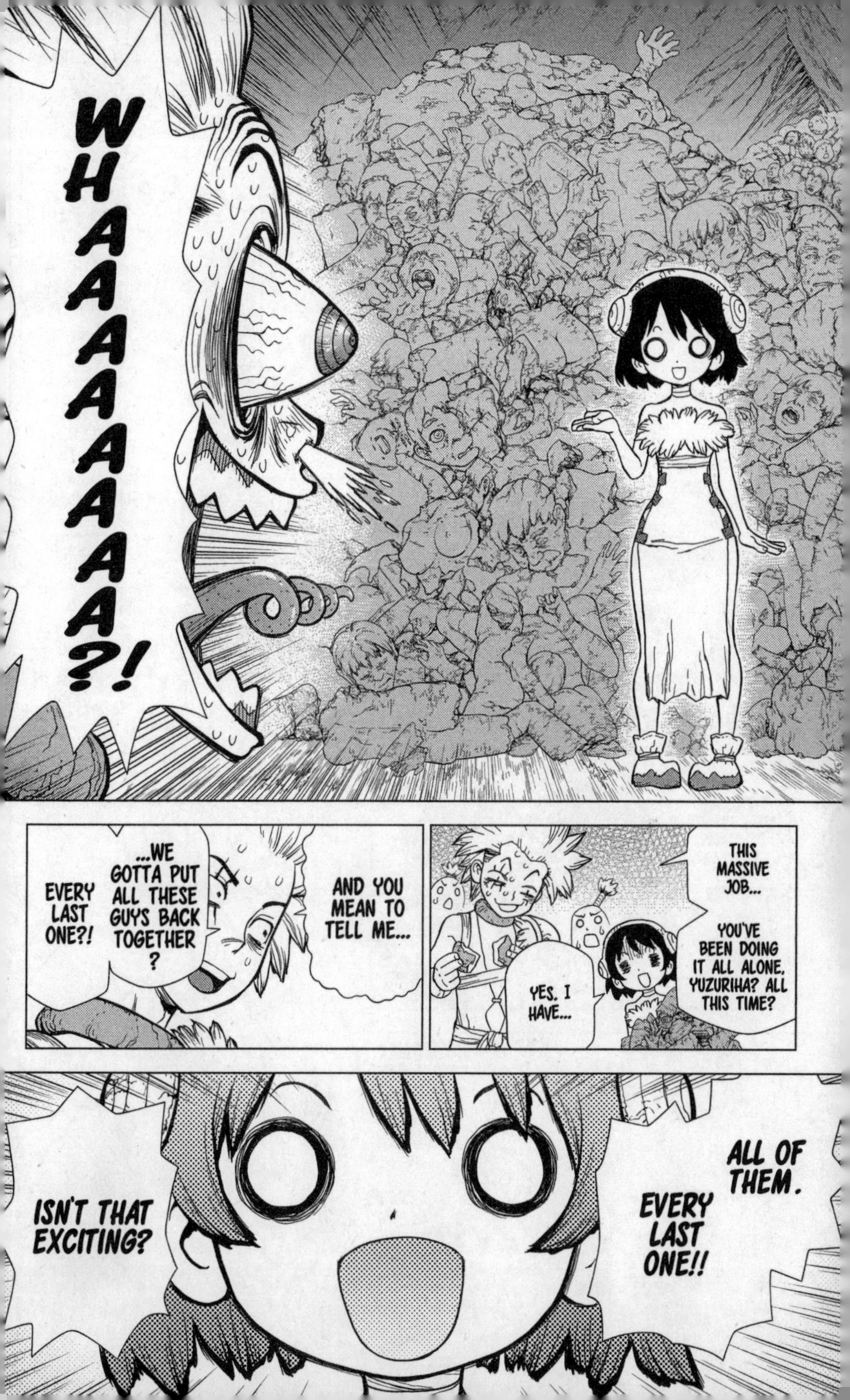
WHAAAAAAAAA?!
THIS MASSIVE JOB...
YOU'VE BEEN DOING IT ALL ALONE, YUZURIHA? ALL THIS TIME?
YES. I HAVE...
AND YOU MEAN TO TELL ME...
...WE GOTTA PUT ALL THESE GUYS BACK TOGETHER?
EVERY LAST ONE?!
ALL OF THEM.
EVERY LAST ONE!!
ISN'T THAT EXCITING?

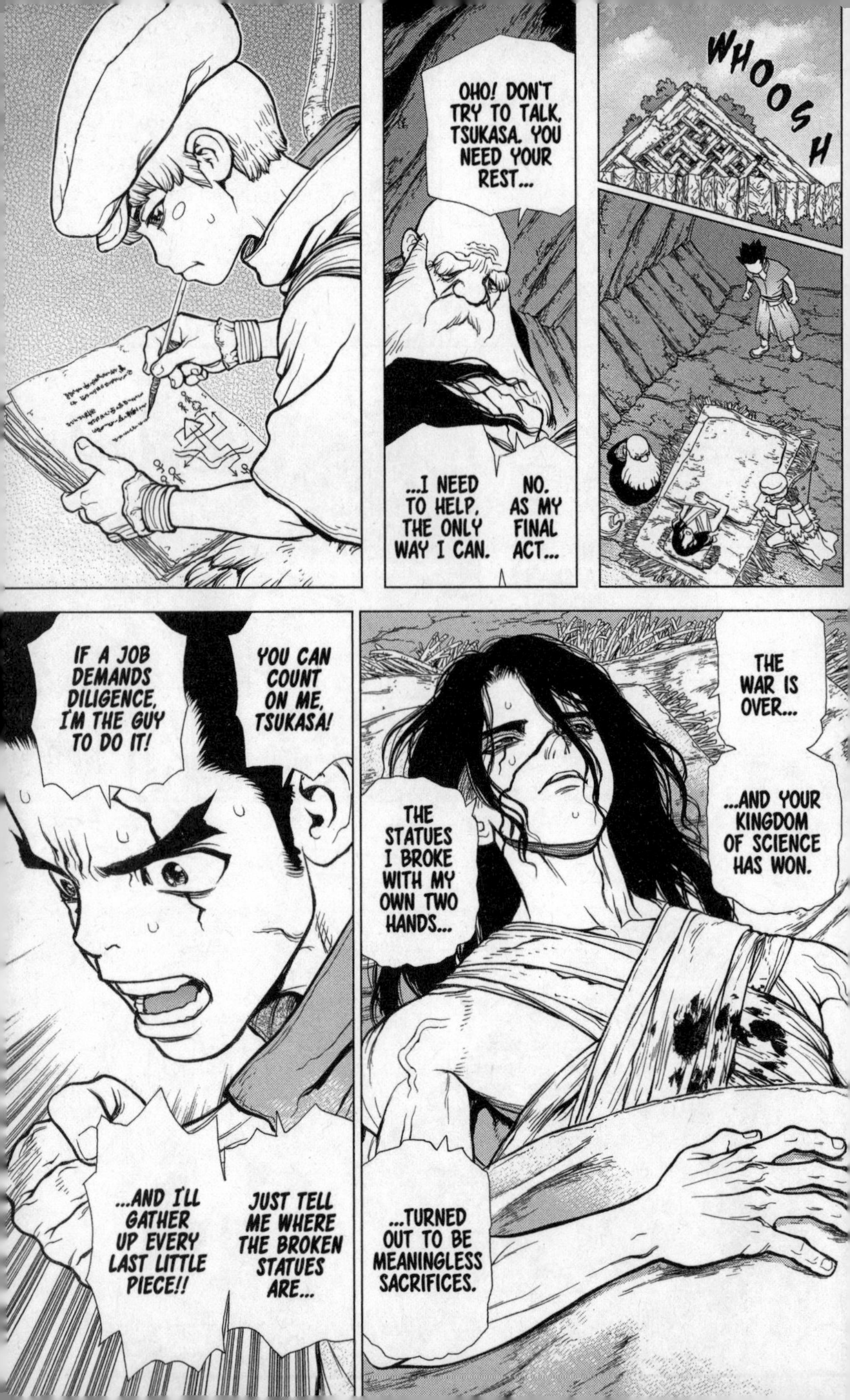
WHOOSH
OHO! DON'T TRY TO TALK, TSUKASA. YOU NEED YOUR REST...
NO. AS MY FINAL ACT...
...I NEED TO HELP, THE ONLY WAY I CAN.
THE WAR IS OVER...
...AND YOUR KINGDOM OF SCIENCE HAS WON.
THE STATUES I BROKE WITH MY OWN TWO HANDS...
...TURNED OUT TO BE MEANINGLESS SACRIFICES.
YOU CAN COUNT ON ME, TSUKASA!
IF A JOB DEMANDS DILIGENCE, I'M THE GUY TO DO IT!
JUST TELL ME WHERE THE BROKEN STATUES ARE...
...AND I'LL GATHER UP EVERY LAST LITTLE PIECE!!

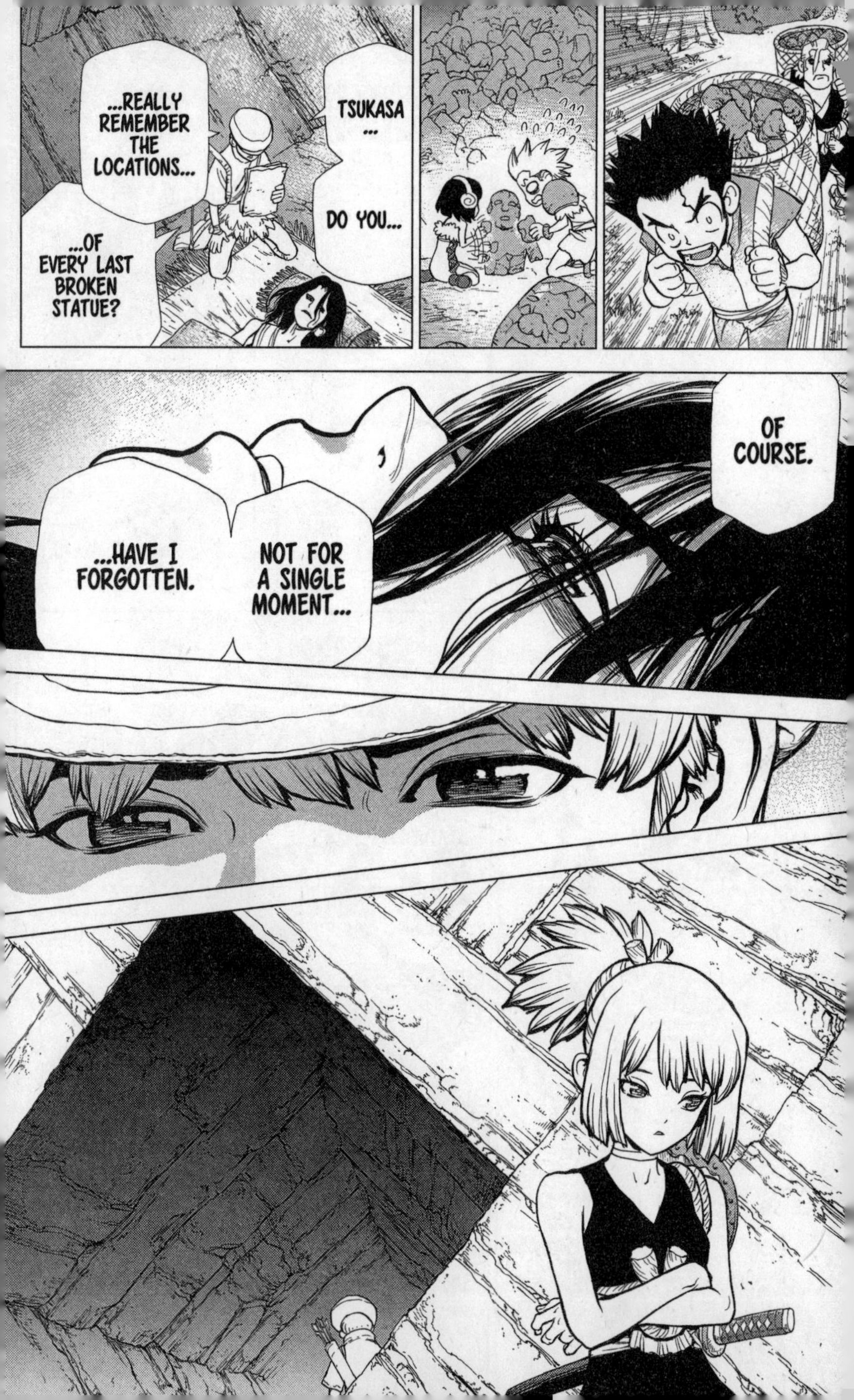
TSUKASA ...
DO YOU...
...REALLY REMEMBER THE LOCATIONS...
...OF EVERY LAST BROKEN STATUE?
OF COURSE.
NOT FOR A SINGLE MOMENT...
...HAVE I FORGOTTEN.

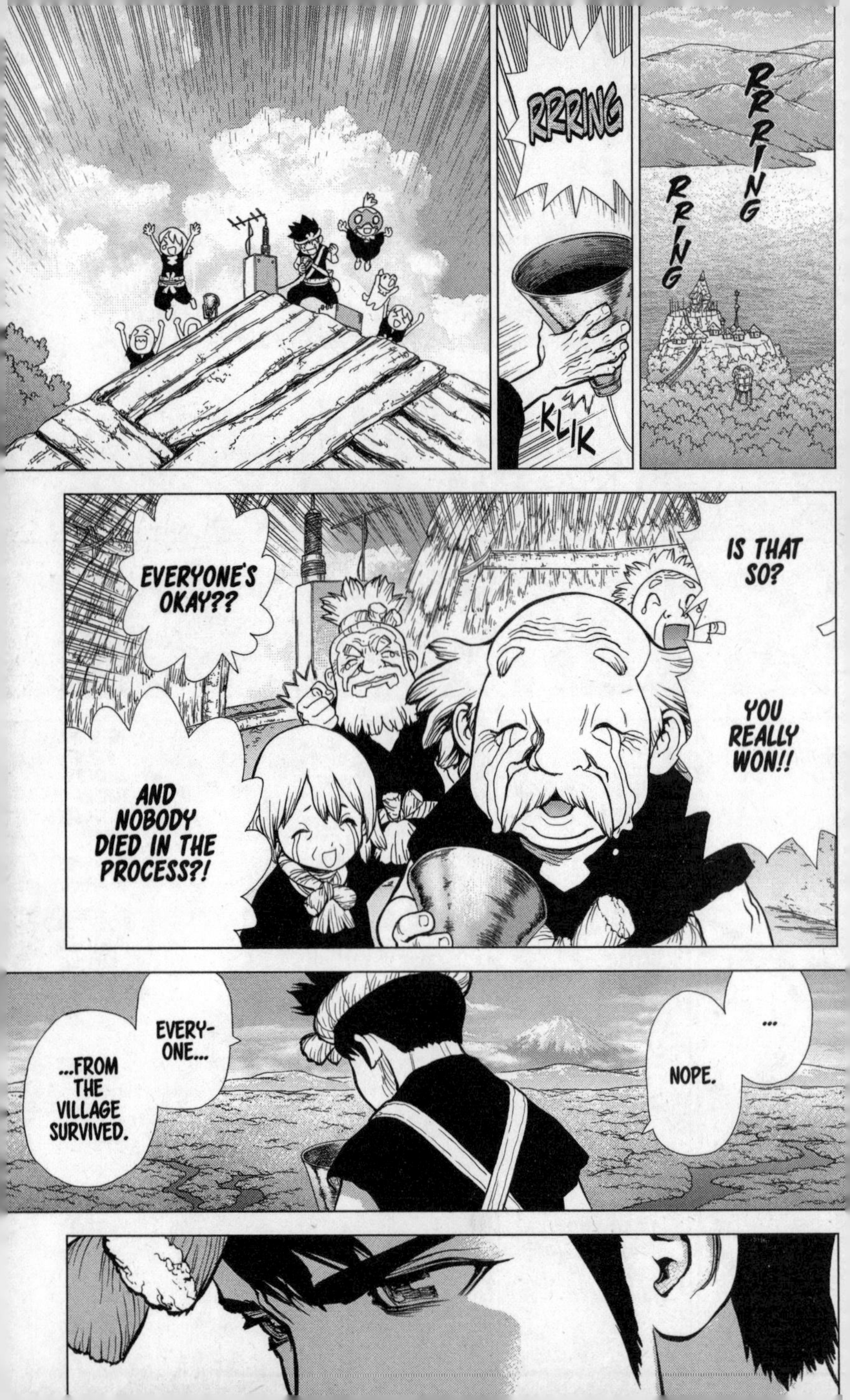

RRRING
RRING
RRRING
KLIK
IS THAT SO?
YOU REALLY WON!!
EVERYONE'S OKAY??
AND NOBODY DIED IN THE PROCESS?!
...
NOPE.
EVERY-ONE...
...FROM THE VILLAGE SURVIVED.

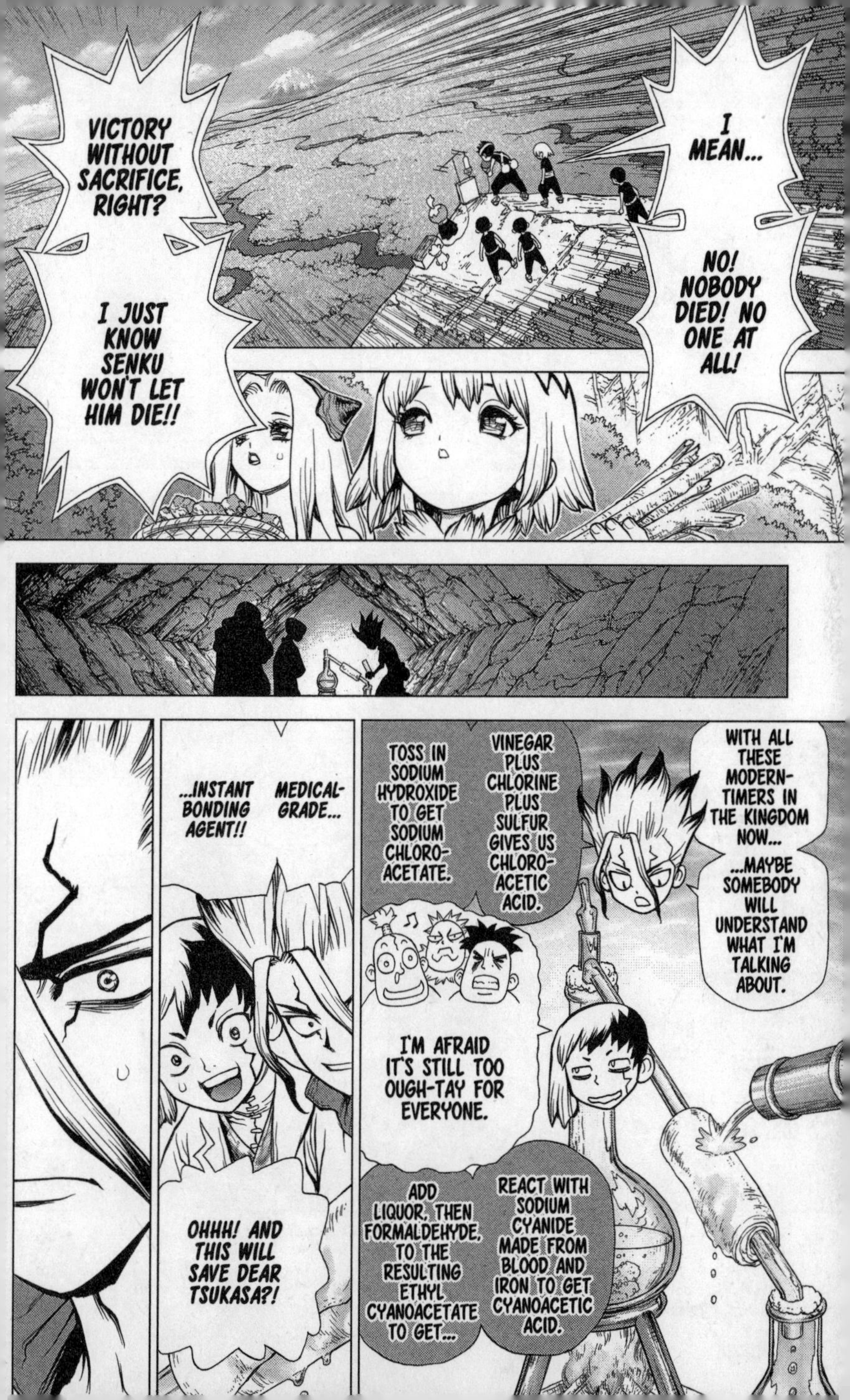
I MEAN...
NO! NOBODY DIED! NO ONE AT ALL!
VICTORY WITHOUT SACRIFICE, RIGHT?
I JUST KNOW SENKU WON'T LET HIM DIE!!
WITH ALL THESE MODERN-TIMERS IN THE KINGDOM NOW...
...MAYBE SOMEBODY WILL UNDERSTAND WHAT I'M TALKING ABOUT.
VINEGAR PLUS CHLORINE PLUS SULFUR GIVES US CHLORO-ACETIC ACID.
TOSS IN SODIUM HYDROXIDE TO GET SODIUM CHLORO-ACETATE.
I'M AFRAID IT'S STILL TOO OUGH-TAY FOR EVERYONE.
REACT WITH SODIUM CYANIDE MADE FROM BLOOD AND IRON TO GET CYANOACETIC ACID.
ADD LIQUOR, THEN FORMALDEHYDE, TO THE RESULTING ETHYL CYANOACETATE TO GET...
MEDICAL-GRADE...
...INSTANT BONDING AGENT!!
OHHH! AND THIS WILL SAVE DEAR TSUKASA?!

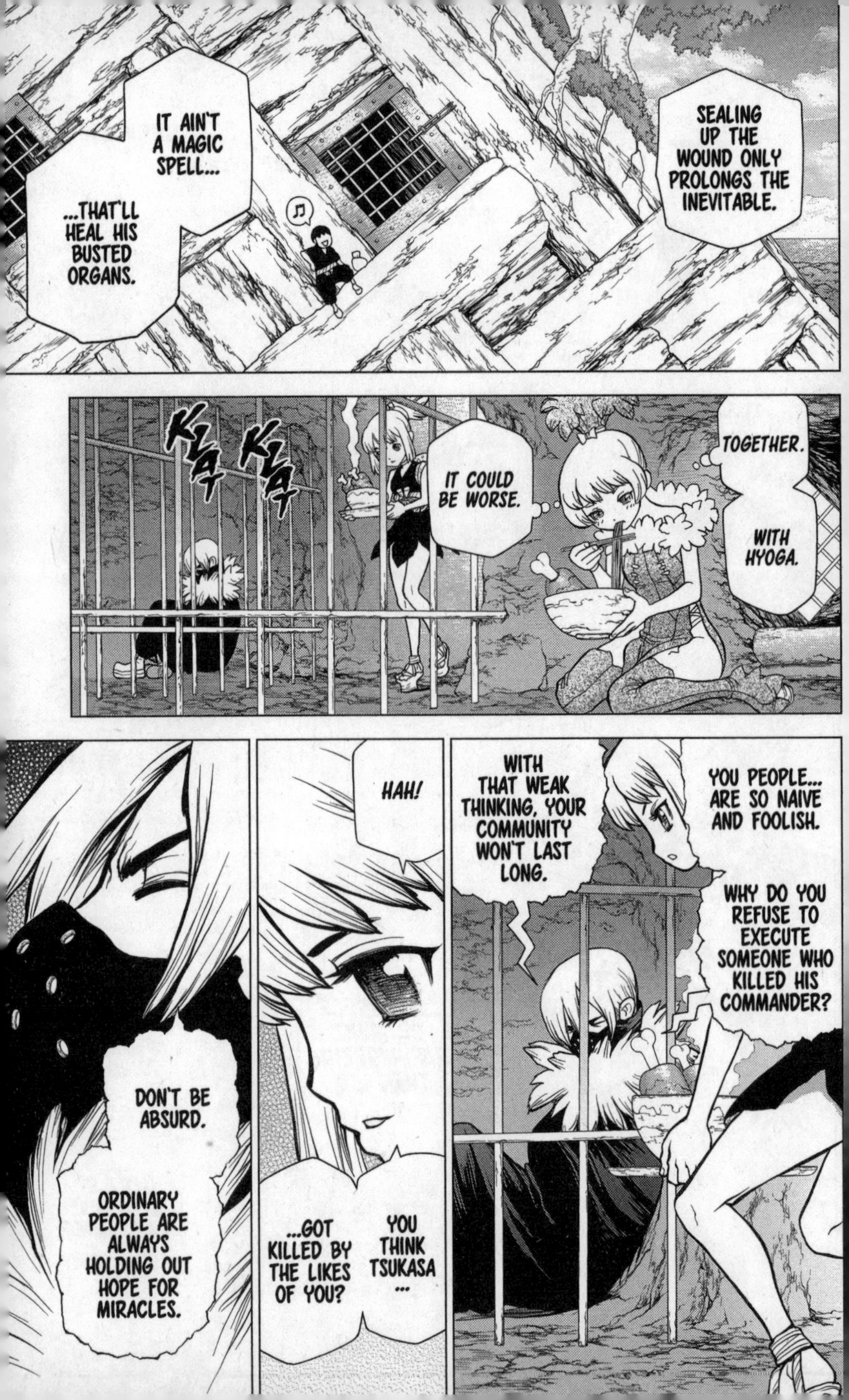
SEALING UP THE WOUND ONLY PROLONGS THE INEVITABLE.
IT AIN'T A MAGIC SPELL...
...THAT'LL HEAL HIS BUSTED ORGANS.
TOGETHER.
WITH HYOGA.
IT COULD BE WORSE.
KLAT
KLAT
YOU PEOPLE... ARE SO NAIVE AND FOOLISH.
WHY DO YOU REFUSE TO EXECUTE SOMEONE WHO KILLED HIS COMMANDER?
WITH THAT WEAK THINKING, YOUR COMMUNITY WON'T LAST LONG.
HAH!
YOU THINK TSUKASA...
...GOT KILLED BY THE LIKES OF YOU?
DON'T BE ABSURD.
ORDINARY PEOPLE ARE ALWAYS HOLDING OUT HOPE FOR MIRACLES.

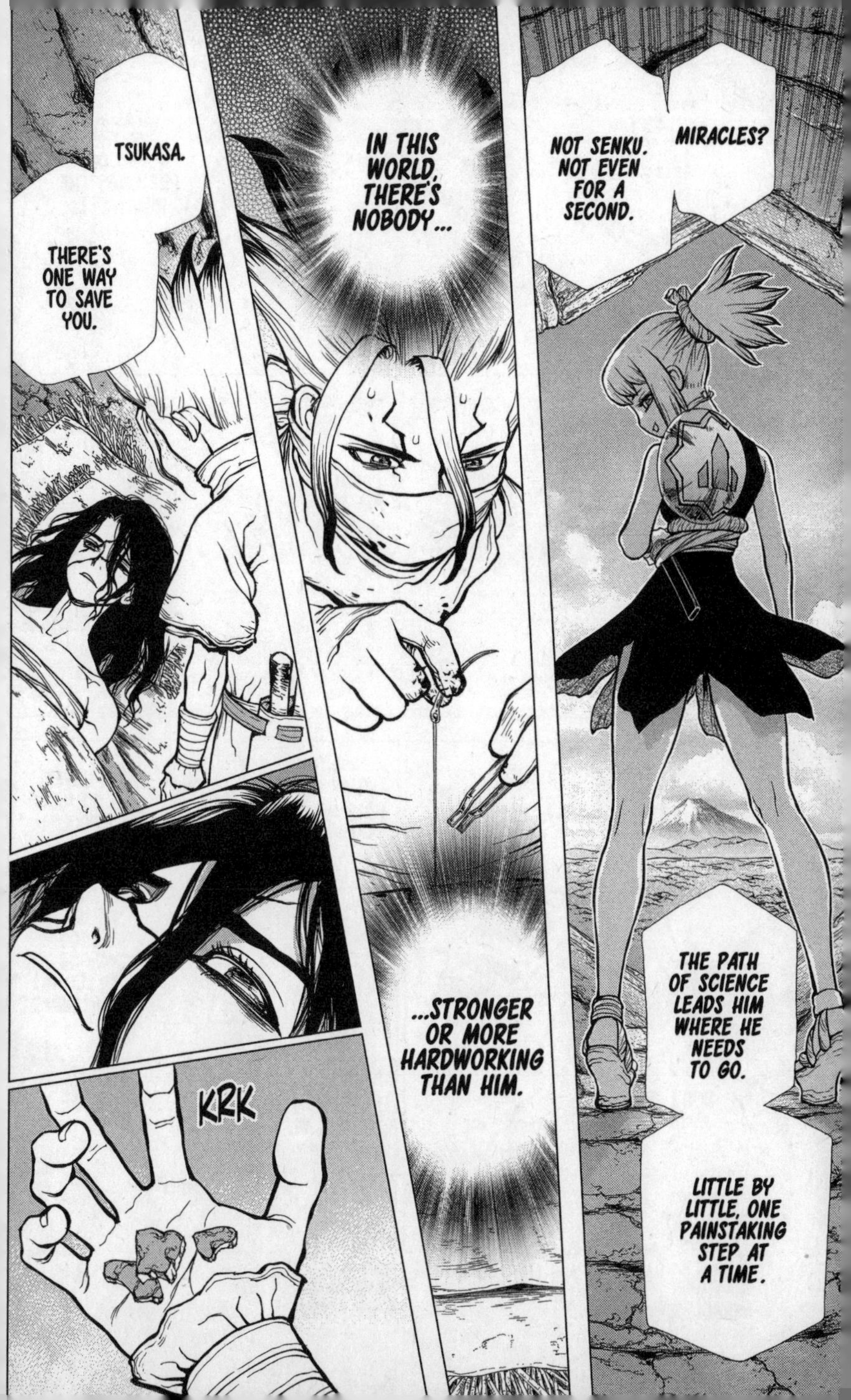
MIRACLES?
NOT SENKU. NOT EVEN FOR A SECOND.
THE PATH OF SCIENCE LEADS HIM WHERE HE NEEDS TO GO.
LITTLE BY LITTLE, ONE PAINSTAKING STEP AT A TIME.
IN THIS WORLD, THERE'S NOBODY...
...STRONGER OR MORE HARDWORKING THAN HIM.
TSUKASA.
THERE'S ONE WAY TO SAVE YOU.
KRK

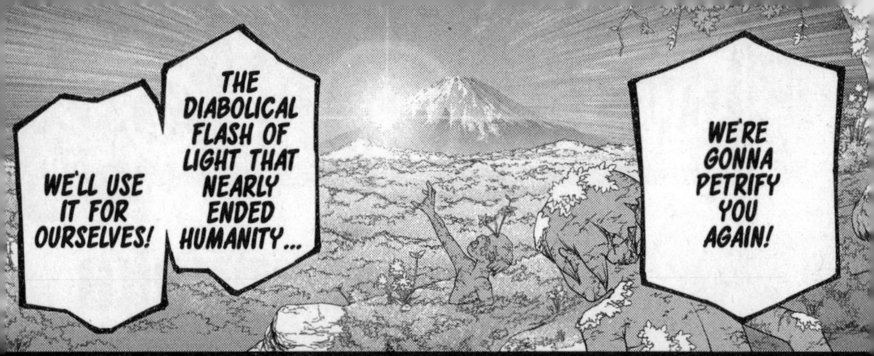
WE'RE GONNA PETRIFY YOU AGAIN!
THE DIABOLICAL FLASH OF LIGHT THAT NEARLY ENDED HUMANITY...
WE'LL USE IT FOR OURSELVES!

Part 3: Dr. STONE

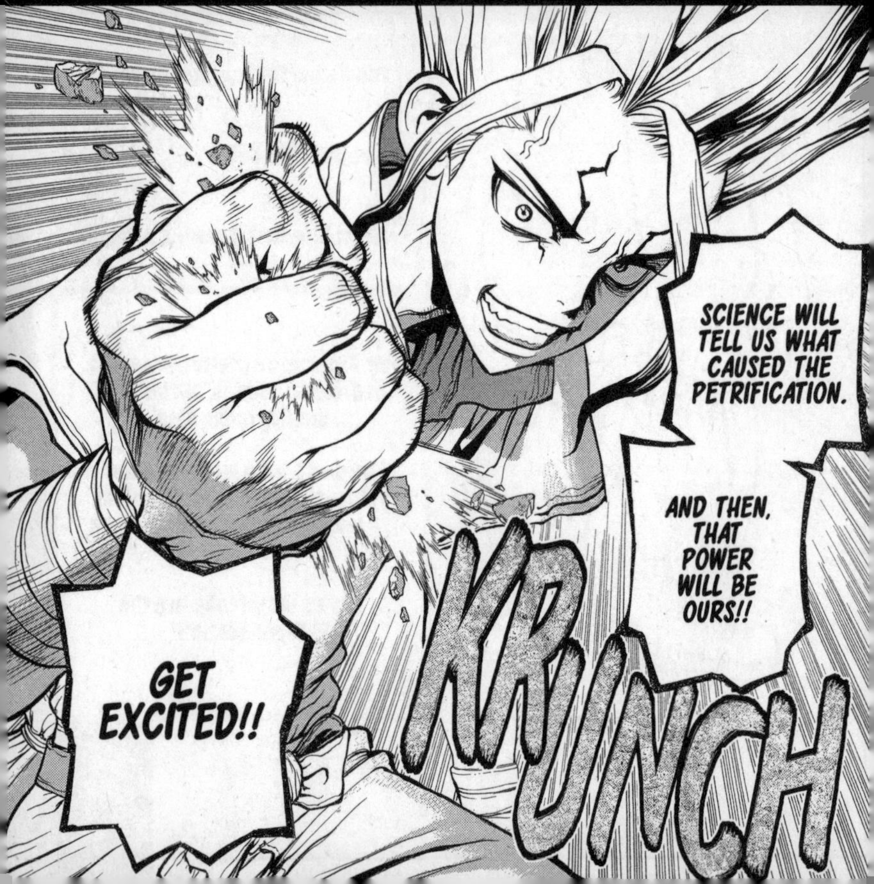
SCIENCE WILL TELL US WHAT CAUSED THE PETRIFICATION.
AND THEN, THAT POWER WILL BE OURS!!
KRUNCH
GET EXCITED!!

Kingdom of Science

WORKER FILE 1

Mr. Mangaka

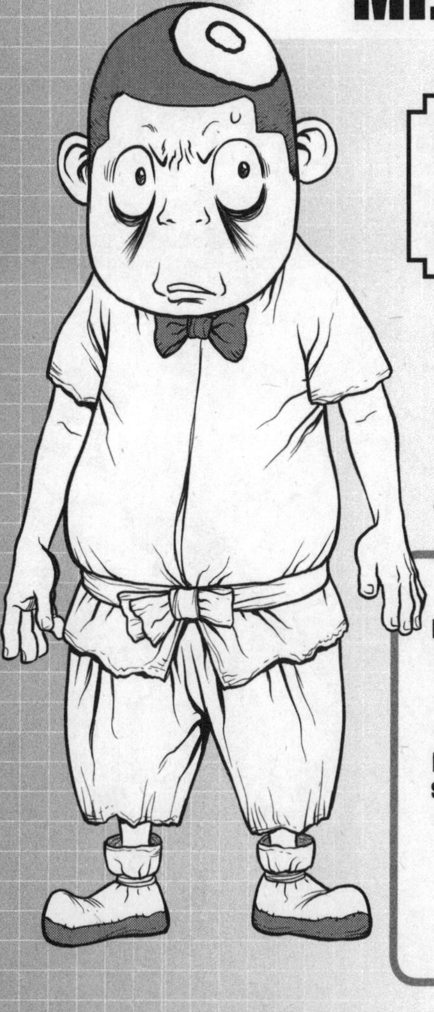

Manga Power:	★★★★
Earnability:	★
All-Nighter Skills:	★★★★★

Full Name: Tetsuya Kinomoto

Height: 155 cm

Job in Kingdom: Drawing pictures

Mr. Kinomoto's pretty darn great at drawing comics, but he's not good at much else.

He was a little let down upon being revived in a world lacking so many amenities, but...then he realized—no more deadlines.

Say no more! Long live the Stone World!!!

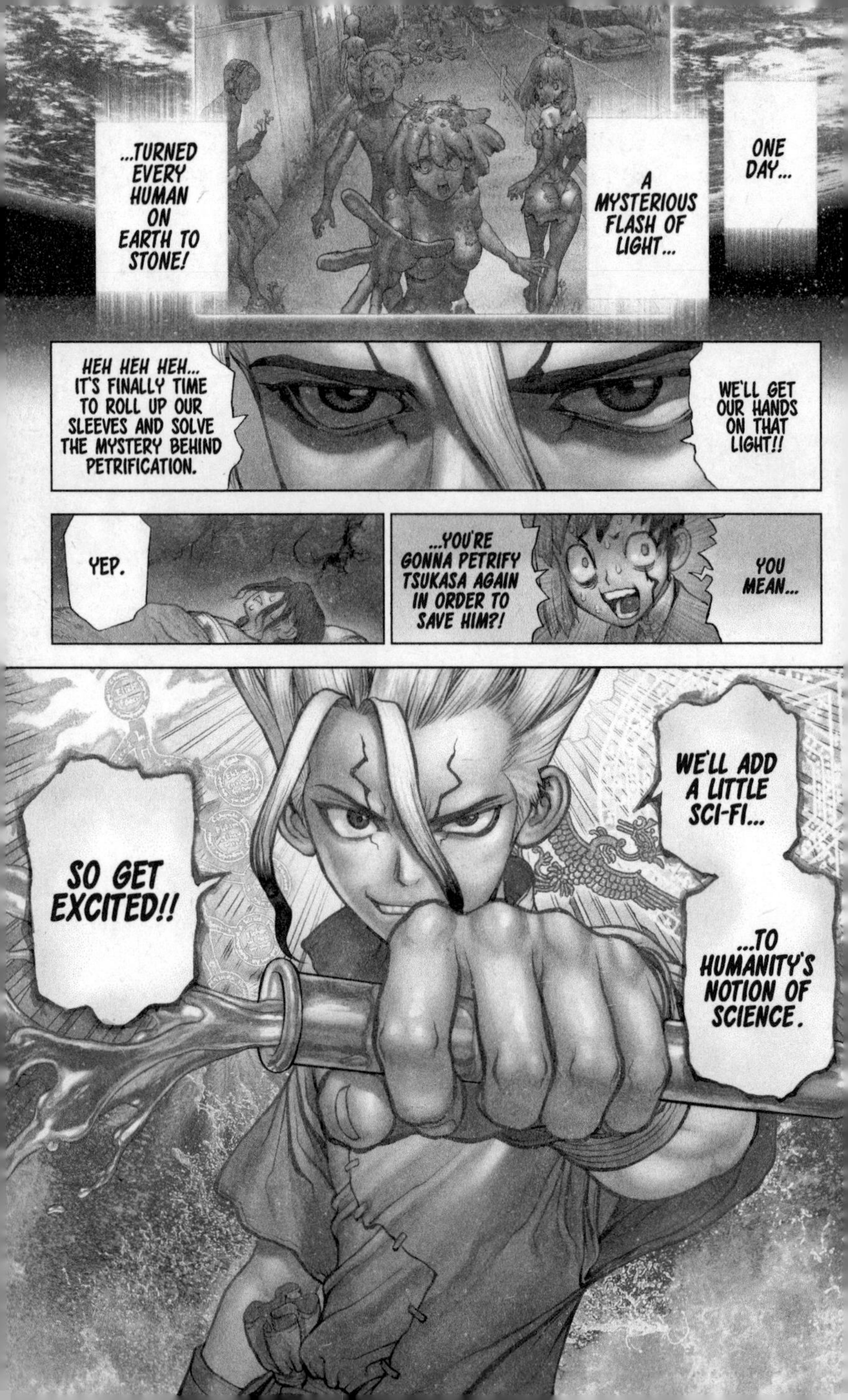
ONE DAY...
A MYSTERIOUS FLASH OF LIGHT...
...TURNED EVERY HUMAN ON EARTH TO STONE!
HEH HEH HEH... IT'S FINALLY TIME TO ROLL UP OUR SLEEVES AND SOLVE THE MYSTERY BEHIND PETRIFICATION.
WE'LL GET OUR HANDS ON THAT LIGHT!!
YOU MEAN...
...YOU'RE GONNA PETRIFY TSUKASA AGAIN IN ORDER TO SAVE HIM?!
YEP.
WE'LL ADD A LITTLE SCI-FI...
...TO HUMANITY'S NOTION OF SCIENCE.
SO GET EXCITED!!

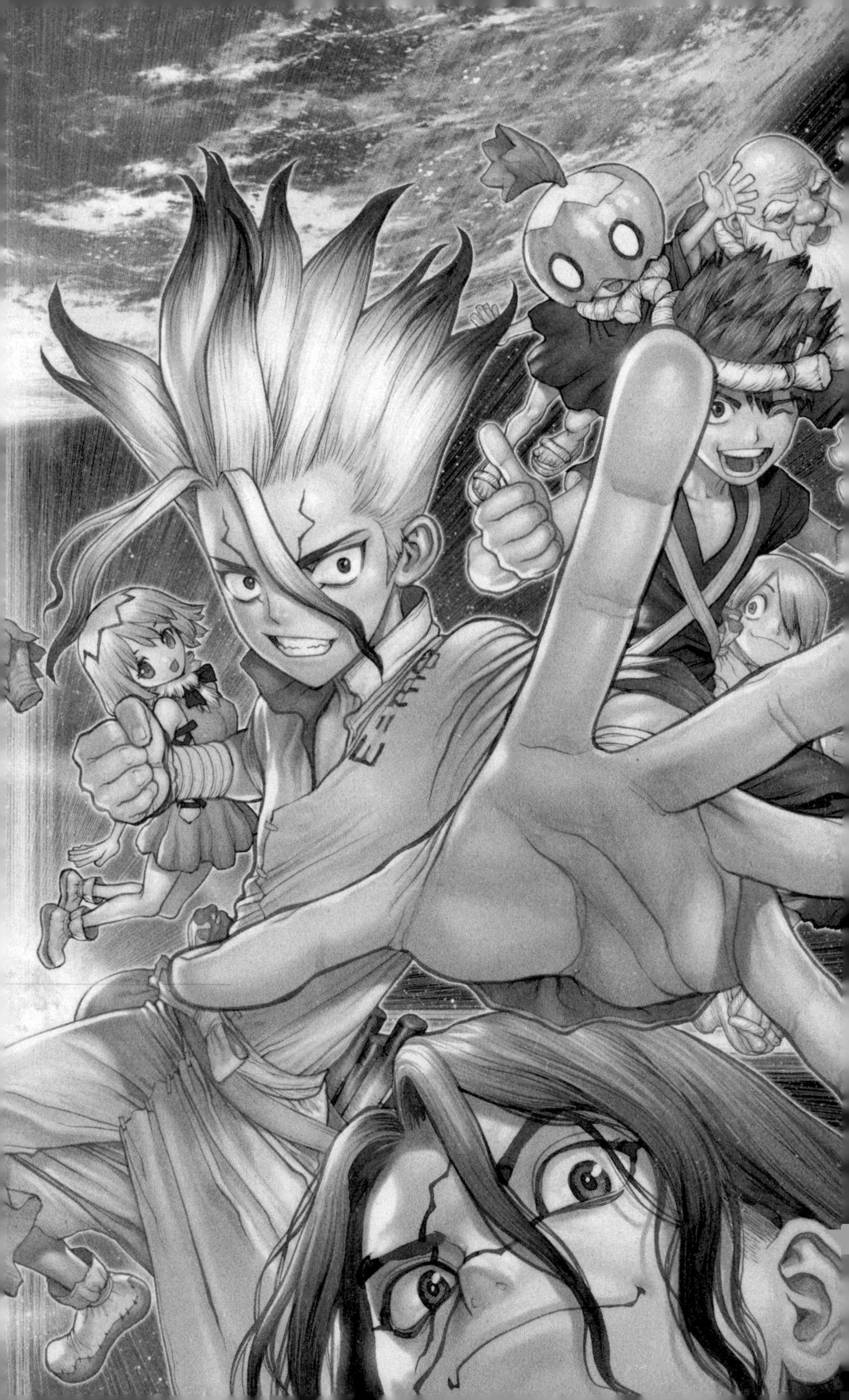

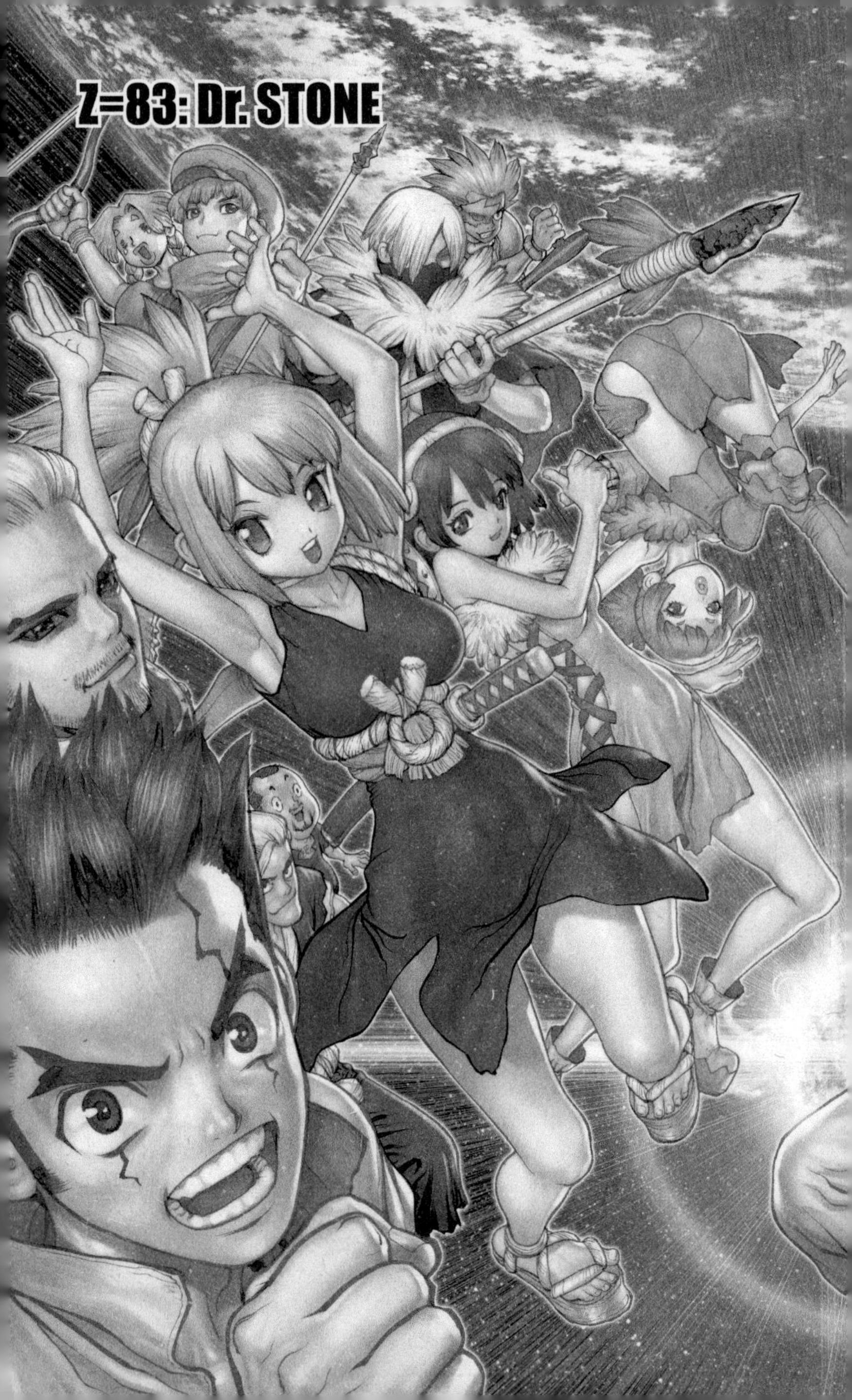
Z=83: Dr. STONE

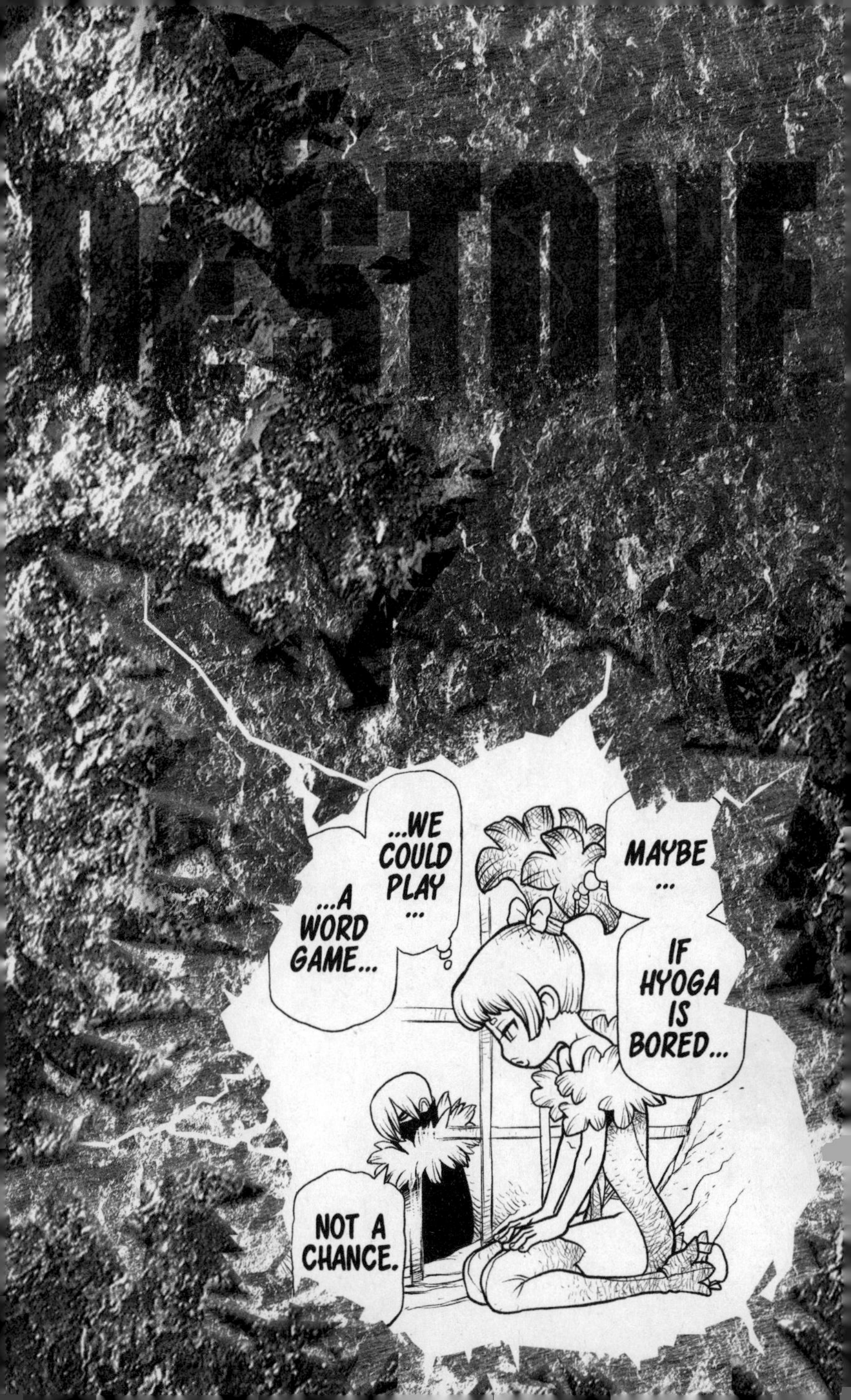
Dr.STONE
MAYBE ... IF HYOGA IS BORED...
...WE COULD PLAY ... ...A WORD GAME...
NOT A CHANCE.

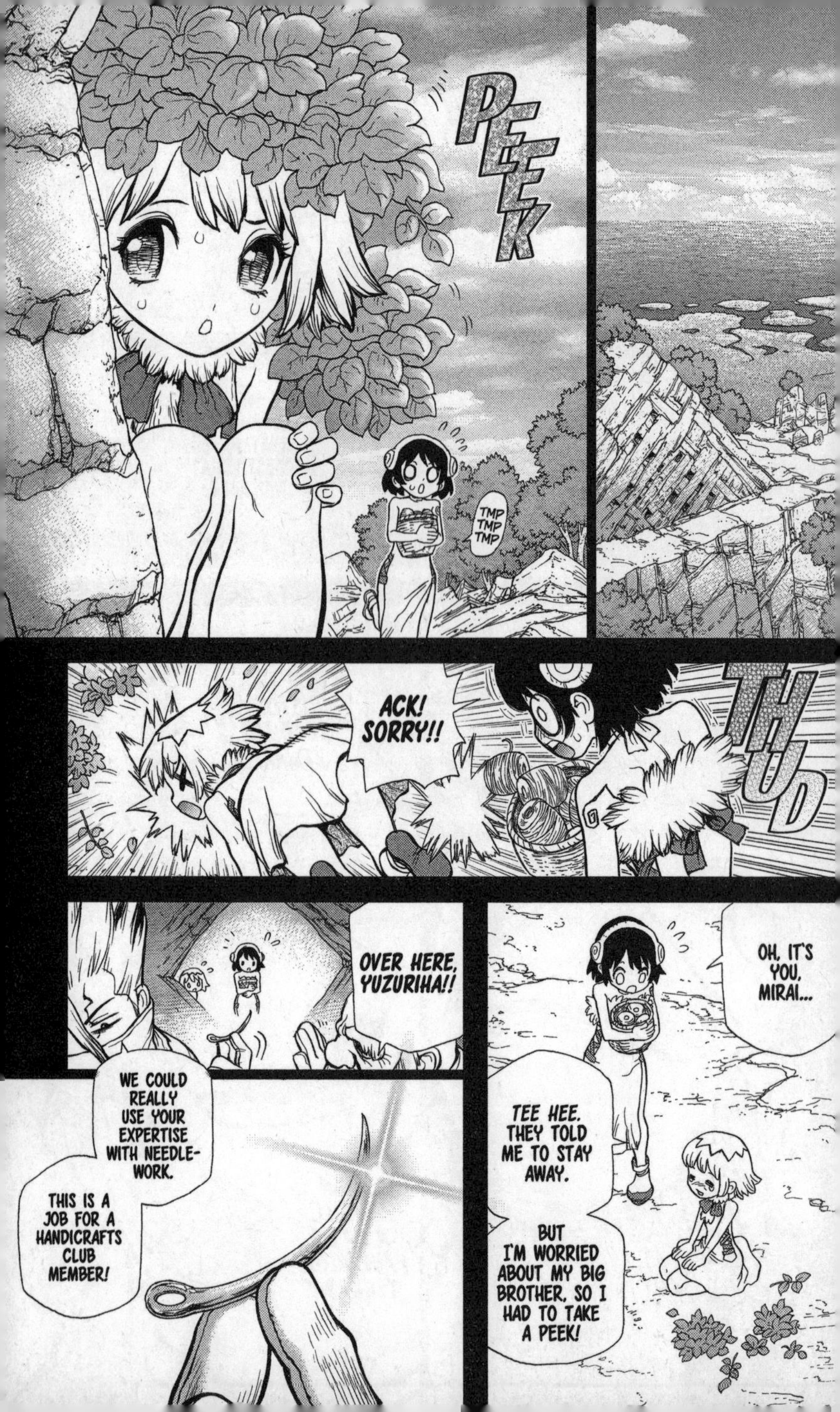
PEEK
TMP TMP TMP
THUD
ACK! SORRY!!
OH, IT'S YOU, MIRAI...
TEE HEE. THEY TOLD ME TO STAY AWAY.
BUT I'M WORRIED ABOUT MY BIG BROTHER, SO I HAD TO TAKE A PEEK!
OVER HERE, YUZURIHA!!
WE COULD REALLY USE YOUR EXPERTISE WITH NEEDLE-WORK.
THIS IS A JOB FOR A HANDICRAFTS CLUB MEMBER!

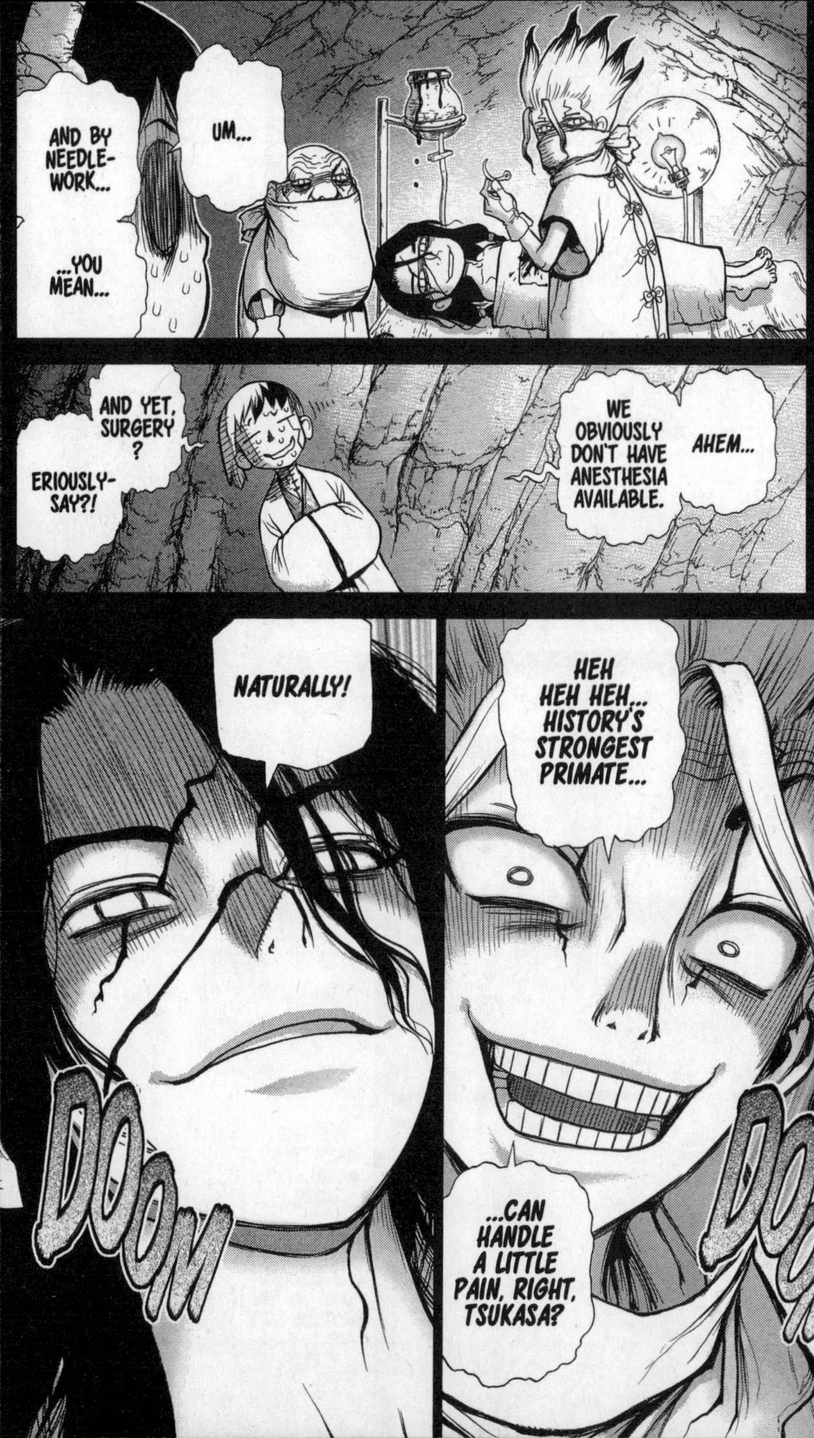
UM...
AND BY NEEDLE-WORK...
...YOU MEAN...
AHEM...
WE OBVIOUSLY DON'T HAVE ANESTHESIA AVAILABLE.
AND YET, SURGERY?
ERIOUSLY-SAY?!
HEH HEH HEH... HISTORY'S STRONGEST PRIMATE...
...CAN HANDLE A LITTLE PAIN, RIGHT, TSUKASA?
DOOM
NATURALLY!
DOOM

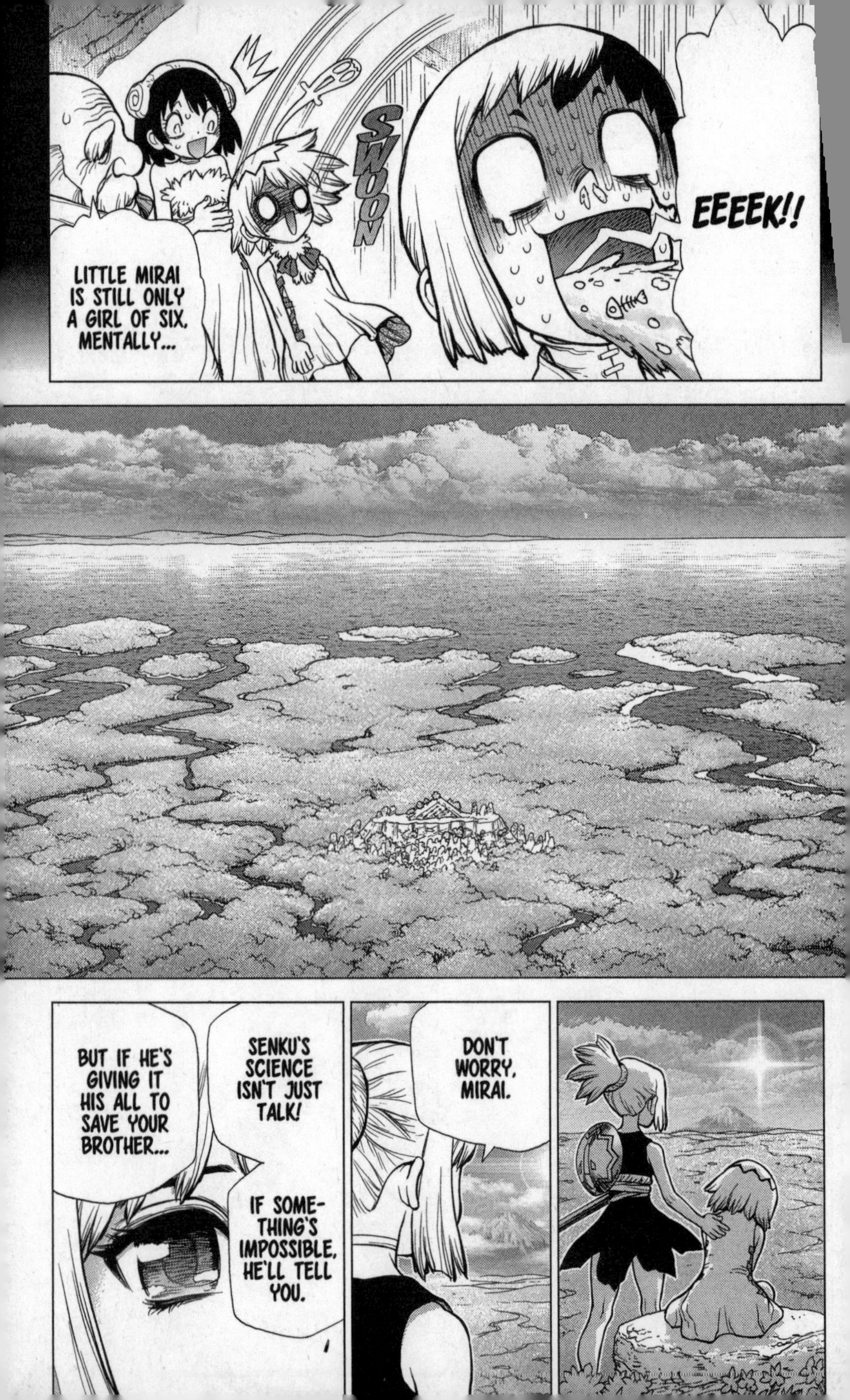
EEEEK!!
SWOOON
LITTLE MIRAI IS STILL ONLY A GIRL OF SIX, MENTALLY...
DON'T WORRY, MIRAI.
SENKU'S SCIENCE ISN'T JUST TALK!
BUT IF HE'S GIVING IT HIS ALL TO SAVE YOUR BROTHER...
IF SOMETHING'S IMPOSSIBLE, HE'LL TELL YOU.

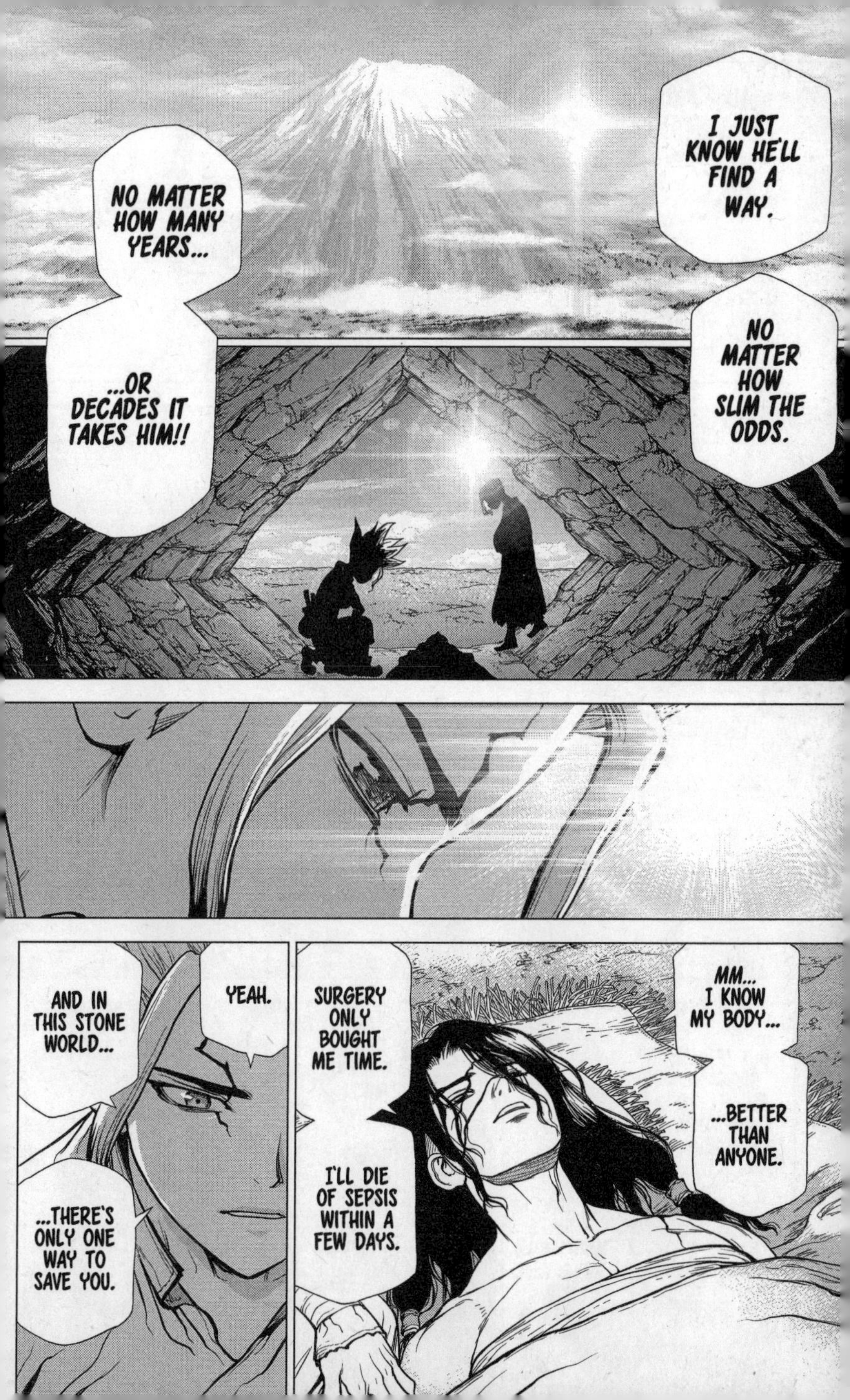
I JUST KNOW HE'LL FIND A WAY.
NO MATTER HOW MANY YEARS...
NO MATTER HOW SLIM THE ODDS.
...OR DECADES IT TAKES HIM!!
MM... I KNOW MY BODY...
...BETTER THAN ANYONE.
SURGERY ONLY BOUGHT ME TIME.
I'LL DIE OF SEPSIS WITHIN A FEW DAYS.
YEAH.
AND IN THIS STONE WORLD...
...THERE'S ONLY ONE WAY TO SAVE YOU.

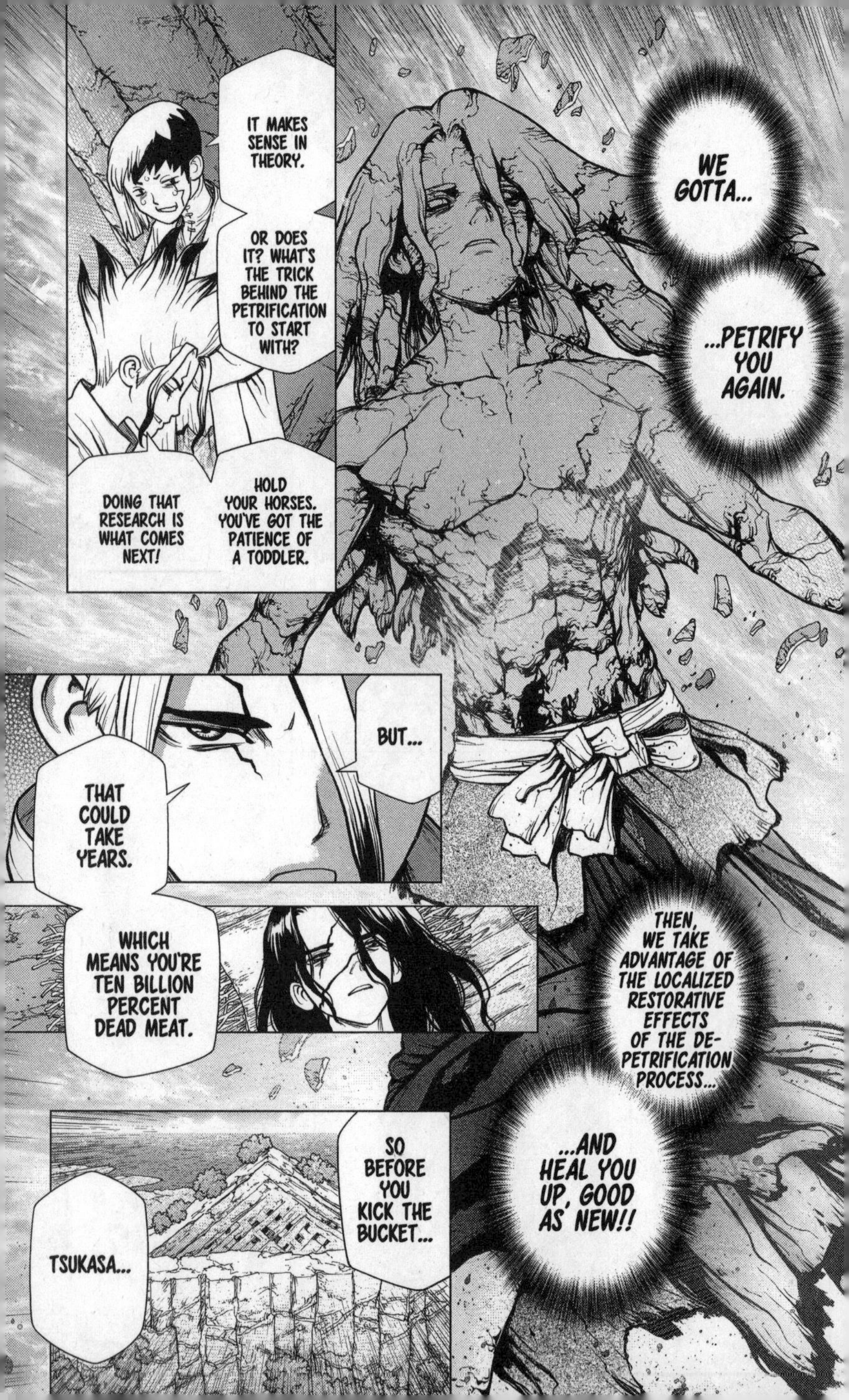

WE GOTTA...
...PETRIFY YOU AGAIN.
THEN, WE TAKE ADVANTAGE OF THE LOCALIZED RESTORATIVE EFFECTS OF THE DE-PETRIFICATION PROCESS...
...AND HEAL YOU UP, GOOD AS NEW!!
IT MAKES SENSE IN THEORY.
OR DOES IT? WHAT'S THE TRICK BEHIND THE PETRIFICATION TO START WITH?
HOLD YOUR HORSES. YOU'VE GOT THE PATIENCE OF A TODDLER.
DOING THAT RESEARCH IS WHAT COMES NEXT!
BUT...
THAT COULD TAKE YEARS.
WHICH MEANS YOU'RE TEN BILLION PERCENT DEAD MEAT.
SO BEFORE YOU KICK THE BUCKET...
TSUKASA...

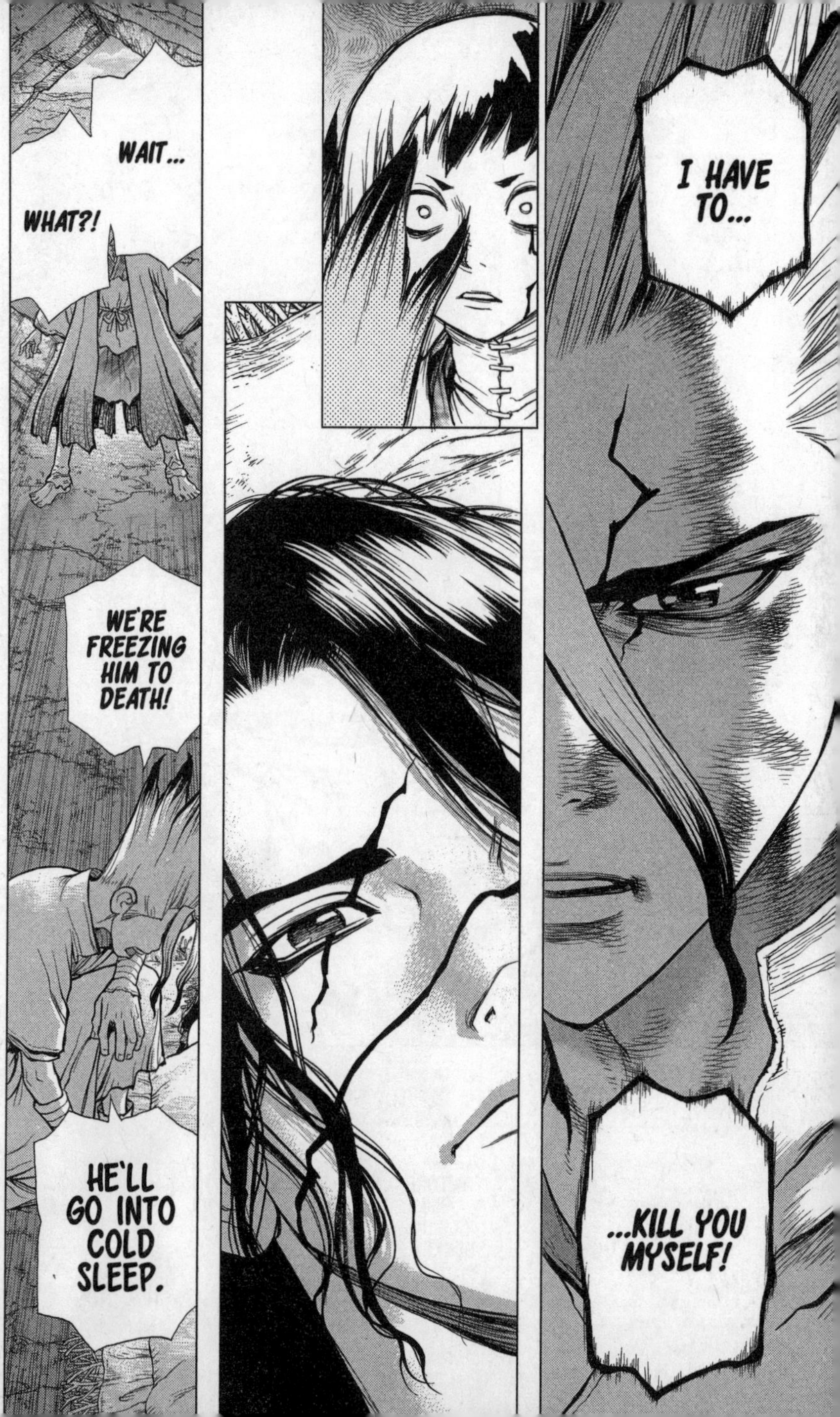
I HAVE TO...
...KILL YOU MYSELF!
WAIT...
WHAT?!
WE'RE FREEZING HIM TO DEATH!
HE'LL GO INTO COLD SLEEP.

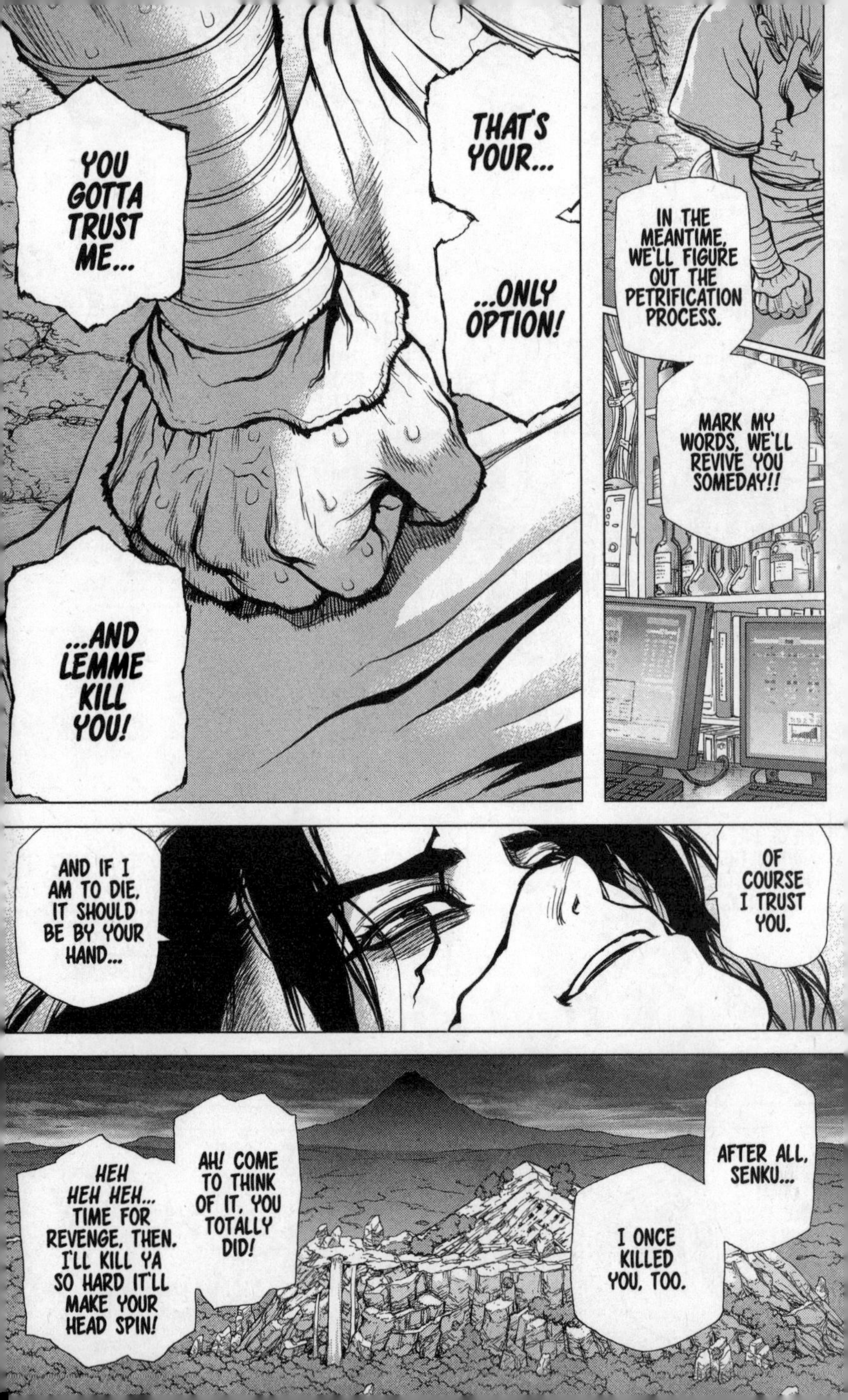
IN THE MEANTIME, WE'LL FIGURE OUT THE PETRIFICATION PROCESS.
MARK MY WORDS, WE'LL REVIVE YOU SOMEDAY!!
THAT'S YOUR...
...ONLY OPTION!
YOU GOTTA TRUST ME...
...AND LEMME KILL YOU!
OF COURSE I TRUST YOU.
AND IF I AM TO DIE, IT SHOULD BE BY YOUR HAND...
AFTER ALL, SENKU...
I ONCE KILLED YOU, TOO.
AH! COME TO THINK OF IT, YOU TOTALLY DID!
HEH HEH HEH... TIME FOR REVENGE, THEN. I'LL KILL YA SO HARD IT'LL MAKE YOUR HEAD SPIN!

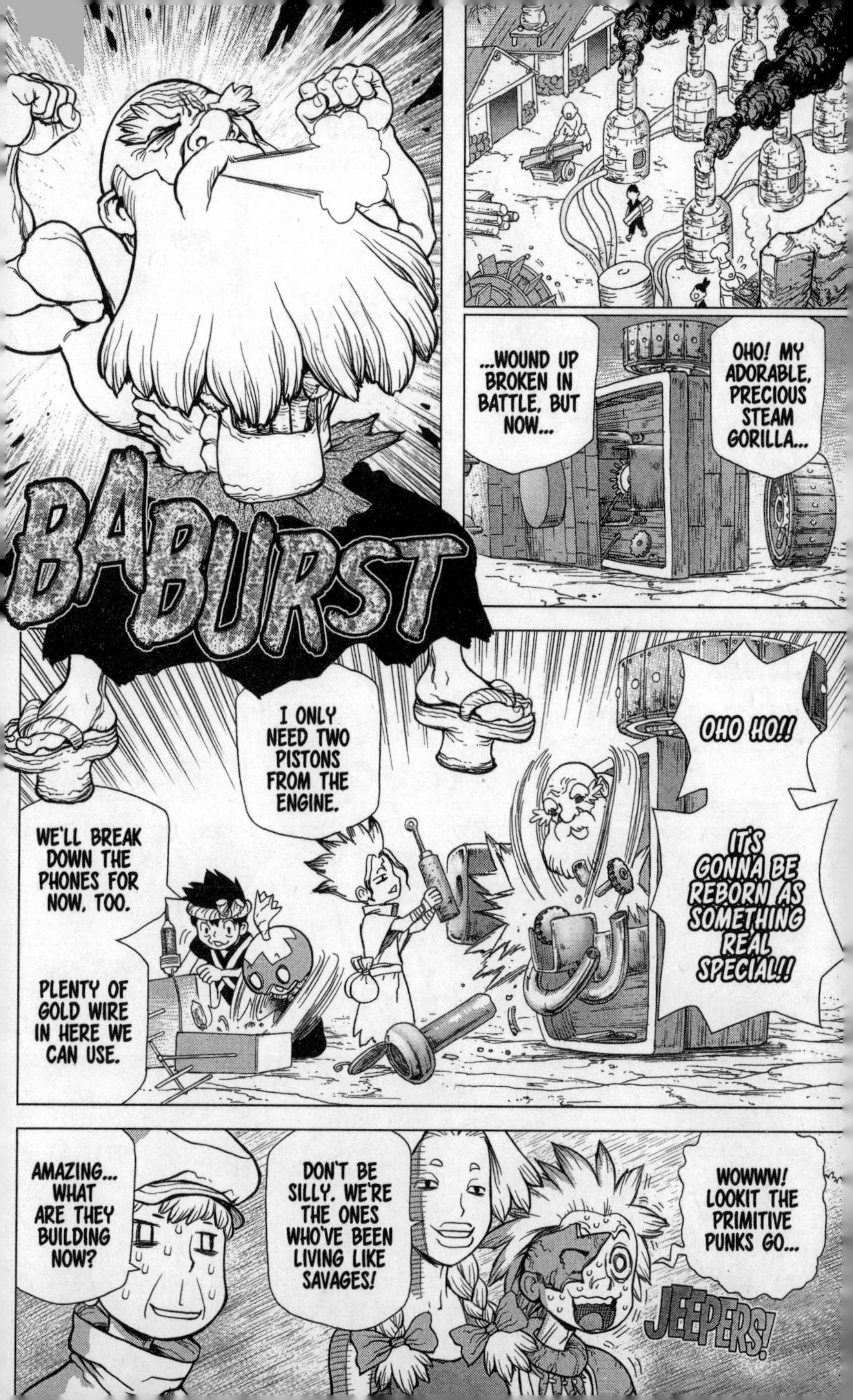
OHO! MY ADORABLE, PRECIOUS STEAM GORILLA...
...WOUND UP BROKEN IN BATTLE, BUT NOW...
BA-BURST
OHO HO!!
IT'S GONNA BE REBORN AS SOMETHING REAL SPECIAL!!
I ONLY NEED TWO PISTONS FROM THE ENGINE.
WE'LL BREAK DOWN THE PHONES FOR NOW, TOO.
PLENTY OF GOLD WIRE IN HERE WE CAN USE.
WOWWW! LOOKIT THE PRIMITIVE PUNKS GO...
JEEPERS!
DON'T BE SILLY. WE'RE THE ONES WHO'VE BEEN LIVING LIKE SAVAGES!
AMAZING... WHAT ARE THEY BUILDING NOW?

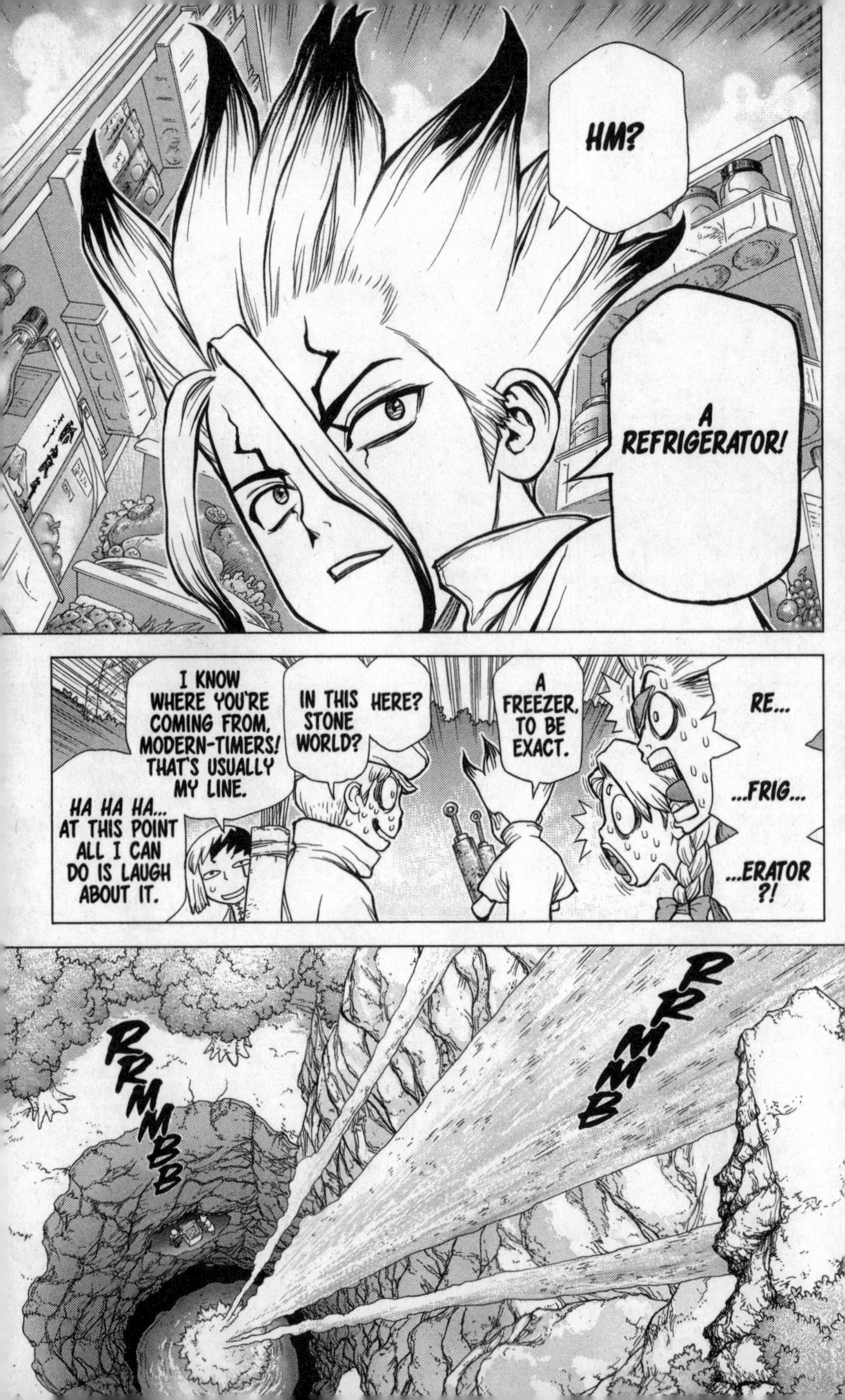
HM?
A REFRIGERATOR!
RE...
...FRIG...
...ERATOR ?!
A FREEZER, TO BE EXACT.
HERE?
IN THIS STONE WORLD?
I KNOW WHERE YOU'RE COMING FROM, MODERN-TIMERS! THAT'S USUALLY MY LINE.
HA HA HA... AT THIS POINT ALL I CAN DO IS LAUGH ABOUT IT.
RRMMB
RRMMBB

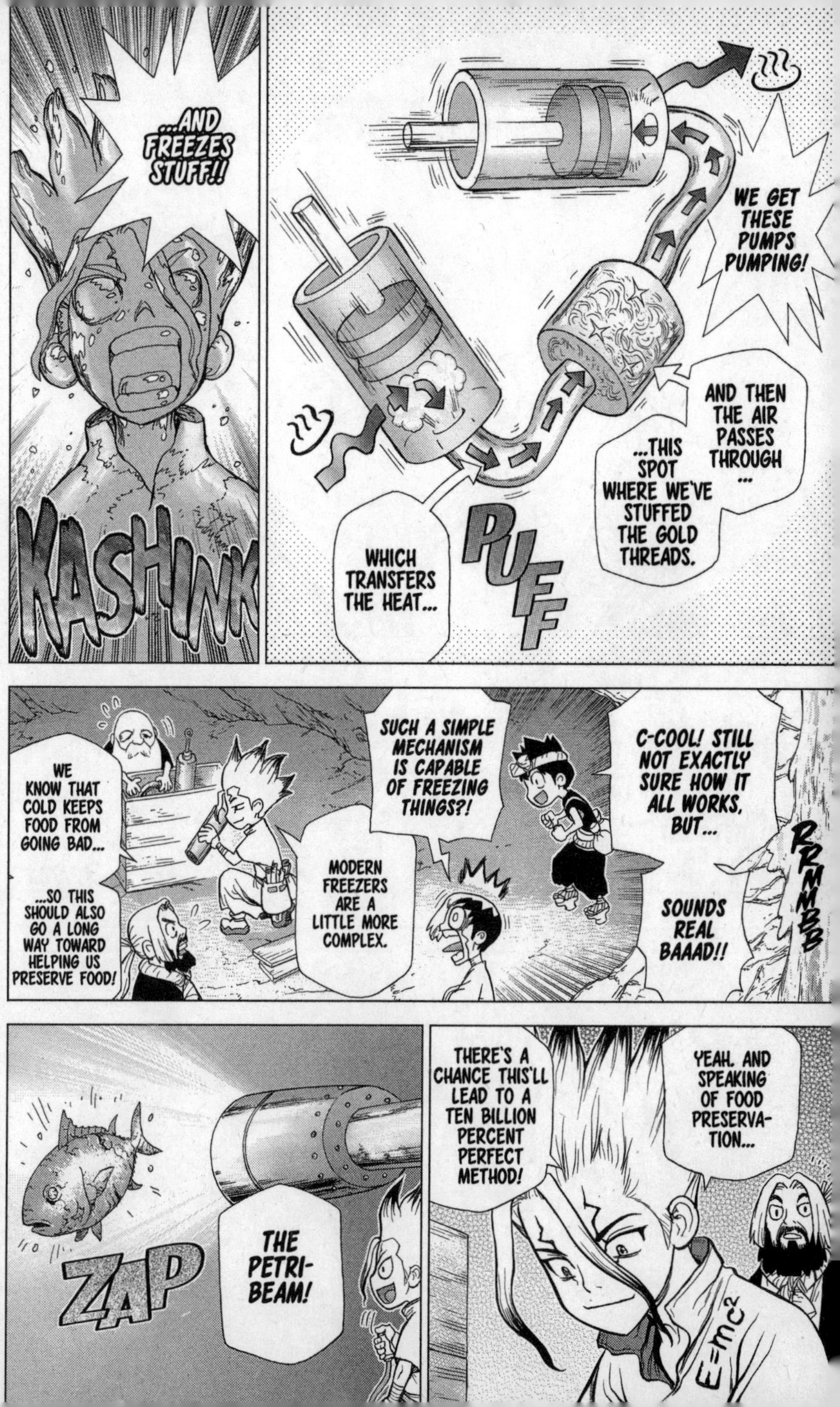
WE GET THESE PUMPS PUMPING!
AND THEN THE AIR PASSES THROUGH ...
...THIS SPOT WHERE WE'VE STUFFED THE GOLD THREADS.
PUFF
WHICH TRANSFERS THE HEAT...
...AND FREEZES STUFF!!
KASHINK
C-COOL! STILL NOT EXACTLY SURE HOW IT ALL WORKS, BUT...
RRMMBB
SOUNDS REAL BAAAD!!
SUCH A SIMPLE MECHANISM IS CAPABLE OF FREEZING THINGS?!
MODERN FREEZERS ARE A LITTLE MORE COMPLEX.
WE KNOW THAT COLD KEEPS FOOD FROM GOING BAD...
...SO THIS SHOULD ALSO GO A LONG WAY TOWARD HELPING US PRESERVE FOOD!
YEAH. AND SPEAKING OF FOOD PRESERVA-TION...
THERE'S A CHANCE THIS'LL LEAD TO A TEN BILLION PERCENT PERFECT METHOD!
E=mc²
THE PETRI-BEAM!
ZAP

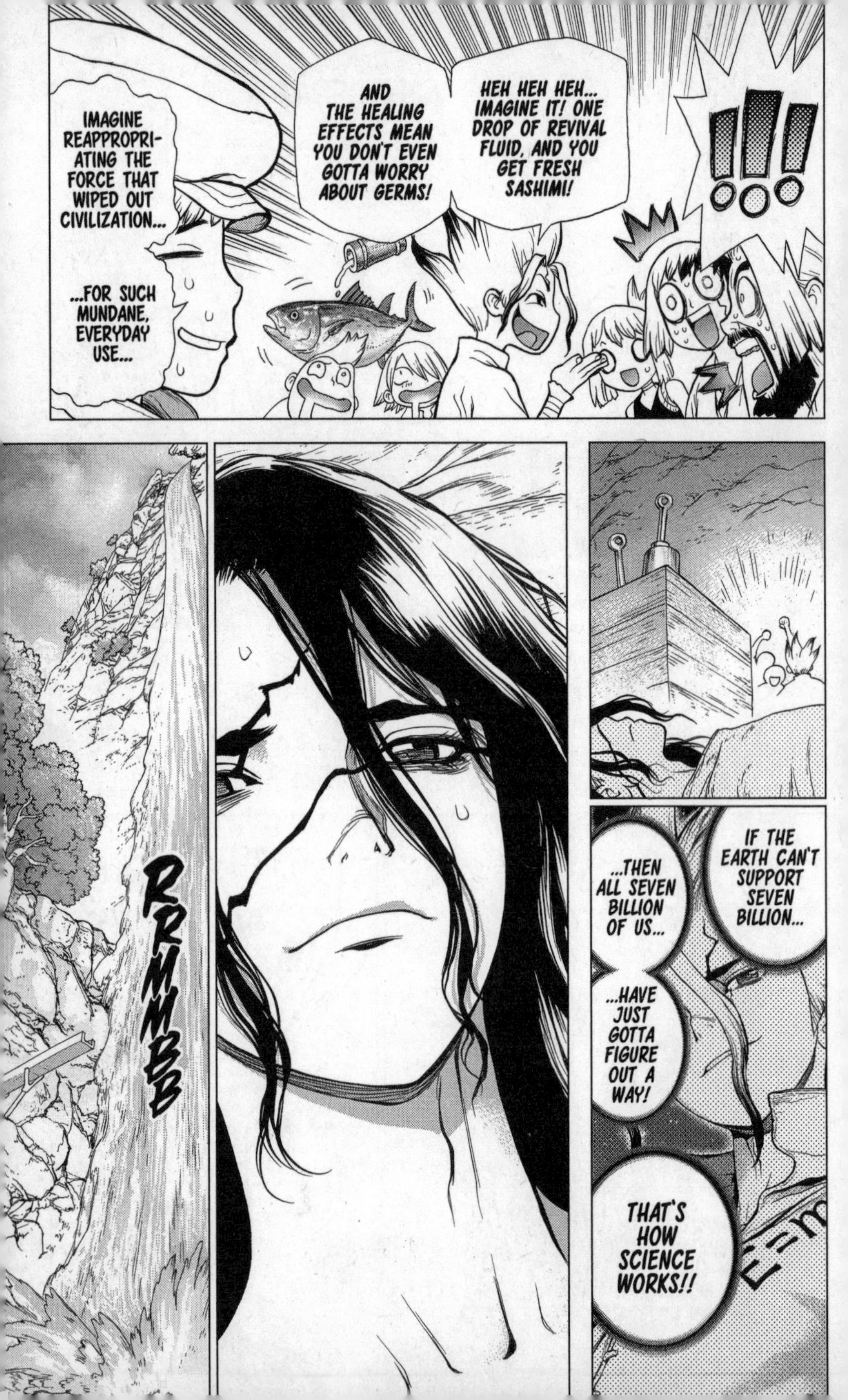
!!!
HEH HEH HEH... IMAGINE IT! ONE DROP OF REVIVAL FLUID, AND YOU GET FRESH SASHIMI!
AND THE HEALING EFFECTS MEAN YOU DON'T EVEN GOTTA WORRY ABOUT GERMS!
IMAGINE REAPPROPRIATING THE FORCE THAT WIPED OUT CIVILIZATION...
...FOR SUCH MUNDANE, EVERYDAY USE...
IF THE EARTH CAN'T SUPPORT SEVEN BILLION...
...THEN ALL SEVEN BILLION OF US...
...HAVE JUST GOTTA FIGURE OUT A WAY!
THAT'S HOW SCIENCE WORKS!!
RRMMBB

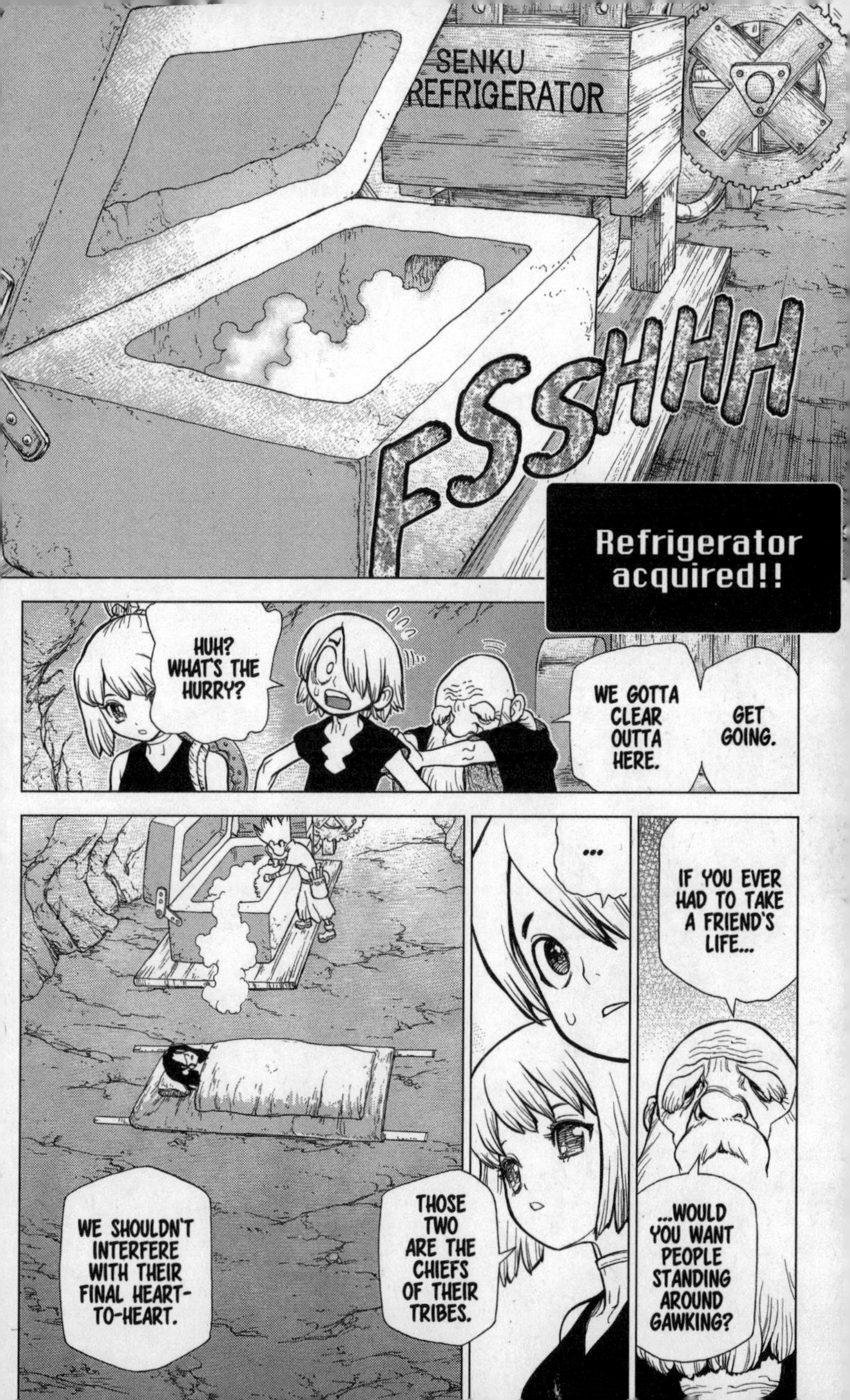
SENKU REFRIGERATOR
FSSHHH
Refrigerator acquired!!
GET GOING.
WE GOTTA CLEAR OUTTA HERE.
HUH? WHAT'S THE HURRY?
IF YOU EVER HAD TO TAKE A FRIEND'S LIFE...
...WOULD YOU WANT PEOPLE STANDING AROUND GAWKING?
...
THOSE TWO ARE THE CHIEFS OF THEIR TRIBES.
WE SHOULDN'T INTERFERE WITH THEIR FINAL HEART-TO-HEART.

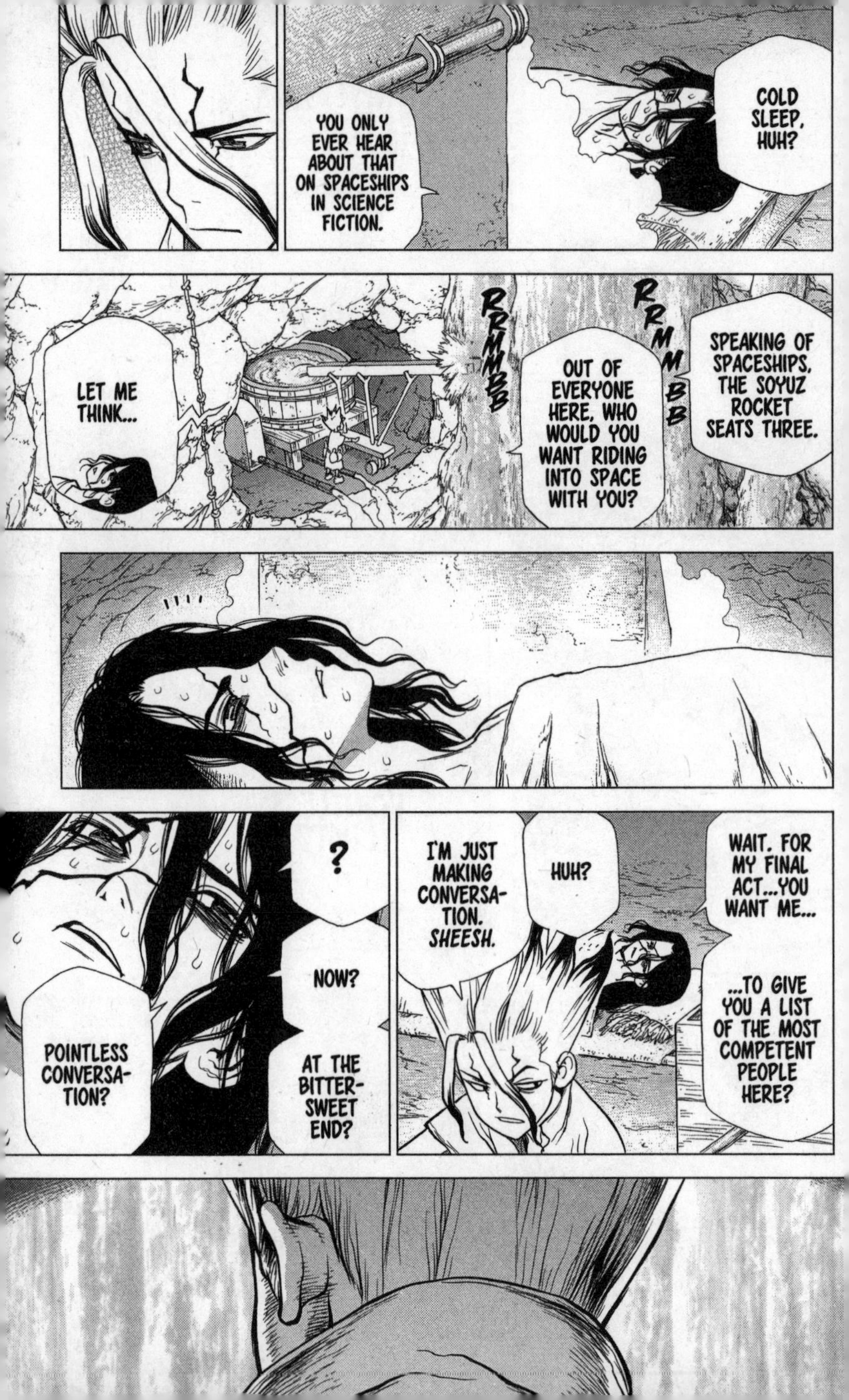
COLD SLEEP, HUH?
YOU ONLY EVER HEAR ABOUT THAT ON SPACESHIPS IN SCIENCE FICTION.
SPEAKING OF SPACESHIPS, THE SOYUZ ROCKET SEATS THREE.
RRMMBB
OUT OF EVERYONE HERE, WHO WOULD YOU WANT RIDING INTO SPACE WITH YOU?
RRMMBB
LET ME THINK...
WAIT. FOR MY FINAL ACT...YOU WANT ME...
...TO GIVE YOU A LIST OF THE MOST COMPETENT PEOPLE HERE?
HUH?
I'M JUST MAKING CONVERSA-TION. SHEESH.
?
NOW?
AT THE BITTER-SWEET END?
POINTLESS CONVERSA-TION?

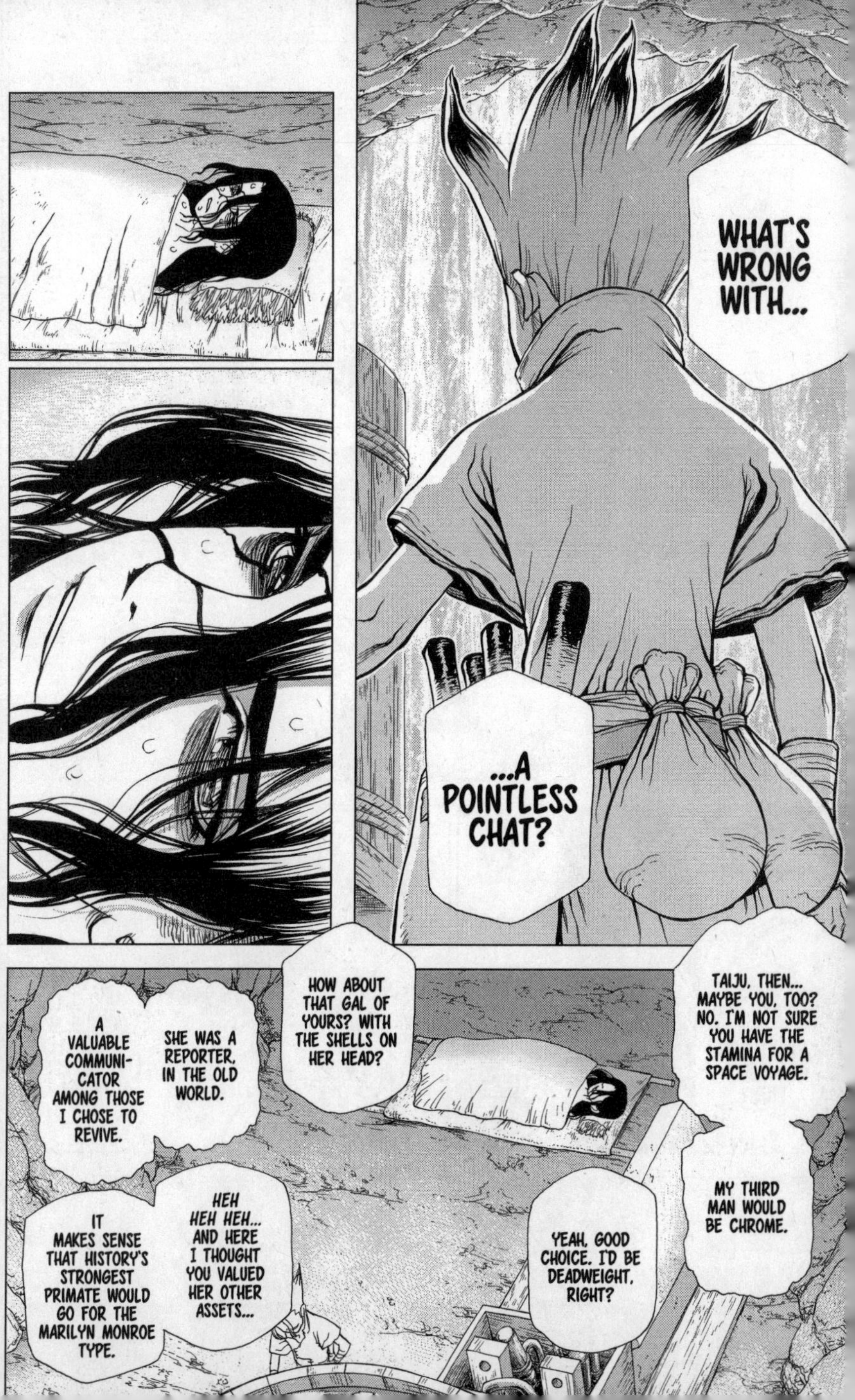
WHAT'S WRONG WITH...
...A POINTLESS CHAT?
TAIJU, THEN... MAYBE YOU, TOO? NO. I'M NOT SURE YOU HAVE THE STAMINA FOR A SPACE VOYAGE.
MY THIRD MAN WOULD BE CHROME.
YEAH, GOOD CHOICE. I'D BE DEADWEIGHT, RIGHT?
HOW ABOUT THAT GAL OF YOURS? WITH THE SHELLS ON HER HEAD?
SHE WAS A REPORTER, IN THE OLD WORLD.
A VALUABLE COMMUNICATOR AMONG THOSE I CHOSE TO REVIVE.
HEH HEH HEH... AND HERE I THOUGHT YOU VALUED HER OTHER ASSETS...
IT MAKES SENSE THAT HISTORY'S STRONGEST PRIMATE WOULD GO FOR THE MARILYN MONROE TYPE.

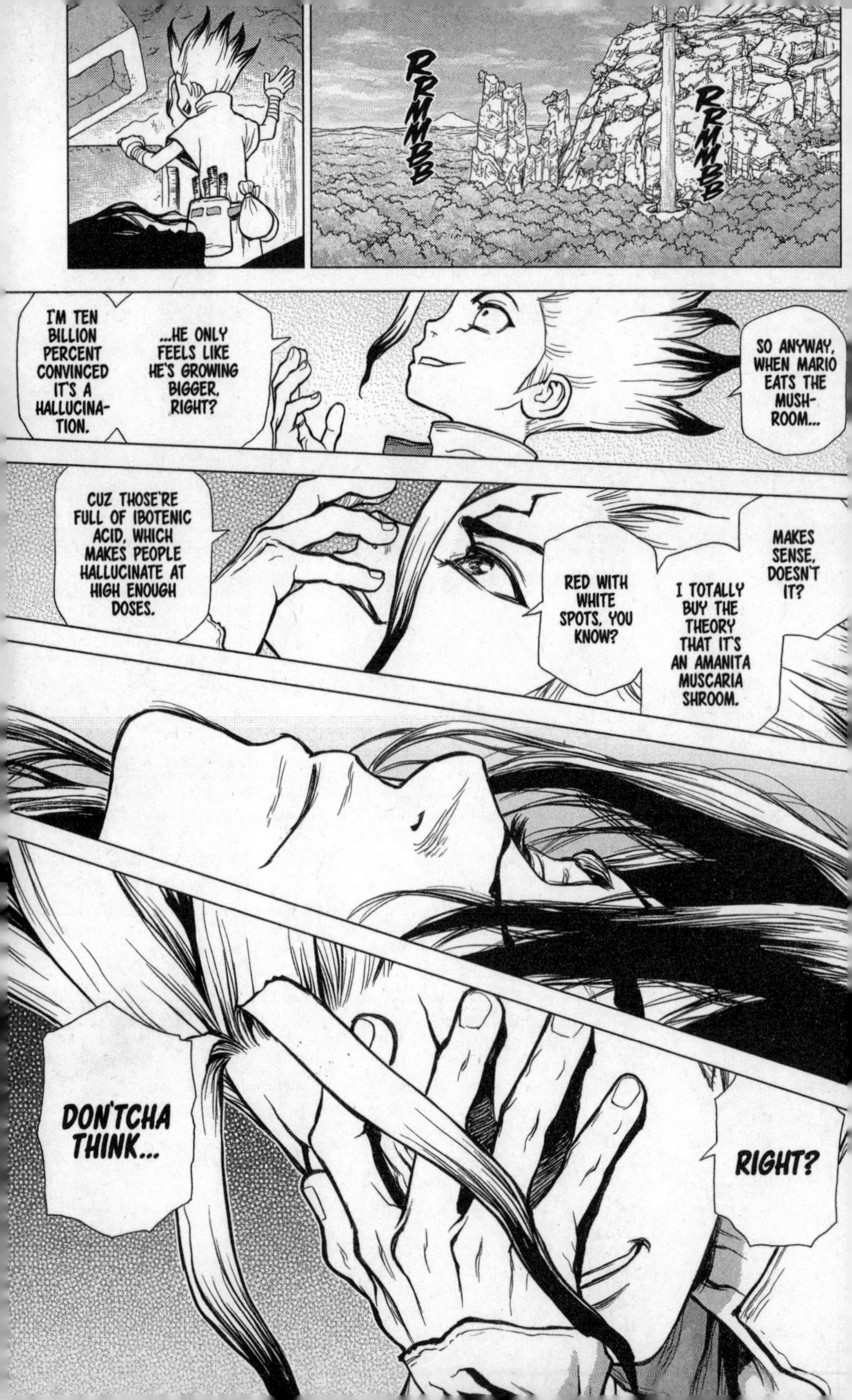
RRMMBB
RRMMBB
SO ANYWAY, WHEN MARIO EATS THE MUSH-ROOM...
...HE ONLY FEELS LIKE HE'S GROWING BIGGER, RIGHT?
I'M TEN BILLION PERCENT CONVINCED IT'S A HALLUCINA-TION.
MAKES SENSE, DOESN'T IT?
I TOTALLY BUY THE THEORY THAT IT'S AN AMANITA MUSCARIA SHROOM.
RED WITH WHITE SPOTS, YOU KNOW?
CUZ THOSE'RE FULL OF IBOTENIC ACID, WHICH MAKES PEOPLE HALLUCINATE AT HIGH ENOUGH DOSES.
RIGHT?
DON'TCHA THINK...

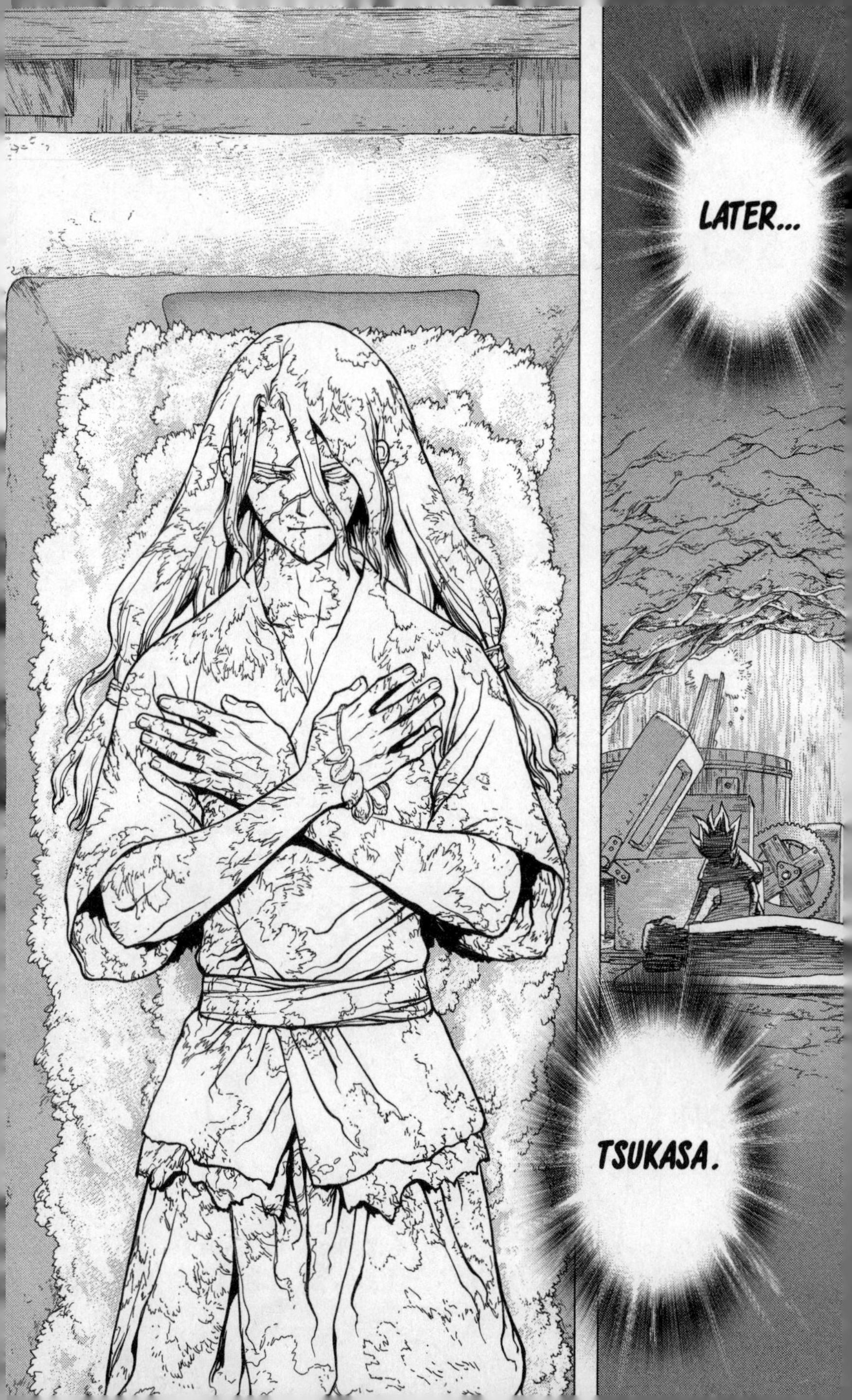
LATER...
TSUKASA.

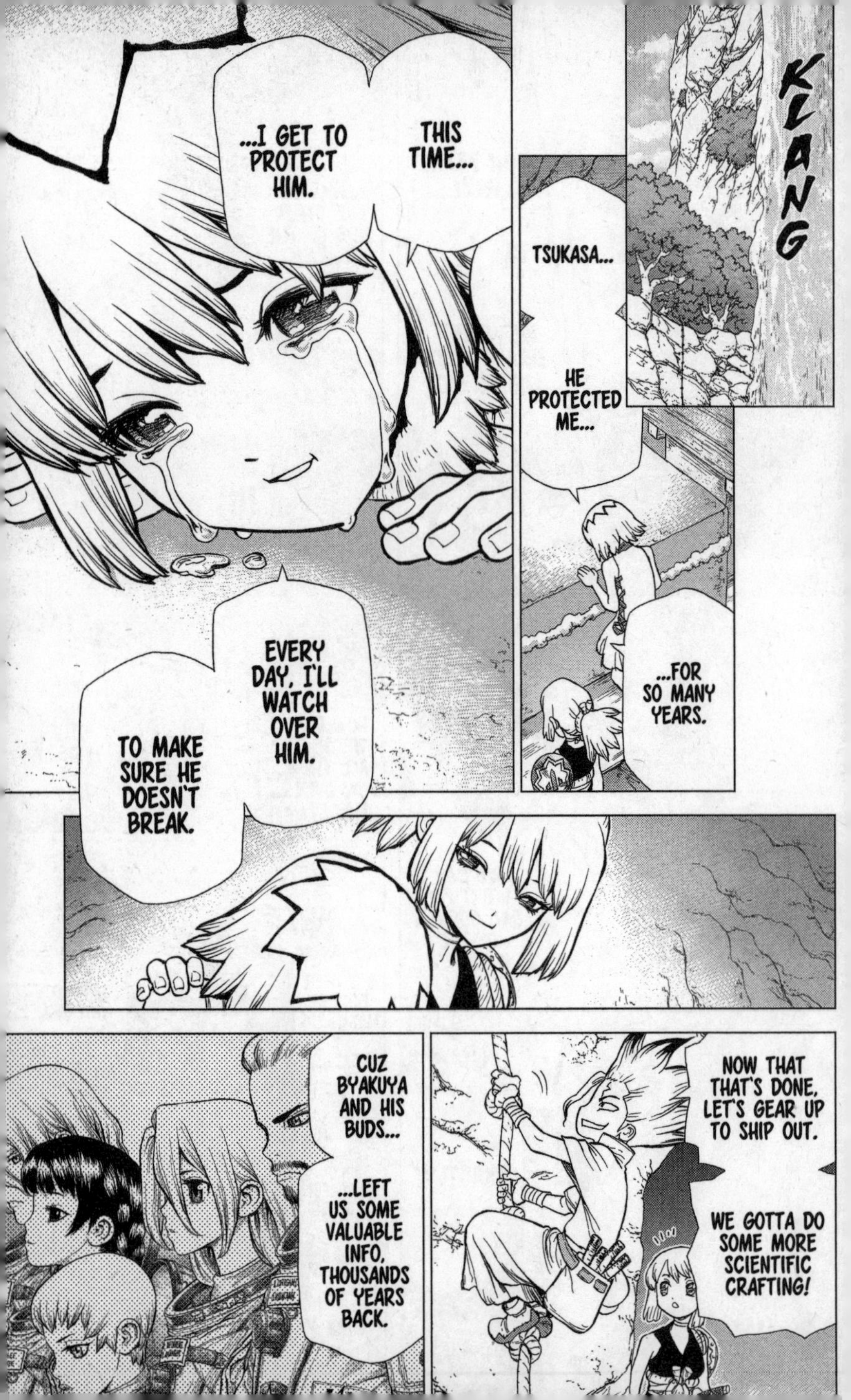
KLANG
TSUKASA...
HE PROTECTED ME...
...FOR SO MANY YEARS.
THIS TIME...
...I GET TO PROTECT HIM.
EVERY DAY, I'LL WATCH OVER HIM.
TO MAKE SURE HE DOESN'T BREAK.
NOW THAT THAT'S DONE, LET'S GEAR UP TO SHIP OUT.
WE GOTTA DO SOME MORE SCIENTIFIC CRAFTING!
CUZ BYAKUYA AND HIS BUDS...
...LEFT US SOME VALUABLE INFO, THOUSANDS OF YEARS BACK.

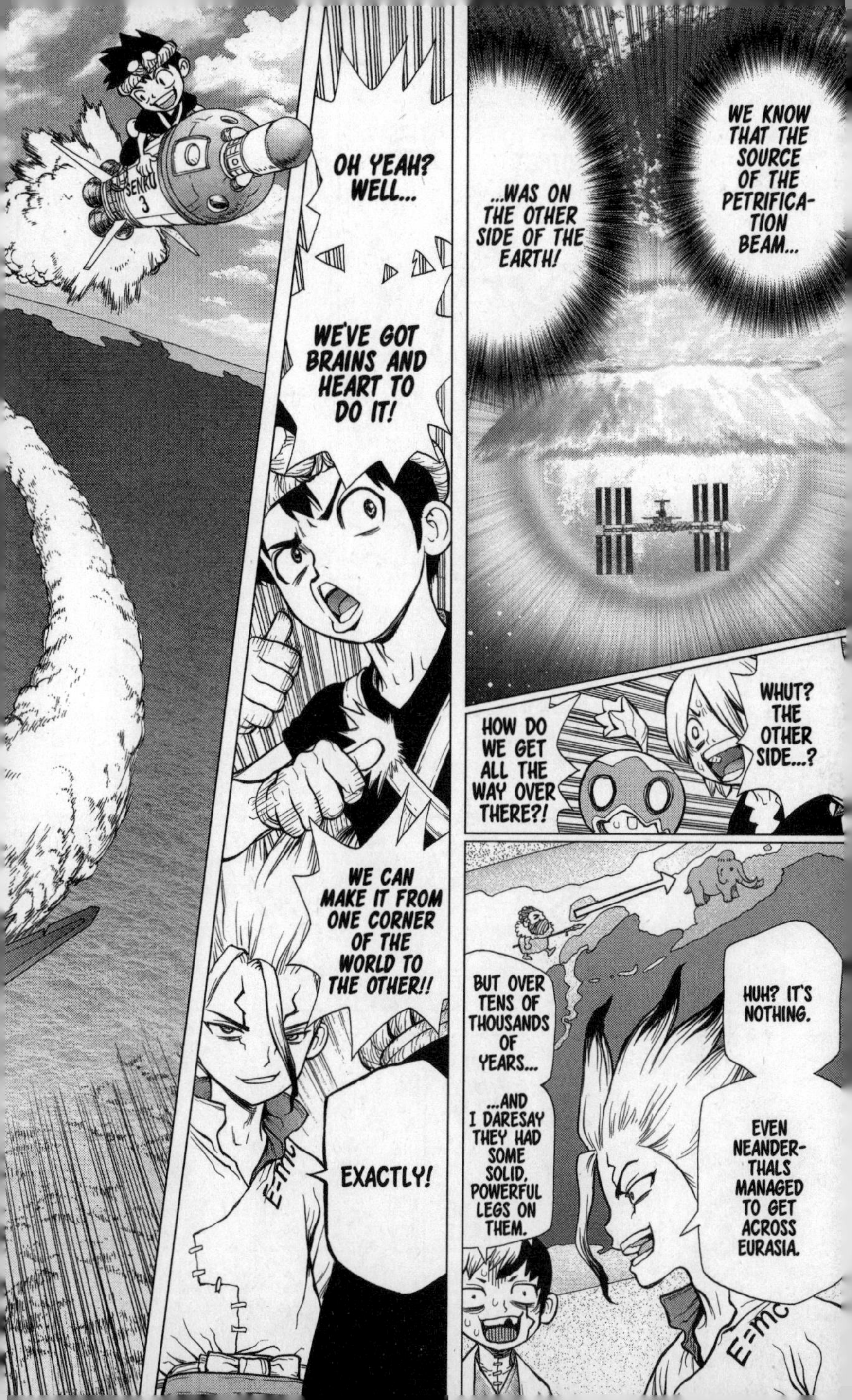
WE KNOW THAT THE SOURCE OF THE PETRIFICATION BEAM...
...WAS ON THE OTHER SIDE OF THE EARTH!
WHUT? THE OTHER SIDE...?
HOW DO WE GET ALL THE WAY OVER THERE?!
HUH? IT'S NOTHING.
EVEN NEANDERTHALS MANAGED TO GET ACROSS EURASIA.
BUT OVER TENS OF THOUSANDS OF YEARS...
...AND I DARESAY THEY HAD SOME SOLID, POWERFUL LEGS ON THEM.
E=mc
OH YEAH? WELL...
WE'VE GOT BRAINS AND HEART TO DO IT!
WE CAN MAKE IT FROM ONE CORNER OF THE WORLD TO THE OTHER!!
EXACTLY!
E=mc
SENKU 3

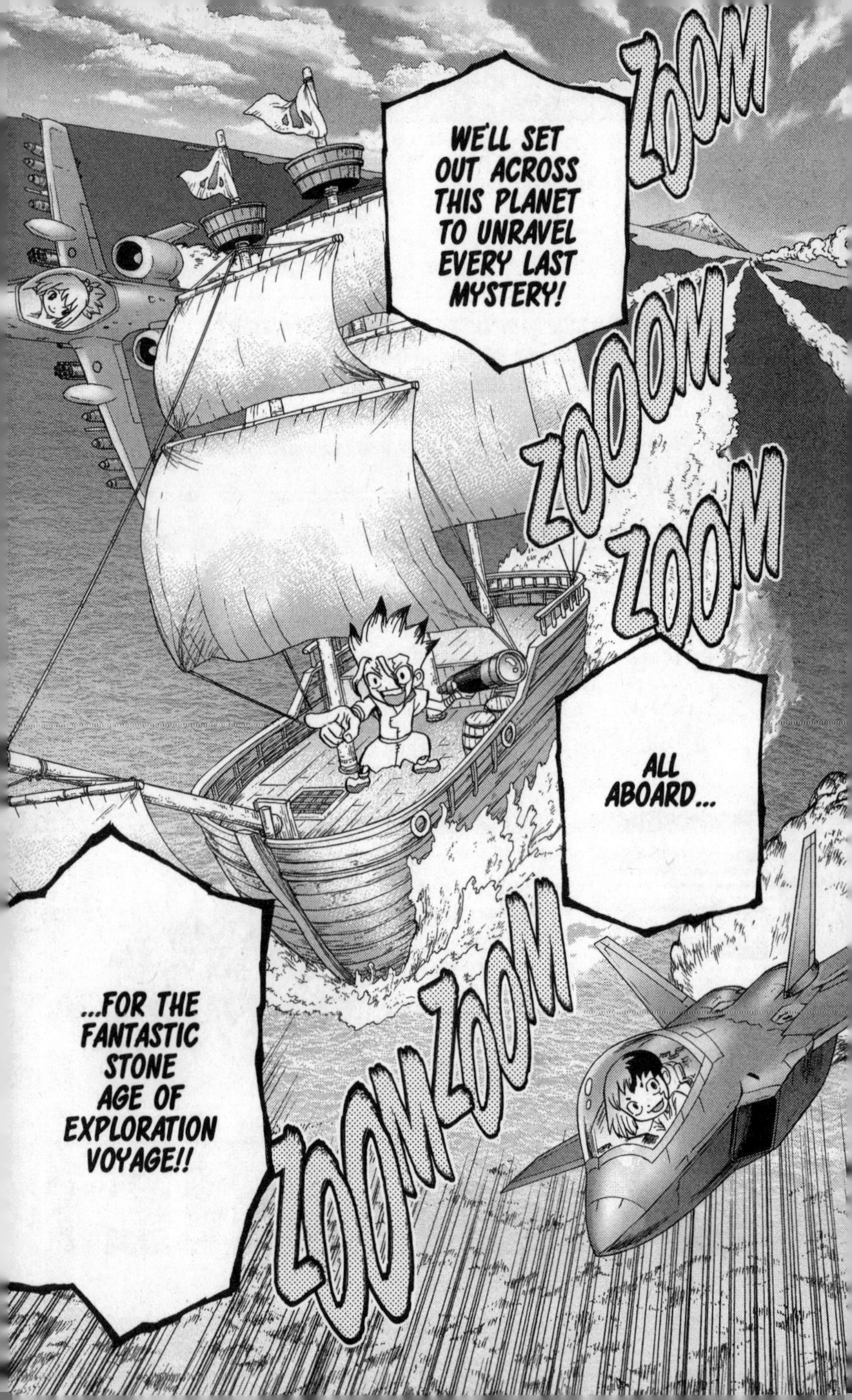
ZOOM
WE'LL SET OUT ACROSS THIS PLANET TO UNRAVEL EVERY LAST MYSTERY!
ZOOOOM
ZOOM ZOOM
ALL ABOARD...
ZOOM ZOOM
...FOR THE FANTASTIC STONE AGE OF EXPLORATION VOYAGE!!

MECHA SENKU Q&A

SEARCH

Question Corner

In the story Tsukasa told in chapter 1, was he actually talking about his own past? And was the little sister who loved mermaids actually Mirai?

K.K. from Kangawa Prefecture SEARCH

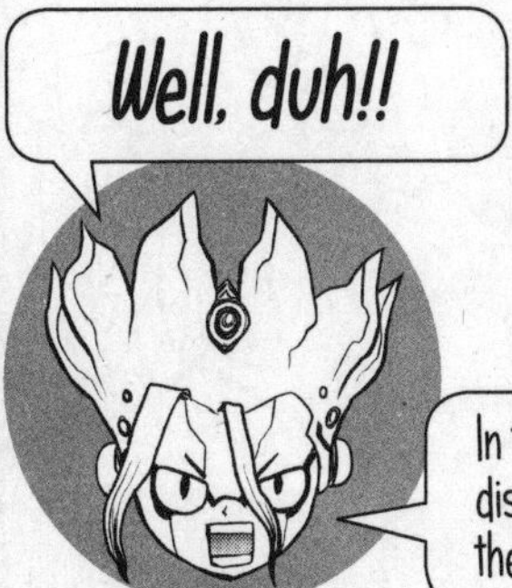
Well, duh!!

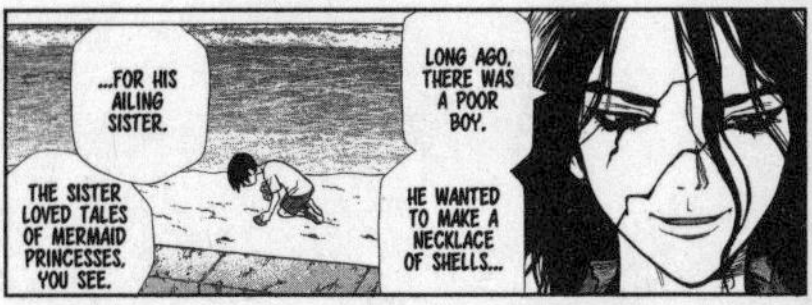
LONG AGO, THERE WAS A POOR BOY.
HE WANTED TO MAKE A NECKLACE OF SHELLS...
...FOR HIS AILING SISTER.
THE SISTER LOVED TALES OF MERMAID PRINCESSES, YOU SEE.

In the original fairy tale about the mermaid, she dissolves into bubbles in the end, but Tsukasa gave the story a happy ending when he told it to Mirai!

Science Questions	How does one make gasoline out of plastic bottle caps?
Character Questions	If Taiju and Tsukasa really fought, who would win?
Questions That Aren't Really Questions	I wanna get petrified and challenge myself to count the seconds...

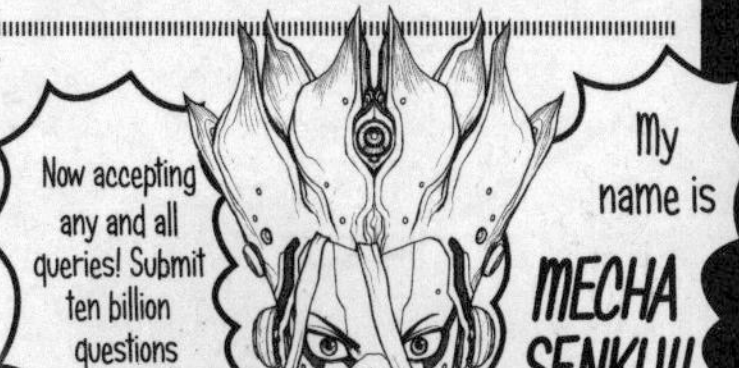
My name is MECHA SENKU!!
Now accepting any and all queries! Submit ten billion questions to me!
KLANG
WHRRR

Dr.STONE

Z=84: People = Power

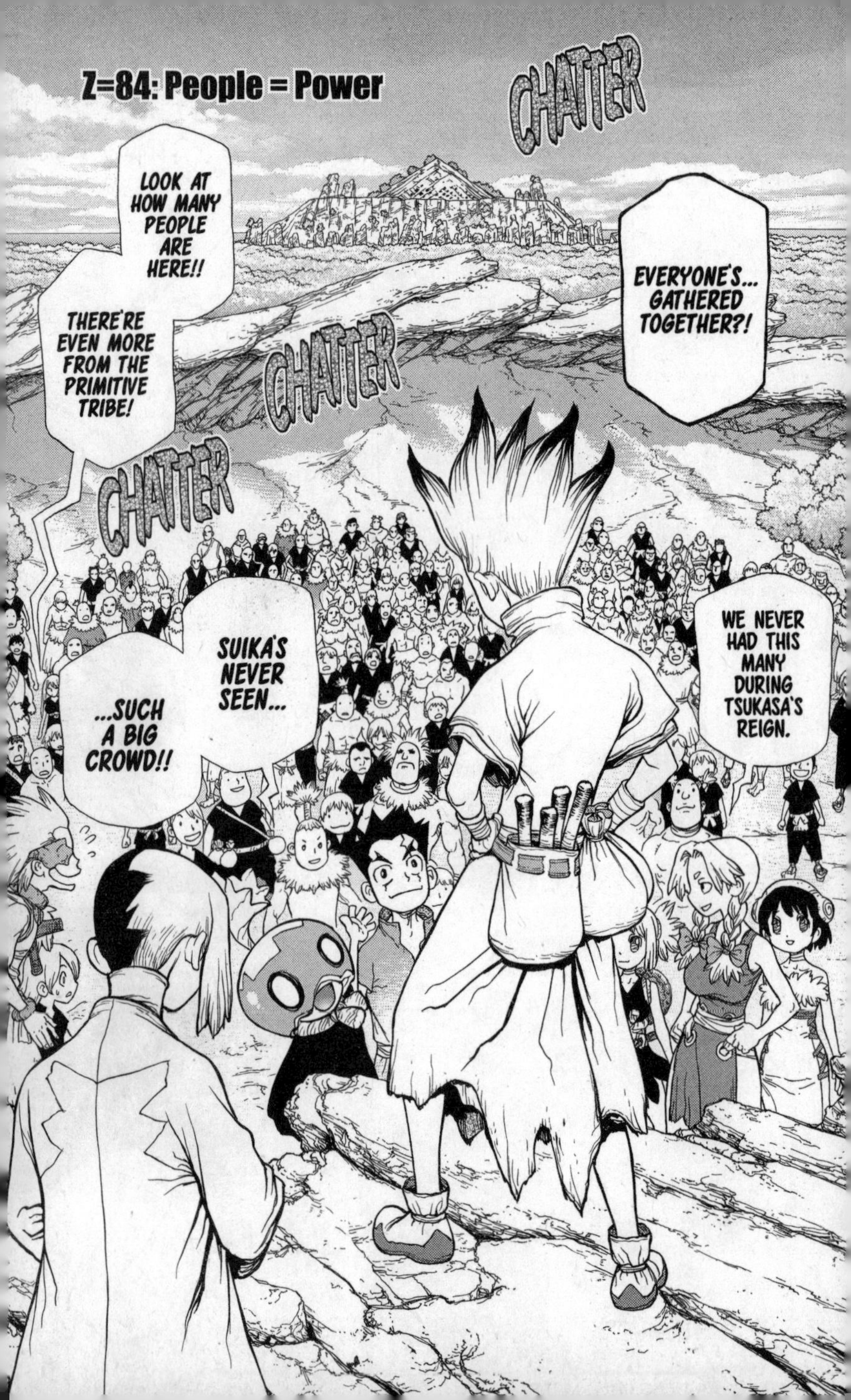
CHATTER
EVERYONE'S... GATHERED TOGETHER?!
LOOK AT HOW MANY PEOPLE ARE HERE!!
THERE'RE EVEN MORE FROM THE PRIMITIVE TRIBE!
CHATTER
CHATTER
WE NEVER HAD THIS MANY DURING TSUKASA'S REIGN.
SUIKA'S NEVER SEEN...
...SUCH A BIG CROWD!!

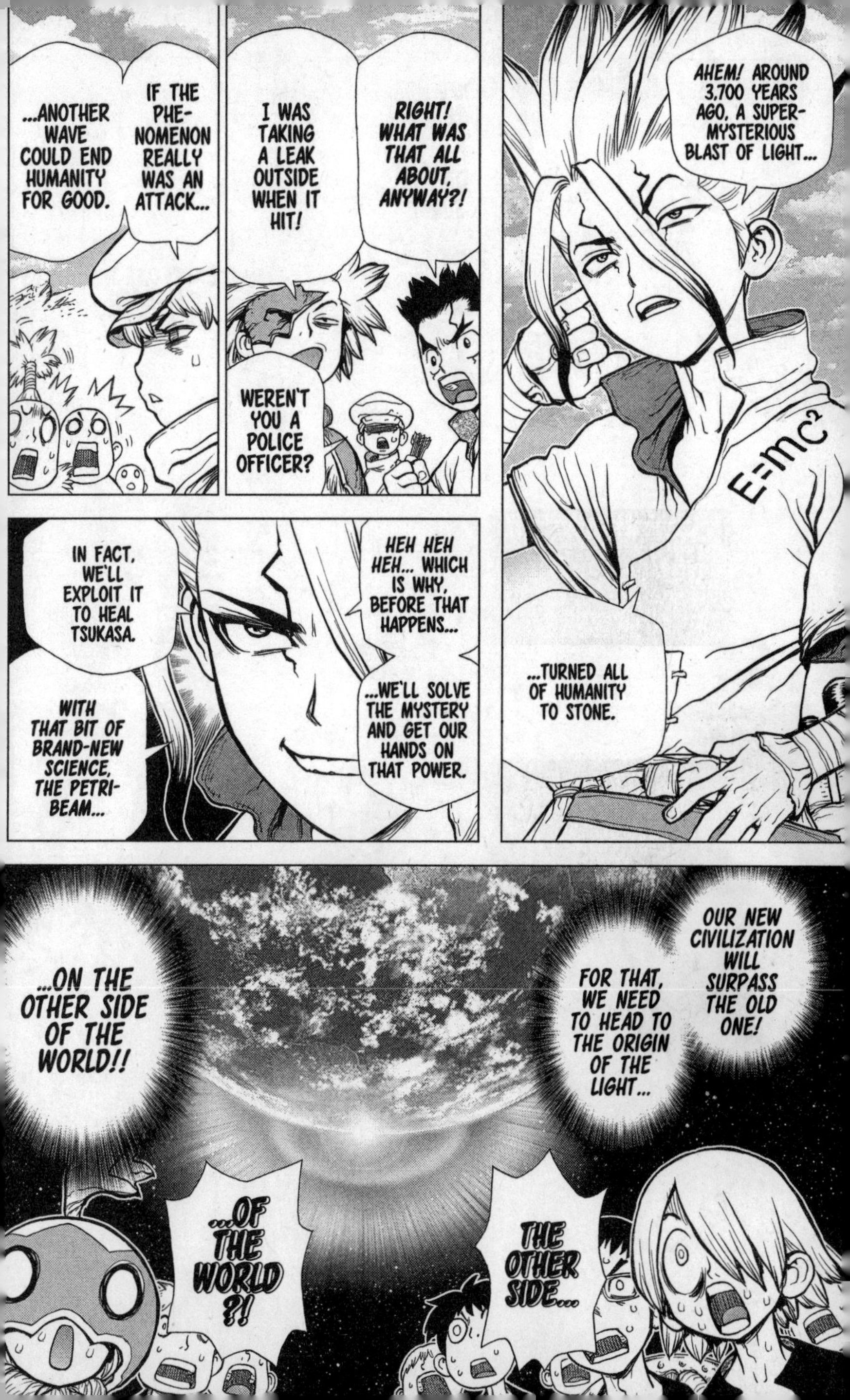
AHEM! AROUND 3,700 YEARS AGO, A SUPER-MYSTERIOUS BLAST OF LIGHT...
$E=mc^2$
...TURNED ALL OF HUMANITY TO STONE.
RIGHT! WHAT WAS THAT ALL ABOUT, ANYWAY?!
I WAS TAKING A LEAK OUTSIDE WHEN IT HIT!
WEREN'T YOU A POLICE OFFICER?
IF THE PHE-NOMENON REALLY WAS AN ATTACK...
...ANOTHER WAVE COULD END HUMANITY FOR GOOD.
HEH HEH HEH... WHICH IS WHY, BEFORE THAT HAPPENS...
...WE'LL SOLVE THE MYSTERY AND GET OUR HANDS ON THAT POWER.
IN FACT, WE'LL EXPLOIT IT TO HEAL TSUKASA.
WITH THAT BIT OF BRAND-NEW SCIENCE, THE PETRI-BEAM...
OUR NEW CIVILIZATION WILL SURPASS THE OLD ONE!
FOR THAT, WE NEED TO HEAD TO THE ORIGIN OF THE LIGHT...
...ON THE OTHER SIDE OF THE WORLD!!
THE OTHER SIDE...
...OF THE WORLD?!

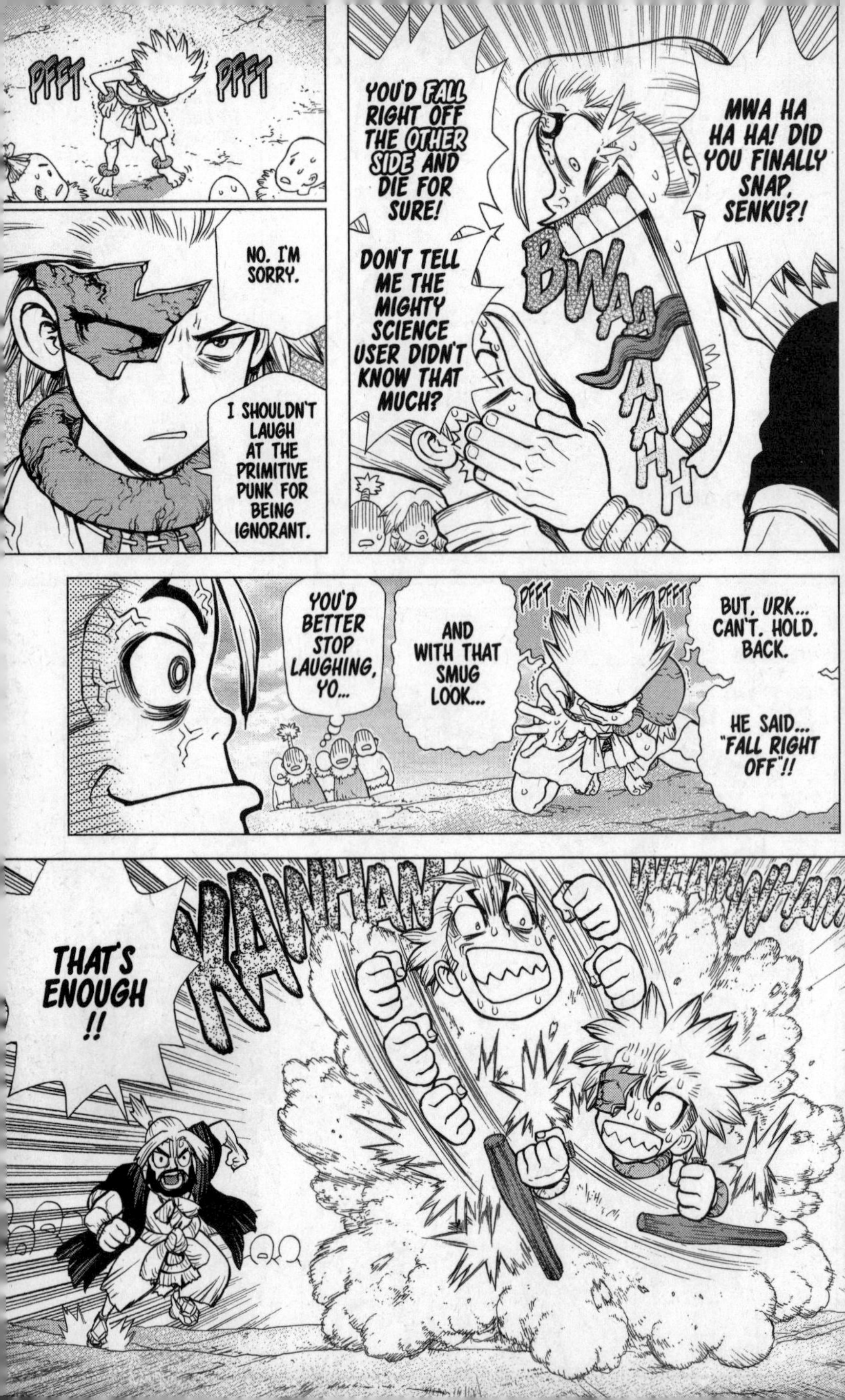
MWA HA HA HA! DID YOU FINALLY SNAP, SENKU?!
BWAAAAHH
YOU'D FALL RIGHT OFF THE OTHER SIDE AND DIE FOR SURE!
DON'T TELL ME THE MIGHTY SCIENCE USER DIDN'T KNOW THAT MUCH?
PFFT
PFFT
NO. I'M SORRY.
I SHOULDN'T LAUGH AT THE PRIMITIVE PUNK FOR BEING IGNORANT.
BUT, URK... CAN'T. HOLD. BACK.
HE SAID... "FALL RIGHT OFF"!!
PFFT
PFFT
AND WITH THAT SMUG LOOK...
YOU'D BETTER STOP LAUGHING, YO...
THAT'S ENOUGH!!

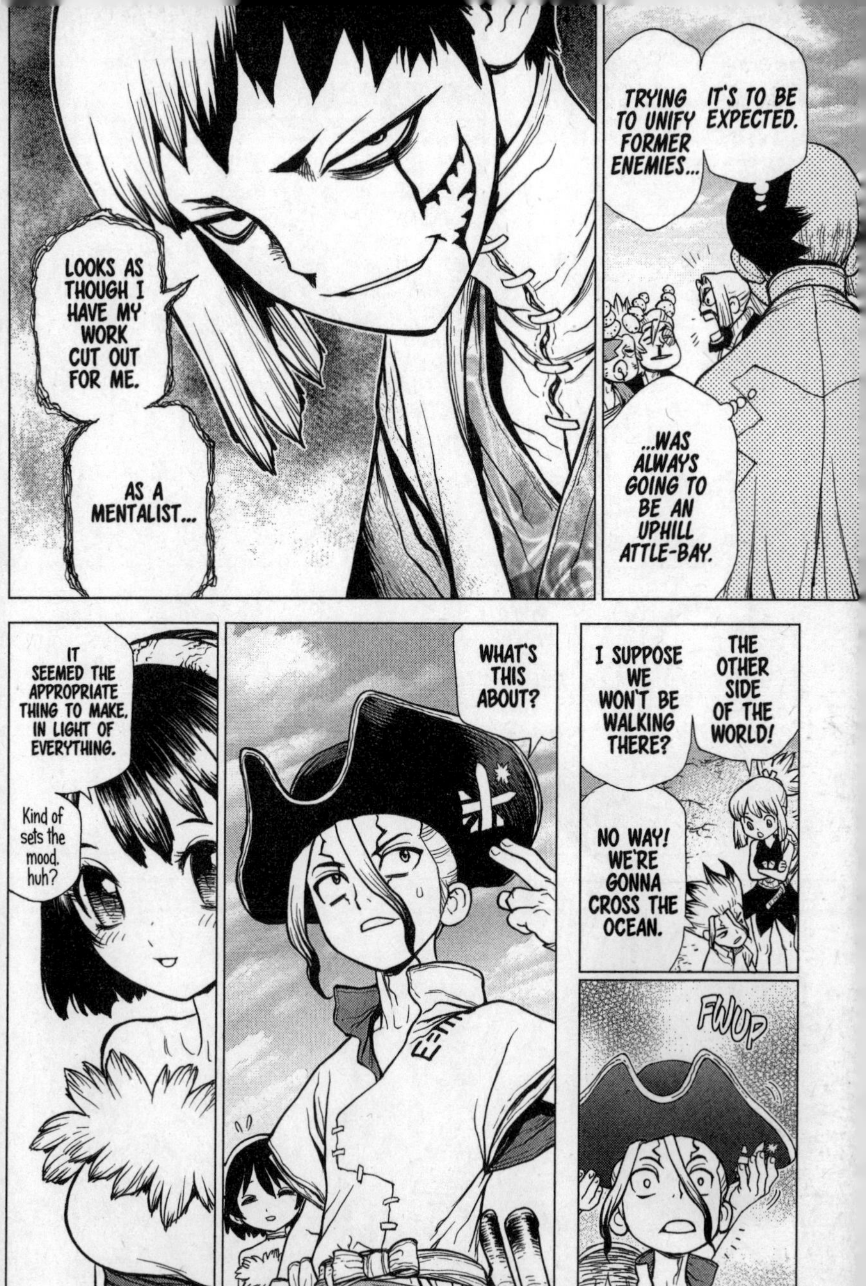
IT'S TO BE EXPECTED.
TRYING TO UNIFY FORMER ENEMIES...
...WAS ALWAYS GOING TO BE AN UPHILL ATTLE-BAY.
LOOKS AS THOUGH I HAVE MY WORK CUT OUT FOR ME.
AS A MENTALIST...
THE OTHER SIDE OF THE WORLD!
I SUPPOSE WE WON'T BE WALKING THERE?
NO WAY! WE'RE GONNA CROSS THE OCEAN.
FWUP
WHAT'S THIS ABOUT?
IT SEEMED THE APPROPRIATE THING TO MAKE, IN LIGHT OF EVERYTHING.
Kind of sets the mood, huh?

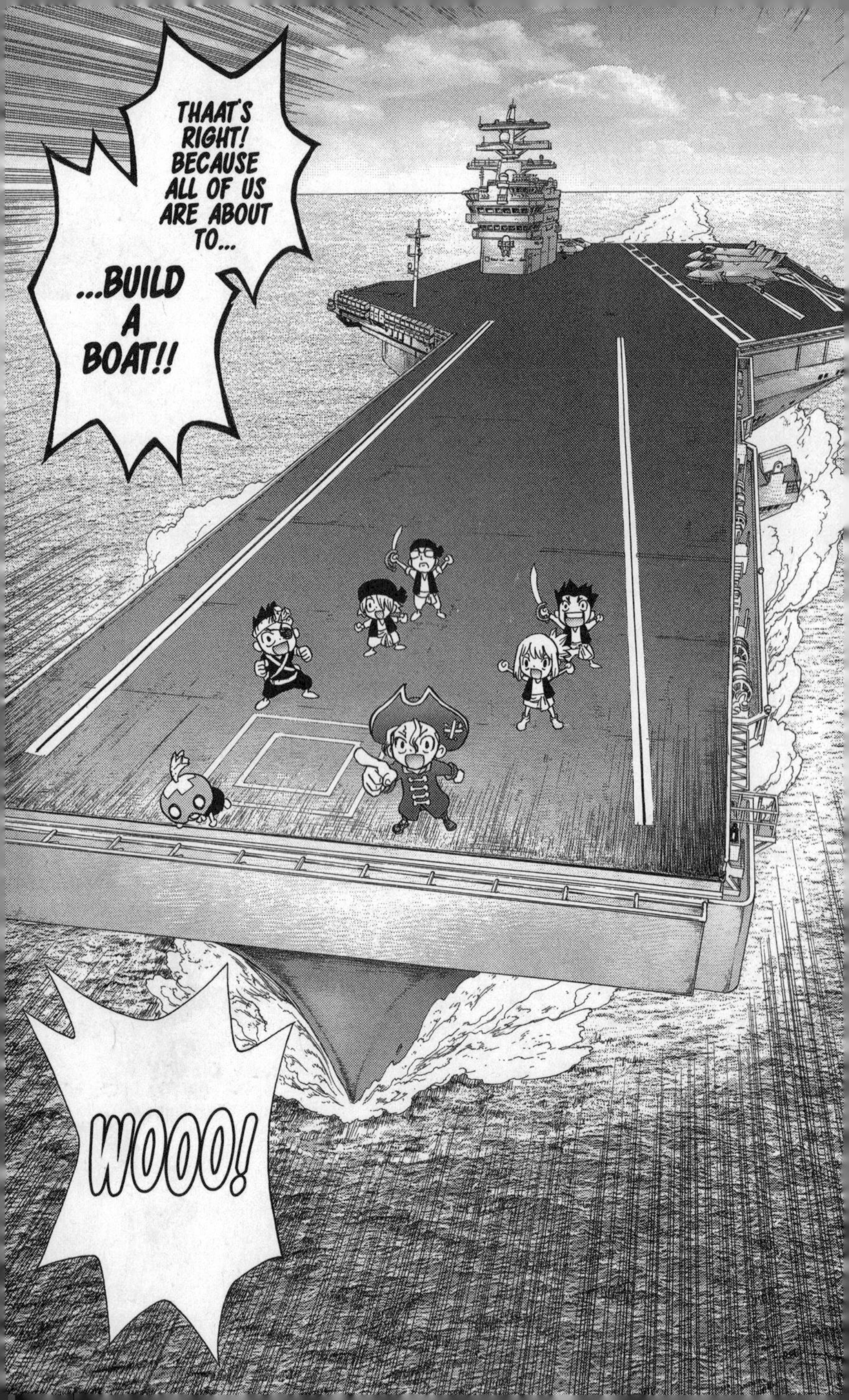
THAAT'S RIGHT! BECAUSE ALL OF US ARE ABOUT TO...
...BUILD A BOAT!!
WOOO!

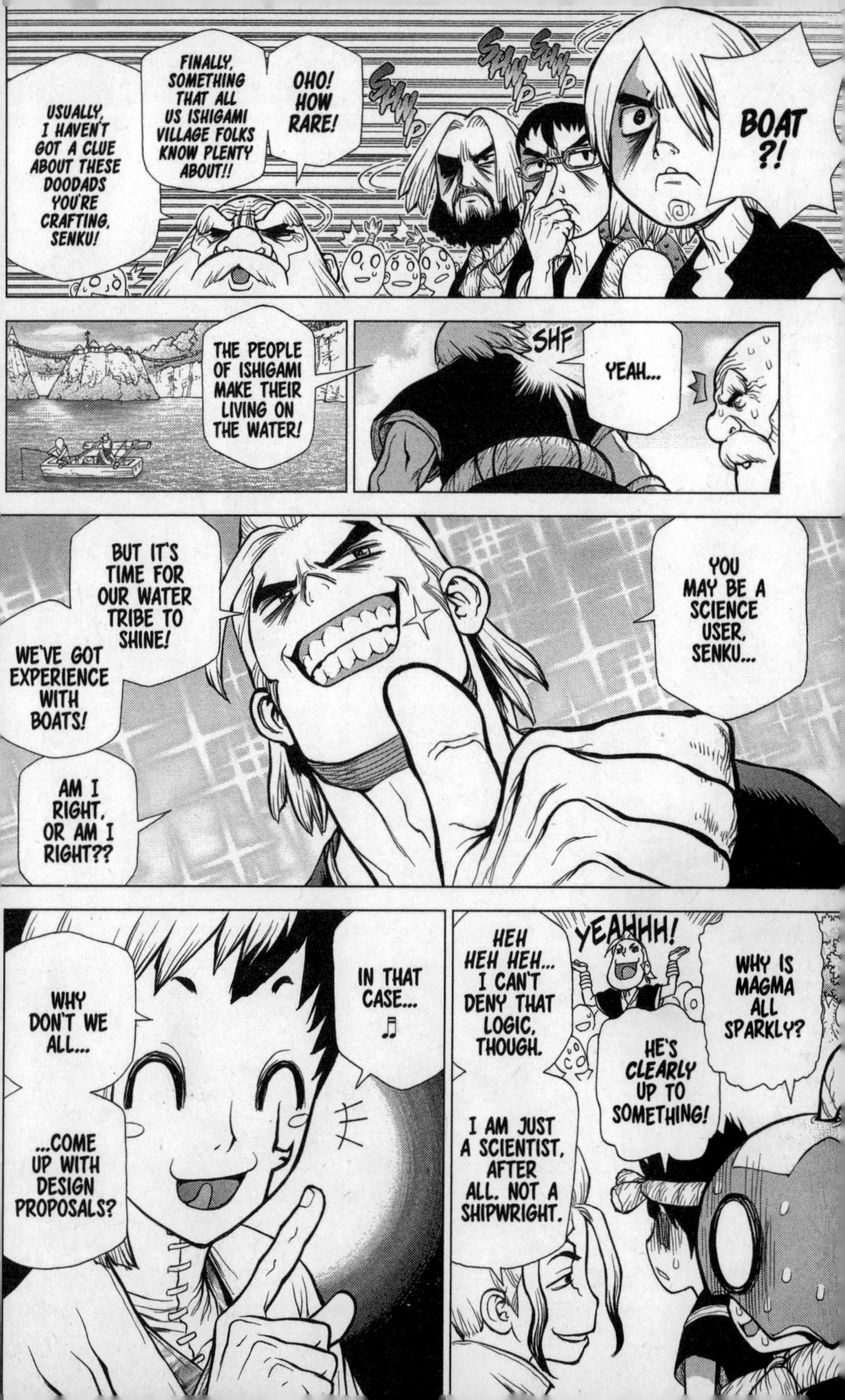
BOAT?!
SHWP SHWP SHWP
OHO! HOW RARE!
FINALLY, SOMETHING THAT ALL US ISHIGAMI VILLAGE FOLKS KNOW PLENTY ABOUT!!
USUALLY, I HAVEN'T GOT A CLUE ABOUT THESE DOODADS YOU'RE CRAFTING, SENKU!
SHF
YEAH...
THE PEOPLE OF ISHIGAMI MAKE THEIR LIVING ON THE WATER!
YOU MAY BE A SCIENCE USER, SENKU...
BUT IT'S TIME FOR OUR WATER TRIBE TO SHINE!
WE'VE GOT EXPERIENCE WITH BOATS!
AM I RIGHT, OR AM I RIGHT??
WHY IS MAGMA ALL SPARKLY?
YEAHHH!
HE'S CLEARLY UP TO SOMETHING!
HEH HEH HEH... I CAN'T DENY THAT LOGIC, THOUGH.
I AM JUST A SCIENTIST, AFTER ALL. NOT A SHIPWRIGHT.
IN THAT CASE... ♫
WHY DON'T WE ALL...
...COME UP WITH DESIGN PROPOSALS?

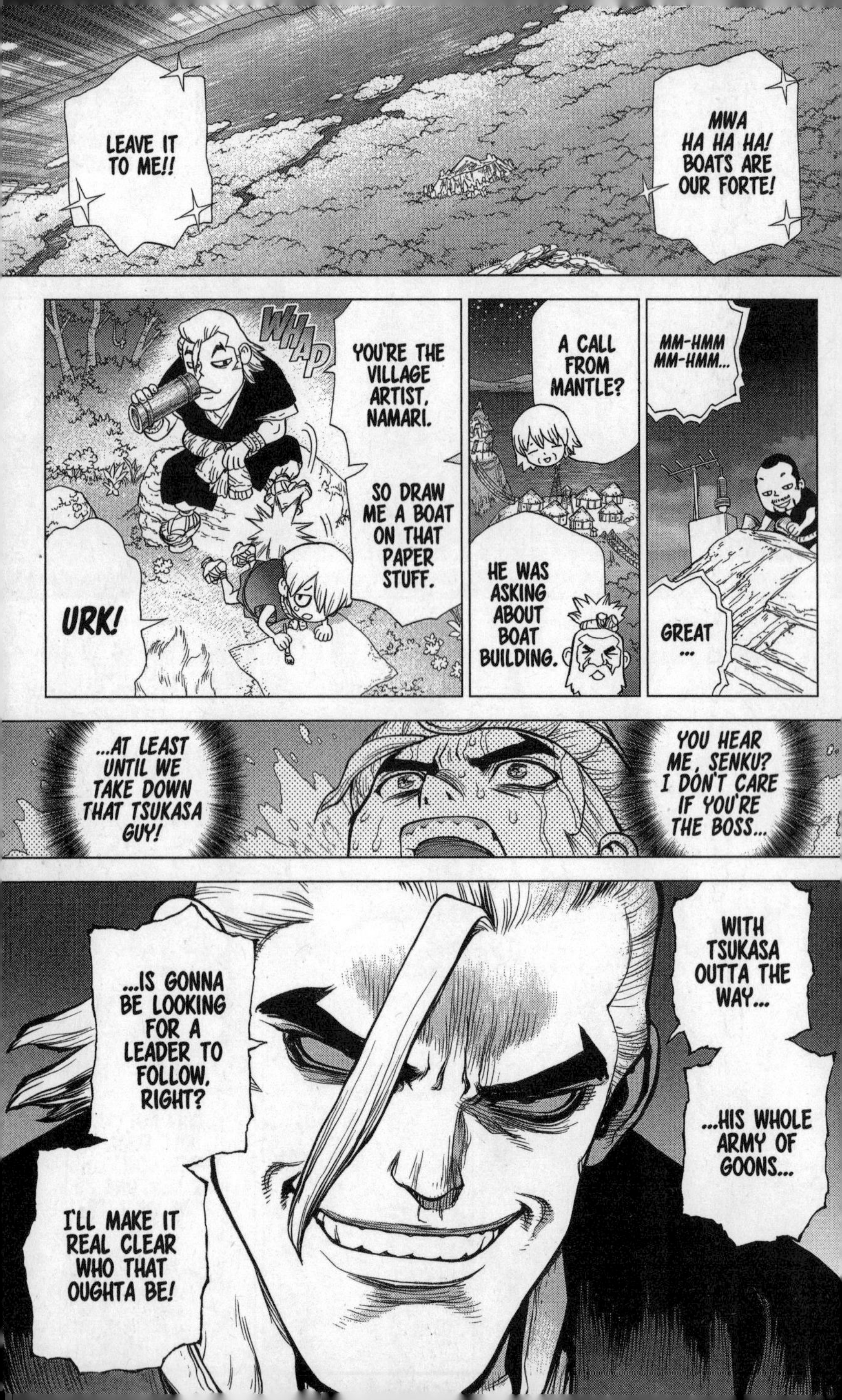
MWA HA HA HA! BOATS ARE OUR FORTE!
LEAVE IT TO ME!!
MM-HMM MM-HMM...
GREAT...
A CALL FROM MANTLE?
HE WAS ASKING ABOUT BOAT BUILDING.
WHAP
YOU'RE THE VILLAGE ARTIST, NAMARI.
SO DRAW ME A BOAT ON THAT PAPER STUFF.
URK!
YOU HEAR ME, SENKU? I DON'T CARE IF YOU'RE THE BOSS...
...AT LEAST UNTIL WE TAKE DOWN THAT TSUKASA GUY!
WITH TSUKASA OUTTA THE WAY...
...HIS WHOLE ARMY OF GOONS...
...IS GONNA BE LOOKING FOR A LEADER TO FOLLOW, RIGHT?
I'LL MAKE IT REAL CLEAR WHO THAT OUGHTA BE!

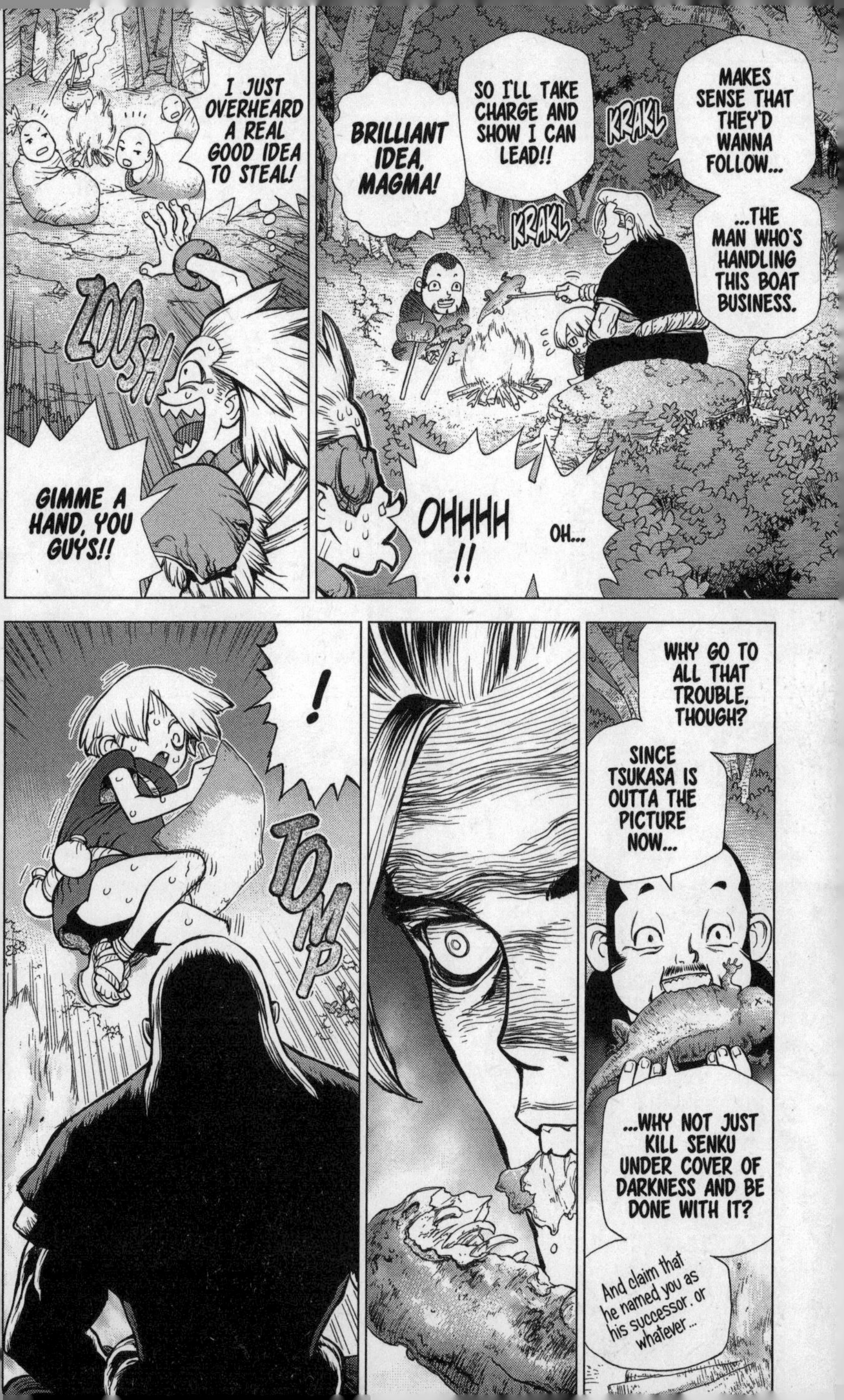

MAKES SENSE THAT THEY'D WANNA FOLLOW...
...THE MAN WHO'S HANDLING THIS BOAT BUSINESS.
KRAKL
SO I'LL TAKE CHARGE AND SHOW I CAN LEAD!!
KRAKL
BRILLIANT IDEA, MAGMA!
OH...
OHHHH!!
I JUST OVERHEARD A REAL GOOD IDEA TO STEAL!
ZOOSH
GIMME A HAND, YOU GUYS!!
WHY GO TO ALL THAT TROUBLE, THOUGH?
SINCE TSUKASA IS OUTTA THE PICTURE NOW...
...WHY NOT JUST KILL SENKU UNDER COVER OF DARKNESS AND BE DONE WITH IT?
And claim that he named you as his successor, or whatever...
!
TOMP

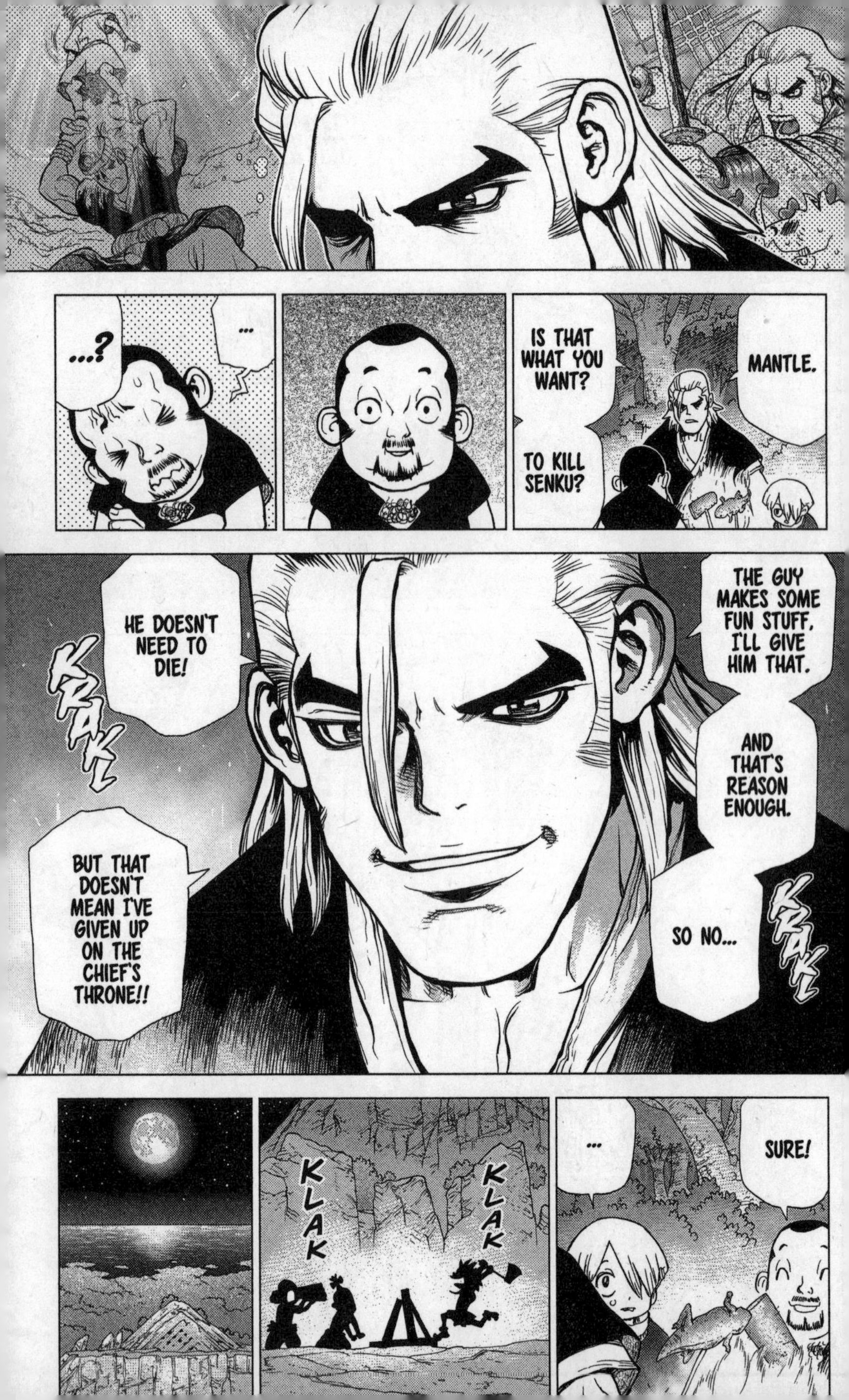
MANTLE.
IS THAT WHAT YOU WANT?
TO KILL SENKU?
...
...?
THE GUY MAKES SOME FUN STUFF, I'LL GIVE HIM THAT.
AND THAT'S REASON ENOUGH.
SO NO...
KRAK
HE DOESN'T NEED TO DIE!
KRAK
BUT THAT DOESN'T MEAN I'VE GIVEN UP ON THE CHIEF'S THRONE!!
SURE!
...
KLAK
KLAK

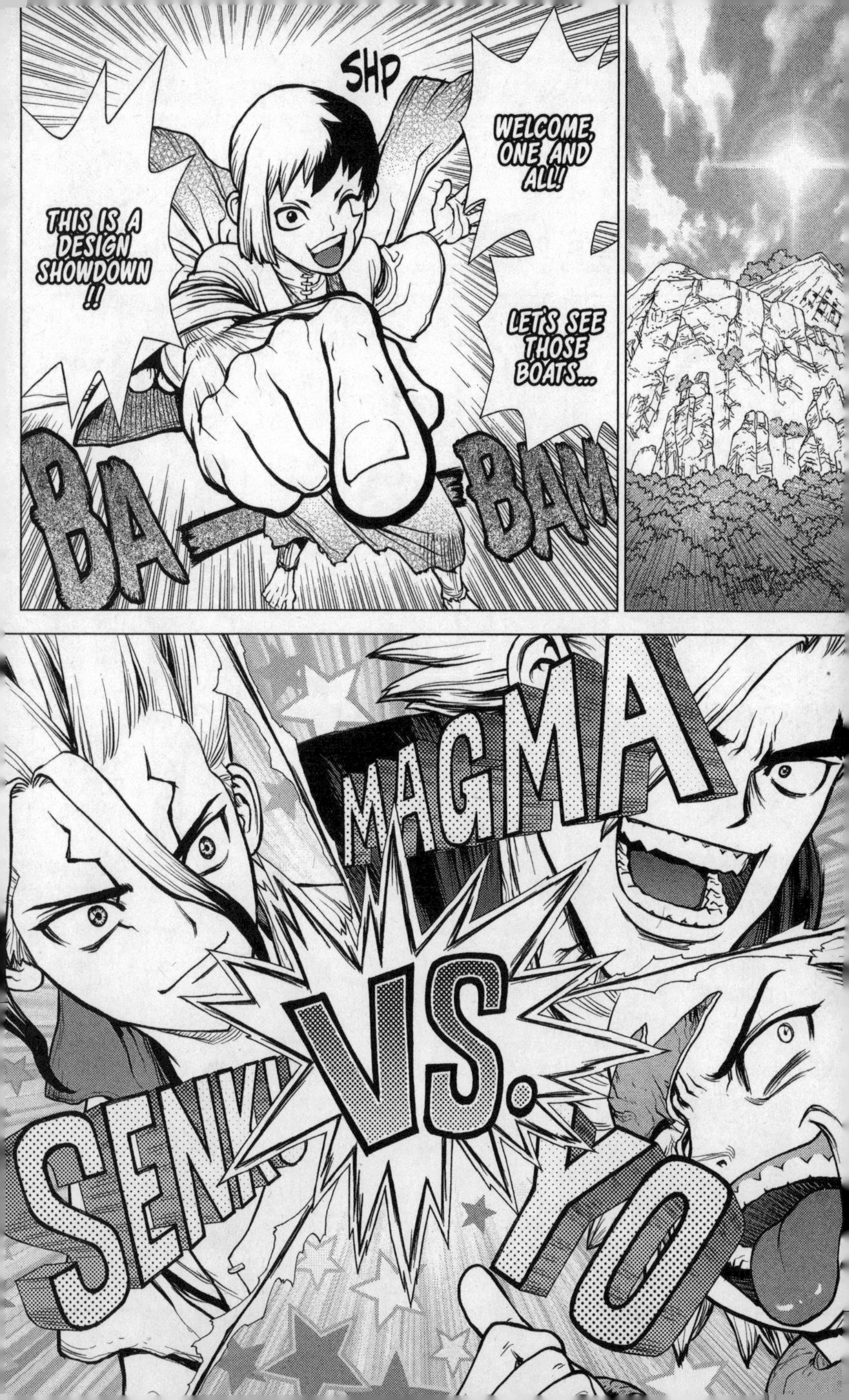
SHP
WELCOME, ONE AND ALL!
THIS IS A DESIGN SHOWDOWN !!
LET'S SEE THOSE BOATS...
BA-BAM
MAGMA
VS.
SENK
YO

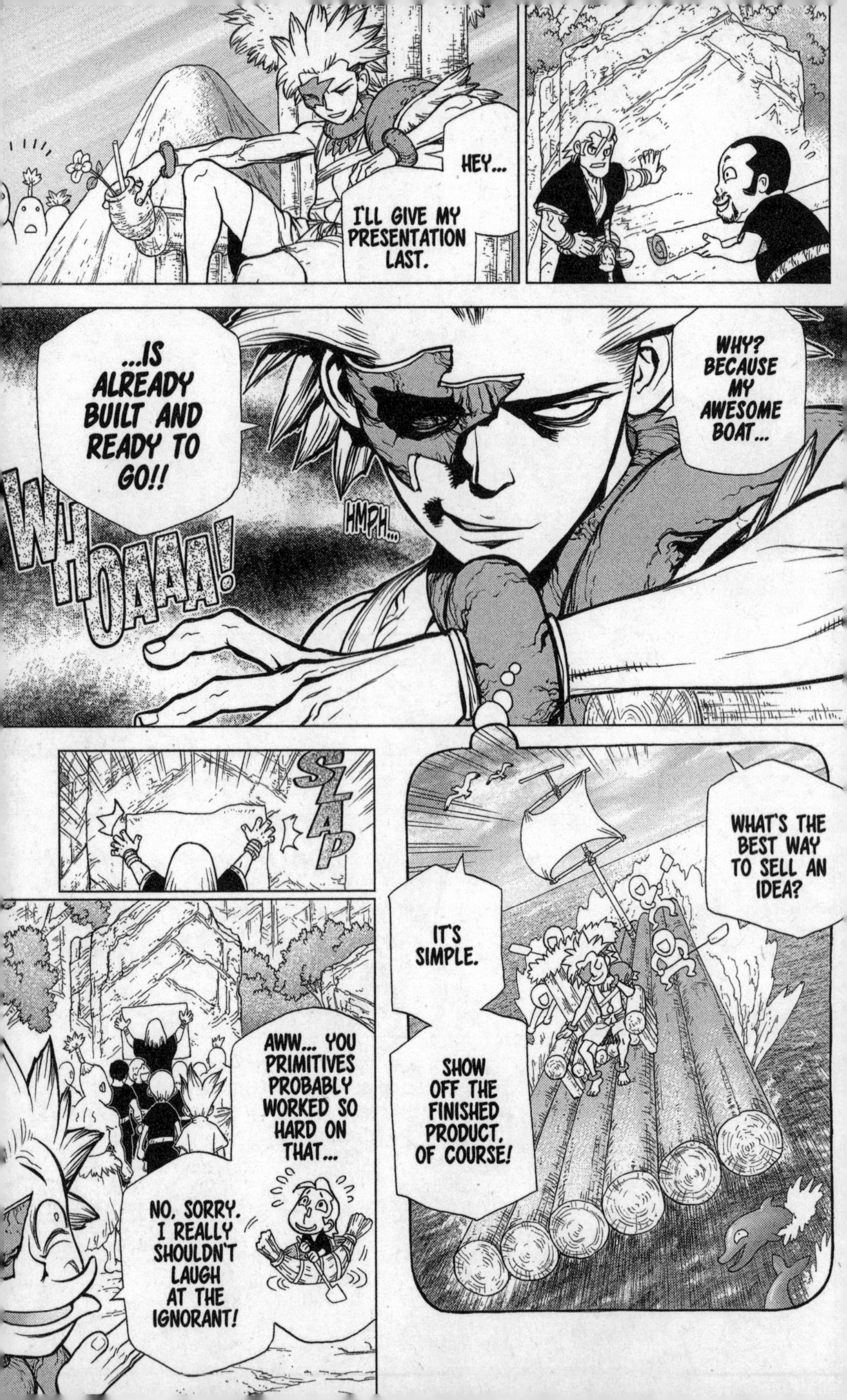
HEY...
I'LL GIVE MY PRESENTATION LAST.
WHY? BECAUSE MY AWESOME BOAT...
...IS ALREADY BUILT AND READY TO GO!!
HMPH...
WHOAAA!
WHAT'S THE BEST WAY TO SELL AN IDEA?
IT'S SIMPLE.
SHOW OFF THE FINISHED PRODUCT, OF COURSE!
SLAP
AWW... YOU PRIMITIVES PROBABLY WORKED SO HARD ON THAT...
NO, SORRY. I REALLY SHOULDN'T LAUGH AT THE IGNORANT!

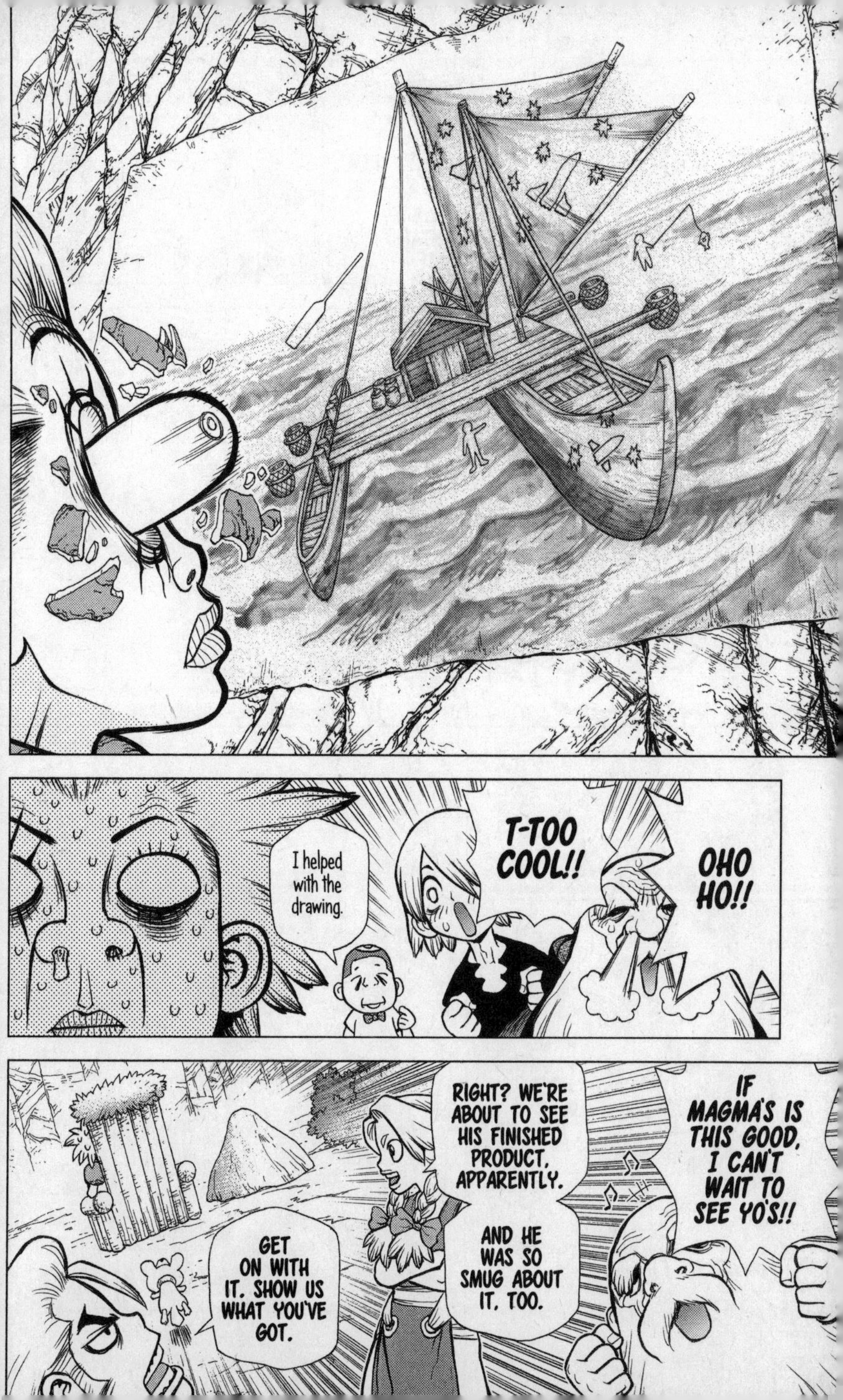
OHO HO!!
T-TOO COOL!!
I helped with the drawing.
IF MAGMA'S IS THIS GOOD, I CAN'T WAIT TO SEE YO'S!!
RIGHT? WE'RE ABOUT TO SEE HIS FINISHED PRODUCT, APPARENTLY.
AND HE WAS SO SMUG ABOUT IT, TOO.
GET ON WITH IT. SHOW US WHAT YOU'VE GOT.

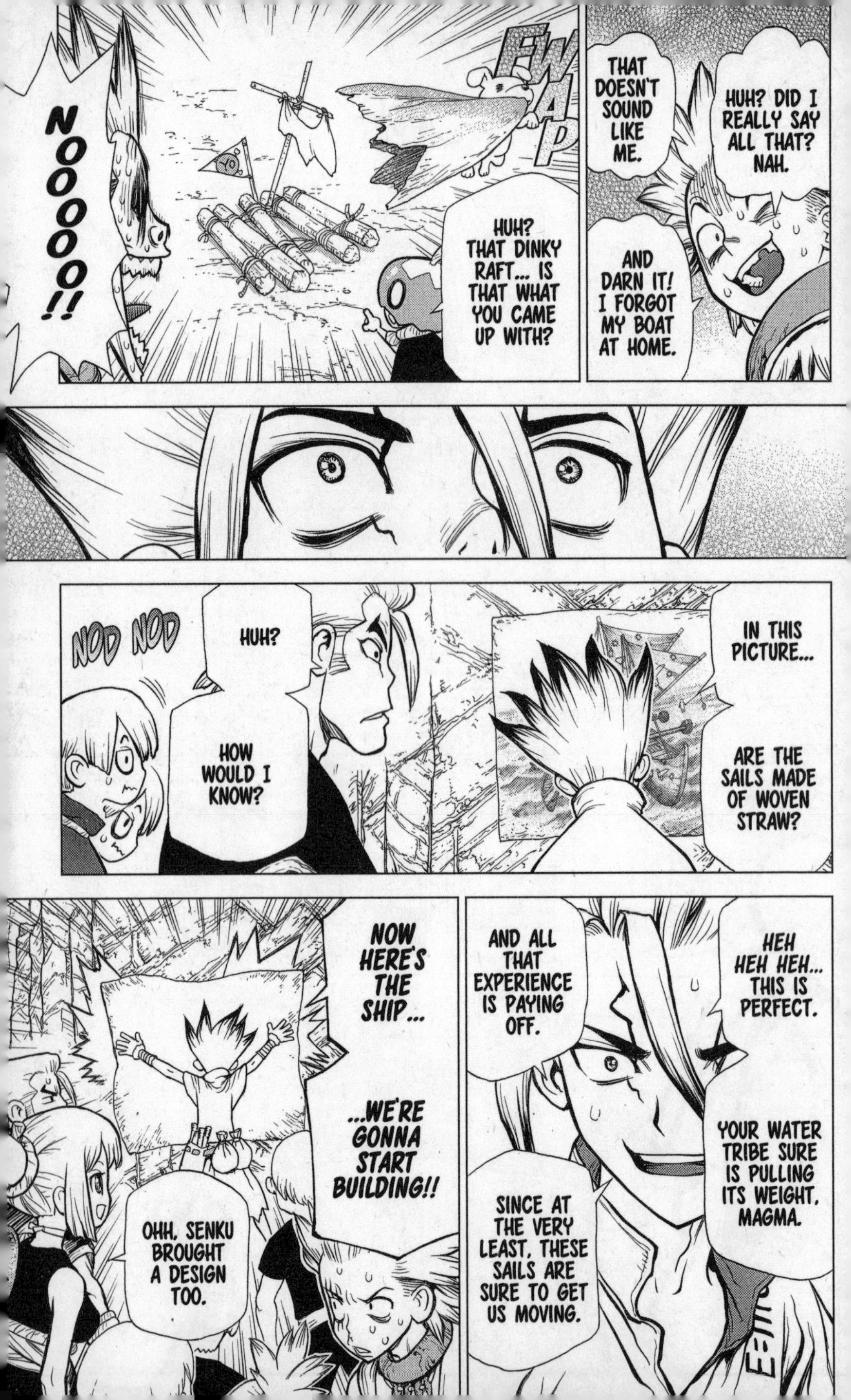
HUH? DID I REALLY SAY ALL THAT? NAH.
THAT DOESN'T SOUND LIKE ME.
AND DARN IT! I FORGOT MY BOAT AT HOME.
FWAP
HUH? THAT DINKY RAFT... IS THAT WHAT YOU CAME UP WITH?
NOOOOOO!!
IN THIS PICTURE...
ARE THE SAILS MADE OF WOVEN STRAW?
HUH?
HOW WOULD I KNOW?
NOD NOD
HEH HEH HEH... THIS IS PERFECT.
AND ALL THAT EXPERIENCE IS PAYING OFF.
YOUR WATER TRIBE SURE IS PULLING ITS WEIGHT, MAGMA.
SINCE AT THE VERY LEAST, THESE SAILS ARE SURE TO GET US MOVING.
NOW HERE'S THE SHIP...
...WE'RE GONNA START BUILDING!!
OHH, SENKU BROUGHT A DESIGN TOO.

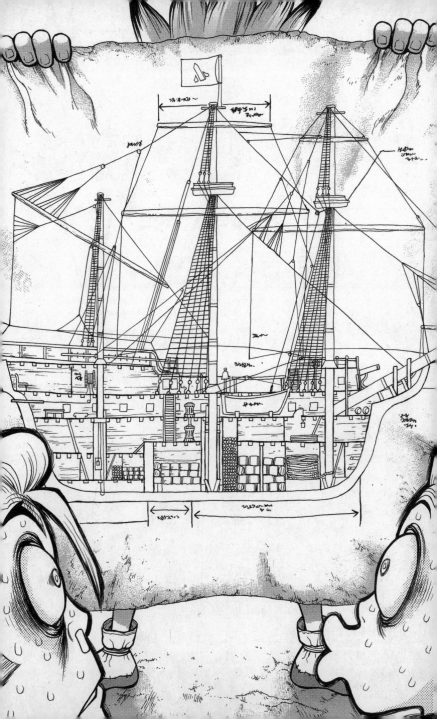

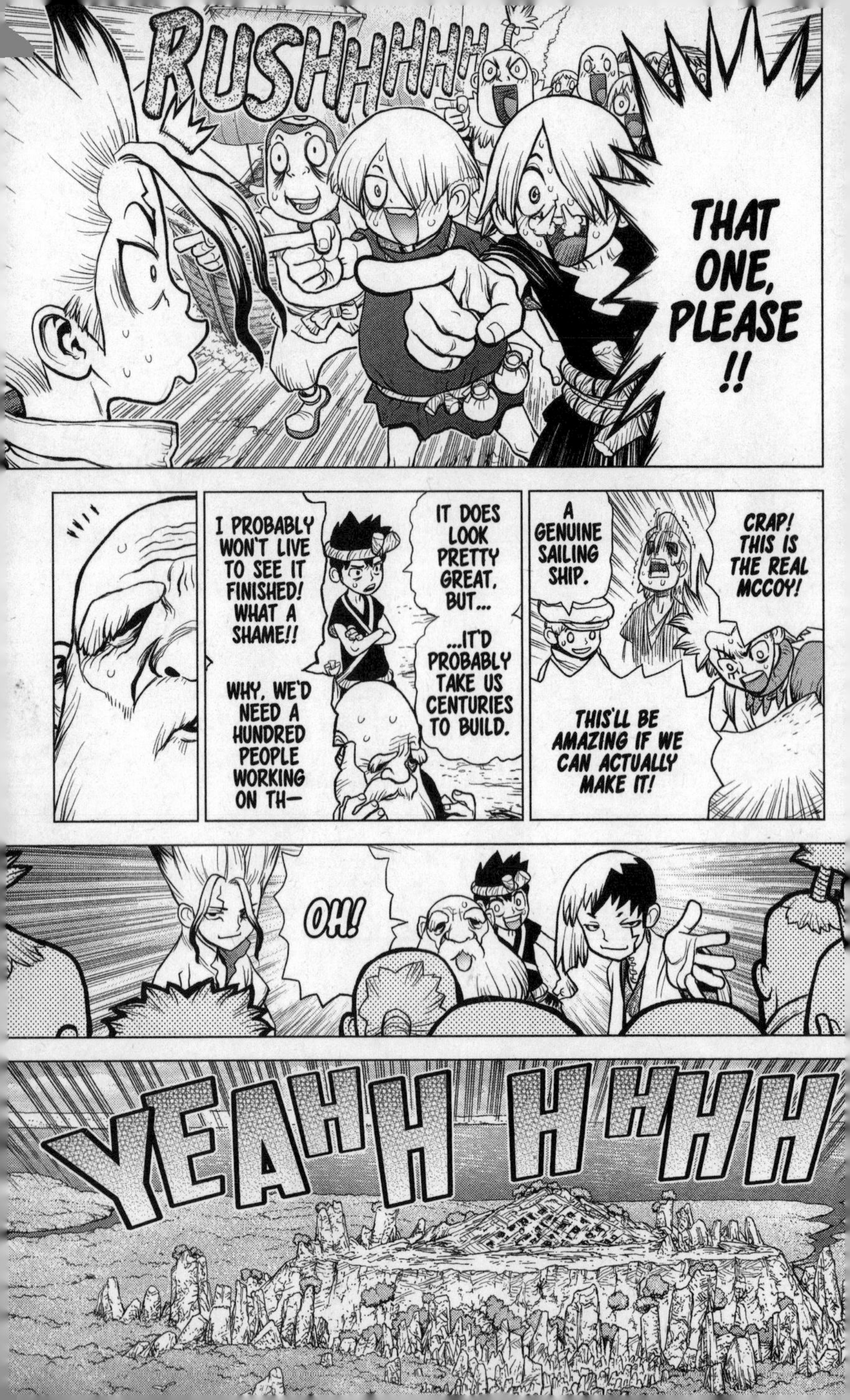
RUSHHHHHH
THAT ONE, PLEASE!!
CRAP! THIS IS THE REAL MCCOY!
A GENUINE SAILING SHIP.
THIS'LL BE AMAZING IF WE CAN ACTUALLY MAKE IT!
IT DOES LOOK PRETTY GREAT, BUT...
...IT'D PROBABLY TAKE US CENTURIES TO BUILD.
I PROBABLY WON'T LIVE TO SEE IT FINISHED! WHAT A SHAME!!
WHY, WE'D NEED A HUNDRED PEOPLE WORKING ON TH—
OH!
YEAHH HHHH

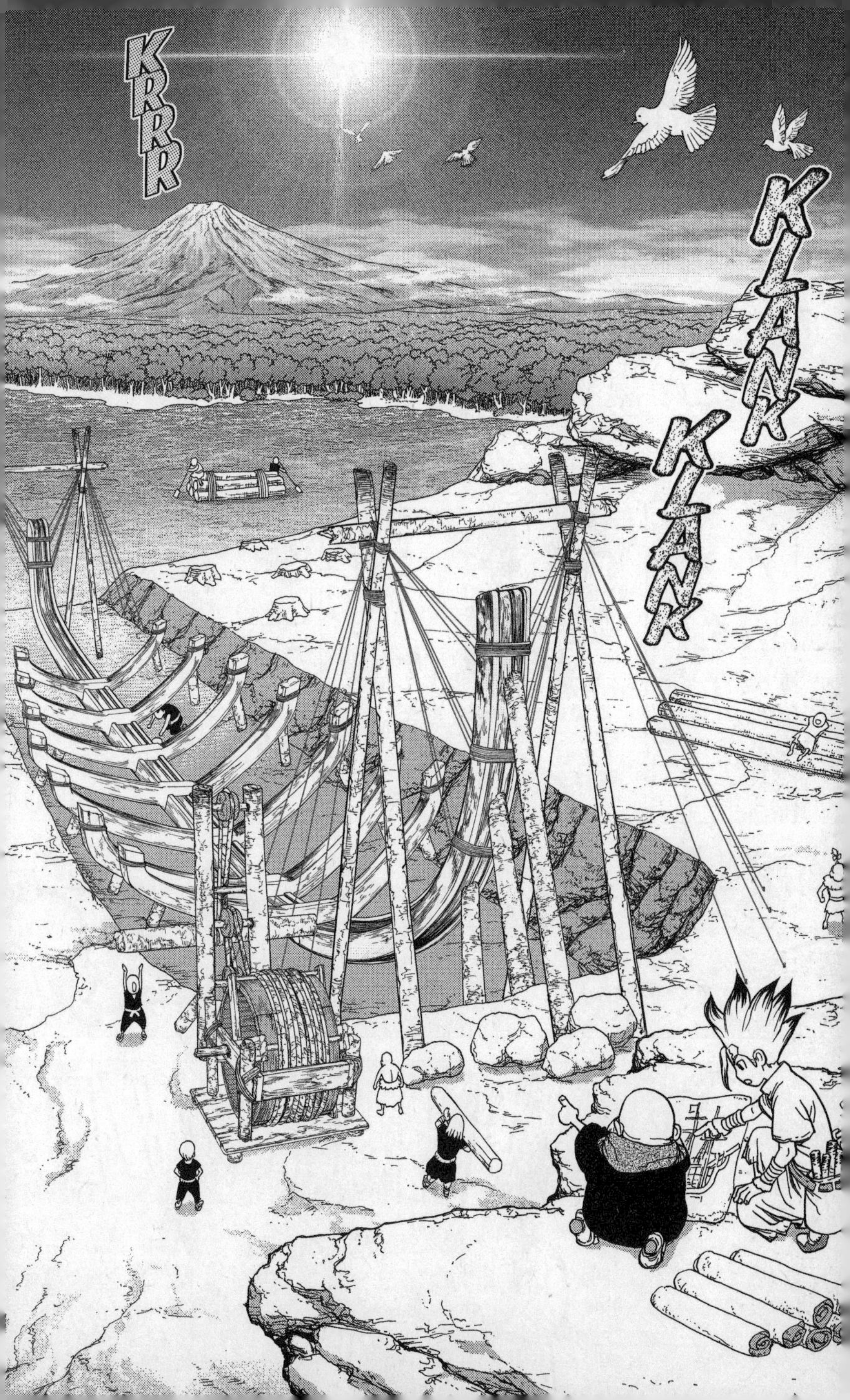
KLANK
KLANK
KRRR

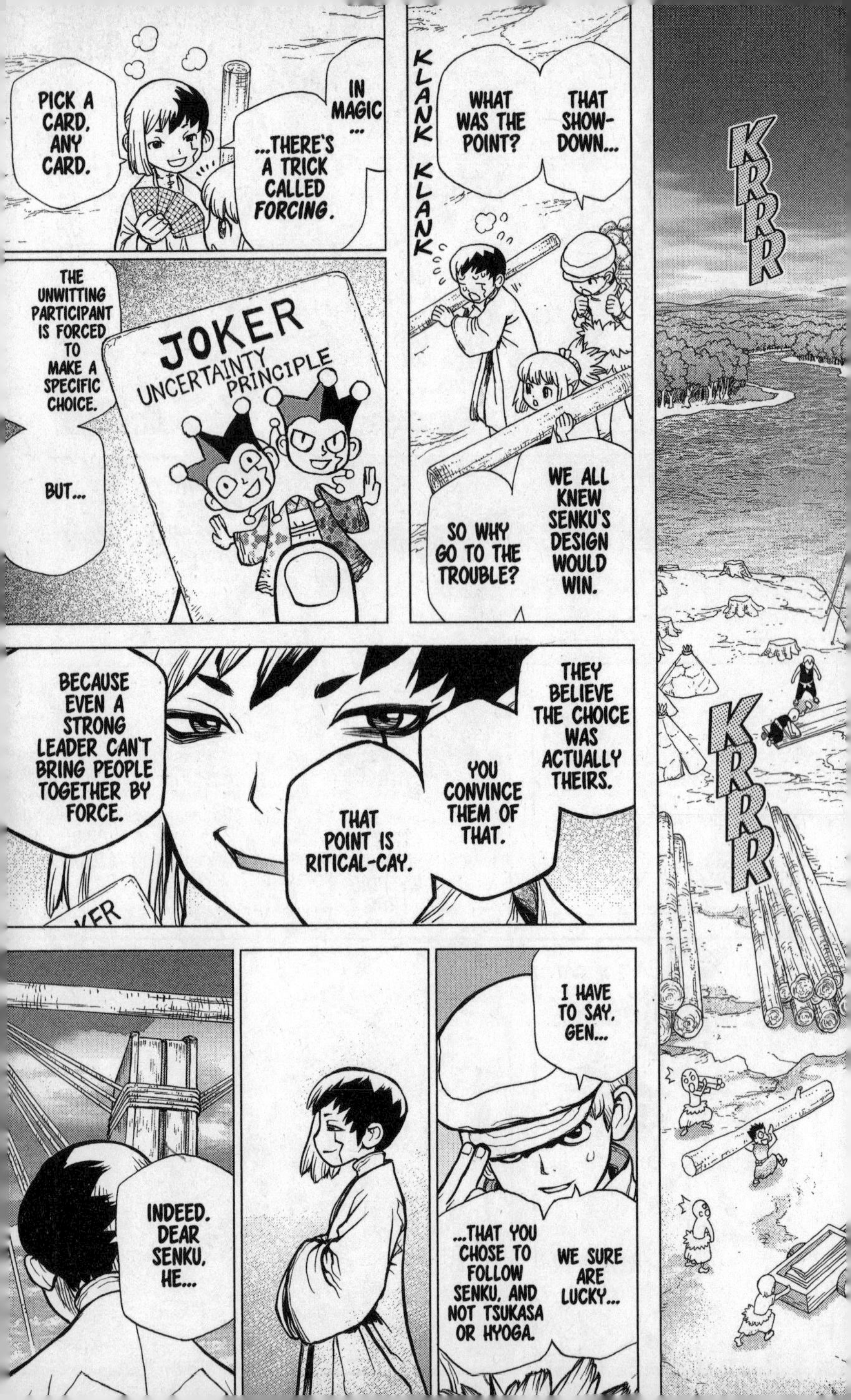
KRRR
KRRR
KLANK KLANK
THAT SHOW-DOWN...
WHAT WAS THE POINT?
WE ALL KNEW SENKU'S DESIGN WOULD WIN.
SO WHY GO TO THE TROUBLE?
IN MAGIC...
...THERE'S A TRICK CALLED FORCING.
PICK A CARD, ANY CARD.
JOKER
UNCERTAINTY PRINCIPLE
THE UNWITTING PARTICIPANT IS FORCED TO MAKE A SPECIFIC CHOICE.
BUT...
THEY BELIEVE THE CHOICE WAS ACTUALLY THEIRS.
YOU CONVINCE THEM OF THAT.
THAT POINT IS RITICAL-CAY.
BECAUSE EVEN A STRONG LEADER CAN'T BRING PEOPLE TOGETHER BY FORCE.
I HAVE TO SAY, GEN...
WE SURE ARE LUCKY...
...THAT YOU CHOSE TO FOLLOW SENKU, AND NOT TSUKASA OR HYOGA.
INDEED. DEAR SENKU, HE...

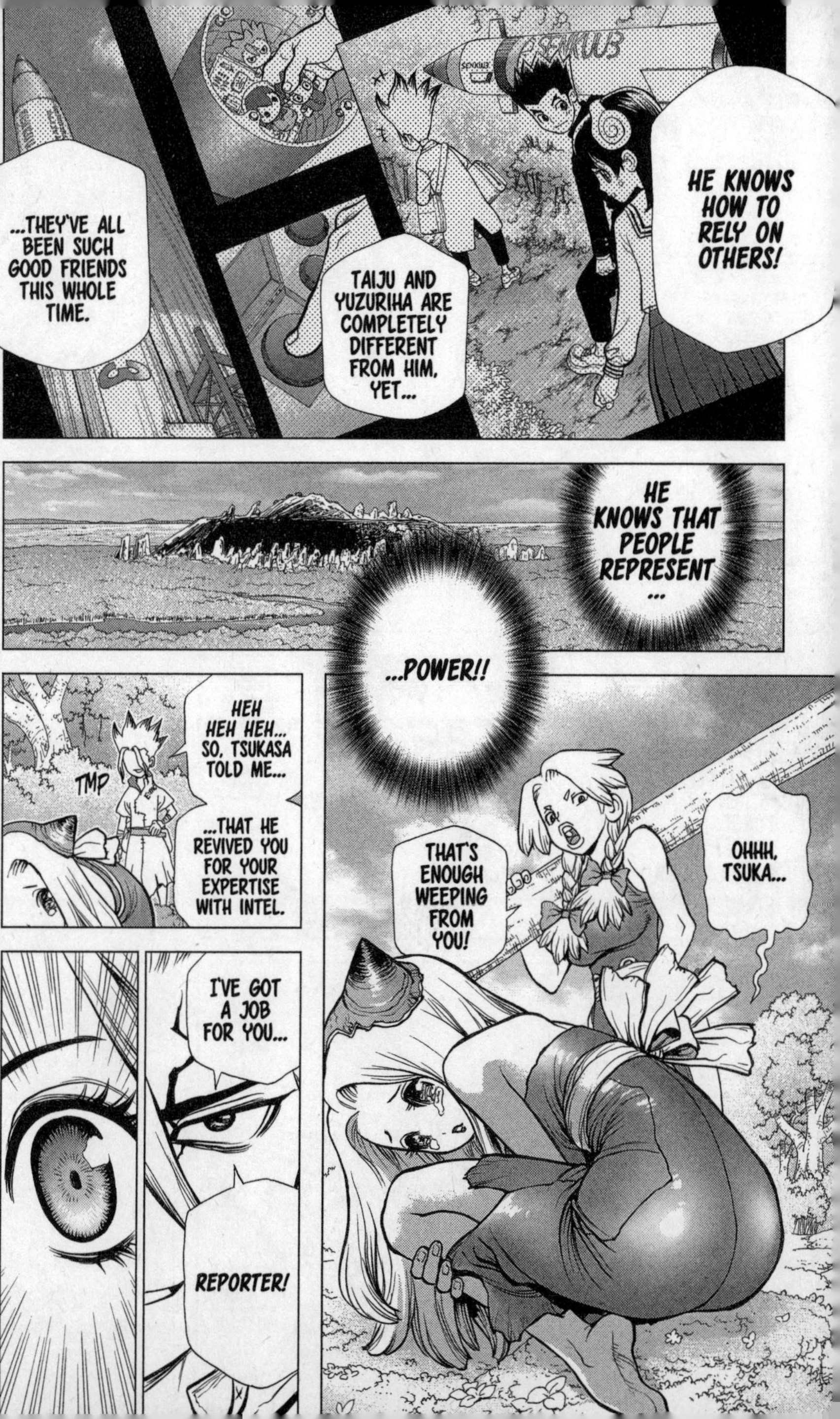
HE KNOWS HOW TO RELY ON OTHERS!
TAIJU AND YUZURIHA ARE COMPLETELY DIFFERENT FROM HIM, YET...
...THEY'VE ALL BEEN SUCH GOOD FRIENDS THIS WHOLE TIME.
HE KNOWS THAT PEOPLE REPRESENT ...
...POWER!!
OHHH, TSUKA...
THAT'S ENOUGH WEEPING FROM YOU!
TMP
HEH HEH HEH... SO, TSUKASA TOLD ME...
...THAT HE REVIVED YOU FOR YOUR EXPERTISE WITH INTEL.
I'VE GOT A JOB FOR YOU...
REPORTER!

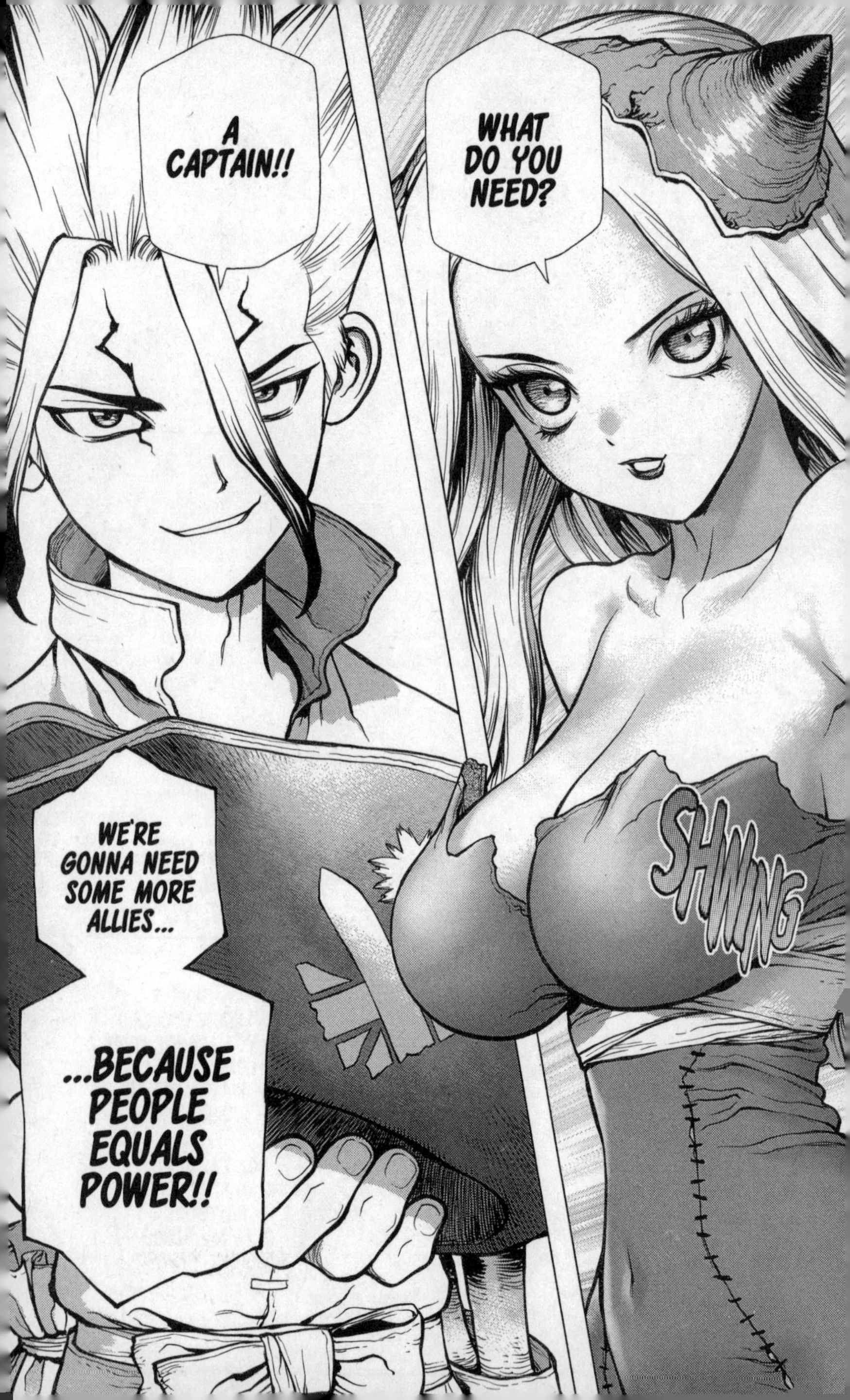
WHAT DO YOU NEED?
A CAPTAIN!!
SHIING
WE'RE GONNA NEED SOME MORE ALLIES...
...BECAUSE PEOPLE EQUALS POWER!!

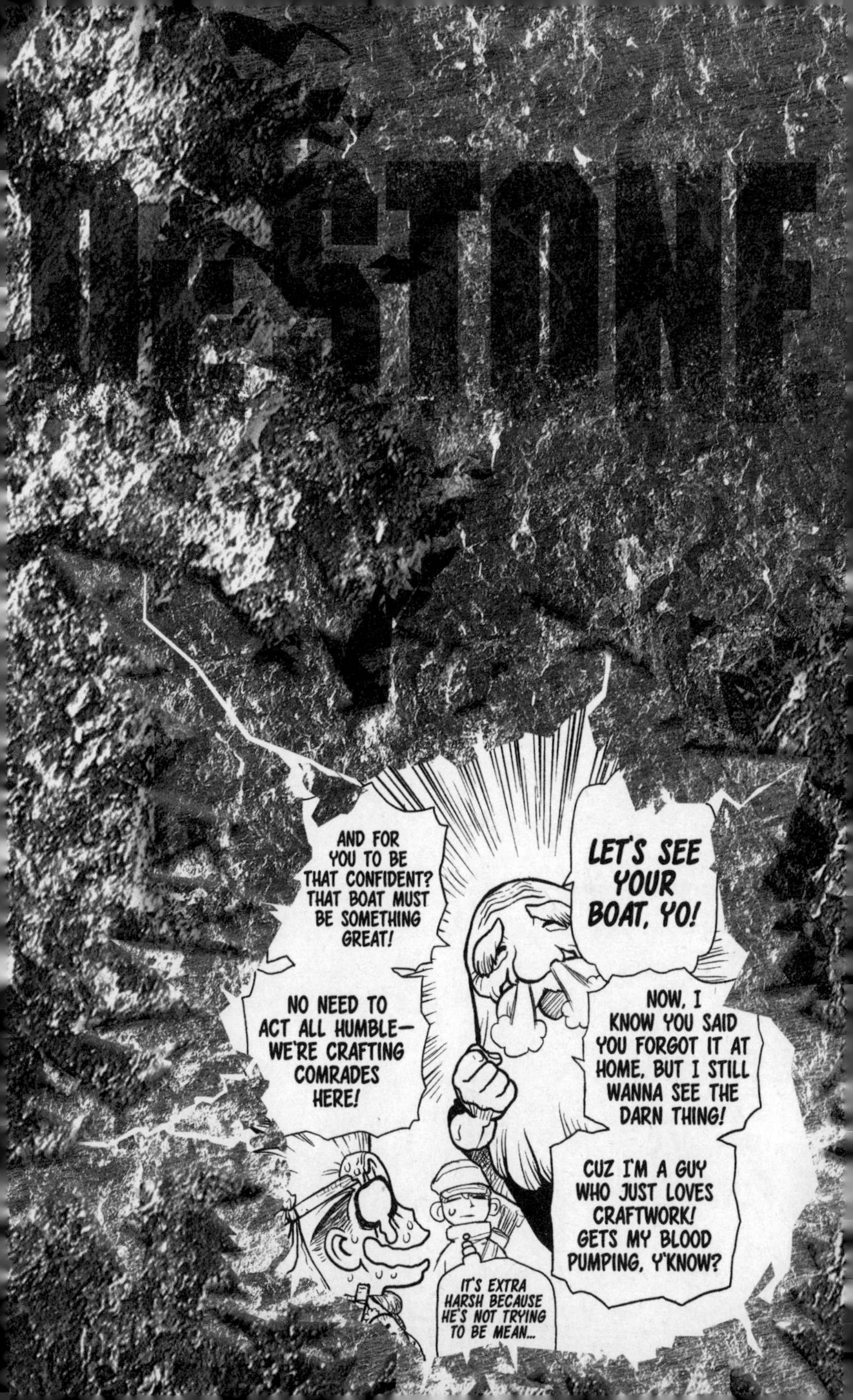
Dr.STONE
LET'S SEE YOUR BOAT, YO!
AND FOR YOU TO BE THAT CONFIDENT? THAT BOAT MUST BE SOMETHING GREAT!
NOW, I KNOW YOU SAID YOU FORGOT IT AT HOME, BUT I STILL WANNA SEE THE DARN THING!
NO NEED TO ACT ALL HUMBLE—WE'RE CRAFTING COMRADES HERE!
CUZ I'M A GUY WHO JUST LOVES CRAFTWORK! GETS MY BLOOD PUMPING, Y'KNOW?
IT'S EXTRA HARSH BECAUSE HE'S NOT TRYING TO BE MEAN...

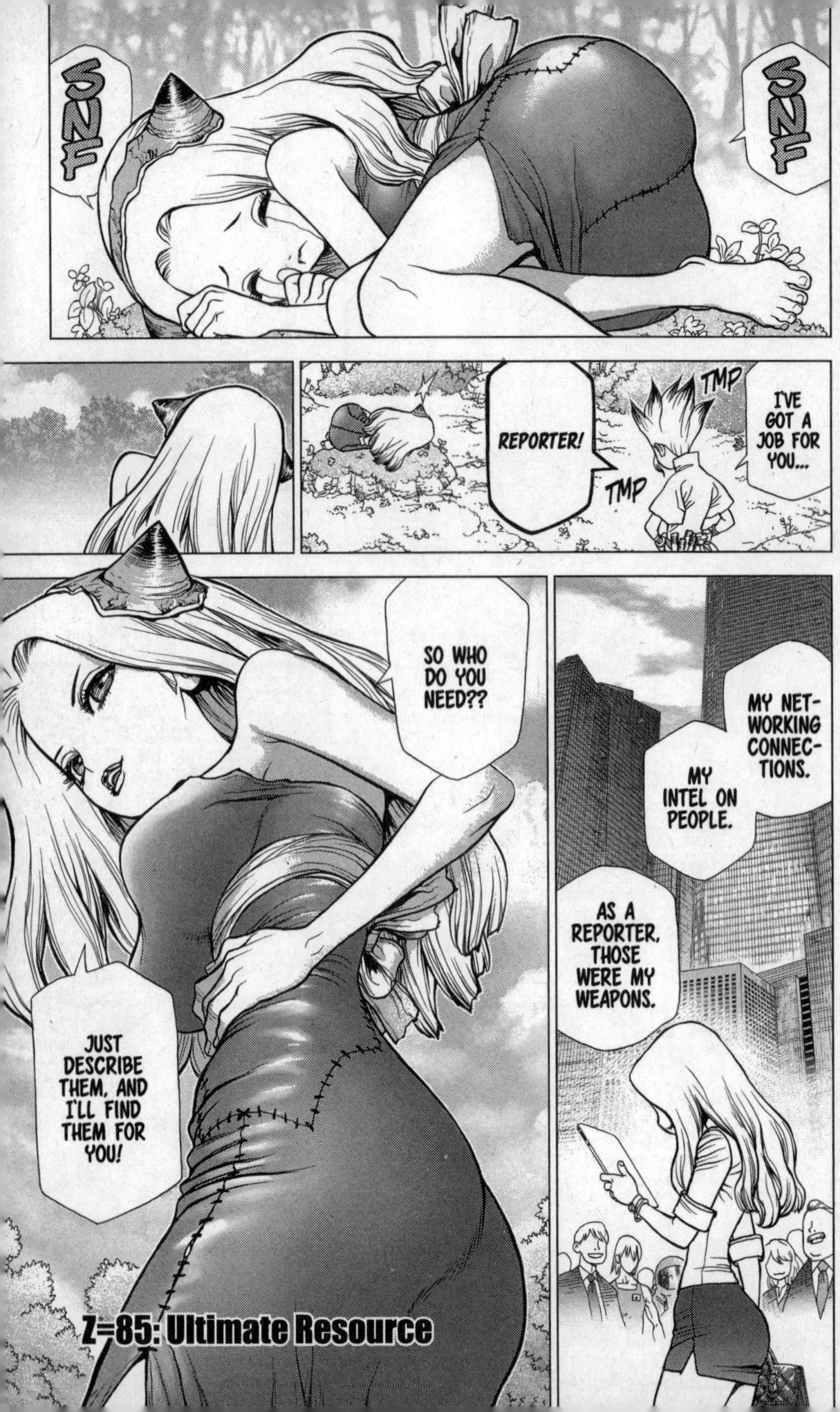
SNF
SNF
TMP
I'VE GOT A JOB FOR YOU...
REPORTER!
TMP
MY NET-WORKING CONNEC-TIONS.
MY INTEL ON PEOPLE.
AS A REPORTER, THOSE WERE MY WEAPONS.
SO WHO DO YOU NEED??
JUST DESCRIBE THEM, AND I'LL FIND THEM FOR YOU!

Z=85: Ultimate Resource

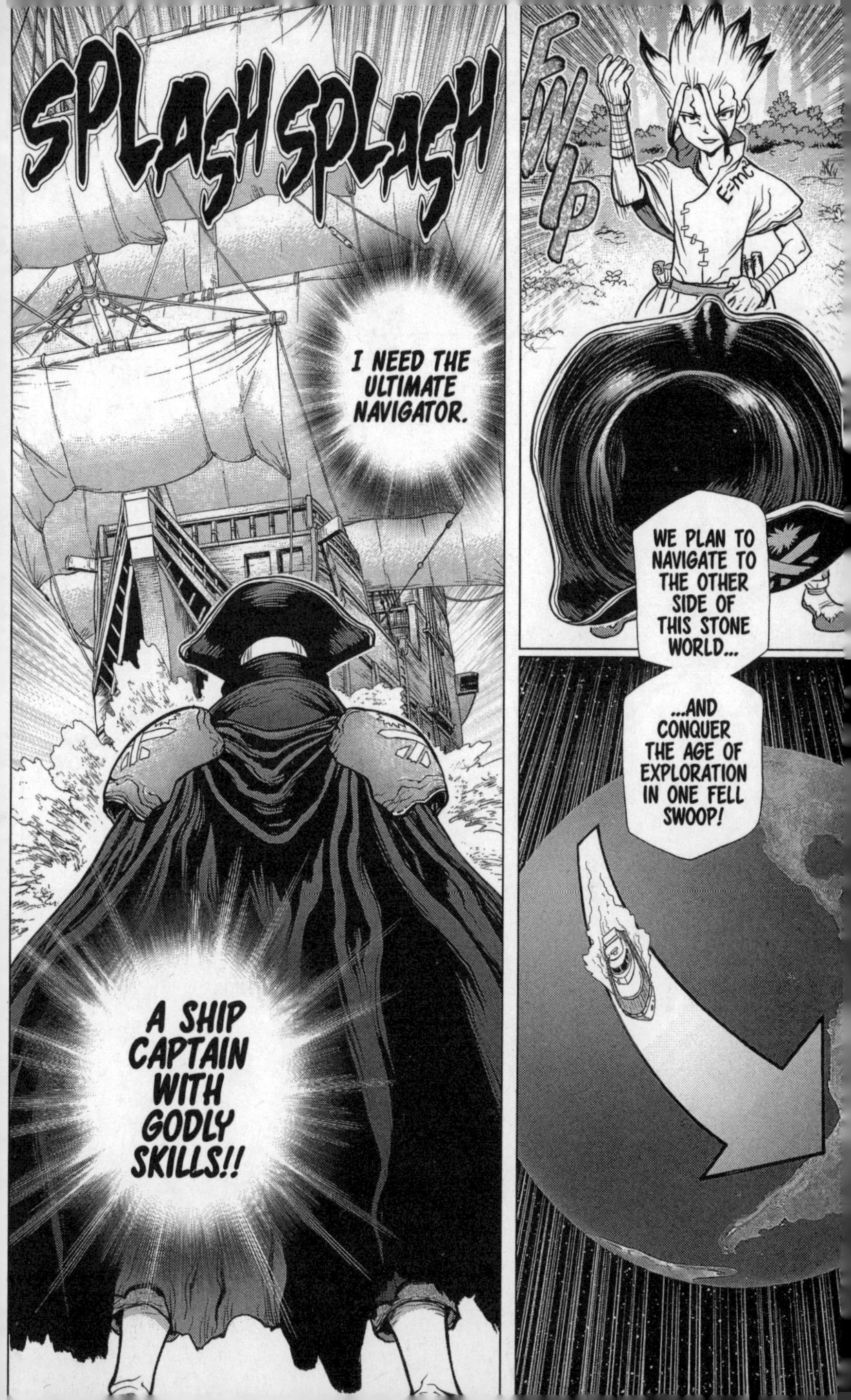
FLIP
$E=mc^2$
WE PLAN TO NAVIGATE TO THE OTHER SIDE OF THIS STONE WORLD...
...AND CONQUER THE AGE OF EXPLORATION IN ONE FELL SWOOP!
SPLASH SPLASH
I NEED THE ULTIMATE NAVIGATOR.
A SHIP CAPTAIN WITH GODLY SKILLS!!

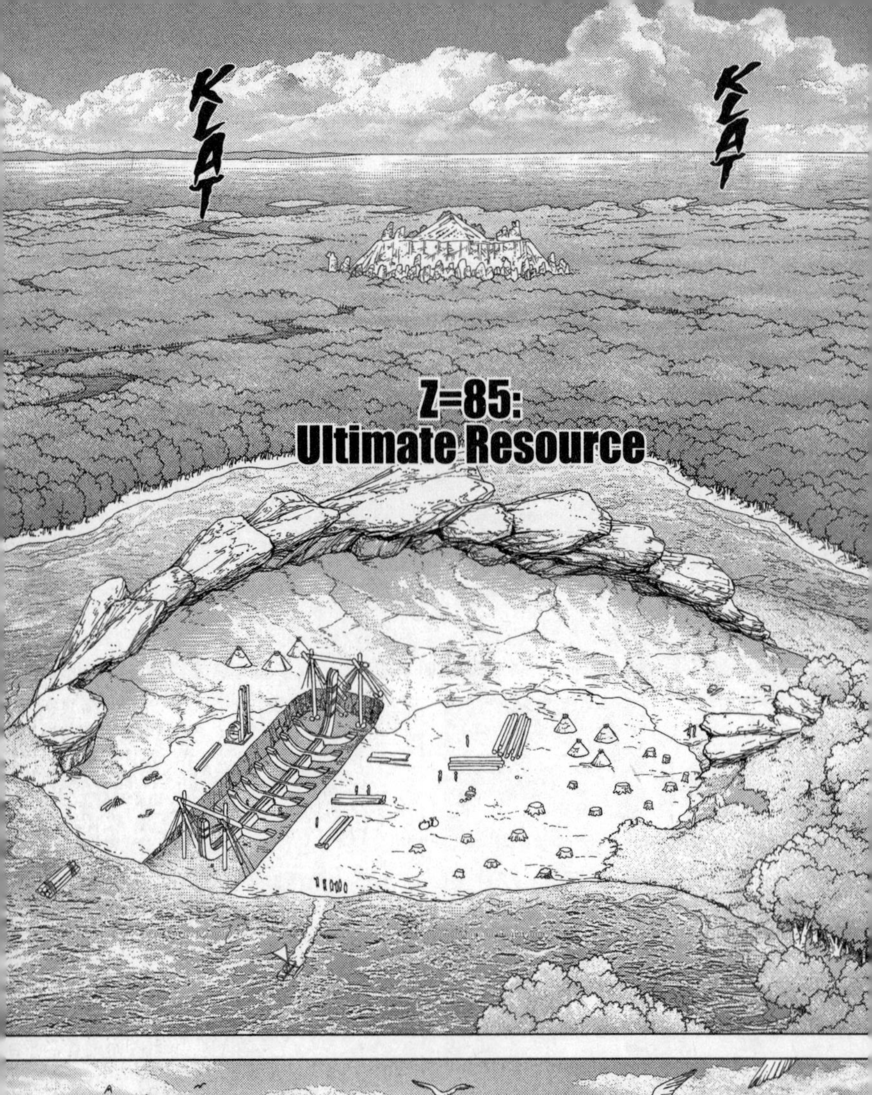
KLAT
KLAT
Z=85:
Ultimate Resource
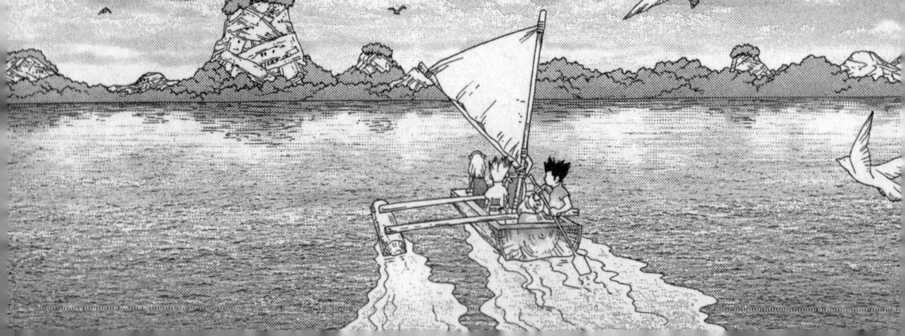

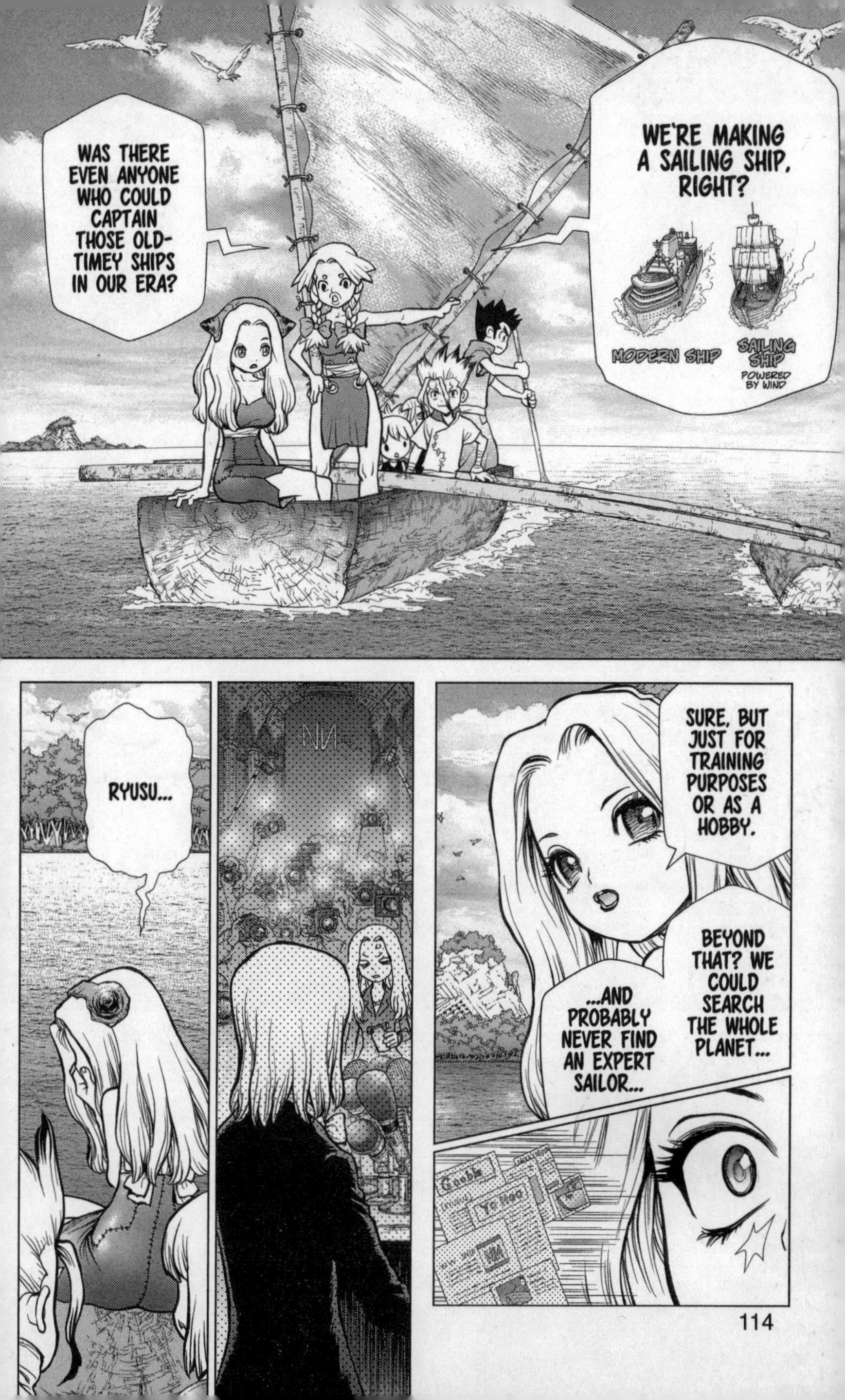
WE'RE MAKING A SAILING SHIP, RIGHT?
MODERN SHIP
SAILING SHIP
POWERED BY WIND
WAS THERE EVEN ANYONE WHO COULD CAPTAIN THOSE OLD-TIMEY SHIPS IN OUR ERA?
SURE, BUT JUST FOR TRAINING PURPOSES OR AS A HOBBY.
BEYOND THAT? WE COULD SEARCH THE WHOLE PLANET...
...AND PROBABLY NEVER FIND AN EXPERT SAILOR...
RYUSU...

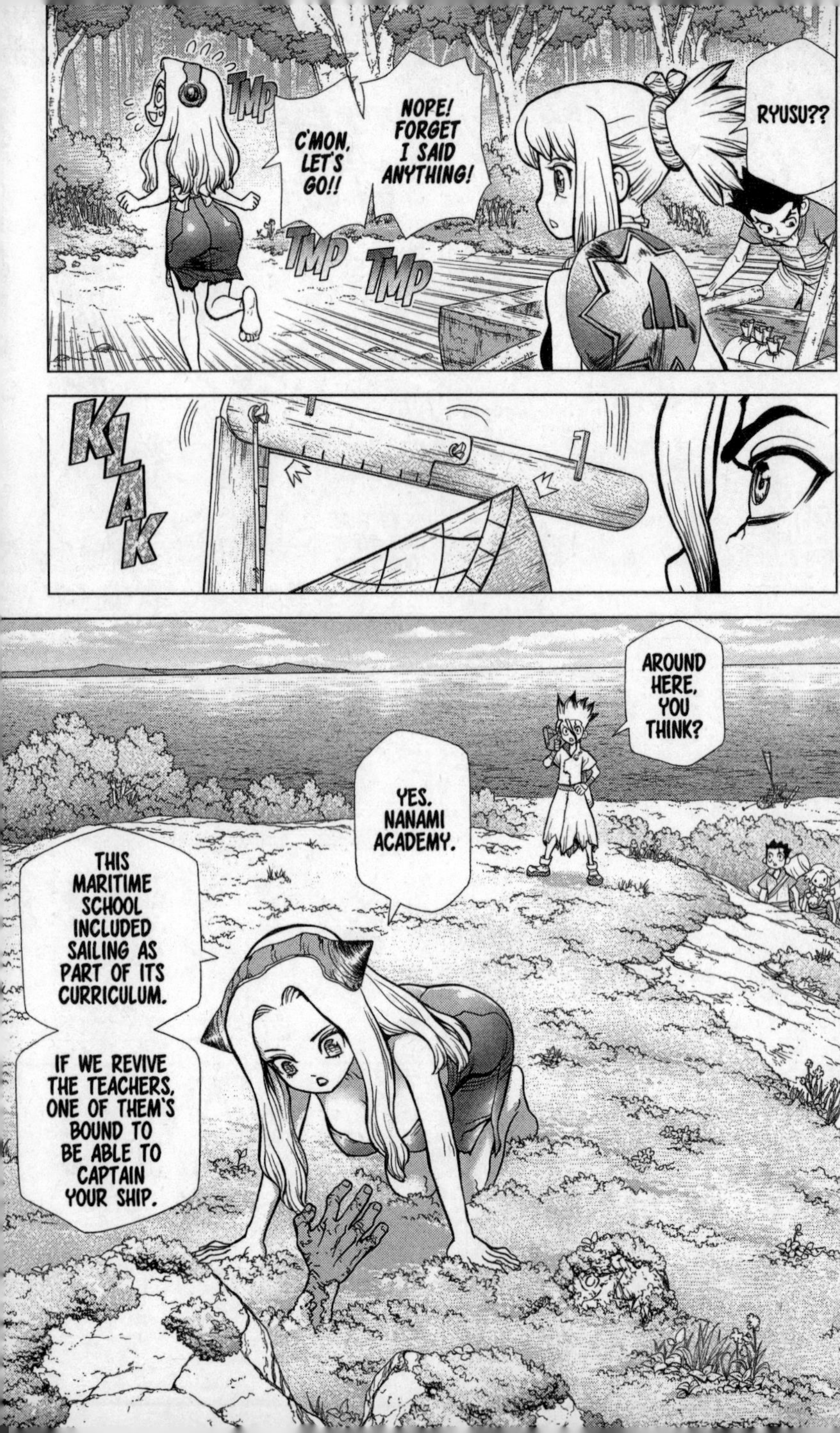
RYUSU??
NOPE! FORGET I SAID ANYTHING!
TMP
TMP
C'MON, LET'S GO!!
TMP
KLAK
AROUND HERE, YOU THINK?
YES. NANAMI ACADEMY.
THIS MARITIME SCHOOL INCLUDED SAILING AS PART OF ITS CURRICULUM.
IF WE REVIVE THE TEACHERS, ONE OF THEM'S BOUND TO BE ABLE TO CAPTAIN YOUR SHIP.

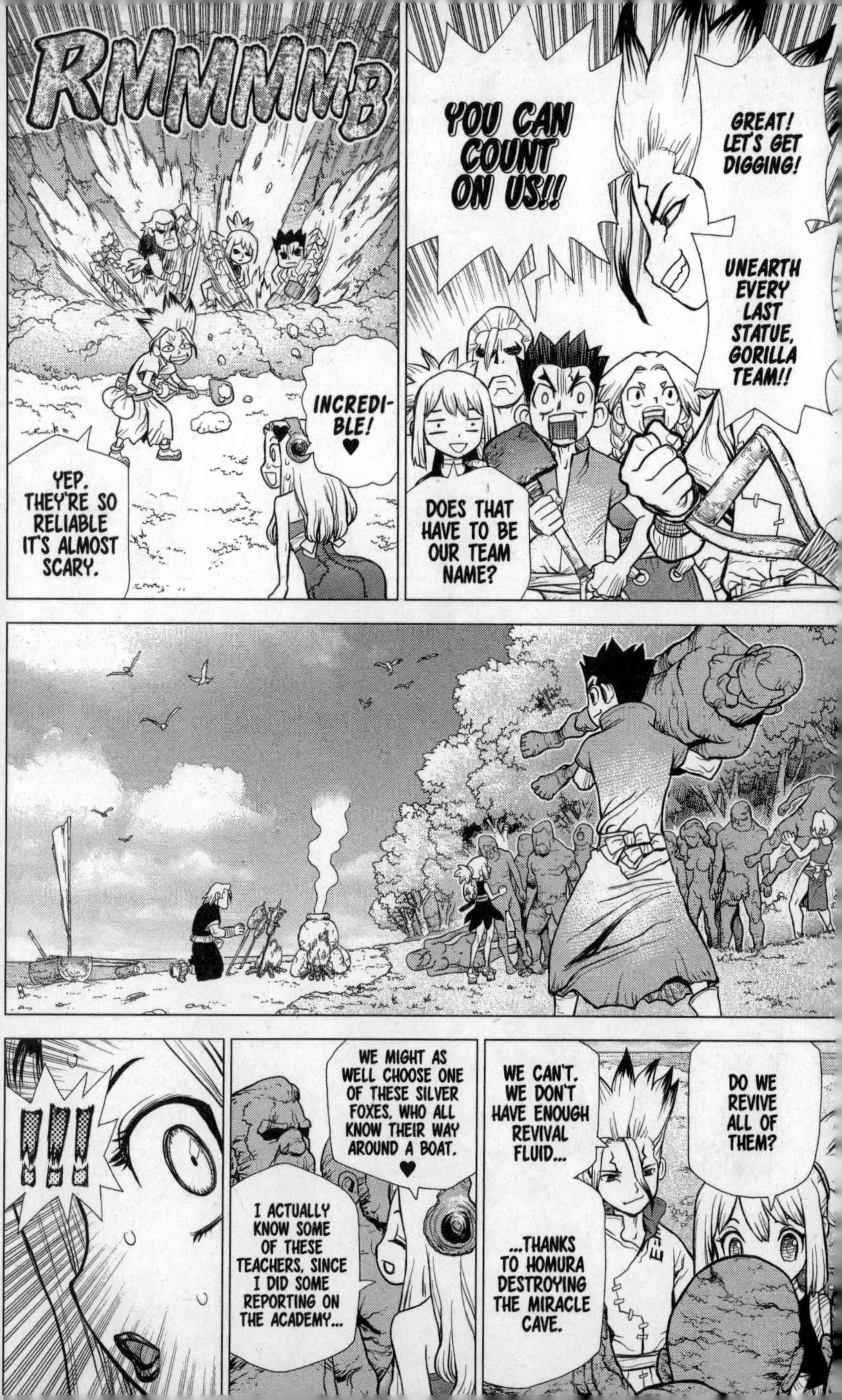
GREAT! LET'S GET DIGGING!
UNEARTH EVERY LAST STATUE, GORILLA TEAM!!
YOU CAN COUNT ON US!!
DOES THAT HAVE TO BE OUR TEAM NAME?
RMMMMMB
INCREDI-BLE! ♥
YEP. THEY'RE SO RELIABLE IT'S ALMOST SCARY.
DO WE REVIVE ALL OF THEM?
WE CAN'T. WE DON'T HAVE ENOUGH REVIVAL FLUID...
...THANKS TO HOMURA DESTROYING THE MIRACLE CAVE.
WE MIGHT AS WELL CHOOSE ONE OF THESE SILVER FOXES, WHO ALL KNOW THEIR WAY AROUND A BOAT. ♥
I ACTUALLY KNOW SOME OF THESE TEACHERS, SINCE I DID SOME REPORTING ON THE ACADEMY...
!!!

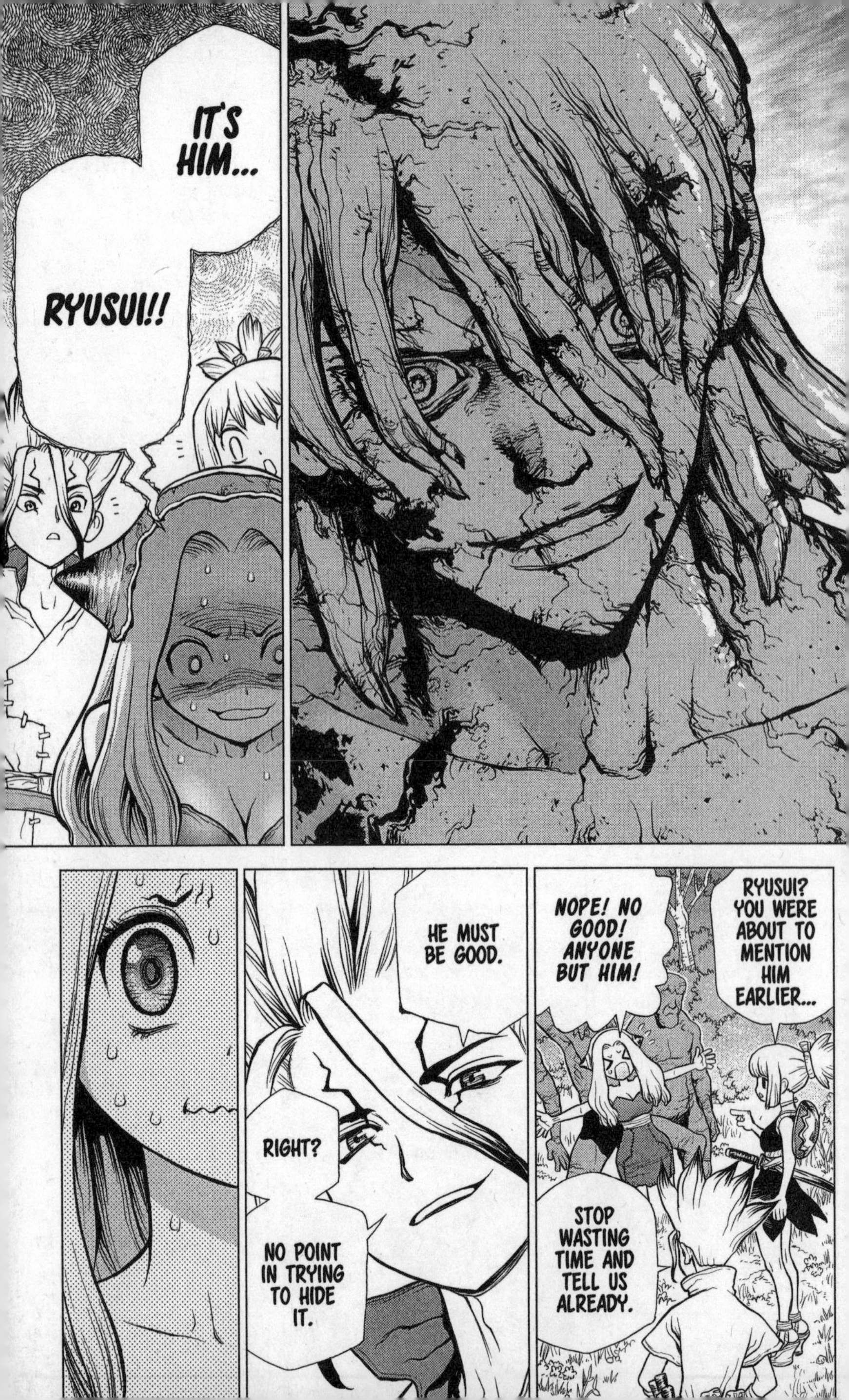
IT'S HIM...
RYUSUI!!
RYUSUI? YOU WERE ABOUT TO MENTION HIM EARLIER...
NOPE! NO GOOD! ANYONE BUT HIM!
STOP WASTING TIME AND TELL US ALREADY.
HE MUST BE GOOD.
RIGHT?
NO POINT IN TRYING TO HIDE IT.

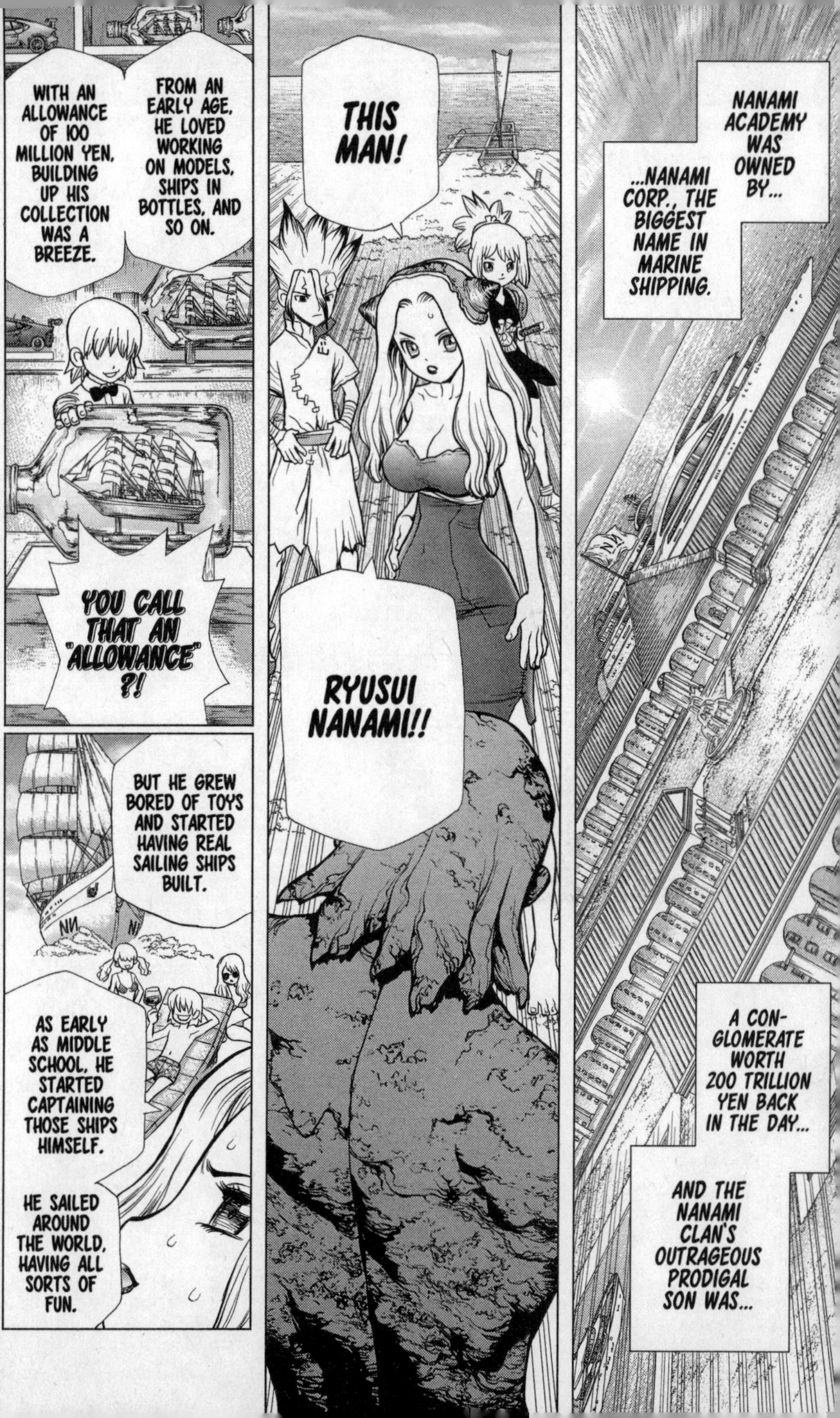
NANAMI ACADEMY WAS OWNED BY...
...NANAMI CORP., THE BIGGEST NAME IN MARINE SHIPPING.
A CONGLOMERATE WORTH 200 TRILLION YEN BACK IN THE DAY...
AND THE NANAMI CLAN'S OUTRAGEOUS PRODIGAL SON WAS...
THIS MAN!
RYUSUI NANAMI!!
FROM AN EARLY AGE, HE LOVED WORKING ON MODELS, SHIPS IN BOTTLES, AND SO ON.
WITH AN ALLOWANCE OF 100 MILLION YEN, BUILDING UP HIS COLLECTION WAS A BREEZE.
YOU CALL THAT AN "ALLOWANCE"?!
BUT HE GREW BORED OF TOYS AND STARTED HAVING REAL SAILING SHIPS BUILT.
AS EARLY AS MIDDLE SCHOOL, HE STARTED CAPTAINING THOSE SHIPS HIMSELF.
HE SAILED AROUND THE WORLD, HAVING ALL SORTS OF FUN.

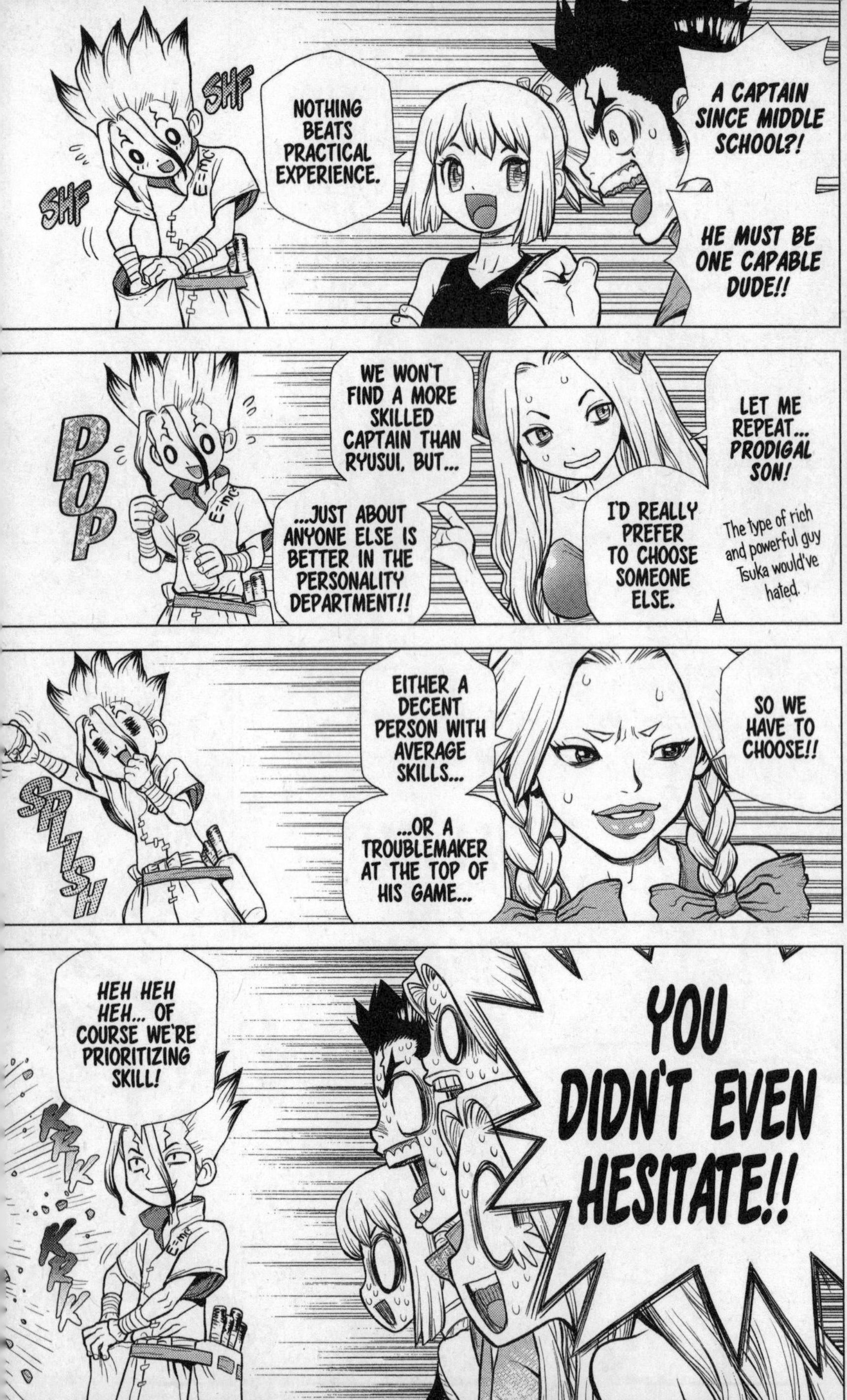
A CAPTAIN SINCE MIDDLE SCHOOL?!
HE MUST BE ONE CAPABLE DUDE!!
NOTHING BEATS PRACTICAL EXPERIENCE.
SHF
SHF
LET ME REPEAT... PRODIGAL SON!
The type of rich and powerful guy Tsuka would've hated.
I'D REALLY PREFER TO CHOOSE SOMEONE ELSE.
WE WON'T FIND A MORE SKILLED CAPTAIN THAN RYUSUI, BUT...
...JUST ABOUT ANYONE ELSE IS BETTER IN THE PERSONALITY DEPARTMENT!!
POP
SO WE HAVE TO CHOOSE!!
EITHER A DECENT PERSON WITH AVERAGE SKILLS...
...OR A TROUBLEMAKER AT THE TOP OF HIS GAME...
SPLISH
YOU DIDN'T EVEN HESITATE!!
HEH HEH HEH... OF COURSE WE'RE PRIORITIZING SKILL!
KRK
KRK

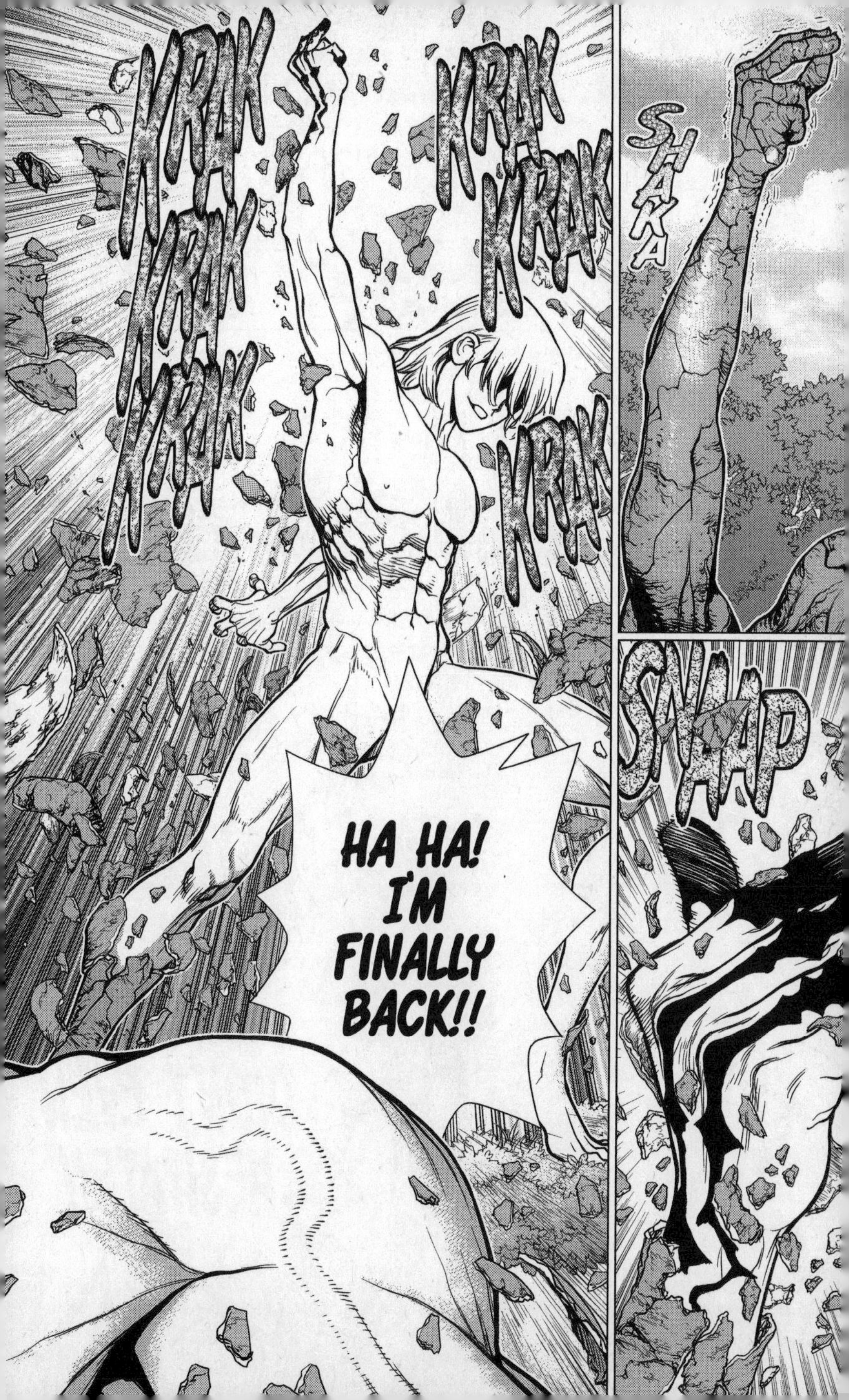
SHAKA
SNAP
KRAK KRAK
KRAK
KRAK KRAK KRAK KRAK
HA HA! I'M FINALLY BACK!!

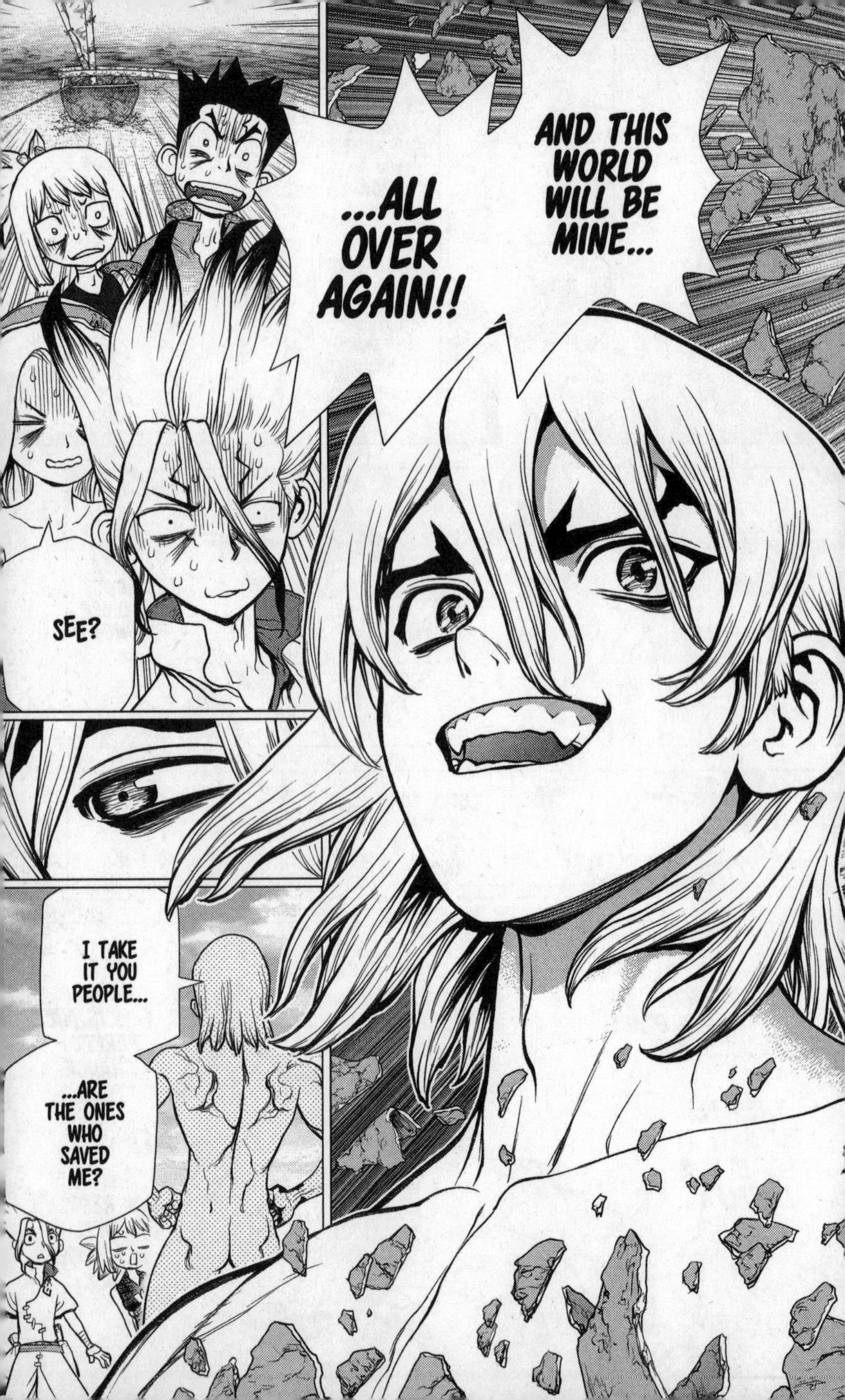
AND THIS WORLD WILL BE MINE...
...ALL OVER AGAIN!!
SEE?
I TAKE IT YOU PEOPLE...
...ARE THE ONES WHO SAVED ME?

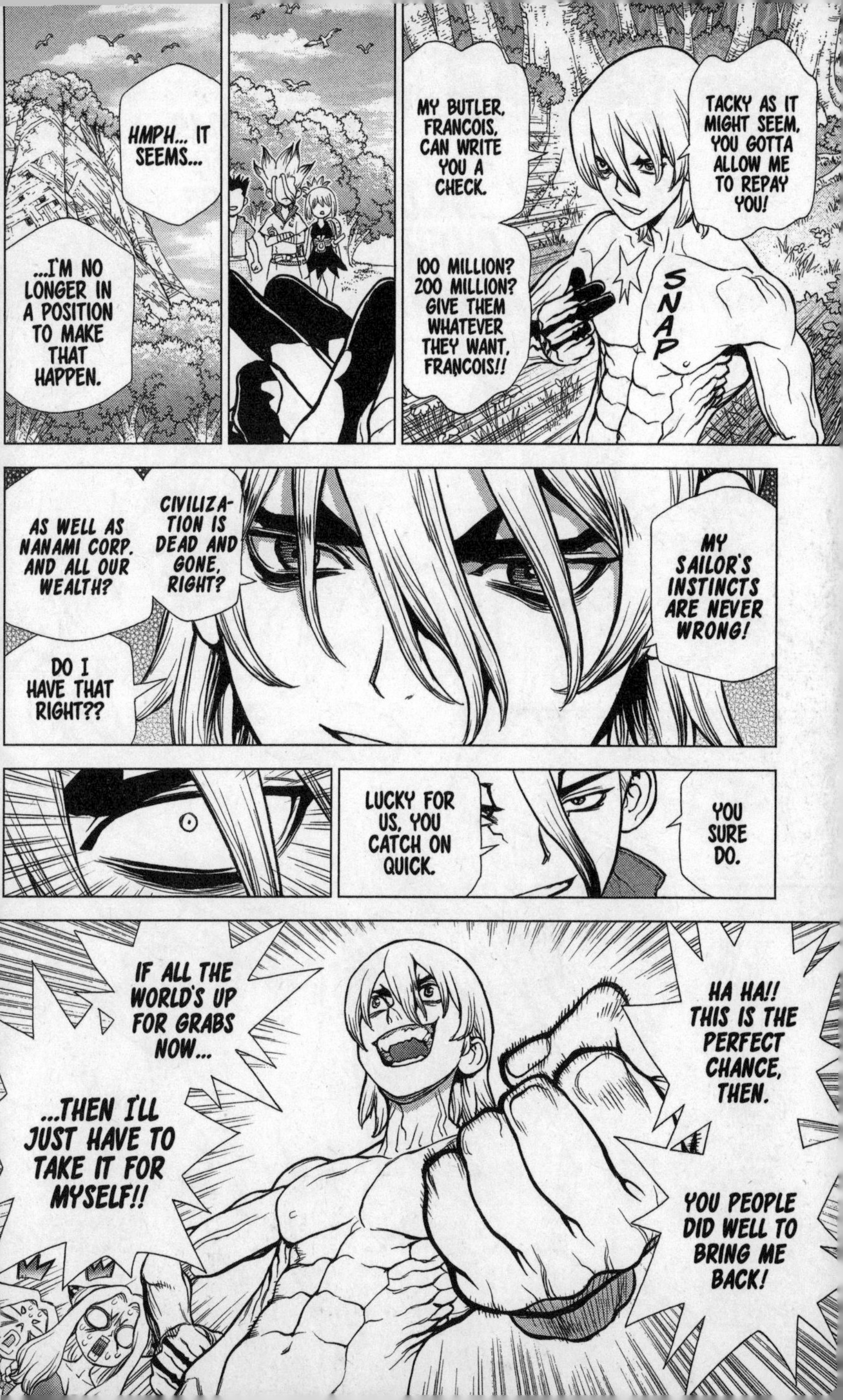

TACKY AS IT MIGHT SEEM, YOU GOTTA ALLOW ME TO REPAY YOU!
MY BUTLER, FRANCOIS, CAN WRITE YOU A CHECK.
SNAP
100 MILLION? 200 MILLION? GIVE THEM WHATEVER THEY WANT, FRANCOIS!!
HMPH... IT SEEMS...
...I'M NO LONGER IN A POSITION TO MAKE THAT HAPPEN.
MY SAILOR'S INSTINCTS ARE NEVER WRONG!
CIVILIZA-TION IS DEAD AND GONE, RIGHT?
AS WELL AS NANAMI CORP. AND ALL OUR WEALTH?
DO I HAVE THAT RIGHT??
YOU SURE DO.
LUCKY FOR US, YOU CATCH ON QUICK.
HA HA!! THIS IS THE PERFECT CHANCE, THEN.
YOU PEOPLE DID WELL TO BRING ME BACK!
IF ALL THE WORLD'S UP FOR GRABS NOW...
...THEN I'LL JUST HAVE TO TAKE IT FOR MYSELF!!

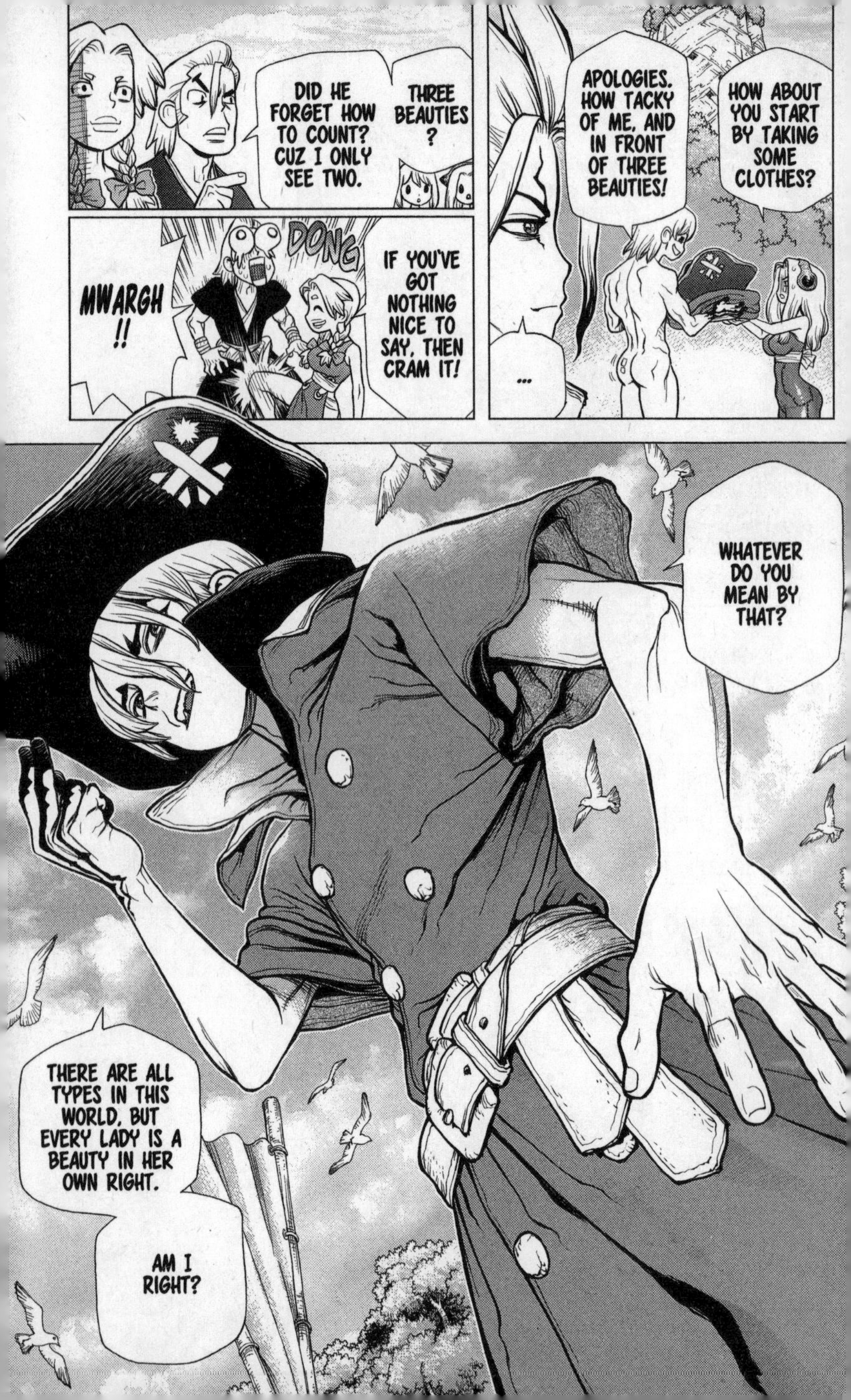
HOW ABOUT YOU START BY TAKING SOME CLOTHES?
APOLOGIES. HOW TACKY OF ME, AND IN FRONT OF THREE BEAUTIES!
...
THREE BEAUTIES ?
DID HE FORGET HOW TO COUNT? CUZ I ONLY SEE TWO.
IF YOU'VE GOT NOTHING NICE TO SAY, THEN CRAM IT!
DONG
MWARGH !!
WHATEVER DO YOU MEAN BY THAT?
THERE ARE ALL TYPES IN THIS WORLD, BUT EVERY LADY IS A BEAUTY IN HER OWN RIGHT.
AM I RIGHT?

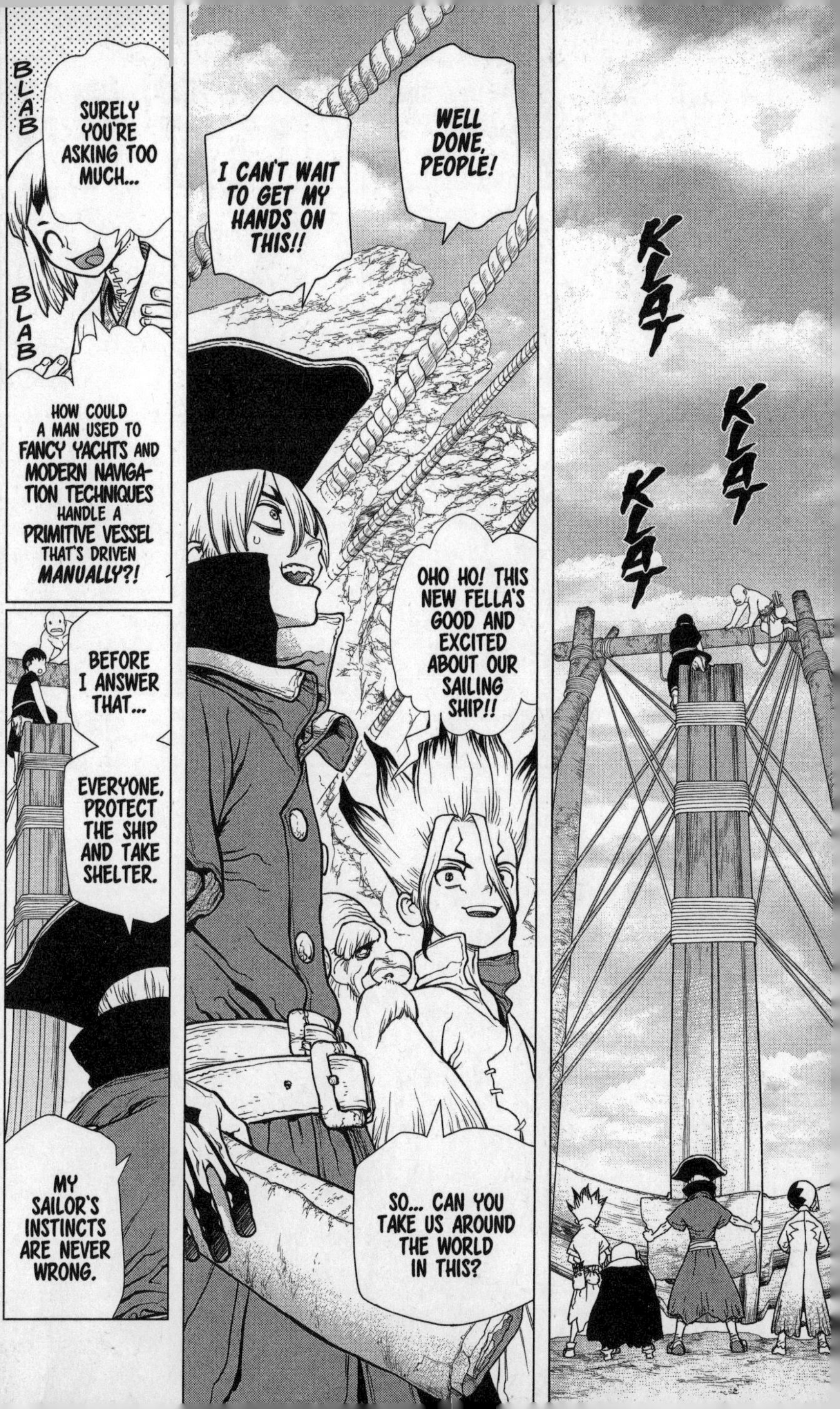
KLAK
KLAK
KLAK
WELL DONE, PEOPLE!
I CAN'T WAIT TO GET MY HANDS ON THIS!!
OHO HO! THIS NEW FELLA'S GOOD AND EXCITED ABOUT OUR SAILING SHIP!!
SO... CAN YOU TAKE US AROUND THE WORLD IN THIS?
BLAB
SURELY YOU'RE ASKING TOO MUCH...
BLAB
HOW COULD A MAN USED TO FANCY YACHTS AND MODERN NAVIGATION TECHNIQUES HANDLE A PRIMITIVE VESSEL THAT'S DRIVEN MANUALLY?!
BEFORE I ANSWER THAT...
EVERYONE, PROTECT THE SHIP AND TAKE SHELTER.
MY SAILOR'S INSTINCTS ARE NEVER WRONG.

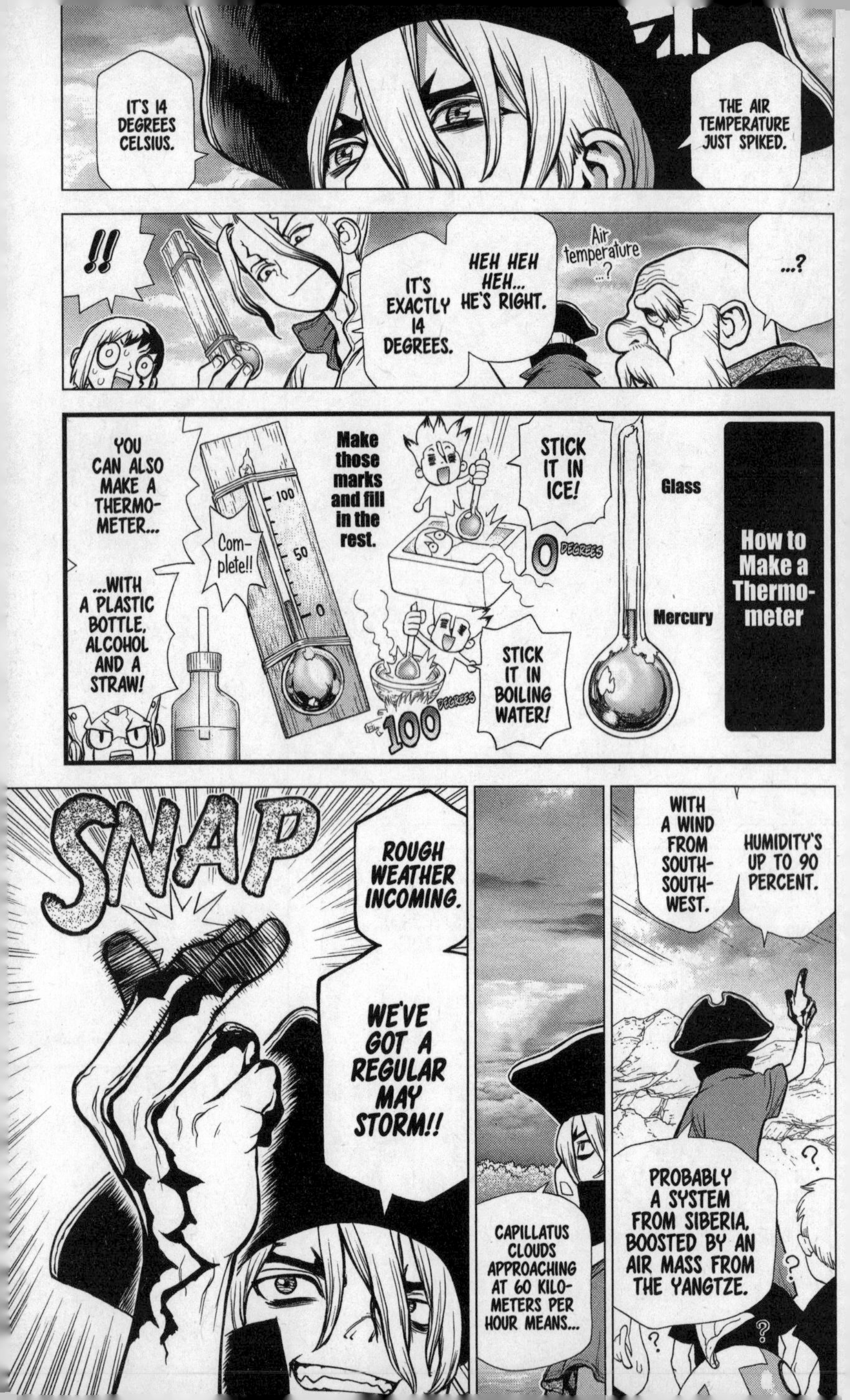
THE AIR TEMPERATURE JUST SPIKED.
IT'S 14 DEGREES CELSIUS.
...?
Air temperature ...?
HEH HEH HEH... HE'S RIGHT.
IT'S EXACTLY 14 DEGREES.
!!
How to Make a Thermometer
Glass
Mercury
STICK IT IN ICE!
0 DEGREES
STICK IT IN BOILING WATER!
100 DEGREES
Make those marks and fill in the rest.
100
50
0
Complete!!
YOU CAN ALSO MAKE A THERMOMETER...
...WITH A PLASTIC BOTTLE, ALCOHOL AND A STRAW!
HUMIDITY'S UP TO 90 PERCENT.
WITH A WIND FROM SOUTH-SOUTHWEST.
PROBABLY A SYSTEM FROM SIBERIA, BOOSTED BY AN AIR MASS FROM THE YANGTZE.
CAPILLATUS CLOUDS APPROACHING AT 60 KILOMETERS PER HOUR MEANS...
ROUGH WEATHER INCOMING.
SNAP
WE'VE GOT A REGULAR MAY STORM!!

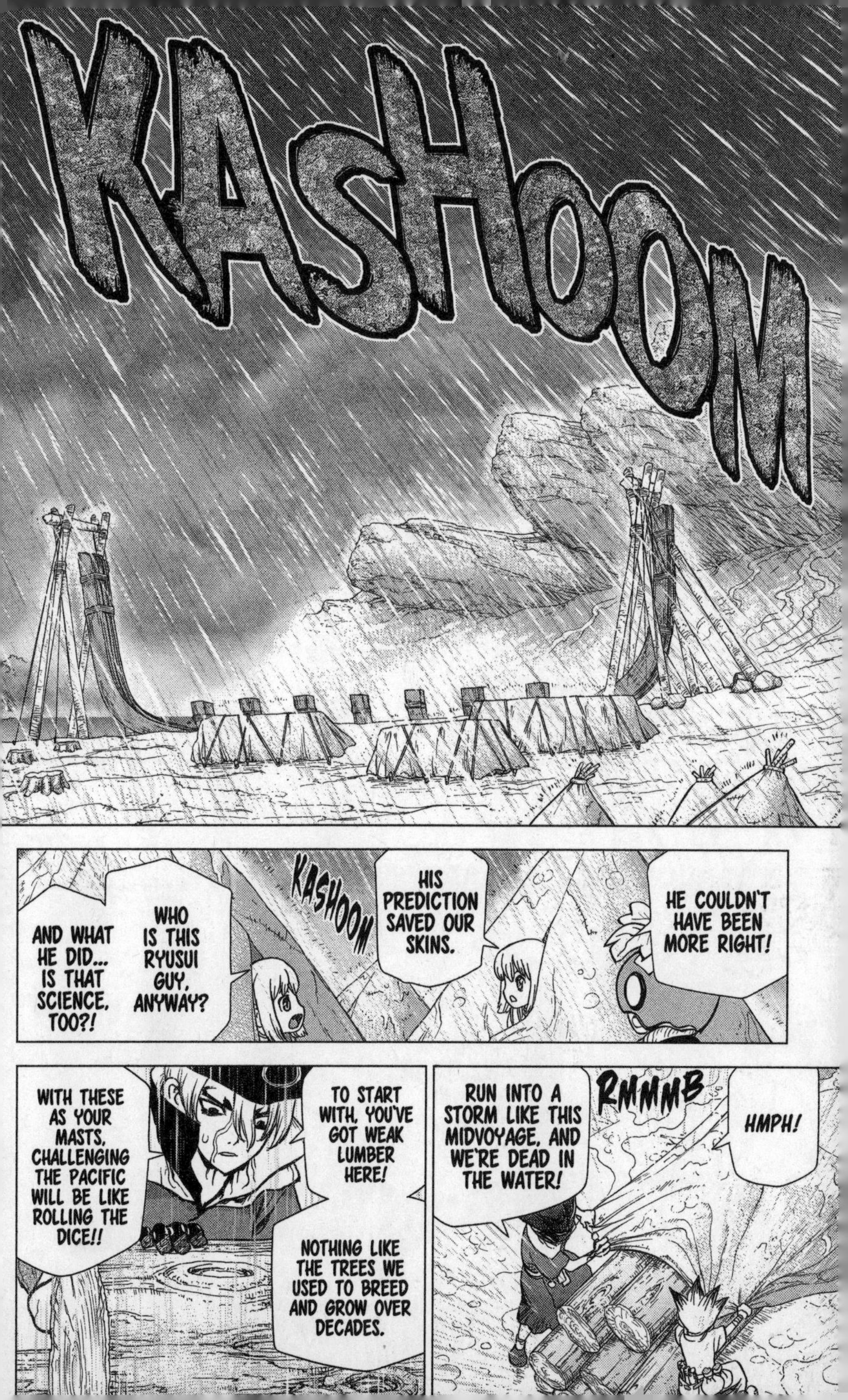
KASHOOM
HE COULDN'T HAVE BEEN MORE RIGHT!
HIS PREDICTION SAVED OUR SKINS.
KASHOOM
WHO IS THIS RYUSUI GUY, ANYWAY?
AND WHAT HE DID... IS THAT SCIENCE, TOO?!
HMPH!
RMMMB
RUN INTO A STORM LIKE THIS MIDVOYAGE, AND WE'RE DEAD IN THE WATER!
TO START WITH, YOU'VE GOT WEAK LUMBER HERE!
WITH THESE AS YOUR MASTS, CHALLENGING THE PACIFIC WILL BE LIKE ROLLING THE DICE!!
NOTHING LIKE THE TREES WE USED TO BREED AND GROW OVER DECADES.

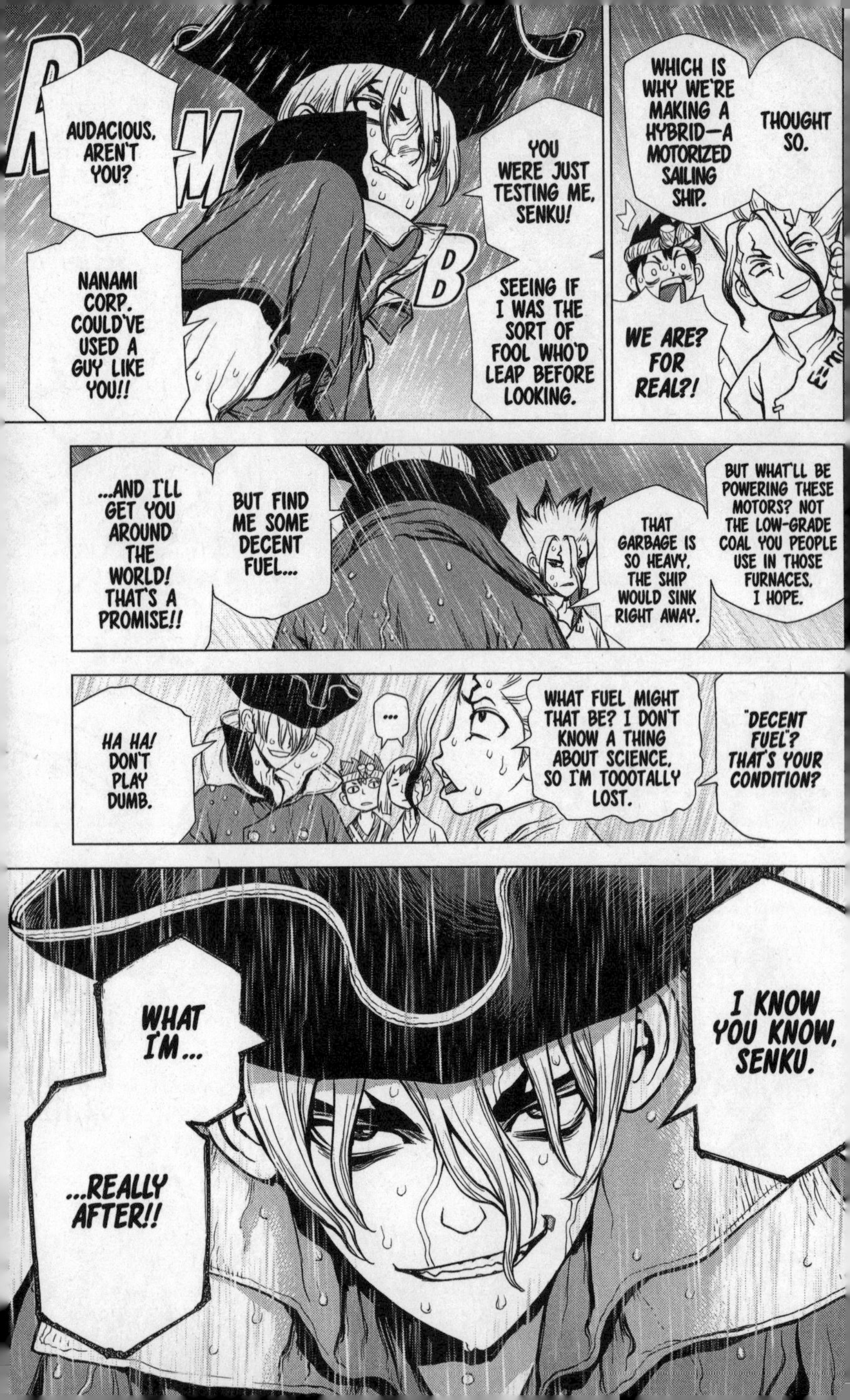
THOUGHT SO.
WHICH IS WHY WE'RE MAKING A HYBRID—A MOTORIZED SAILING SHIP.
WE ARE? FOR REAL?!
YOU WERE JUST TESTING ME, SENKU!
SEEING IF I WAS THE SORT OF FOOL WHO'D LEAP BEFORE LOOKING.
AUDACIOUS, AREN'T YOU?
NANAMI CORP. COULD'VE USED A GUY LIKE YOU!!
BUT WHAT'LL BE POWERING THESE MOTORS? NOT THE LOW-GRADE COAL YOU PEOPLE USE IN THOSE FURNACES, I HOPE.
THAT GARBAGE IS SO HEAVY, THE SHIP WOULD SINK RIGHT AWAY.
BUT FIND ME SOME DECENT FUEL...
...AND I'LL GET YOU AROUND THE WORLD! THAT'S A PROMISE!!
"DECENT FUEL"? THAT'S YOUR CONDITION?
WHAT FUEL MIGHT THAT BE? I DON'T KNOW A THING ABOUT SCIENCE, SO I'M TOOOTALLY LOST.
...
HA HA! DON'T PLAY DUMB.
I KNOW YOU KNOW, SENKU.
WHAT I'M...
...REALLY AFTER!!

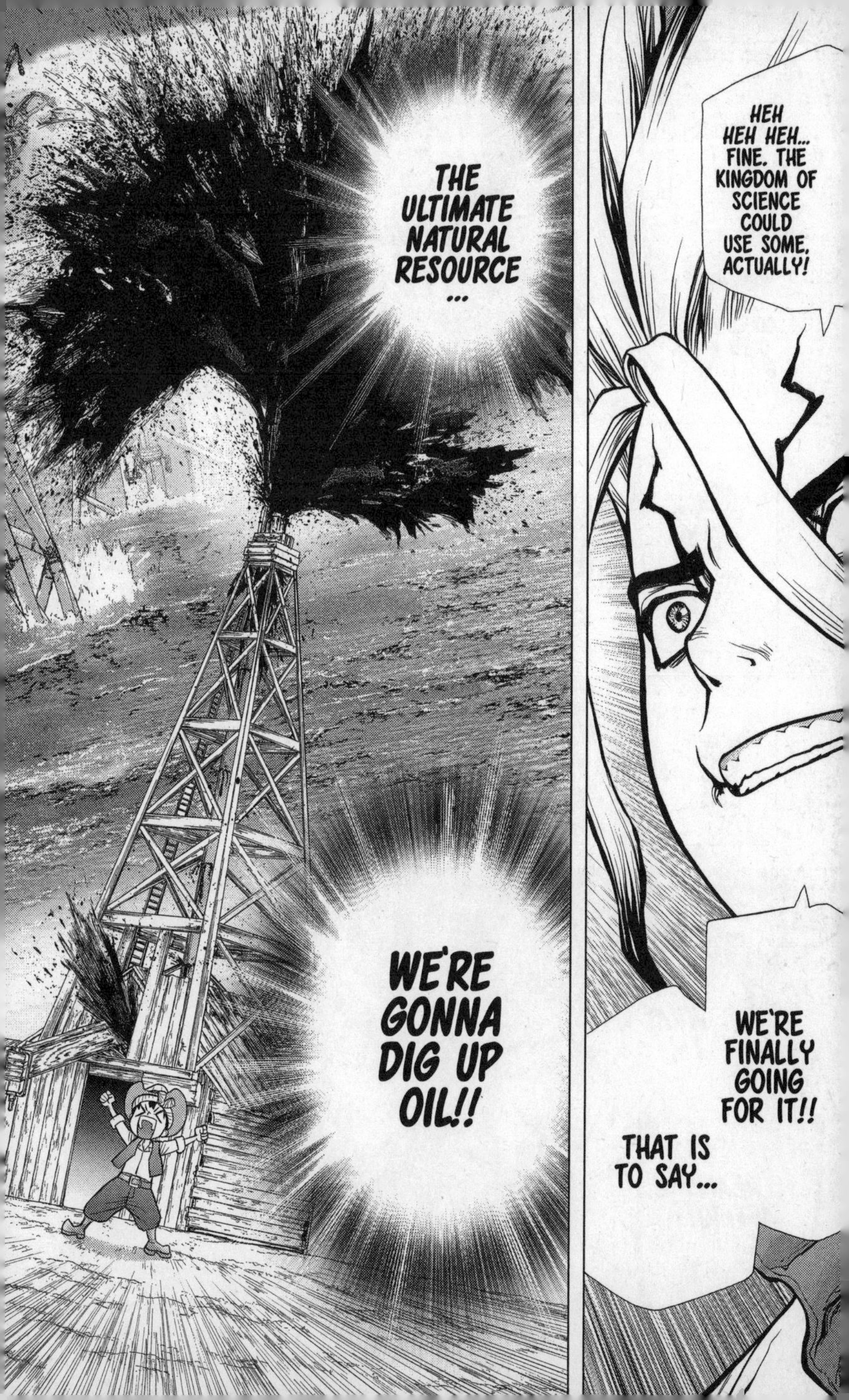
HEH HEH HEH... FINE. THE KINGDOM OF SCIENCE COULD USE SOME, ACTUALLY!
WE'RE FINALLY GOING FOR IT!!
THAT IS TO SAY...
THE ULTIMATE NATURAL RESOURCE...
WE'RE GONNA DIG UP OIL!!

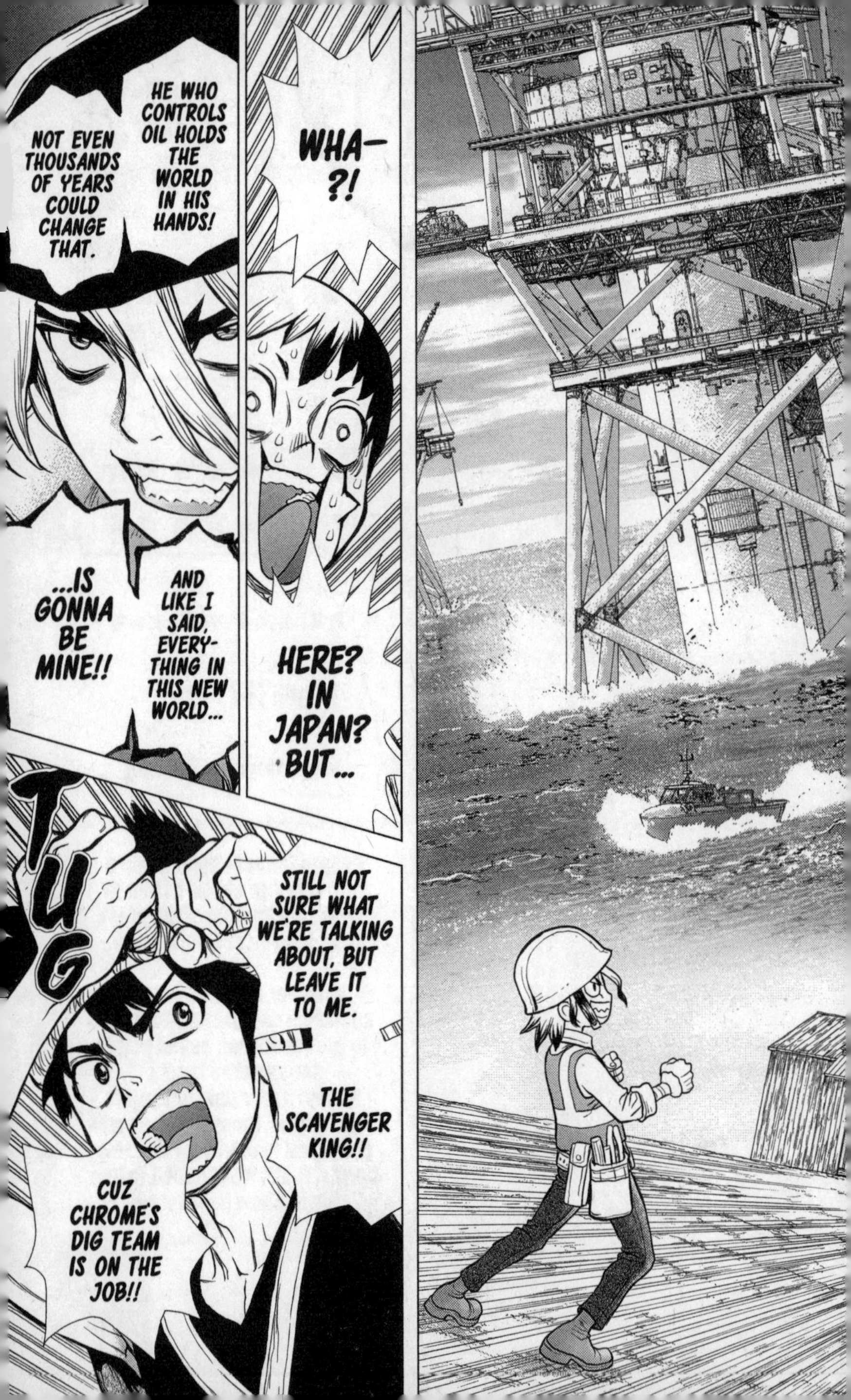
WHA-?!
HERE? IN JAPAN? BUT...
HE WHO CONTROLS OIL HOLDS THE WORLD IN HIS HANDS!
NOT EVEN THOUSANDS OF YEARS COULD CHANGE THAT.
AND LIKE I SAID, EVERY-THING IN THIS NEW WORLD...
...IS GONNA BE MINE!!
TUG
STILL NOT SURE WHAT WE'RE TALKING ABOUT, BUT LEAVE IT TO ME.
THE SCAVENGER KING!!
CUZ CHROME'S DIG TEAM IS ON THE JOB!!

Kingdom of Science

WORKER FILE ②

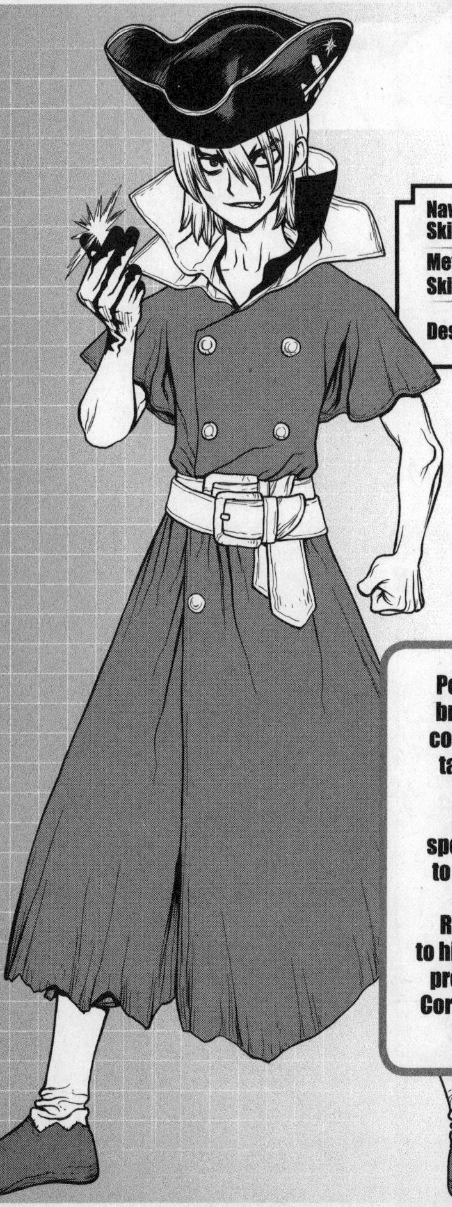

Ryusui

Navigation Skills	★★★★★
Meteorology Skills:	★★★★★
Desire:	★★★★★

Full Name: Ryusui Nanami

Height: 187 cm

Job in Kingdom: Captain

People thought Ryusui had a bright future ahead of him in corporate business due to his talents even at a young age.

However, his extravagant spending and greedy ways led to his reputation as the black sheep of the family.
Ryusui never paid any mind to his critics, though, and he was prepared to take over Nanami Corp. if that's what it took to live his life how he wanted!

Z=86: Money

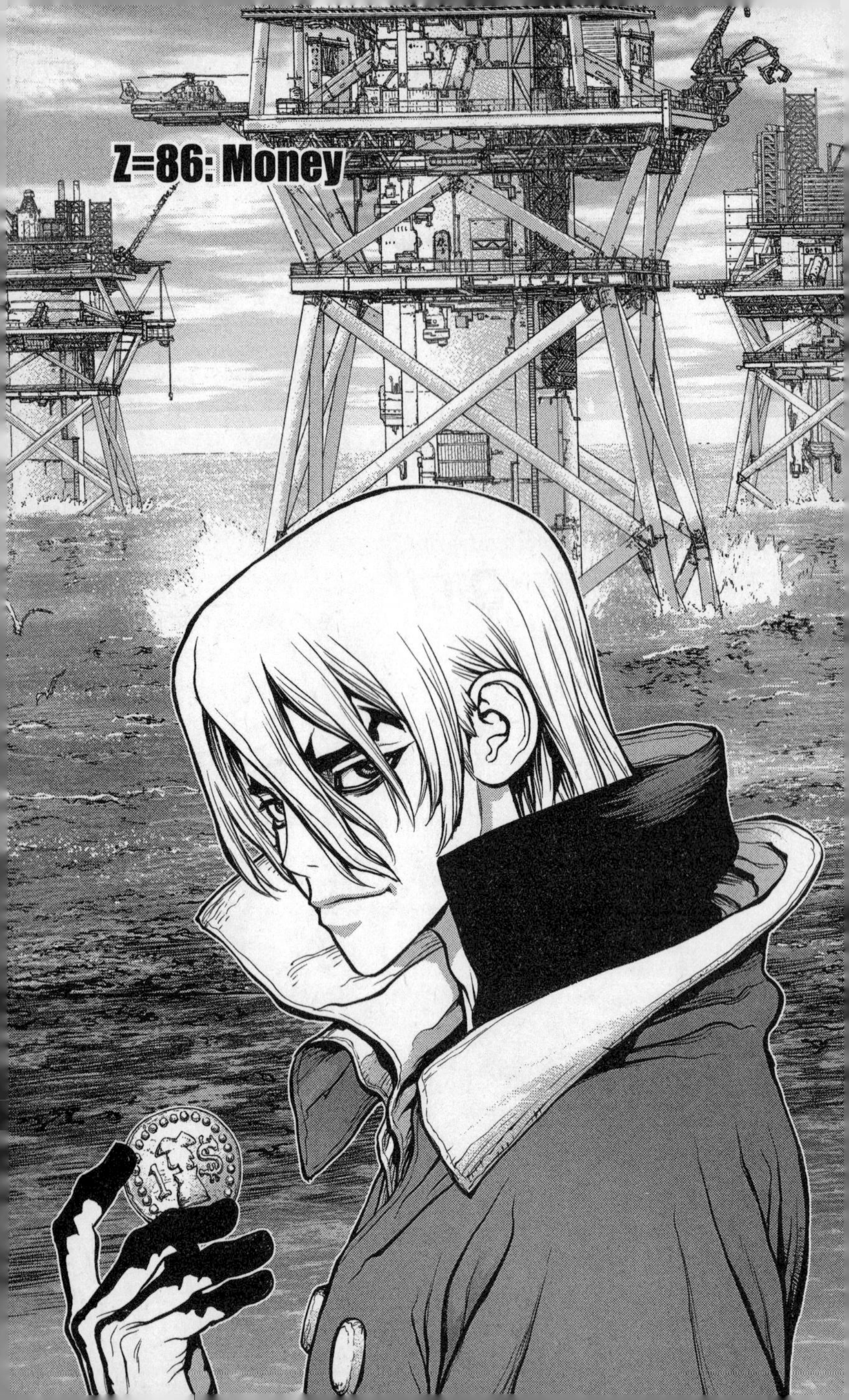

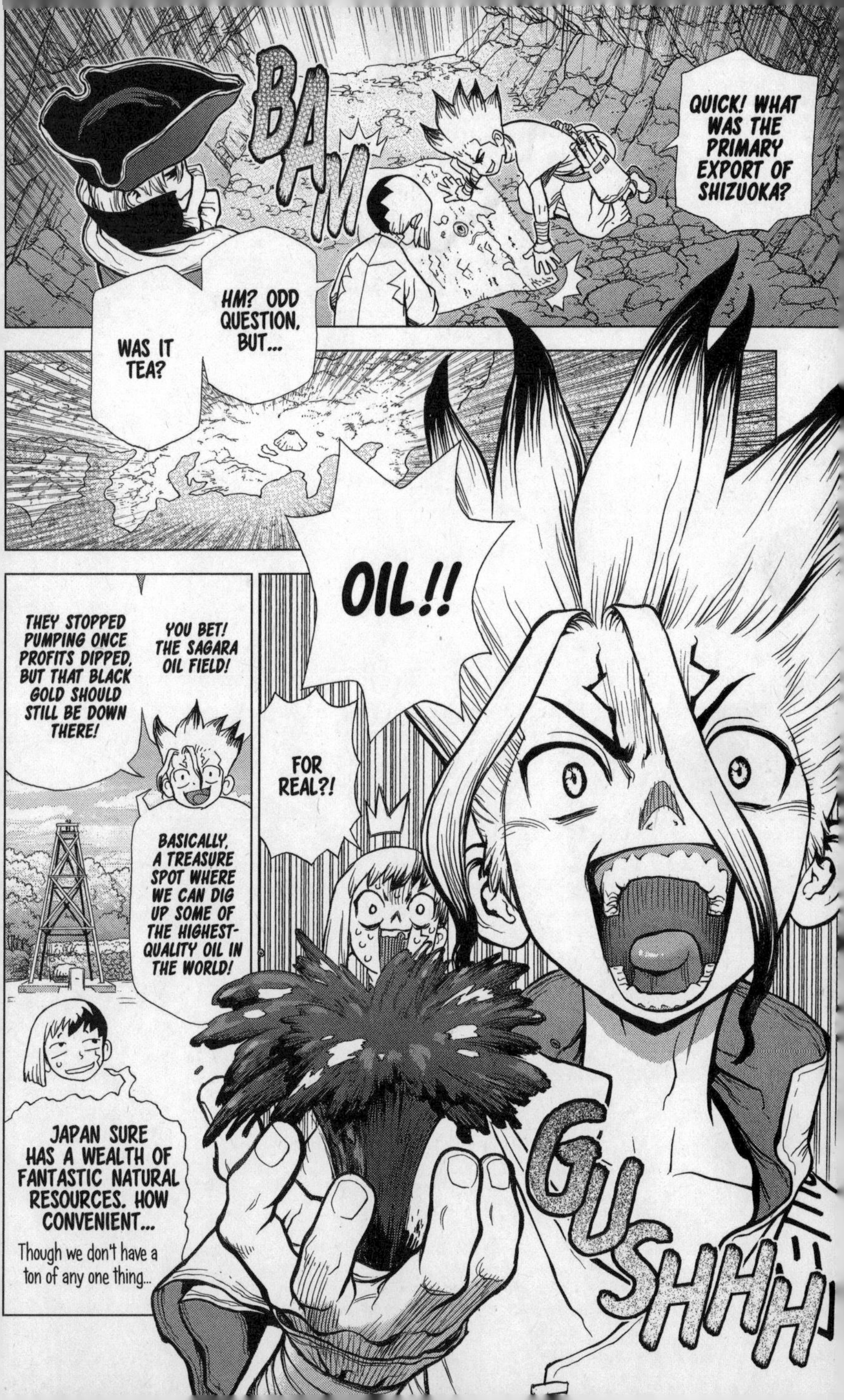
QUICK! WHAT WAS THE PRIMARY EXPORT OF SHIZUOKA?
BAM
HM? ODD QUESTION, BUT...
WAS IT TEA?
OIL!!
FOR REAL?!
GUSHHH
YOU BET! THE SAGARA OIL FIELD!
THEY STOPPED PUMPING ONCE PROFITS DIPPED, BUT THAT BLACK GOLD SHOULD STILL BE DOWN THERE!
BASICALLY, A TREASURE SPOT WHERE WE CAN DIG UP SOME OF THE HIGHEST-QUALITY OIL IN THE WORLD!
JAPAN SURE HAS A WEALTH OF FANTASTIC NATURAL RESOURCES. HOW CONVENIENT...
Though we don't have a ton of any one thing...

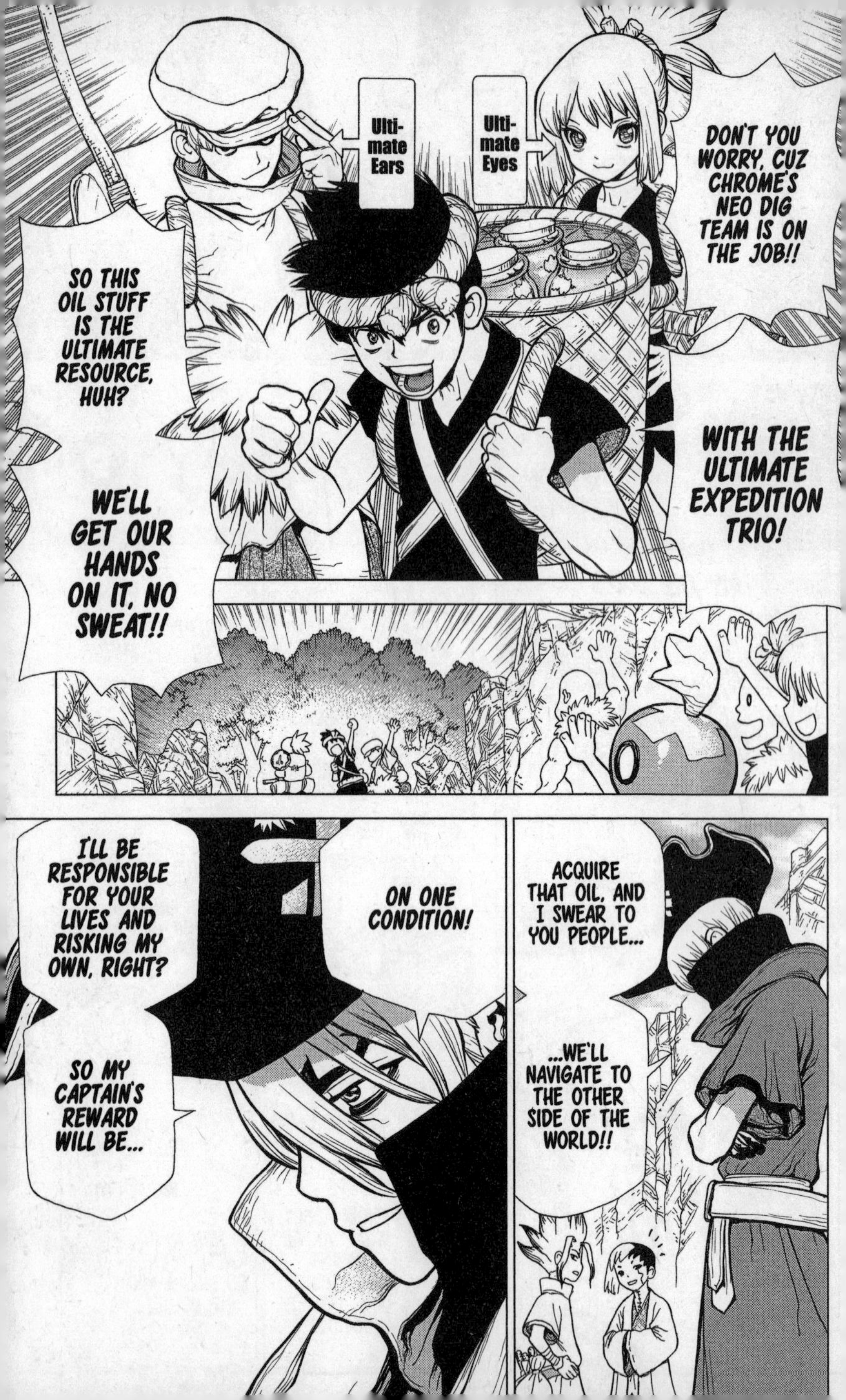
DON'T YOU WORRY, CUZ CHROME'S NEO DIG TEAM IS ON THE JOB!!
Ulti-mate Eyes
Ulti-mate Ears
WITH THE ULTIMATE EXPEDITION TRIO!
SO THIS OIL STUFF IS THE ULTIMATE RESOURCE, HUH?
WE'LL GET OUR HANDS ON IT, NO SWEAT!!
ACQUIRE THAT OIL, AND I SWEAR TO YOU PEOPLE...
...WE'LL NAVIGATE TO THE OTHER SIDE OF THE WORLD!!
ON ONE CONDITION!
I'LL BE RESPONSIBLE FOR YOUR LIVES AND RISKING MY OWN, RIGHT?
SO MY CAPTAIN'S REWARD WILL BE...

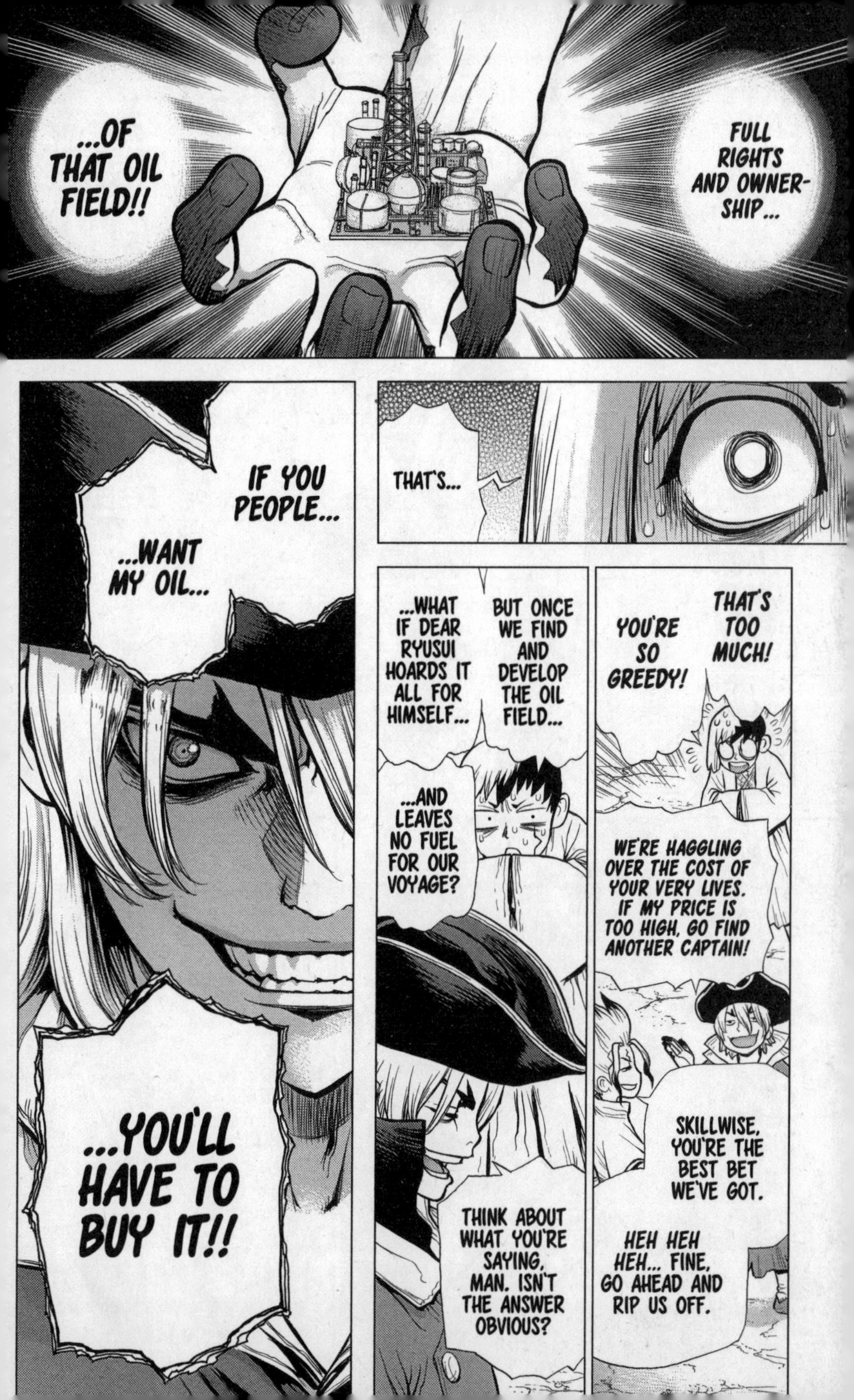
FULL RIGHTS AND OWNER-SHIP...
...OF THAT OIL FIELD!!
THAT'S...
THAT'S TOO MUCH!
YOU'RE SO GREEDY!
WE'RE HAGGLING OVER THE COST OF YOUR VERY LIVES. IF MY PRICE IS TOO HIGH, GO FIND ANOTHER CAPTAIN!
SKILLWISE, YOU'RE THE BEST BET WE'VE GOT.
HEH HEH HEH... FINE, GO AHEAD AND RIP US OFF.
BUT ONCE WE FIND AND DEVELOP THE OIL FIELD...
...WHAT IF DEAR RYUSUI HOARDS IT ALL FOR HIMSELF...
...AND LEAVES NO FUEL FOR OUR VOYAGE?
THINK ABOUT WHAT YOU'RE SAYING, MAN. ISN'T THE ANSWER OBVIOUS?
IF YOU PEOPLE...
...WANT MY OIL...
...YOU'LL HAVE TO BUY IT!!

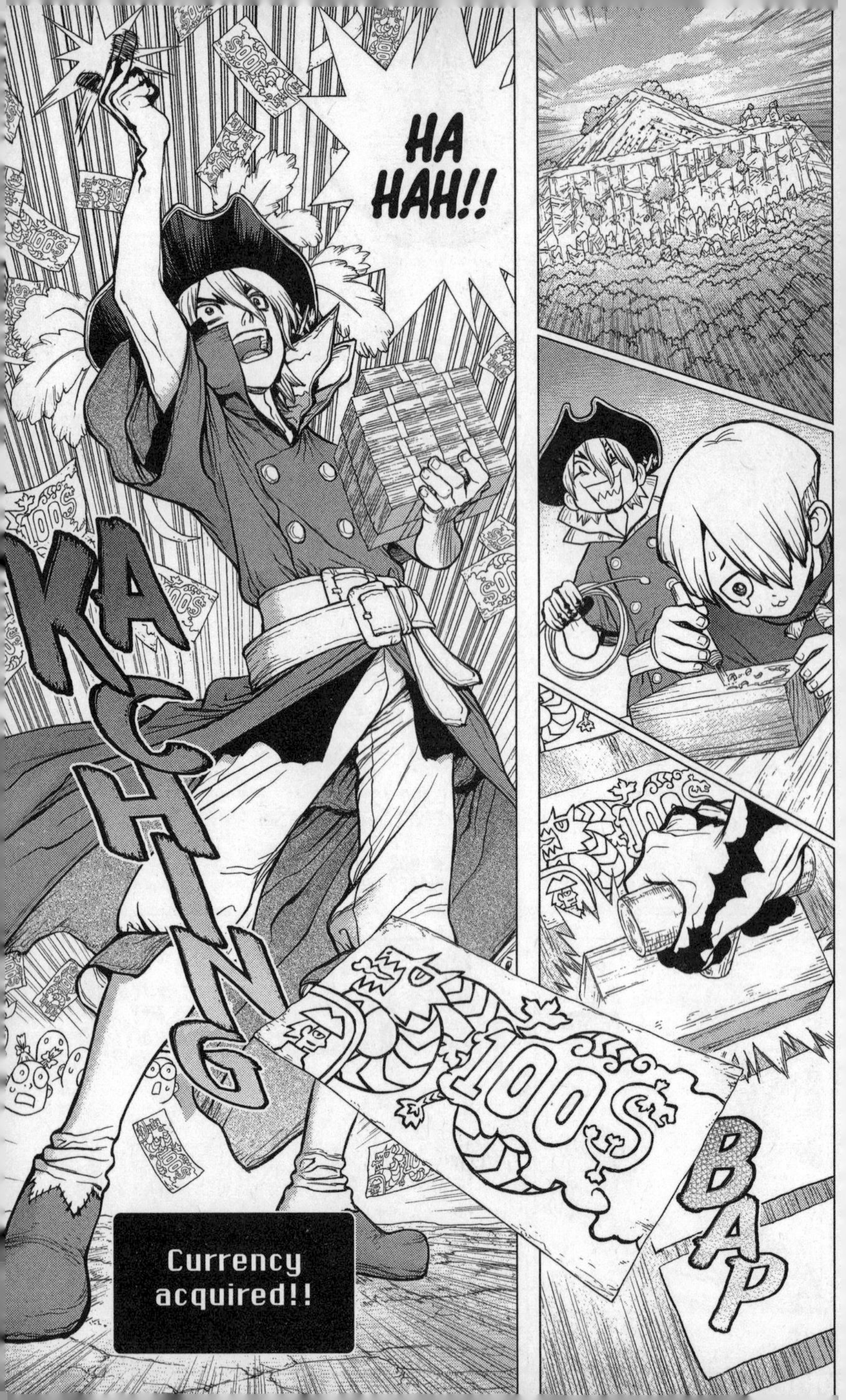
BAP
HA HAH!!
KA-CHING
Currency acquired!!

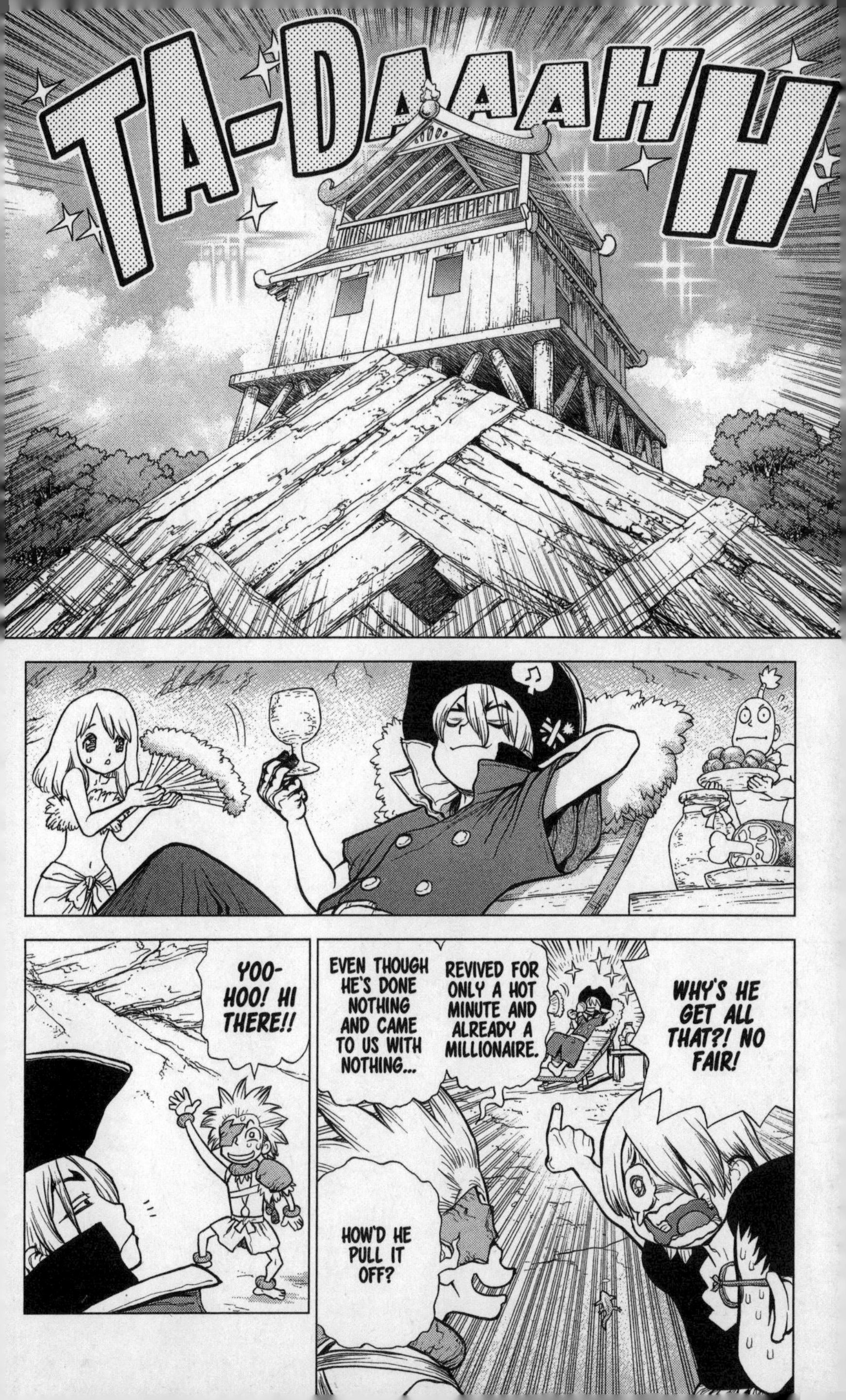
TA-DAAAHH
WHY'S HE GET ALL THAT?! NO FAIR!
REVIVED FOR ONLY A HOT MINUTE AND ALREADY A MILLIONAIRE.
EVEN THOUGH HE'S DONE NOTHING AND CAME TO US WITH NOTHING...
HOW'D HE PULL IT OFF?
YOO-HOO! HI THERE!!

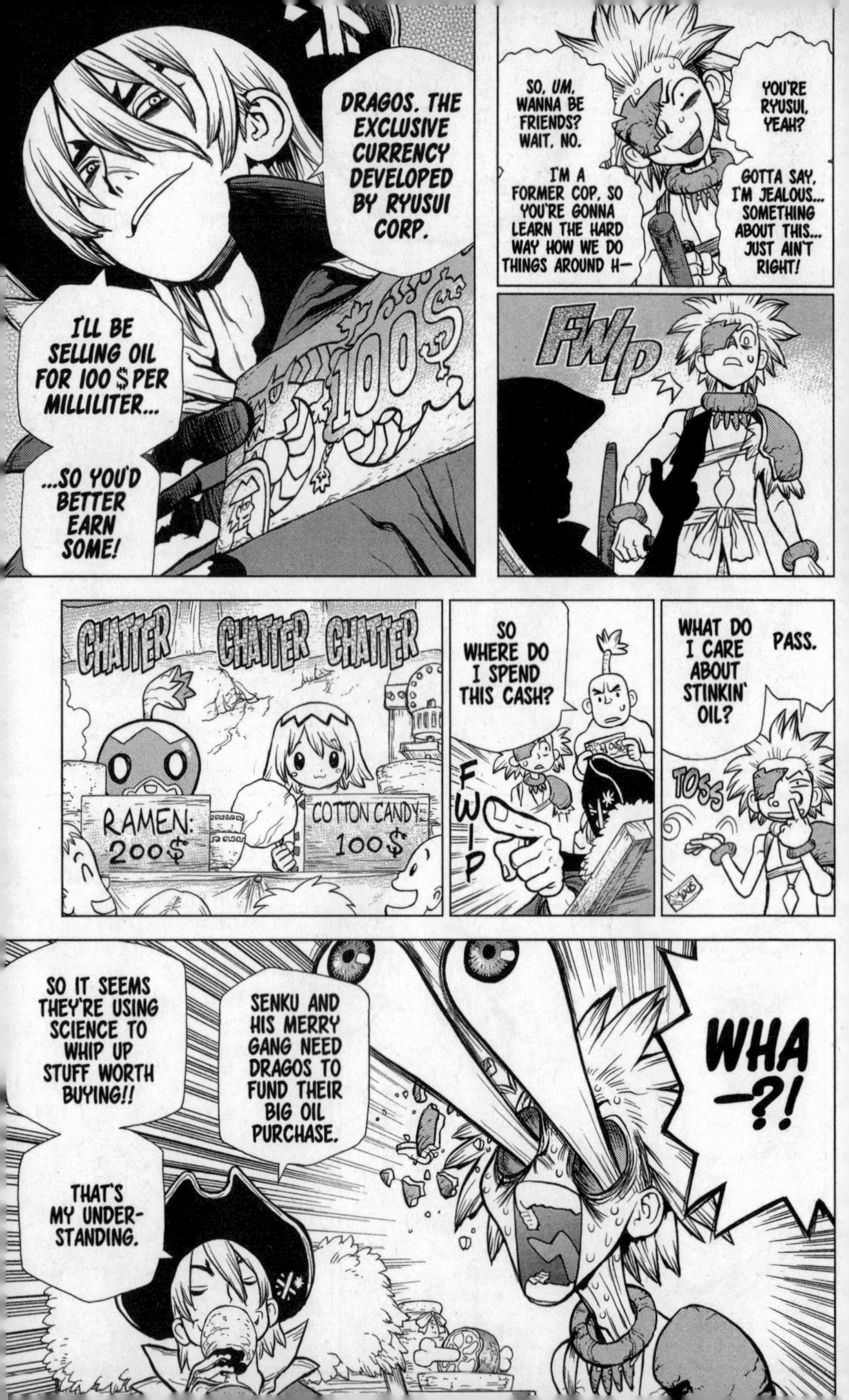
YOU'RE RYUSUI, YEAH?
GOTTA SAY, I'M JEALOUS... SOMETHING ABOUT THIS... JUST AIN'T RIGHT!
SO, UM, WANNA BE FRIENDS? WAIT, NO.
I'M A FORMER COP, SO YOU'RE GONNA LEARN THE HARD WAY HOW WE DO THINGS AROUND H—
FWIP
DRAGOS. THE EXCLUSIVE CURRENCY DEVELOPED BY RYUSUI CORP.
100$
I'LL BE SELLING OIL FOR 100$ PER MILLILITER...
...SO YOU'D BETTER EARN SOME!
WHAT DO I CARE ABOUT STINKIN' OIL?
PASS.
TOSS
SO WHERE DO I SPEND THIS CASH?
FWIP
CHATTER
CHATTER CHATTER
RAMEN: 200$
COTTON CANDY 100$
WHA—?!
SENKU AND HIS MERRY GANG NEED DRAGOS TO FUND THEIR BIG OIL PURCHASE.
SO IT SEEMS THEY'RE USING SCIENCE TO WHIP UP STUFF WORTH BUYING!!
THAT'S MY UNDER-STANDING.

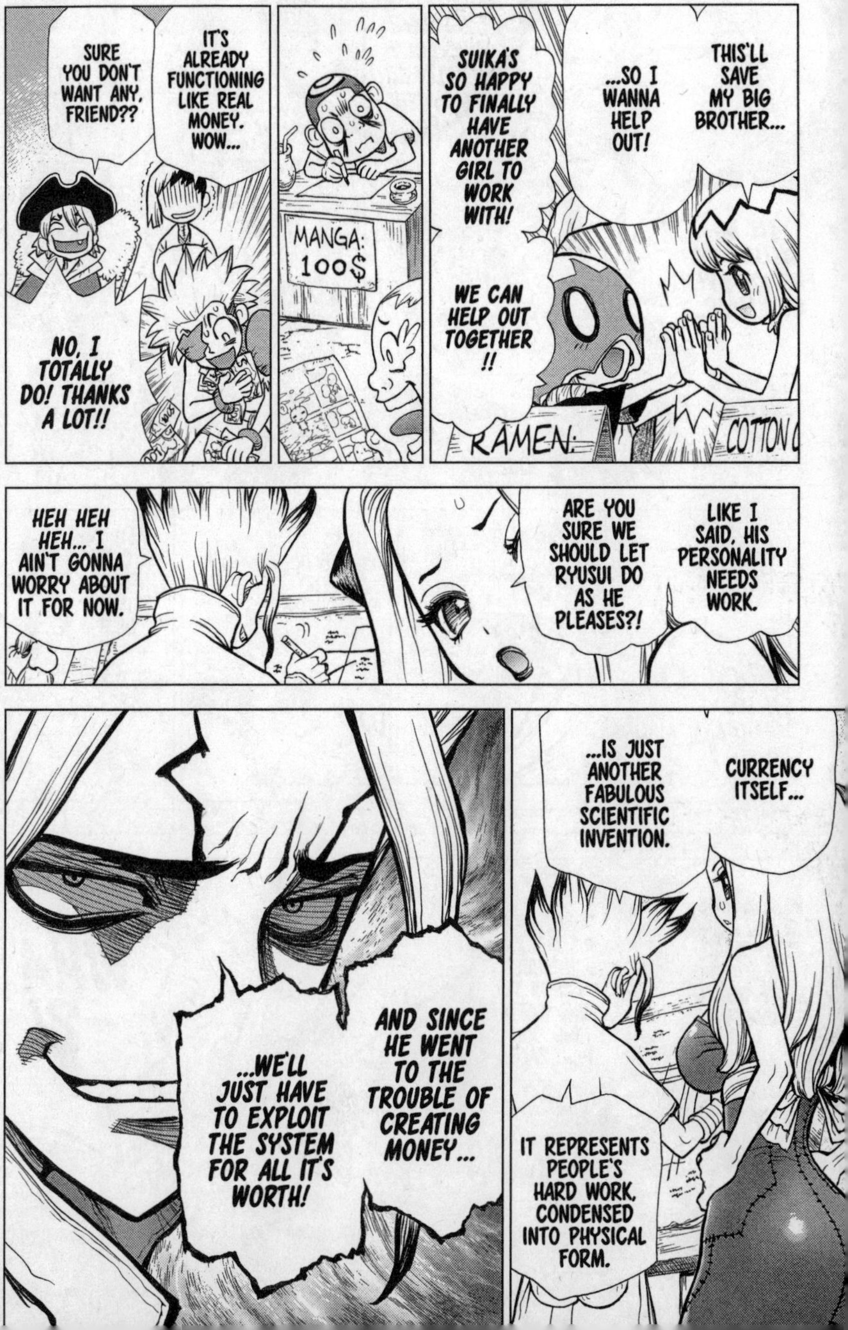
THIS'LL SAVE MY BIG BROTHER...
...SO I WANNA HELP OUT!
SUIKA'S SO HAPPY TO FINALLY HAVE ANOTHER GIRL TO WORK WITH!
WE CAN HELP OUT TOGETHER!!
COTTON
RAMEN:
MANGA: 100$
IT'S ALREADY FUNCTIONING LIKE REAL MONEY. WOW...
SURE YOU DON'T WANT ANY, FRIEND??
NO, I TOTALLY DO! THANKS A LOT!!
LIKE I SAID, HIS PERSONALITY NEEDS WORK.
ARE YOU SURE WE SHOULD LET RYUSUI DO AS HE PLEASES?!
HEH HEH HEH... I AIN'T GONNA WORRY ABOUT IT FOR NOW.
CURRENCY ITSELF...
...IS JUST ANOTHER FABULOUS SCIENTIFIC INVENTION.
IT REPRESENTS PEOPLE'S HARD WORK, CONDENSED INTO PHYSICAL FORM.
AND SINCE HE WENT TO THE TROUBLE OF CREATING MONEY...
...WE'LL JUST HAVE TO EXPLOIT THE SYSTEM FOR ALL IT'S WORTH!

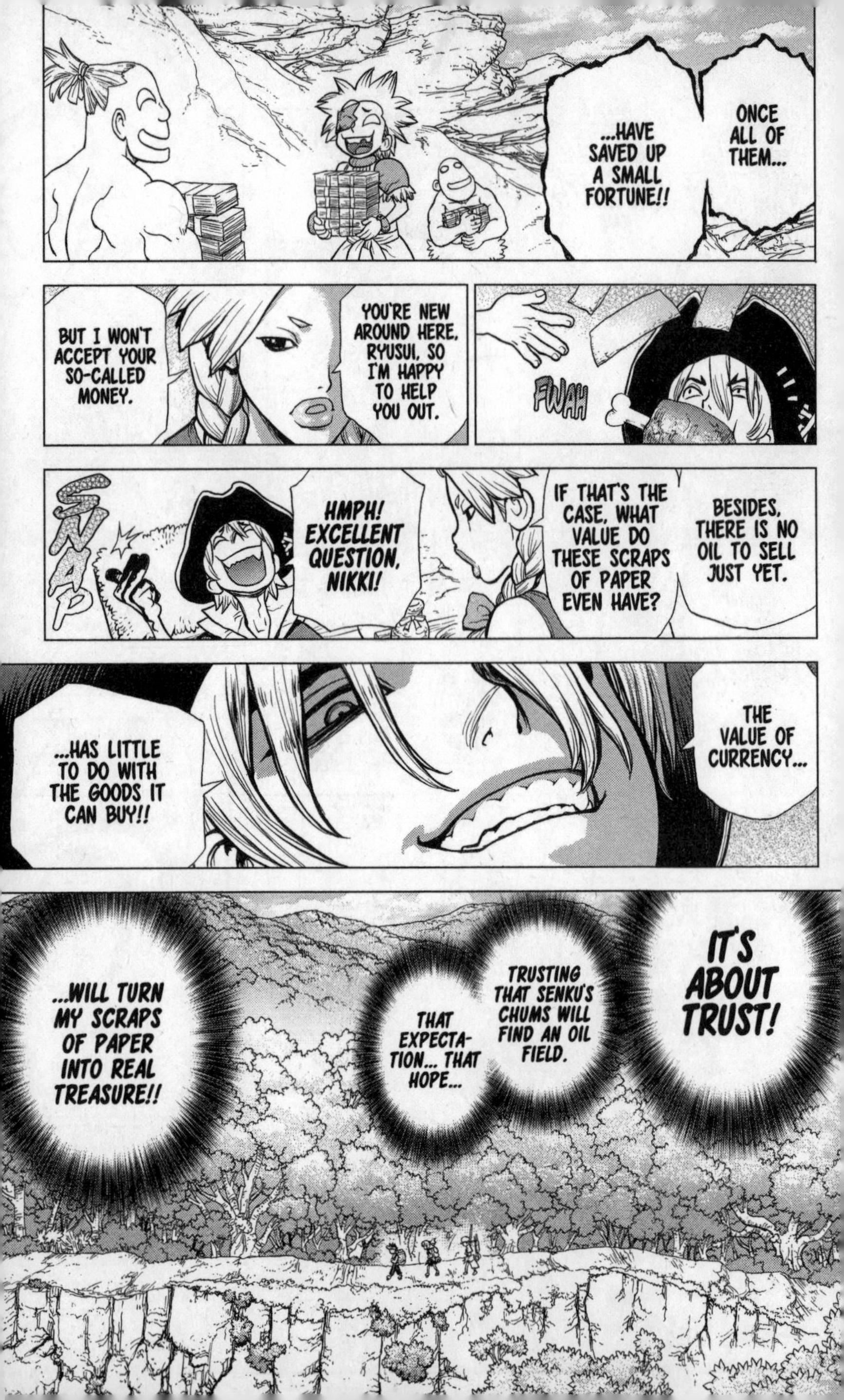
ONCE ALL OF THEM...
...HAVE SAVED UP A SMALL FORTUNE!!
FWAH
YOU'RE NEW AROUND HERE, RYUSUI, SO I'M HAPPY TO HELP YOU OUT.
BUT I WON'T ACCEPT YOUR SO-CALLED MONEY.
BESIDES, THERE IS NO OIL TO SELL JUST YET.
IF THAT'S THE CASE, WHAT VALUE DO THESE SCRAPS OF PAPER EVEN HAVE?
HMPH! EXCELLENT QUESTION, NIKKI!
SNAP
THE VALUE OF CURRENCY...
...HAS LITTLE TO DO WITH THE GOODS IT CAN BUY!!
IT'S ABOUT TRUST!
TRUSTING THAT SENKU'S CHUMS WILL FIND AN OIL FIELD.
THAT EXPECTA-TION... THAT HOPE...
...WILL TURN MY SCRAPS OF PAPER INTO REAL TREASURE!!

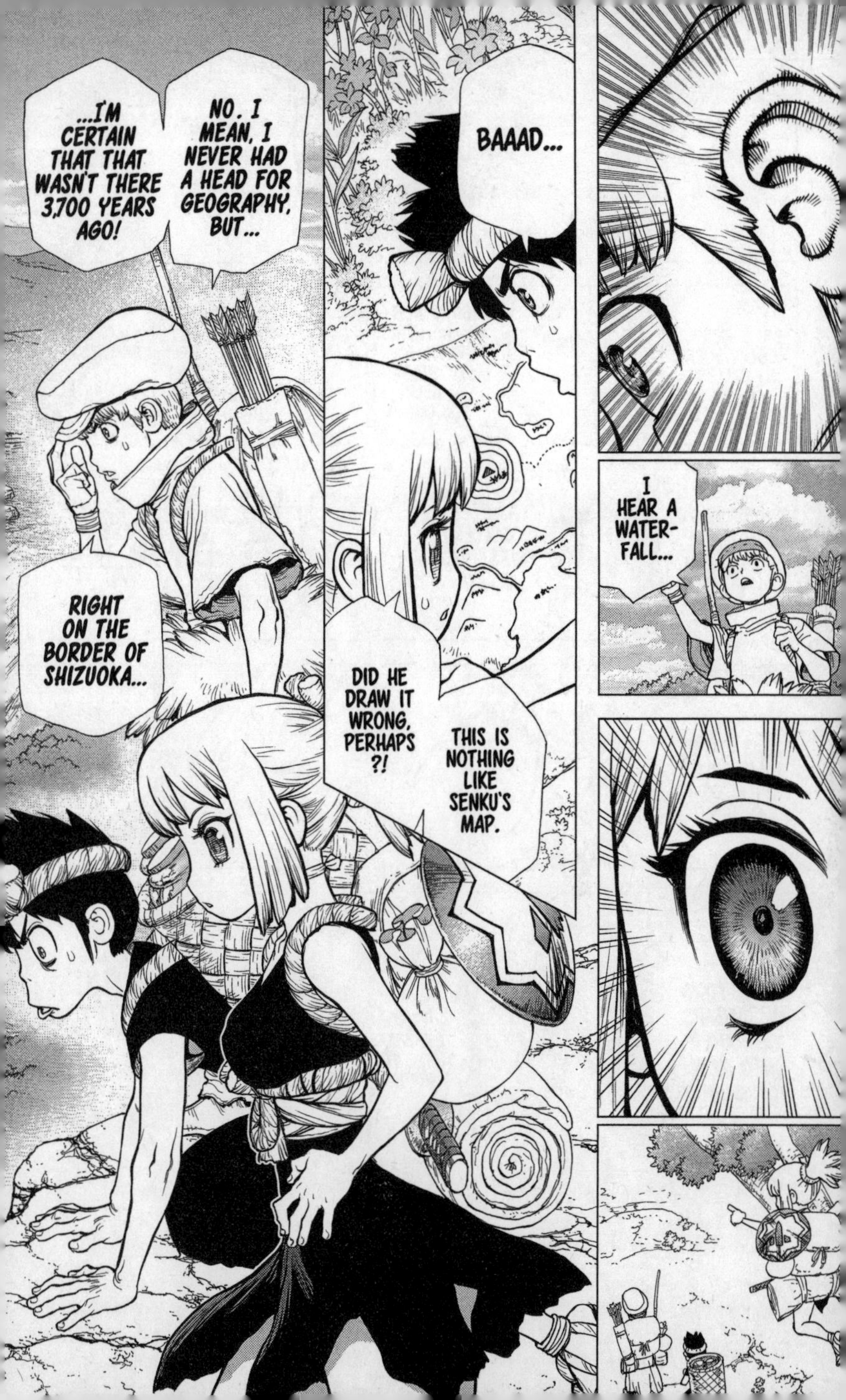
I HEAR A WATER-FALL...
BAAAD...
THIS IS NOTHING LIKE SENKU'S MAP.
DID HE DRAW IT WRONG, PERHAPS?!
NO. I MEAN, I NEVER HAD A HEAD FOR GEOGRAPHY, BUT...
...I'M CERTAIN THAT THAT WASN'T THERE 3,700 YEARS AGO!
RIGHT ON THE BORDER OF SHIZUOKA...

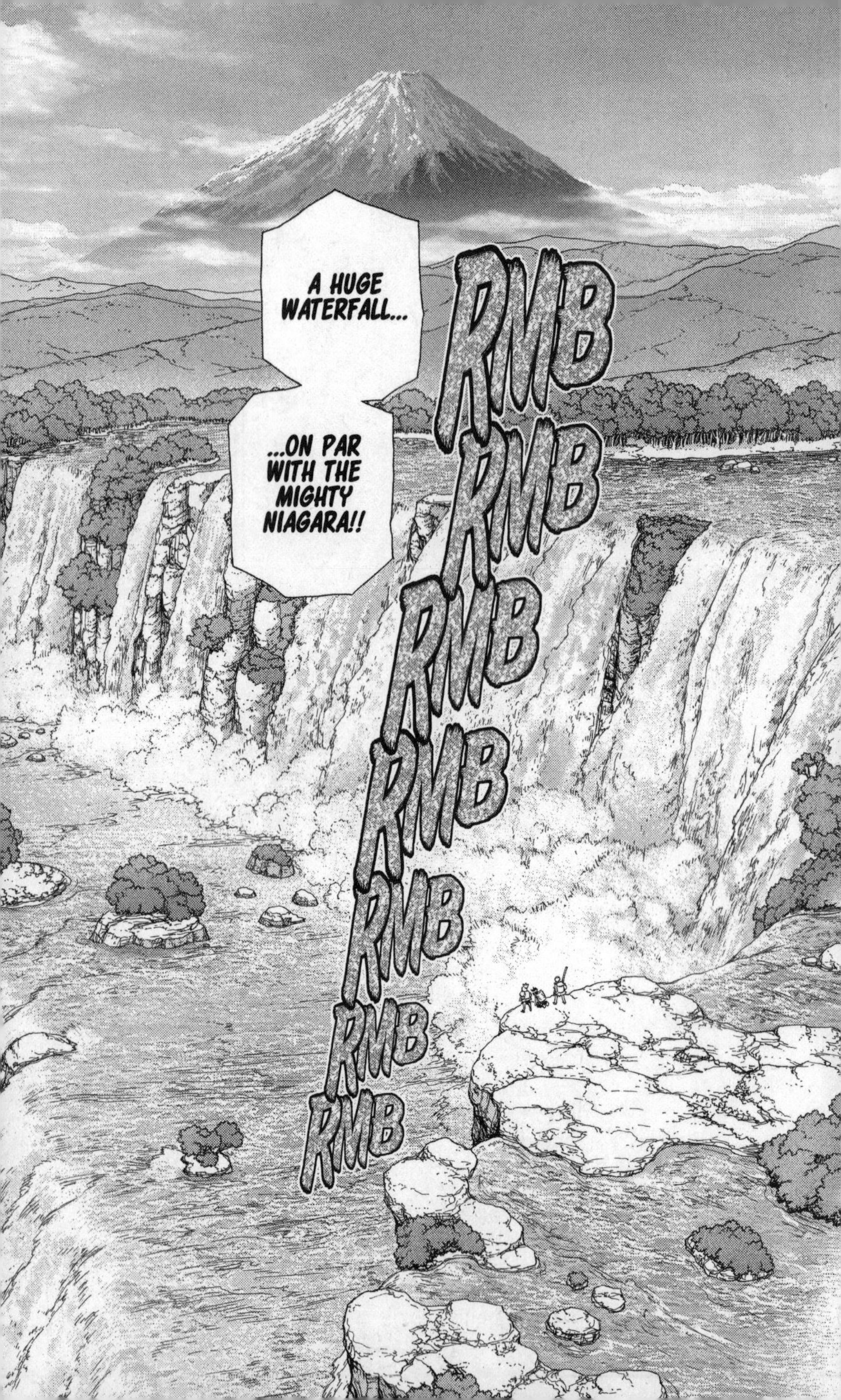
A HUGE WATERFALL...
...ON PAR WITH THE MIGHTY NIAGARA!!
RMB RMB RMB RMB RMB RMB RMB

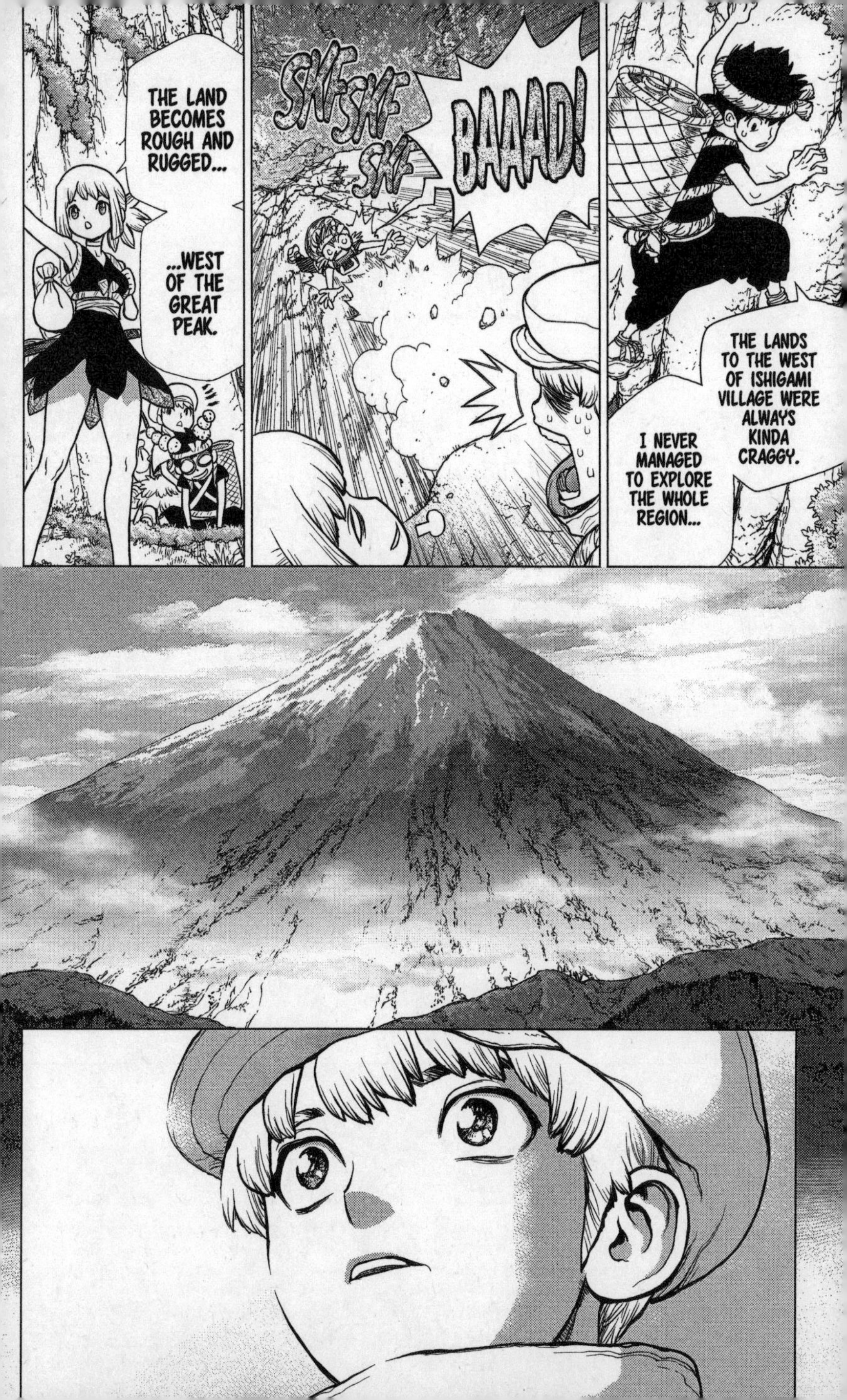
THE LANDS TO THE WEST OF ISHIGAMI VILLAGE WERE ALWAYS KINDA CRAGGY.
I NEVER MANAGED TO EXPLORE THE WHOLE REGION...
BAAAD!
SKF SKF SKF
THE LAND BECOMES ROUGH AND RUGGED...
...WEST OF THE GREAT PEAK.

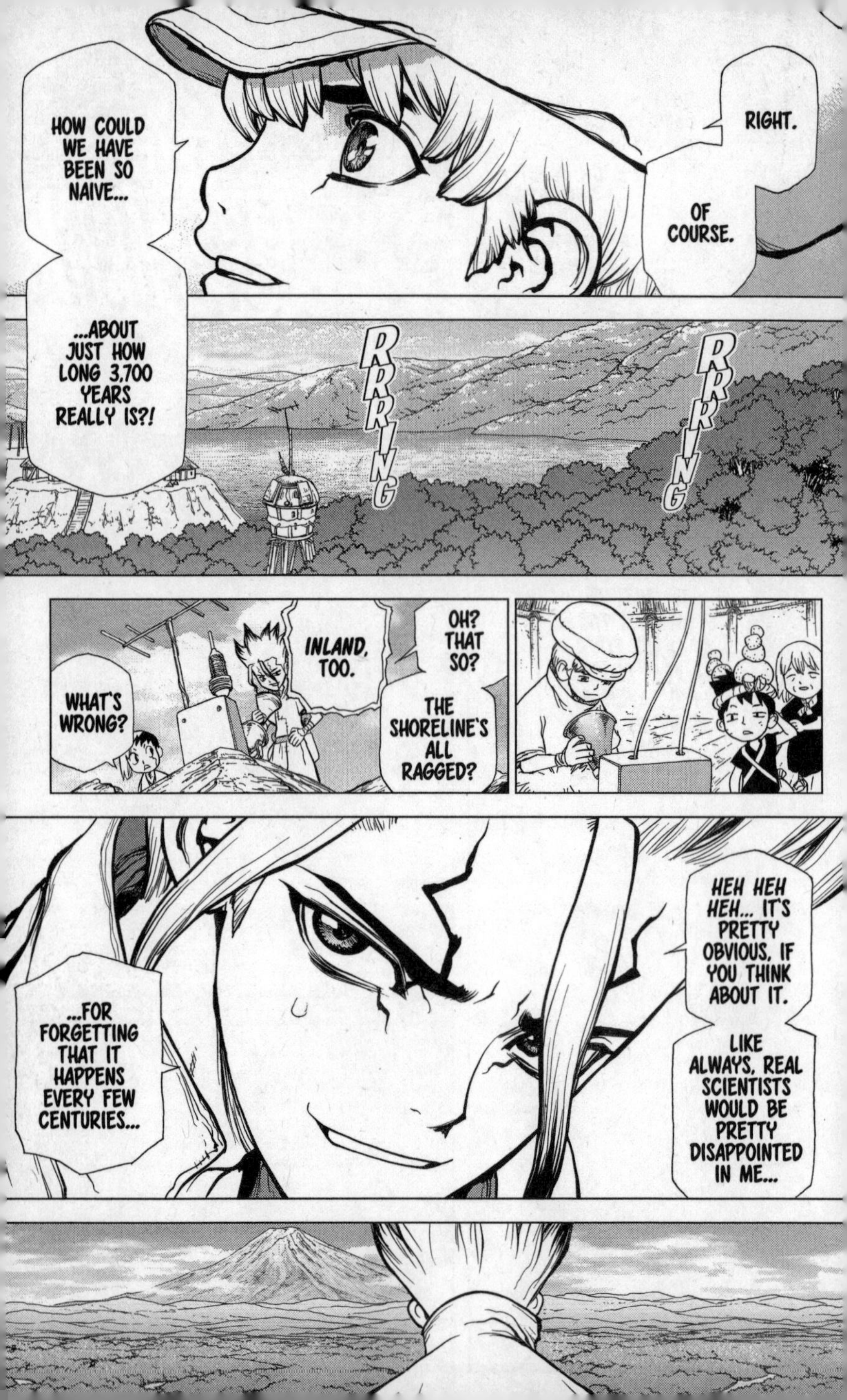
RIGHT.
OF COURSE.
HOW COULD WE HAVE BEEN SO NAIVE...
...ABOUT JUST HOW LONG 3,700 YEARS REALLY IS?!
RRRING
RRRING
OH? THAT SO?
THE SHORELINE'S ALL RAGGED?
INLAND, TOO.
WHAT'S WRONG?
HEH HEH HEH... IT'S PRETTY OBVIOUS, IF YOU THINK ABOUT IT.
LIKE ALWAYS, REAL SCIENTISTS WOULD BE PRETTY DISAPPOINTED IN ME...
...FOR FORGETTING THAT IT HAPPENS EVERY FEW CENTURIES...

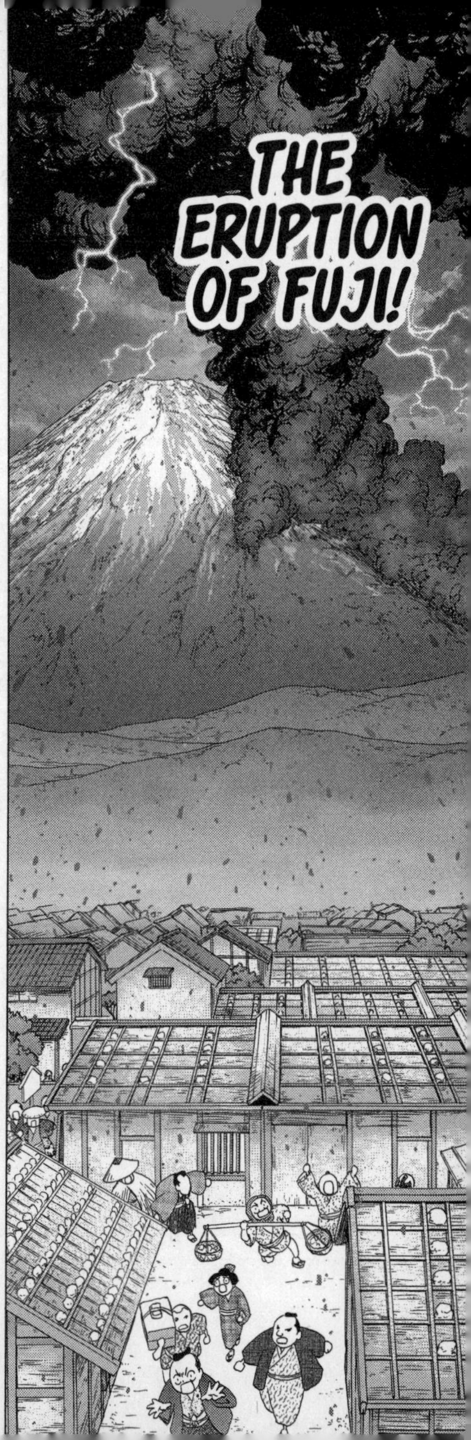
THE ERUPTION OF FUJI!

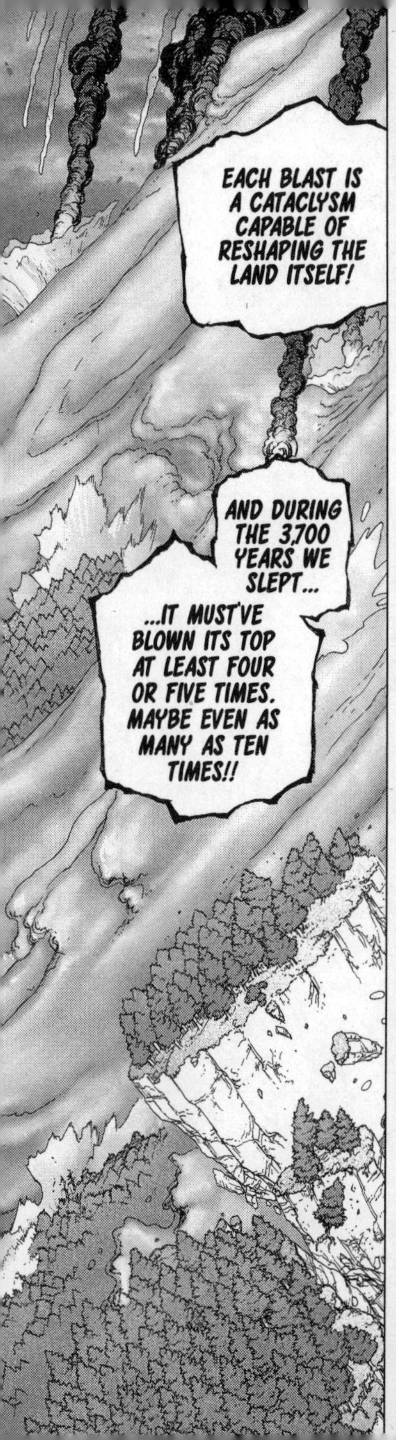
EACH BLAST IS A CATACLYSM CAPABLE OF RESHAPING THE LAND ITSELF!
AND DURING THE 3,700 YEARS WE SLEPT...
...IT MUST'VE BLOWN ITS TOP AT LEAST FOUR OR FIVE TIMES. MAYBE EVEN AS MANY AS TEN TIMES!!

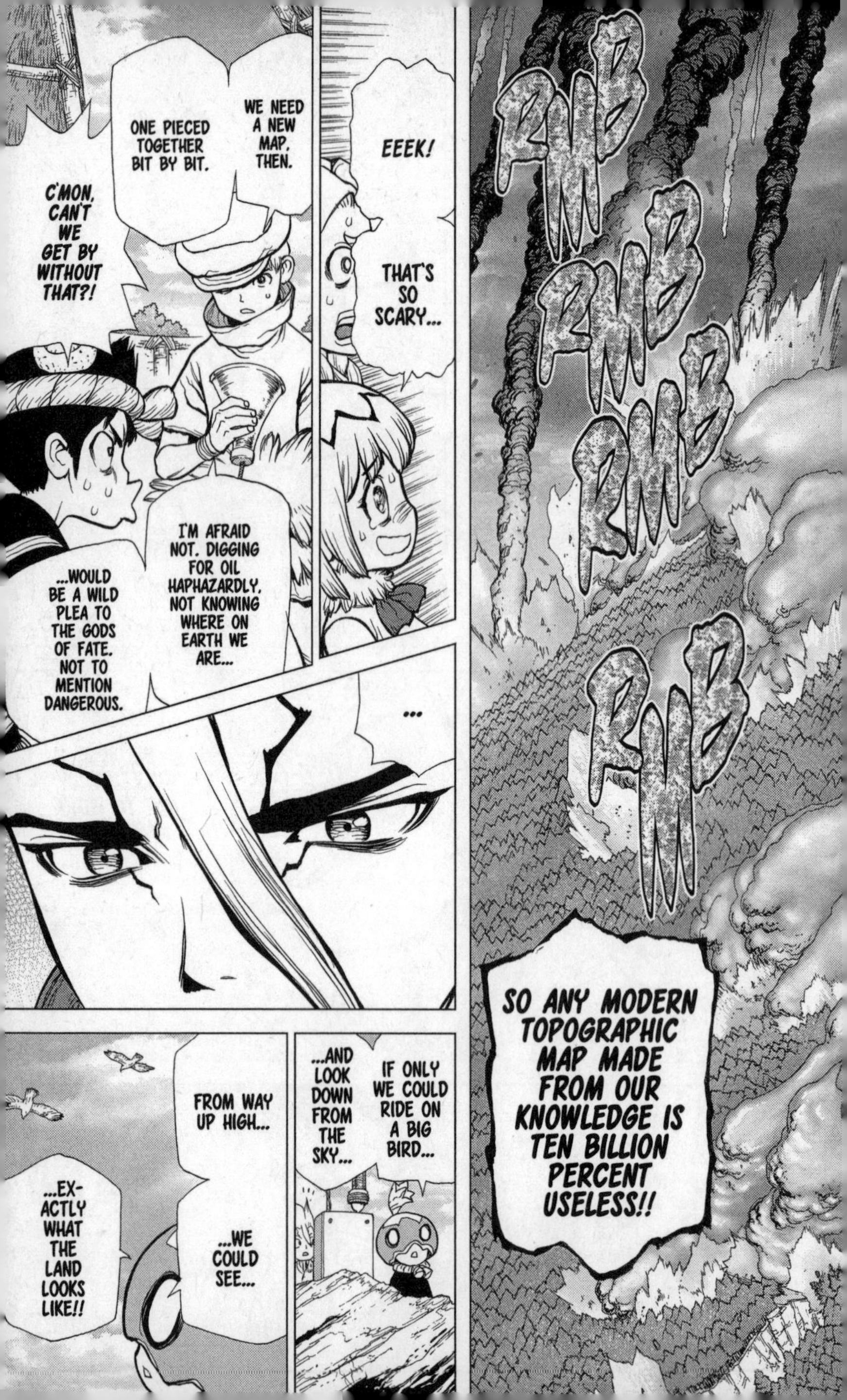
RMB RMB RMB RMB
SO ANY MODERN TOPOGRAPHIC MAP MADE FROM OUR KNOWLEDGE IS TEN BILLION PERCENT USELESS!!
EEEK!
THAT'S SO SCARY...
WE NEED A NEW MAP, THEN.
ONE PIECED TOGETHER BIT BY BIT.
C'MON, CAN'T WE GET BY WITHOUT THAT?!
I'M AFRAID NOT. DIGGING FOR OIL HAPHAZARDLY, NOT KNOWING WHERE ON EARTH WE ARE...
...WOULD BE A WILD PLEA TO THE GODS OF FATE. NOT TO MENTION DANGEROUS.
...
IF ONLY WE COULD RIDE ON A BIG BIRD...
...AND LOOK DOWN FROM THE SKY...
FROM WAY UP HIGH...
...WE COULD SEE...
...EX-ACTLY WHAT THE LAND LOOKS LIKE!!

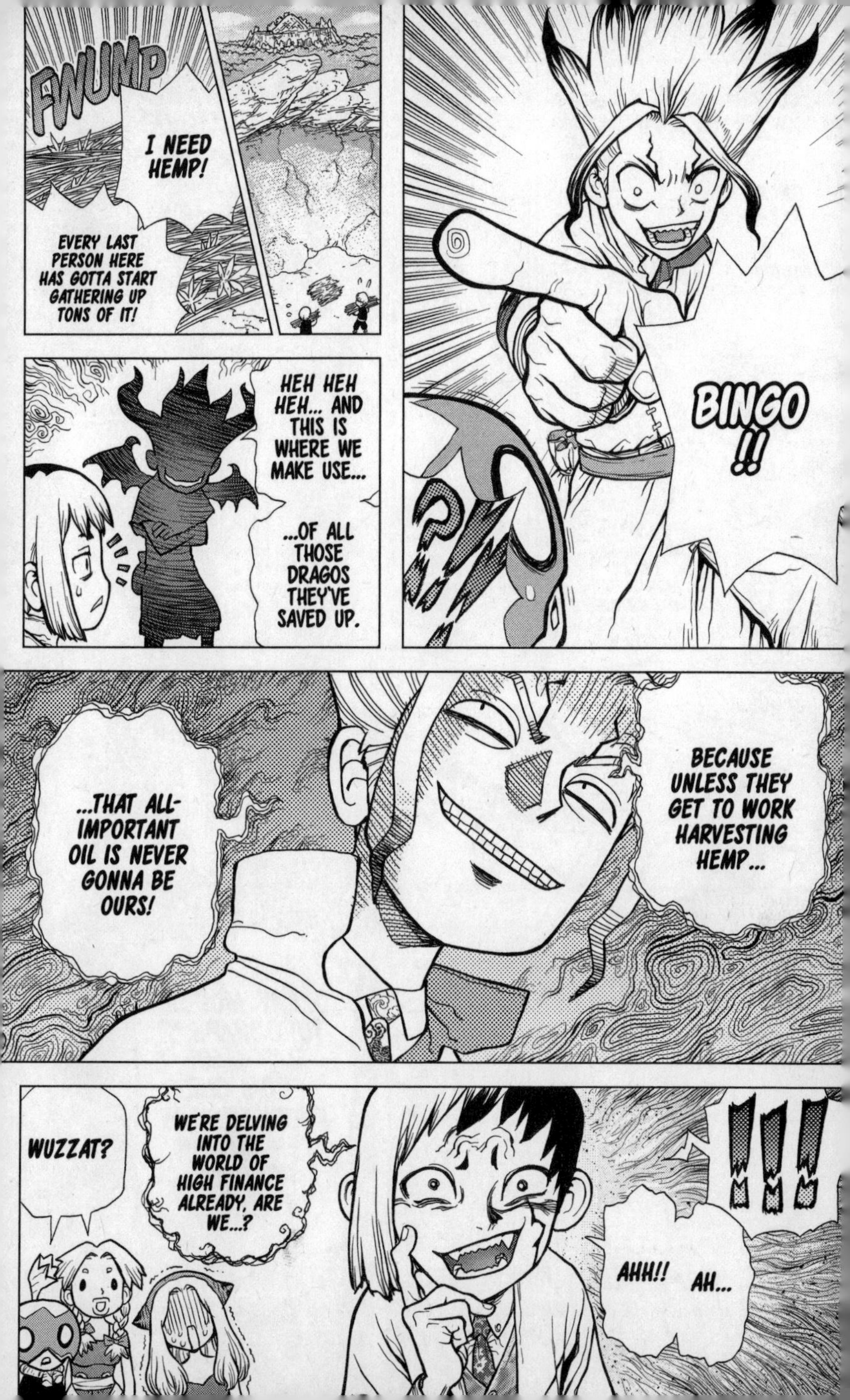
BINGO !!
FWUMP
I NEED HEMP!
EVERY LAST PERSON HERE HAS GOTTA START GATHERING UP TONS OF IT!
HEH HEH HEH... AND THIS IS WHERE WE MAKE USE...
...OF ALL THOSE DRAGOS THEY'VE SAVED UP.
BECAUSE UNLESS THEY GET TO WORK HARVESTING HEMP...
...THAT ALL-IMPORTANT OIL IS NEVER GONNA BE OURS!
!!!
AHH!! AH...
WE'RE DELVING INTO THE WORLD OF HIGH FINANCE ALREADY, ARE WE...?
WUZZAT?

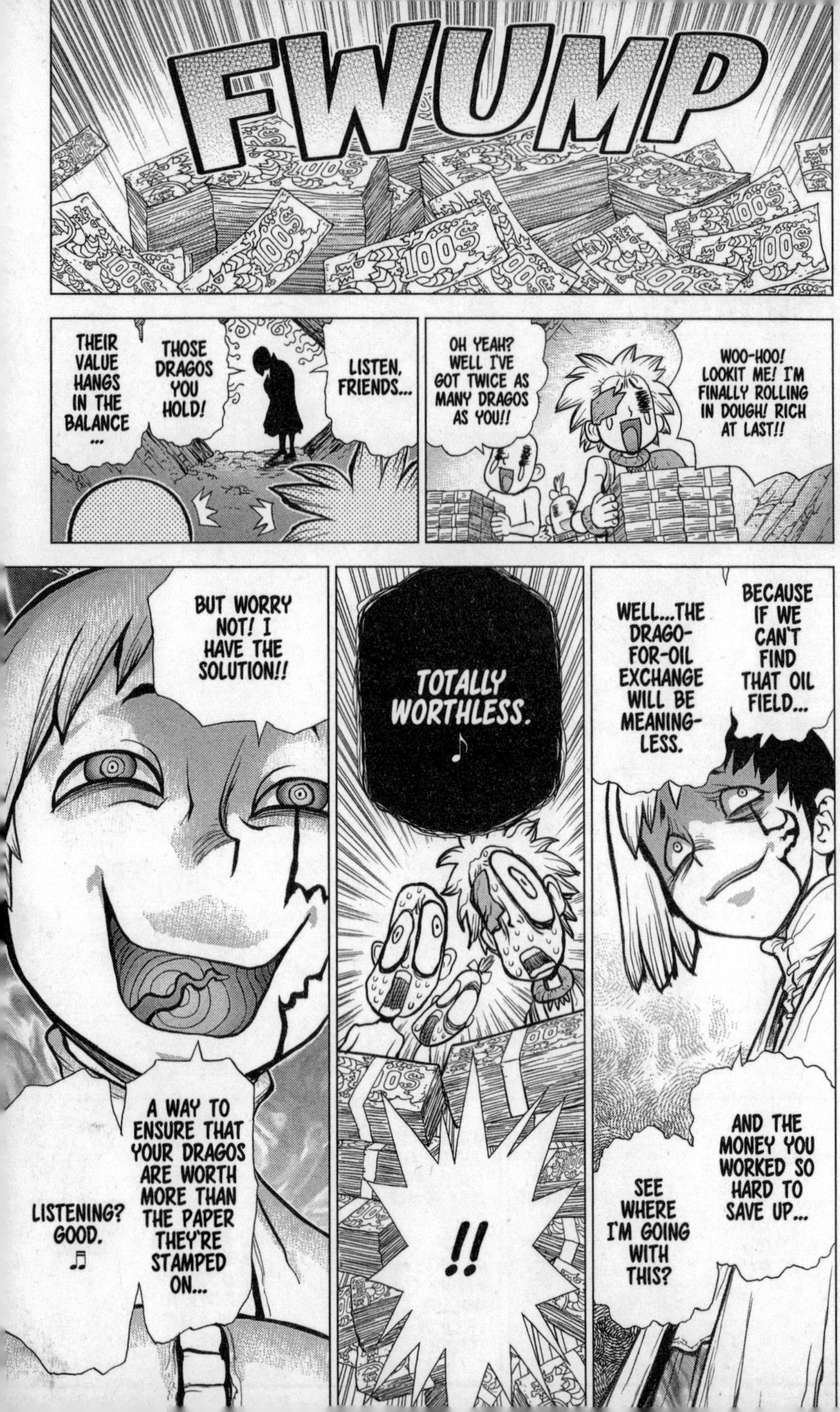
FWUMP
WOO-HOO! LOOKIT ME! I'M FINALLY ROLLING IN DOUGH! RICH AT LAST!!
OH YEAH? WELL I'VE GOT TWICE AS MANY DRAGOS AS YOU!!
LISTEN, FRIENDS...
THOSE DRAGOS YOU HOLD!
THEIR VALUE HANGS IN THE BALANCE...
BECAUSE IF WE CAN'T FIND THAT OIL FIELD...
WELL...THE DRAGO-FOR-OIL EXCHANGE WILL BE MEANING-LESS.
AND THE MONEY YOU WORKED SO HARD TO SAVE UP...
SEE WHERE I'M GOING WITH THIS?
TOTALLY WORTHLESS. ♪
!!
BUT WORRY NOT! I HAVE THE SOLUTION!!
A WAY TO ENSURE THAT YOUR DRAGOS ARE WORTH MORE THAN THE PAPER THEY'RE STAMPED ON...
LISTENING? GOOD. ♫

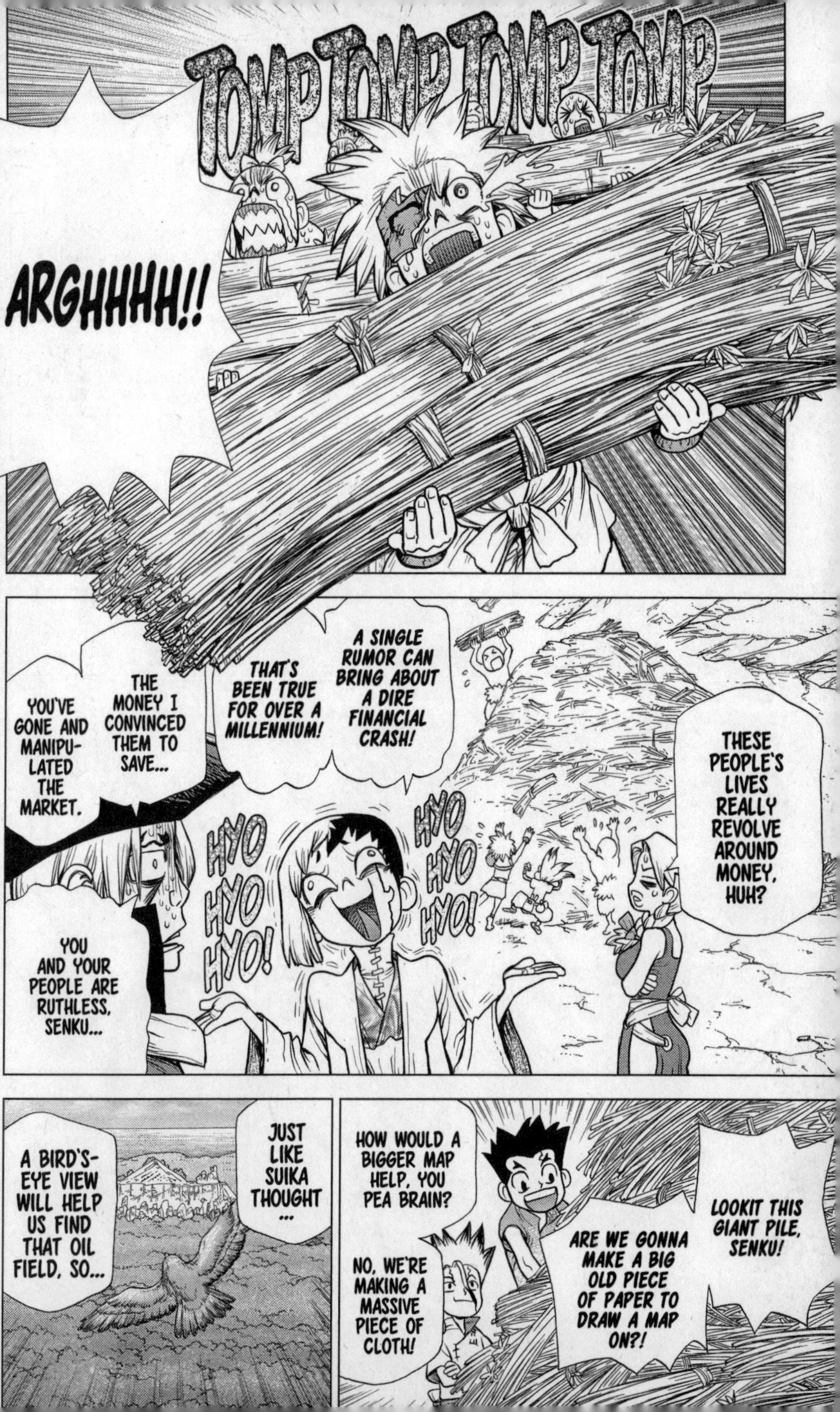

TOMP TOMP TOMP TOMP
ARGHHHH!!
THESE PEOPLE'S LIVES REALLY REVOLVE AROUND MONEY, HUH?
A SINGLE RUMOR CAN BRING ABOUT A DIRE FINANCIAL CRASH!
THAT'S BEEN TRUE FOR OVER A MILLENNIUM!
HYO HYO HYO!
HYO HYO HYO!
THE MONEY I CONVINCED THEM TO SAVE...
YOU'VE GONE AND MANIPU-LATED THE MARKET.
YOU AND YOUR PEOPLE ARE RUTHLESS, SENKU...
LOOKIT THIS GIANT PILE, SENKU!
ARE WE GONNA MAKE A BIG OLD PIECE OF PAPER TO DRAW A MAP ON?!
HOW WOULD A BIGGER MAP HELP, YOU PEA BRAIN?
NO, WE'RE MAKING A MASSIVE PIECE OF CLOTH!
JUST LIKE SUIKA THOUGHT...
A BIRD'S-EYE VIEW WILL HELP US FIND THAT OIL FIELD, SO...

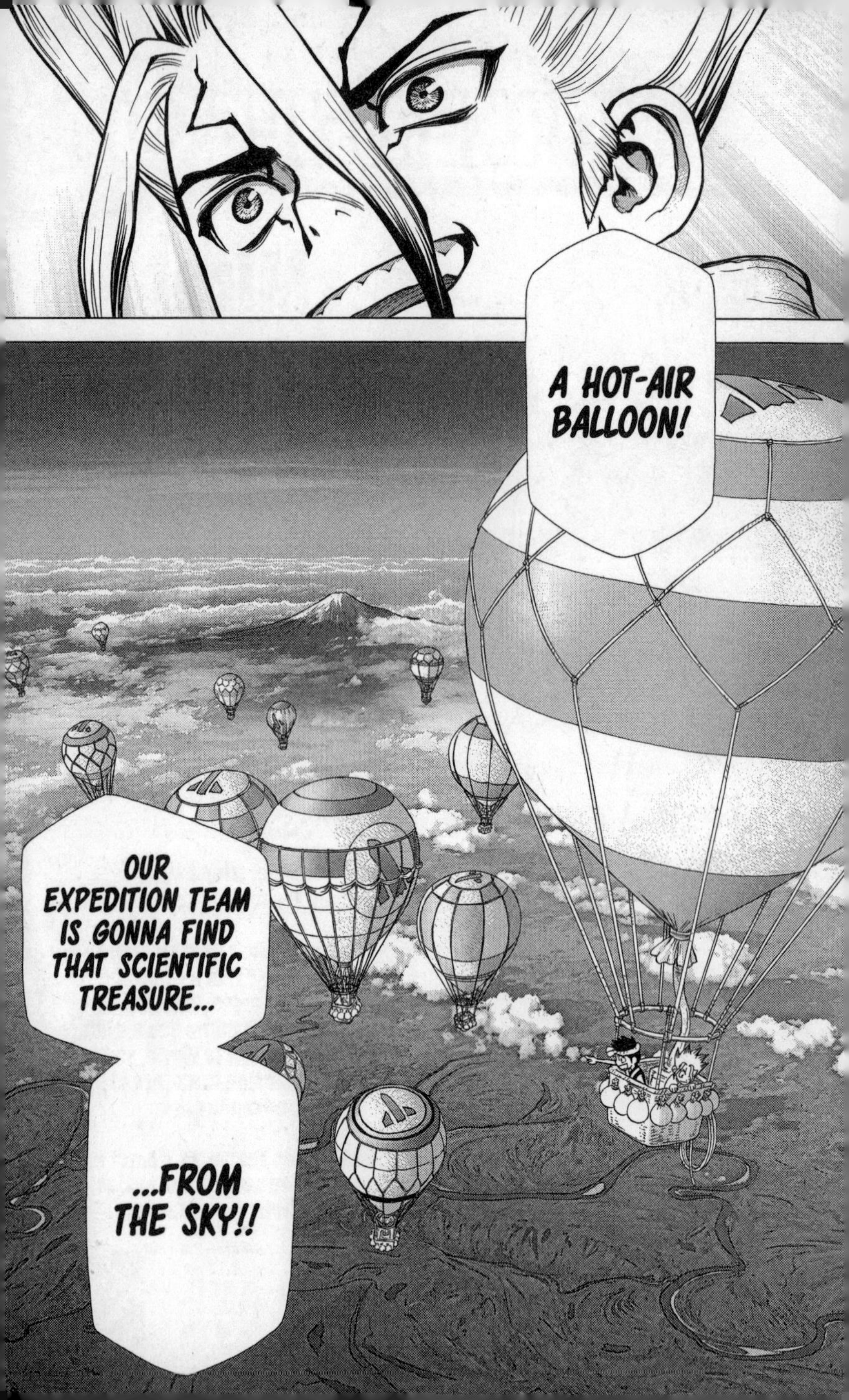
A HOT-AIR BALLOON!
OUR EXPEDITION TEAM IS GONNA FIND THAT SCIENTIFIC TREASURE...
...FROM THE SKY!!

Kingdom of Science

WORKER FILE 3

Mirai

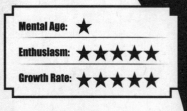

Mental Age: ★

Enthusiasm: ★★★★★

Growth Rate: ★★★★★

Full Name: Mirai Shishio

Height: 139 cm

Job in Kingdom: Cotton candy vendor

Mirai and her friend Suika love running the food stalls together!

Mentally, she's only six years old, because that's when she went into a coma. However, by successfully holding down a job in the brutal Stone World, she's already started to mature at a breakneck pace.

Monitoring Tsukasa's freezer is another one of Mirai's jobs, so she's actually quite busy.

Z=87: Senku's Department Store

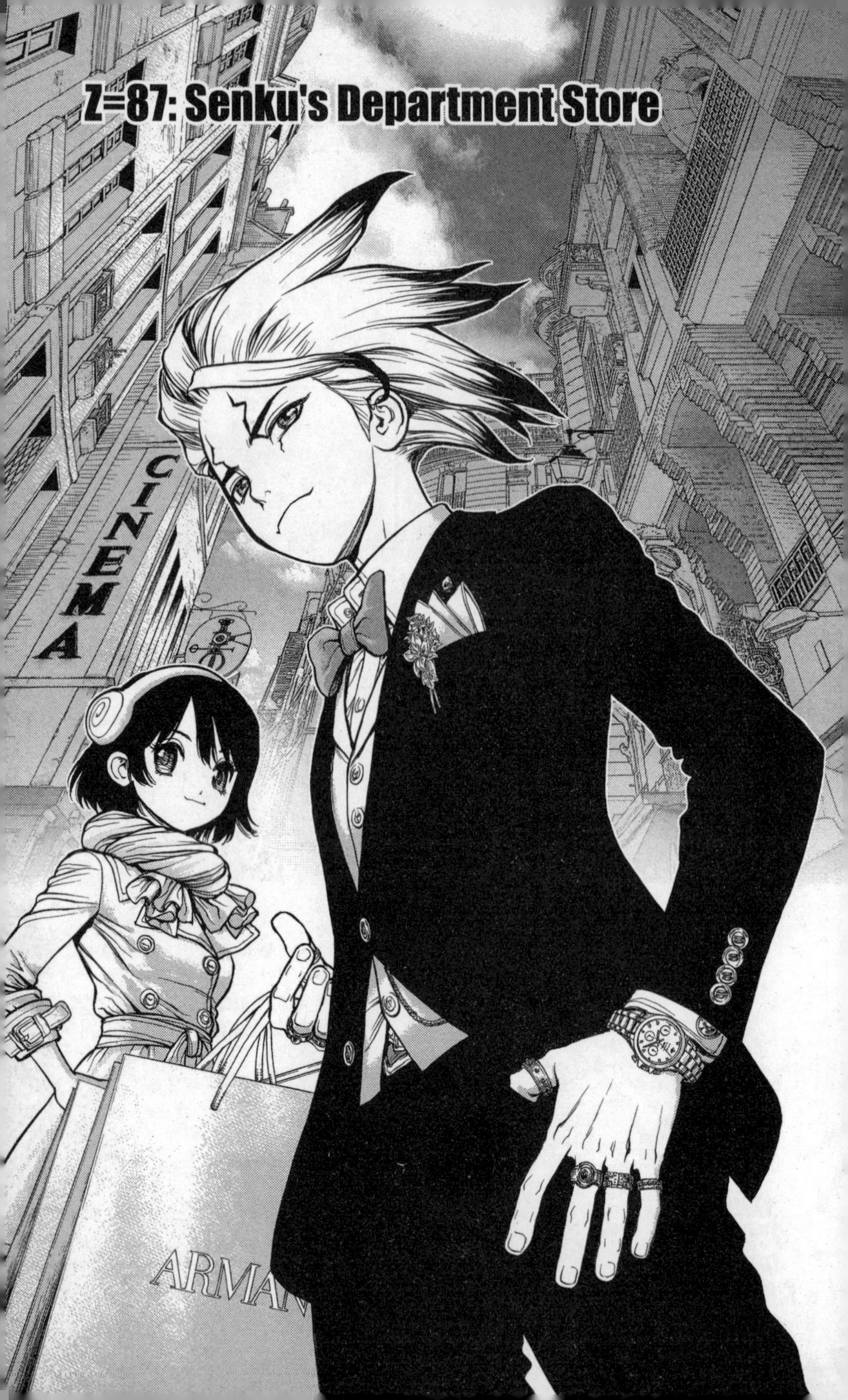

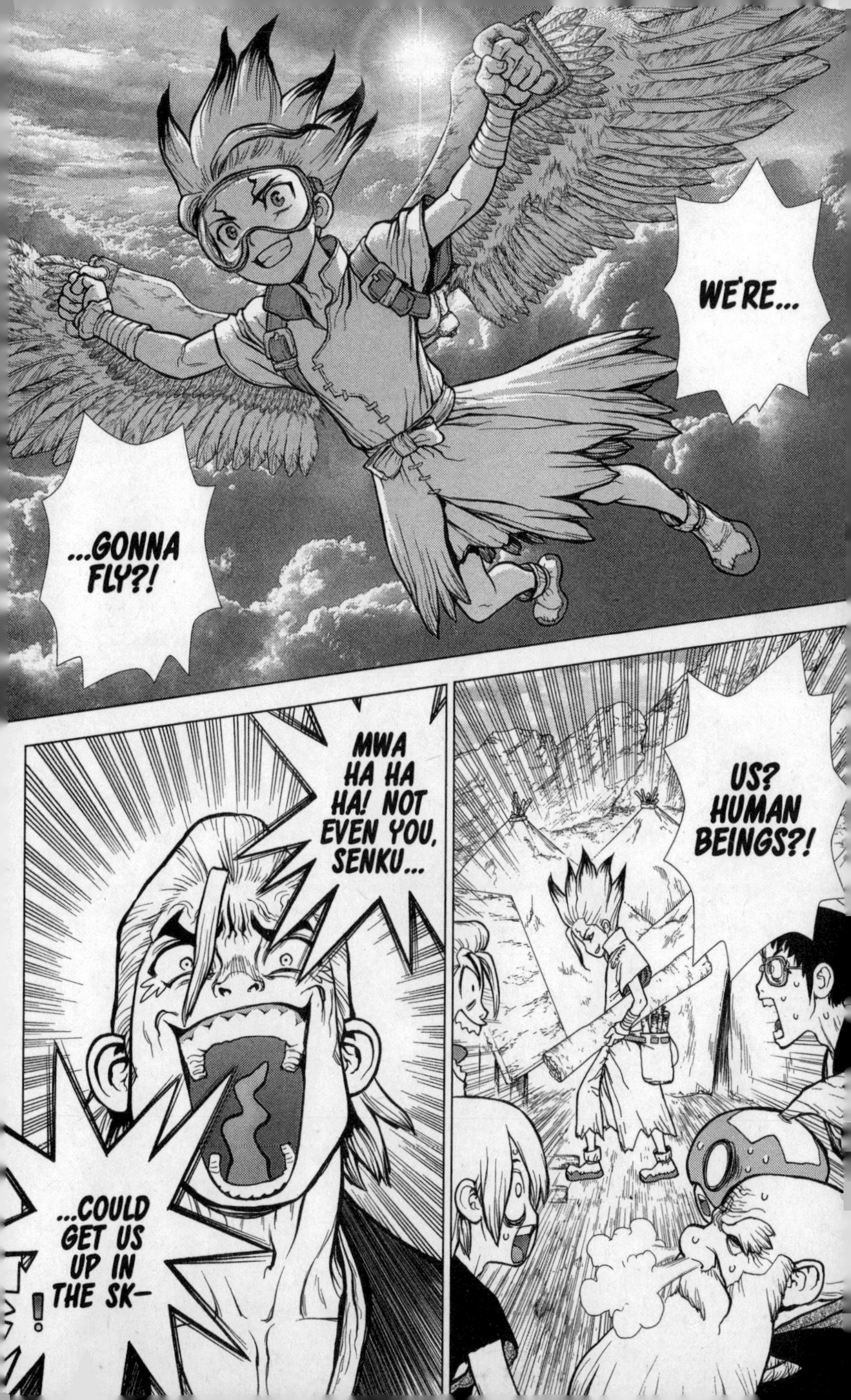
WE'RE...
...GONNA FLY?!
US? HUMAN BEINGS?!
MWA HA HA HA! NOT EVEN YOU, SENKU...
...COULD GET US UP IN THE SK—

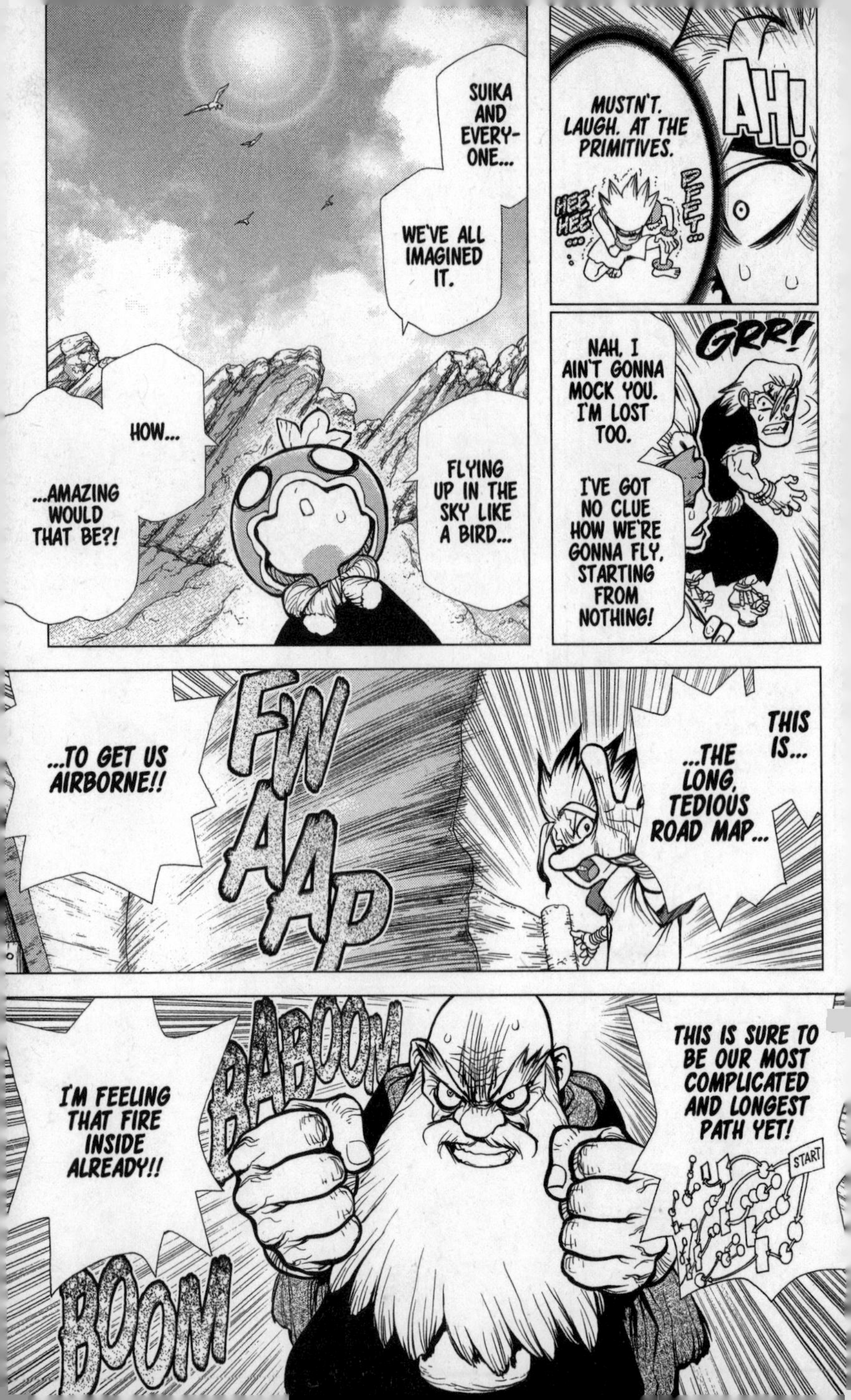
AH!
MUSTN'T. LAUGH. AT THE PRIMITIVES.
PFFT...
HEE HEE...
GRR!
NAH, I AIN'T GONNA MOCK YOU. I'M LOST TOO.
I'VE GOT NO CLUE HOW WE'RE GONNA FLY, STARTING FROM NOTHING!
SUIKA AND EVERY-ONE...
WE'VE ALL IMAGINED IT.
FLYING UP IN THE SKY LIKE A BIRD...
HOW...
...AMAZING WOULD THAT BE?!
THIS IS...
...THE LONG, TEDIOUS ROAD MAP...
FWAAAP
...TO GET US AIRBORNE!!
THIS IS SURE TO BE OUR MOST COMPLICATED AND LONGEST PATH YET!
START
BABOOM
I'M FEELING THAT FIRE INSIDE ALREADY!!
BOOM

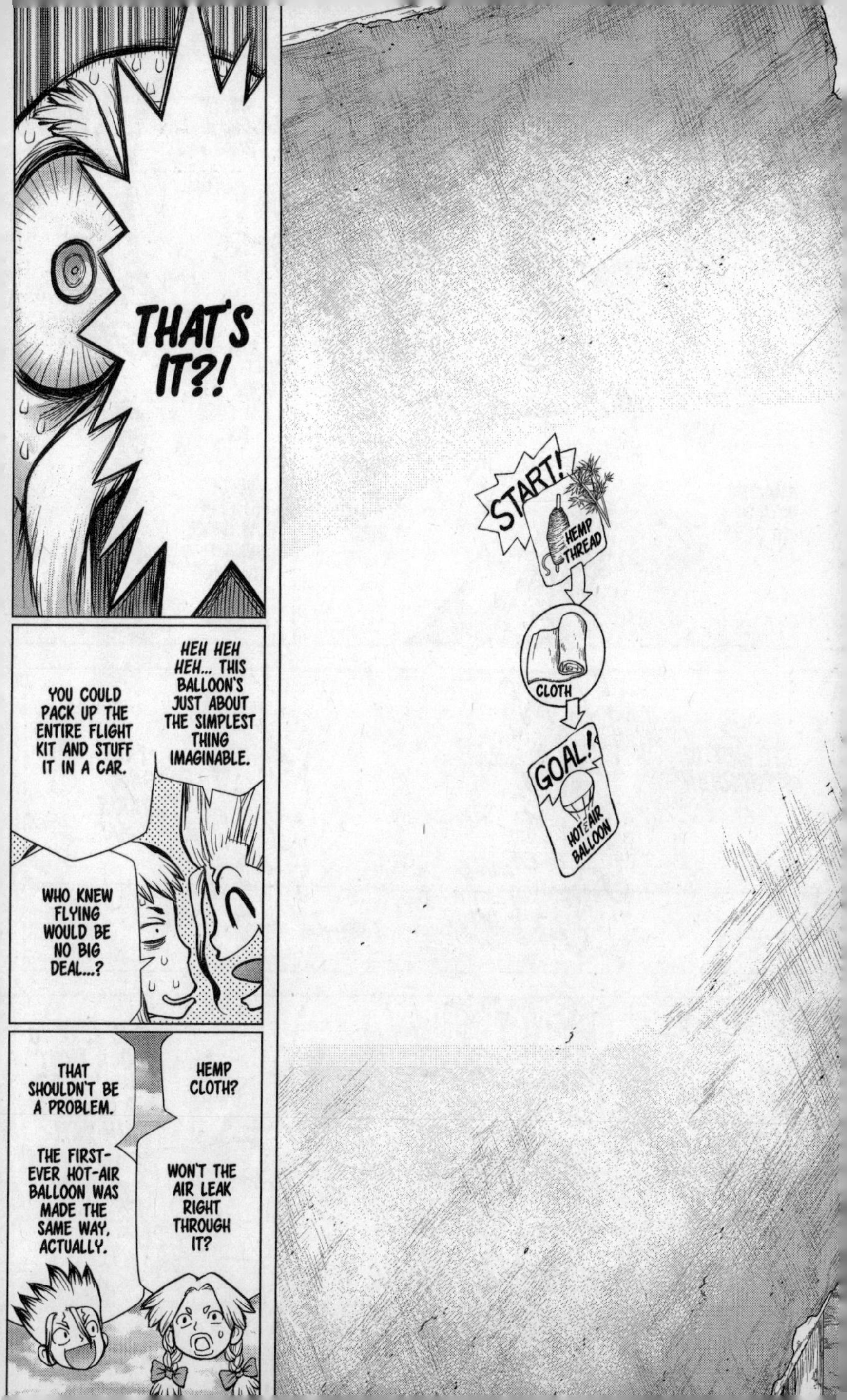
START!
HEMP THREAD
CLOTH
GOAL!
HOT-AIR BALLOON
THAT'S IT?!
HEH HEH HEH... THIS BALLOON'S JUST ABOUT THE SIMPLEST THING IMAGINABLE.
YOU COULD PACK UP THE ENTIRE FLIGHT KIT AND STUFF IT IN A CAR.
WHO KNEW FLYING WOULD BE NO BIG DEAL...?
HEMP CLOTH?
WON'T THE AIR LEAK RIGHT THROUGH IT?
THAT SHOULDN'T BE A PROBLEM.
THE FIRST-EVER HOT-AIR BALLOON WAS MADE THE SAME WAY, ACTUALLY.

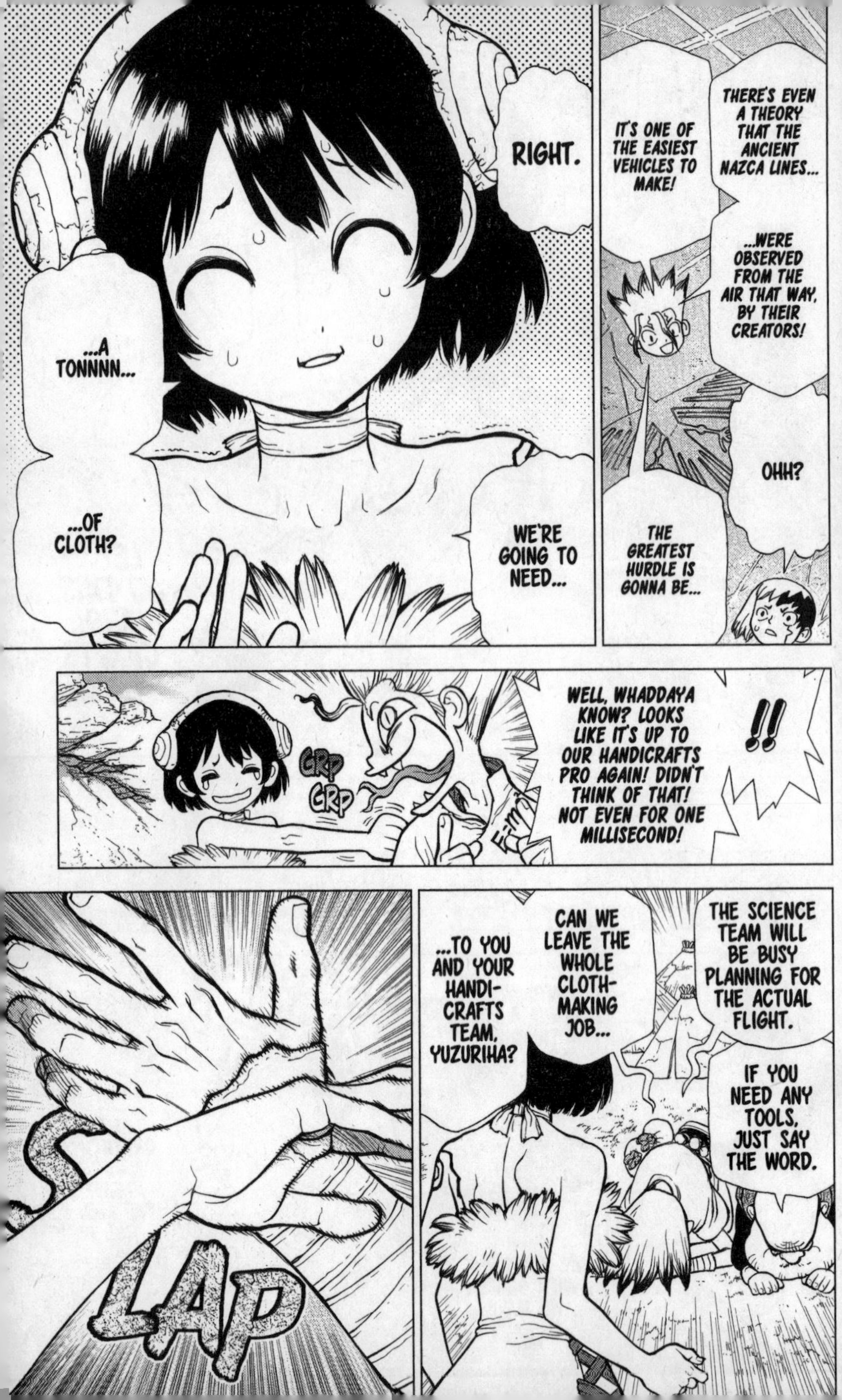
IT'S ONE OF THE EASIEST VEHICLES TO MAKE!
THERE'S EVEN A THEORY THAT THE ANCIENT NAZCA LINES...
...WERE OBSERVED FROM THE AIR THAT WAY, BY THEIR CREATORS!
OHH?
THE GREATEST HURDLE IS GONNA BE...
WE'RE GOING TO NEED...
...A TONNNN...
...OF CLOTH?
RIGHT.
!!
WELL, WHADDAYA KNOW? LOOKS LIKE IT'S UP TO OUR HANDICRAFTS PRO AGAIN! DIDN'T THINK OF THAT! NOT EVEN FOR ONE MILLISECOND!
GRP
GRP
THE SCIENCE TEAM WILL BE BUSY PLANNING FOR THE ACTUAL FLIGHT.
CAN WE LEAVE THE WHOLE CLOTH-MAKING JOB...
...TO YOU AND YOUR HANDI-CRAFTS TEAM, YUZURIHA?
IF YOU NEED ANY TOOLS, JUST SAY THE WORD.
LAP

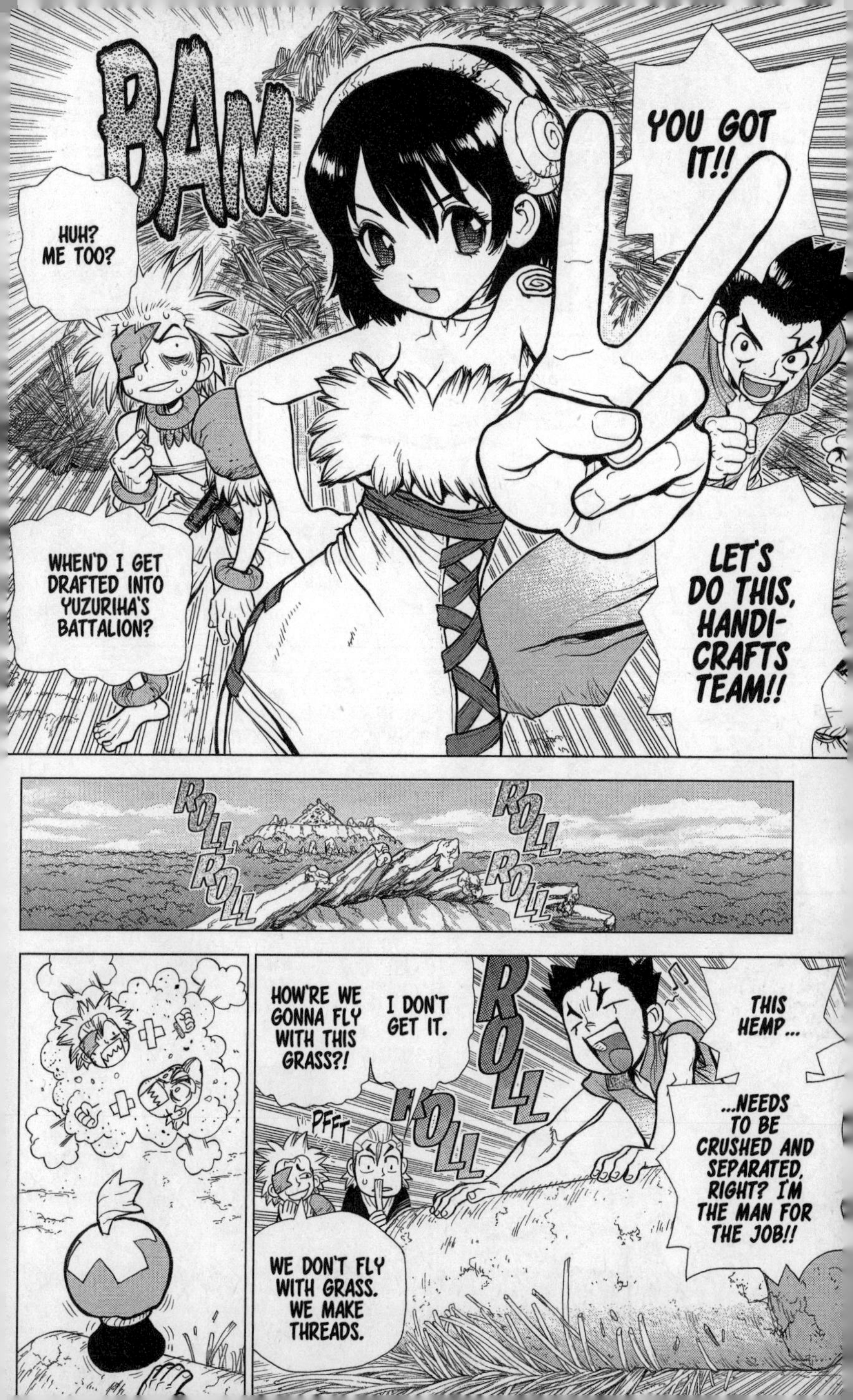
YOU GOT IT!!
BAM
LET'S DO THIS, HANDICRAFTS TEAM!!
HUH? ME TOO?
WHEN'D I GET DRAFTED INTO YUZURIHA'S BATTALION?
ROLL ROLL
ROLL ROLL
THIS HEMP...
...NEEDS TO BE CRUSHED AND SEPARATED, RIGHT? I'M THE MAN FOR THE JOB!!
ROLL ROLL
I DON'T GET IT.
HOW'RE WE GONNA FLY WITH THIS GRASS?!
PFFT
WE DON'T FLY WITH GRASS. WE MAKE THREADS.

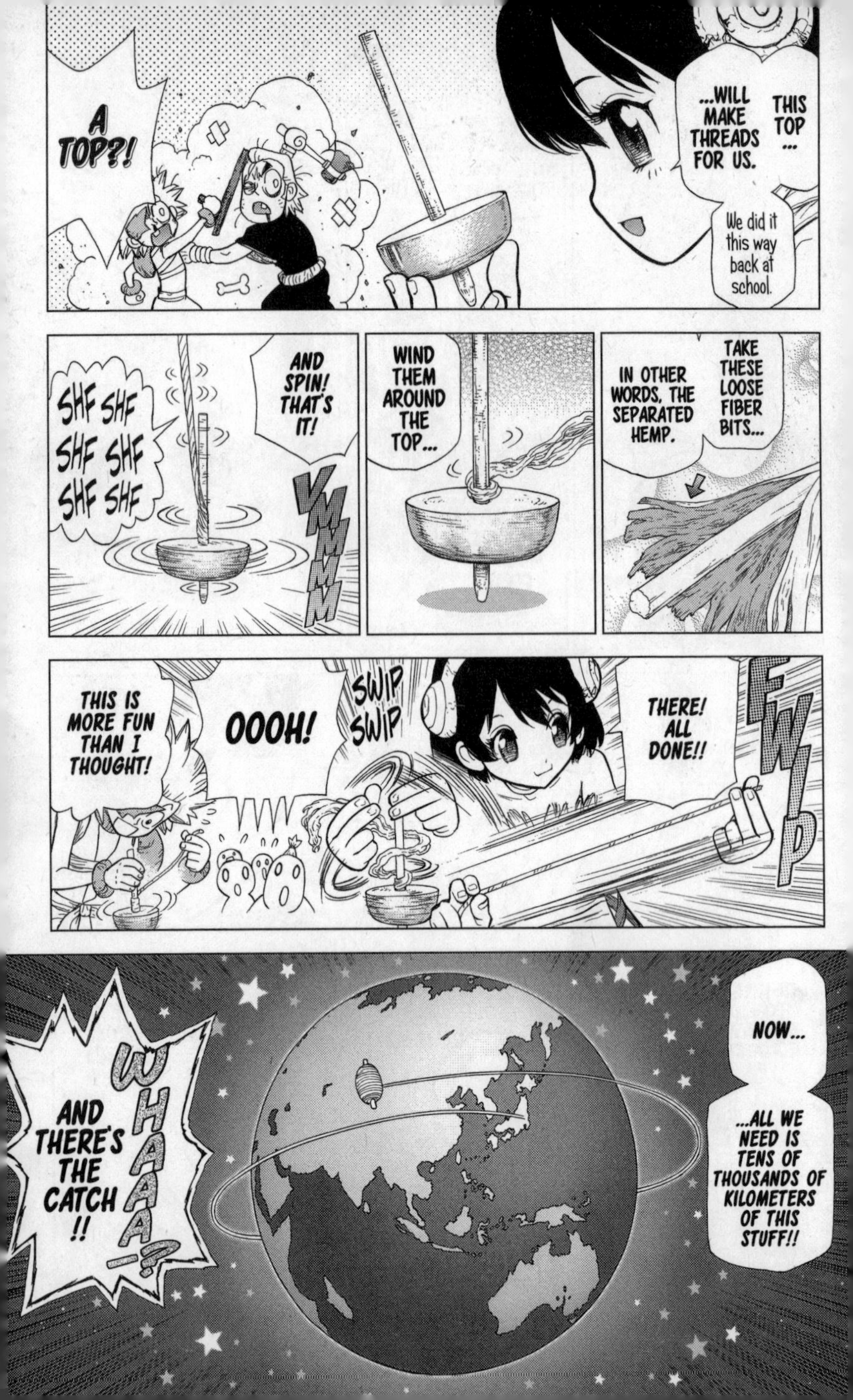
THIS TOP...
...WILL MAKE THREADS FOR US.
We did it this way back at school.
A TOP?!
TAKE THESE LOOSE FIBER BITS...
IN OTHER WORDS, THE SEPARATED HEMP.
WIND THEM AROUND THE TOP...
AND SPIN! THAT'S IT!
VMMMMM
SHF SHF SHF SHF SHF SHF
FWIP
THERE! ALL DONE!!
SWIP SWIP
OOOH!
THIS IS MORE FUN THAN I THOUGHT!
NOW...
...ALL WE NEED IS TENS OF THOUSANDS OF KILOMETERS OF THIS STUFF!!
WHAAAA-?
AND THERE'S THE CATCH!!

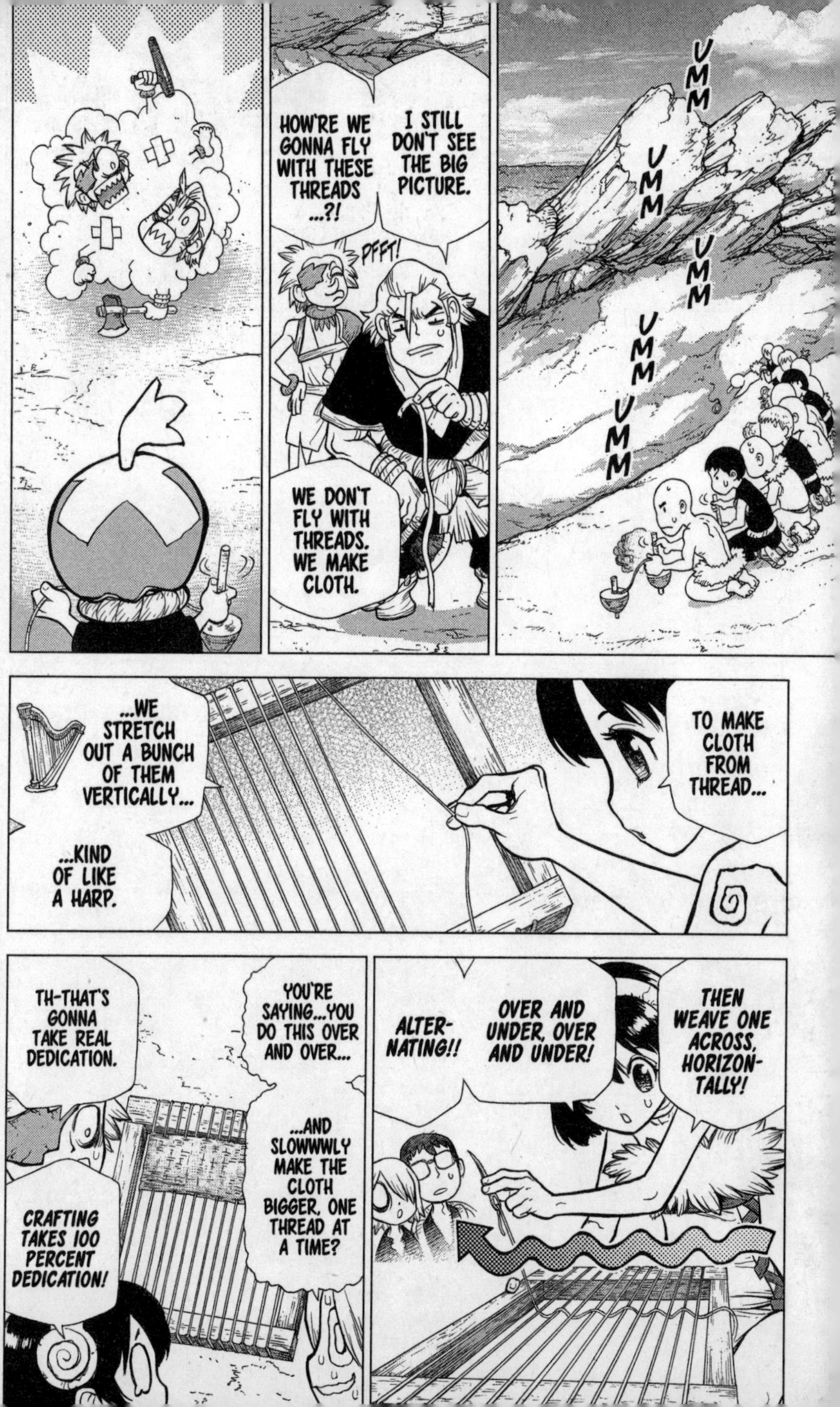
UMM UMM UMM UMM UMM UMM
I STILL DON'T SEE THE BIG PICTURE.
HOW'RE WE GONNA FLY WITH THESE THREADS ...?!
PFFT!
WE DON'T FLY WITH THREADS. WE MAKE CLOTH.
TO MAKE CLOTH FROM THREAD...
...WE STRETCH OUT A BUNCH OF THEM VERTICALLY...
...KIND OF LIKE A HARP.
THEN WEAVE ONE ACROSS, HORIZON-TALLY!
OVER AND UNDER, OVER AND UNDER!
ALTER-NATING!!
YOU'RE SAYING...YOU DO THIS OVER AND OVER...
TH-THAT'S GONNA TAKE REAL DEDICATION.
...AND SLOWWWLY MAKE THE CLOTH BIGGER, ONE THREAD AT A TIME?
CRAFTING TAKES 100 PERCENT DEDICATION!

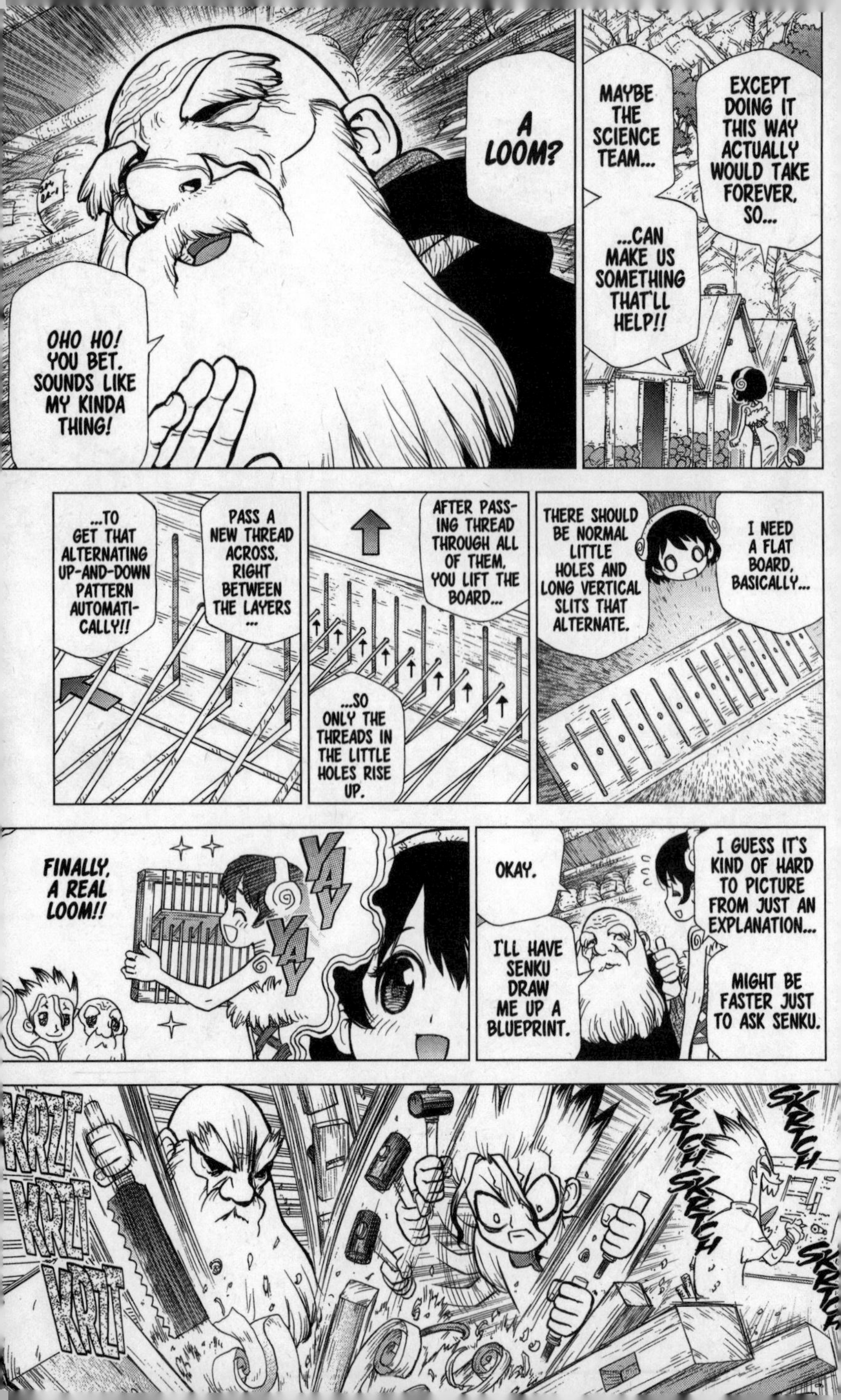
EXCEPT DOING IT THIS WAY ACTUALLY WOULD TAKE FOREVER, SO...
MAYBE THE SCIENCE TEAM...
...CAN MAKE US SOMETHING THAT'LL HELP!!
A LOOM?
OHO HO! YOU BET. SOUNDS LIKE MY KINDA THING!
I NEED A FLAT BOARD, BASICALLY...
THERE SHOULD BE NORMAL LITTLE HOLES AND LONG VERTICAL SLITS THAT ALTERNATE.
AFTER PASSING THREAD THROUGH ALL OF THEM, YOU LIFT THE BOARD...
...SO ONLY THE THREADS IN THE LITTLE HOLES RISE UP.
PASS A NEW THREAD ACROSS, RIGHT BETWEEN THE LAYERS...
...TO GET THAT ALTERNATING UP-AND-DOWN PATTERN AUTOMATICALLY!!
I GUESS IT'S KIND OF HARD TO PICTURE FROM JUST AN EXPLANATION...
MIGHT BE FASTER JUST TO ASK SENKU.
OKAY.
I'LL HAVE SENKU DRAW ME UP A BLUEPRINT.
YAY
YAY
FINALLY, A REAL LOOM!!
SKRTCH
SKRTCH
SKRTCH
SKRTCH
KRZT
KRZT
KRZT

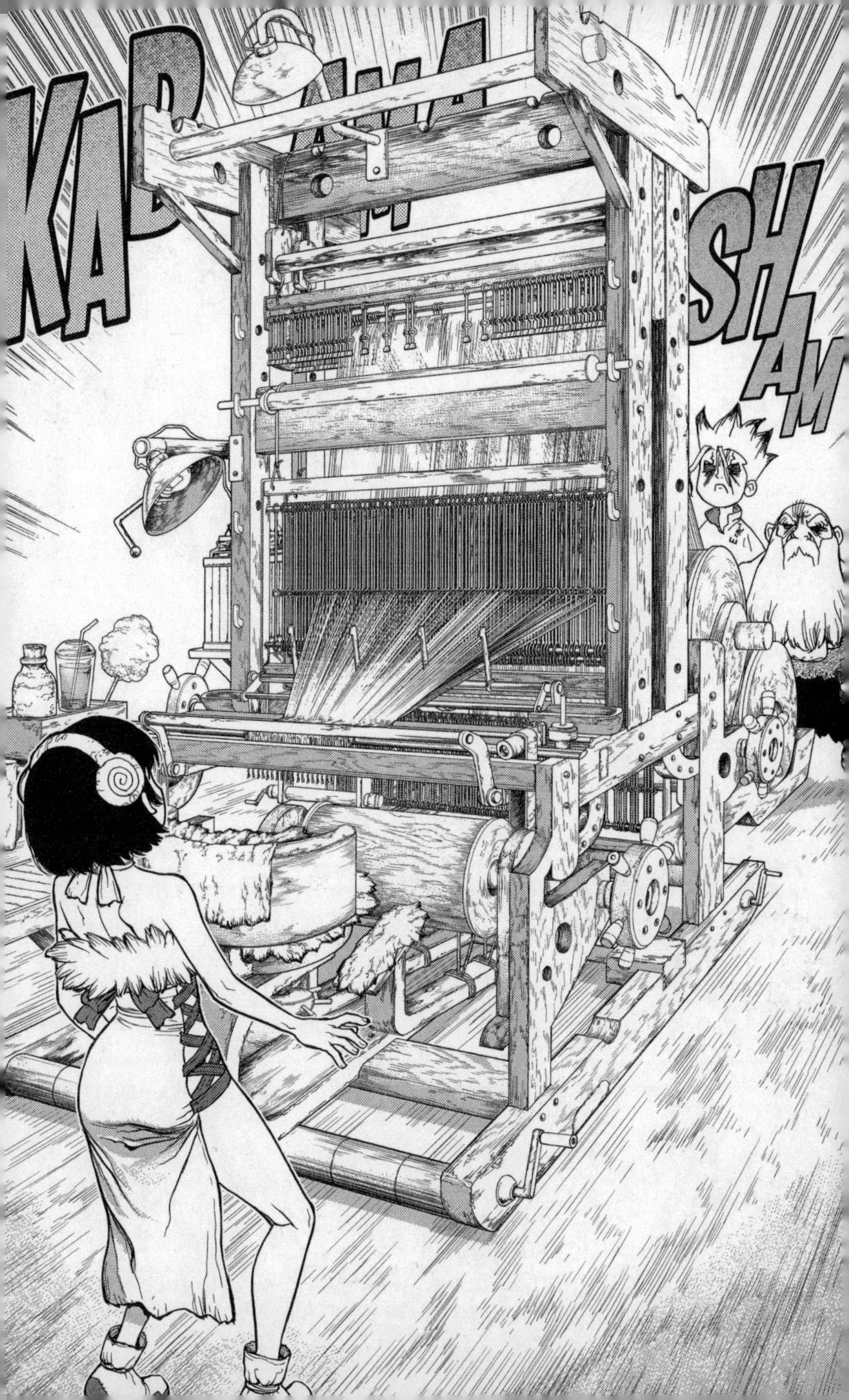
KAB
SHAM

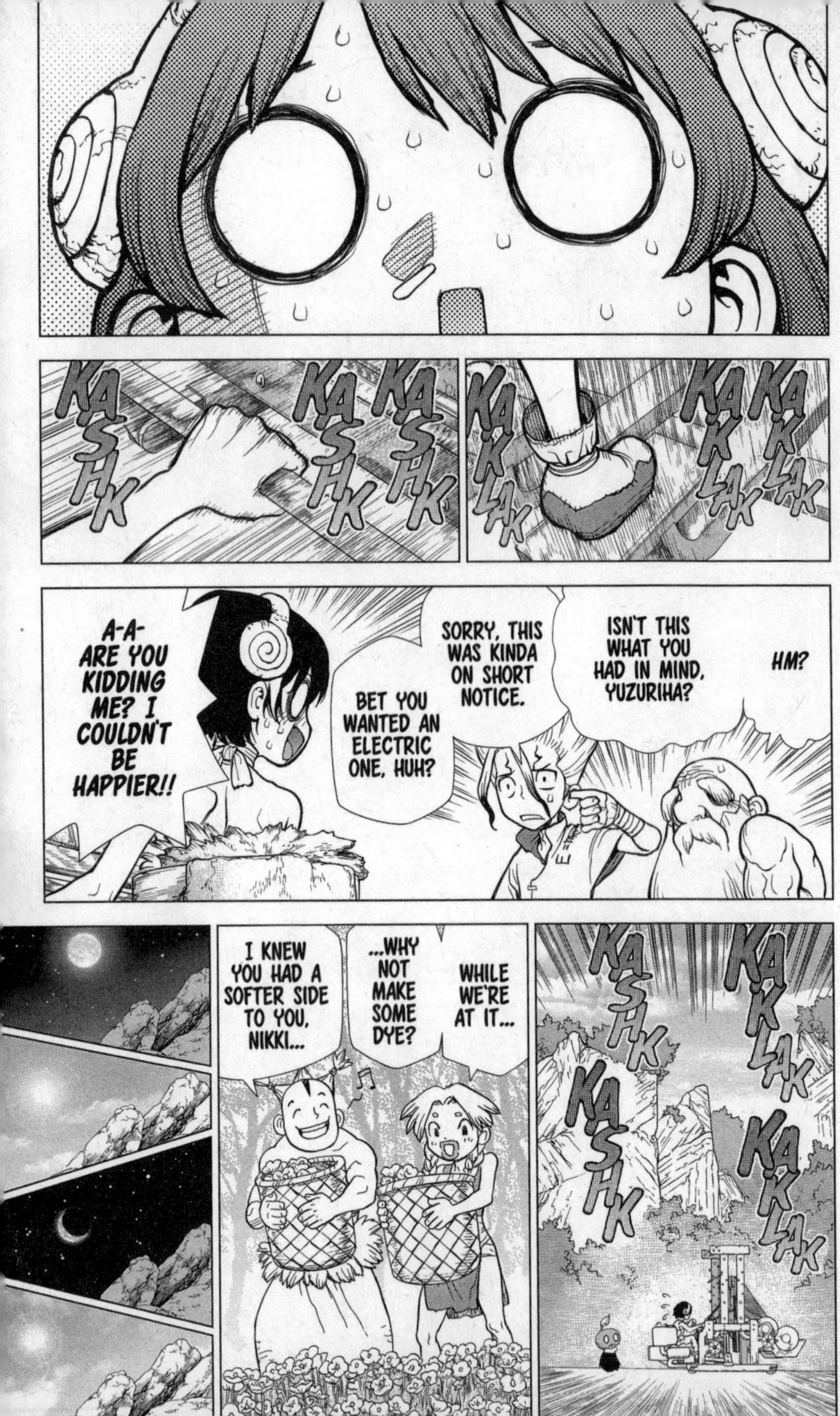
KAKLAK
KAKLAK
KAKLAK
KASHK
KASHK
KASHK
HM?
ISN'T THIS WHAT YOU HAD IN MIND, YUZURIHA?
SORRY, THIS WAS KINDA ON SHORT NOTICE.
BET YOU WANTED AN ELECTRIC ONE, HUH?
A-A-ARE YOU KIDDING ME? I COULDN'T BE HAPPIER!!
KAKLAK
KAKLAK
KASHK
KASHK
WHILE WE'RE AT IT...
...WHY NOT MAKE SOME DYE?
I KNEW YOU HAD A SOFTER SIDE TO YOU, NIKKI...

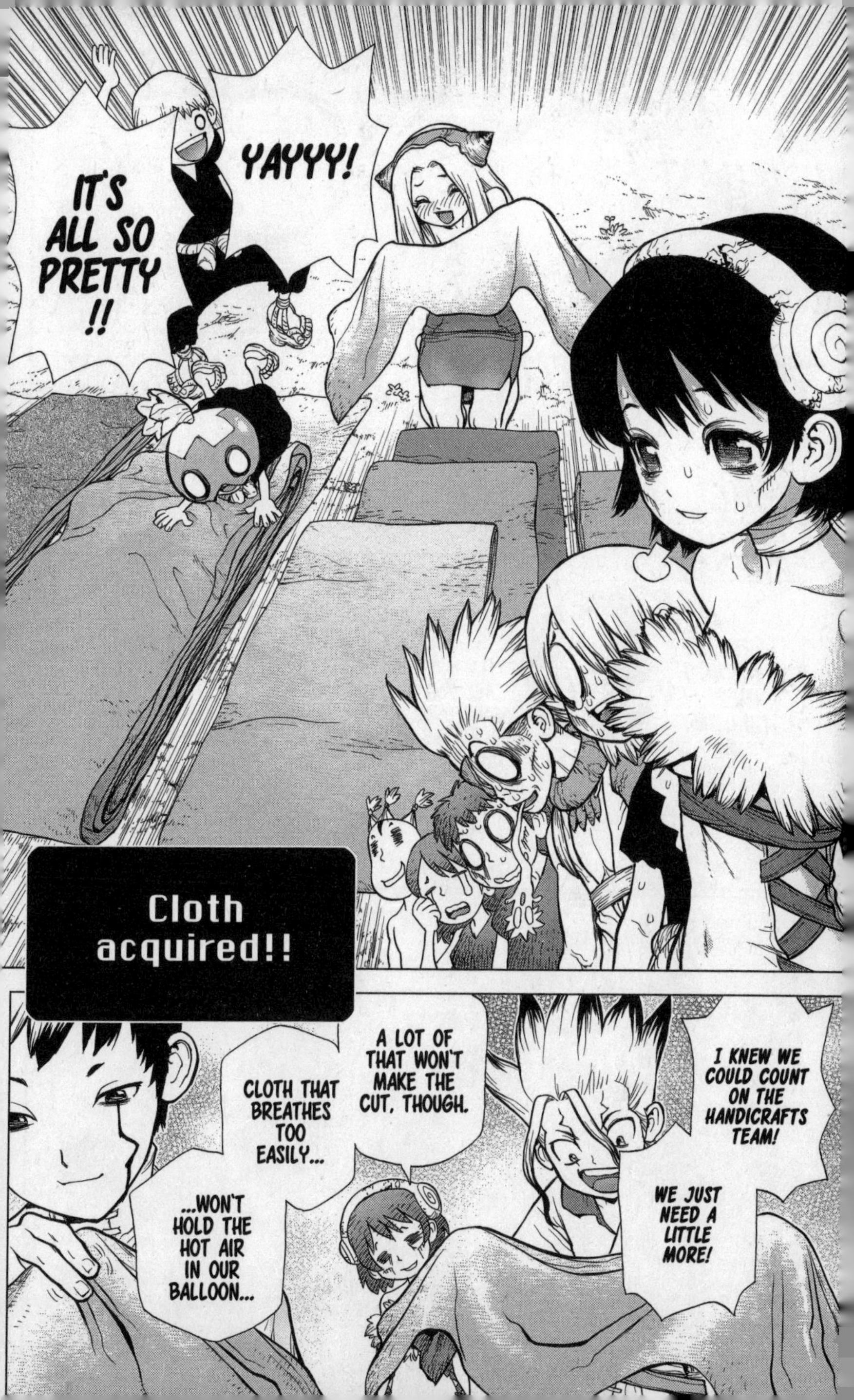
YAYYY!
IT'S ALL SO PRETTY !!
Cloth acquired!!
I KNEW WE COULD COUNT ON THE HANDICRAFTS TEAM!
WE JUST NEED A LITTLE MORE!
A LOT OF THAT WON'T MAKE THE CUT, THOUGH.
CLOTH THAT BREATHES TOO EASILY...
...WON'T HOLD THE HOT AIR IN OUR BALLOON...

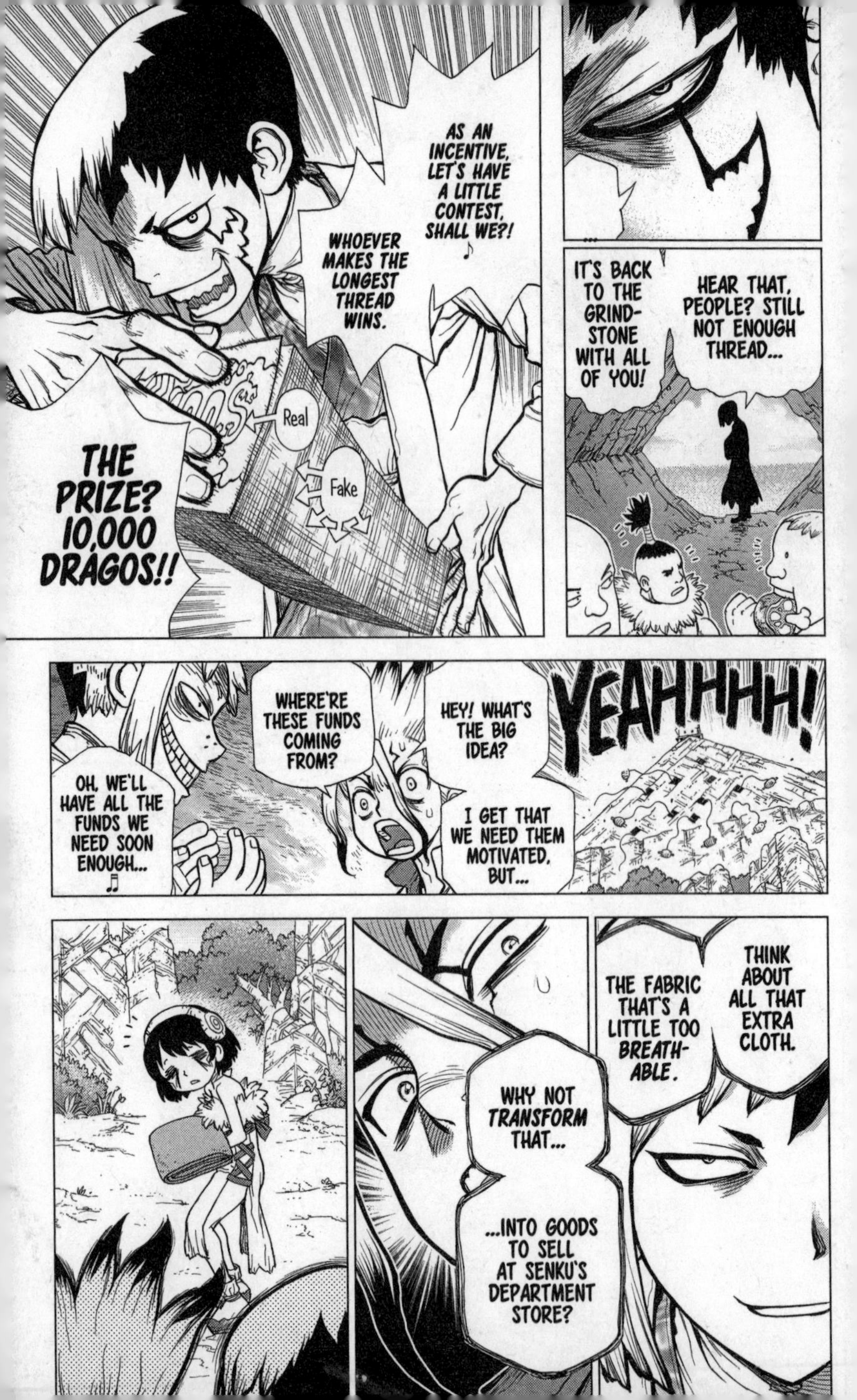
...
HEAR THAT, PEOPLE? STILL NOT ENOUGH THREAD...
IT'S BACK TO THE GRIND-STONE WITH ALL OF YOU!
AS AN INCENTIVE, LET'S HAVE A LITTLE CONTEST, SHALL WE?! ♪
WHOEVER MAKES THE LONGEST THREAD WINS.
Real
Fake
THE PRIZE? 10,000 DRAGOS!!
YEAHHHH!
HEY! WHAT'S THE BIG IDEA?
I GET THAT WE NEED THEM MOTIVATED, BUT...
WHERE'RE THESE FUNDS COMING FROM?
OH, WE'LL HAVE ALL THE FUNDS WE NEED SOON ENOUGH... ♫
THINK ABOUT ALL THAT EXTRA CLOTH.
THE FABRIC THAT'S A LITTLE TOO BREATHABLE.
WHY NOT TRANSFORM THAT...
...INTO GOODS TO SELL AT SENKU'S DEPARTMENT STORE?

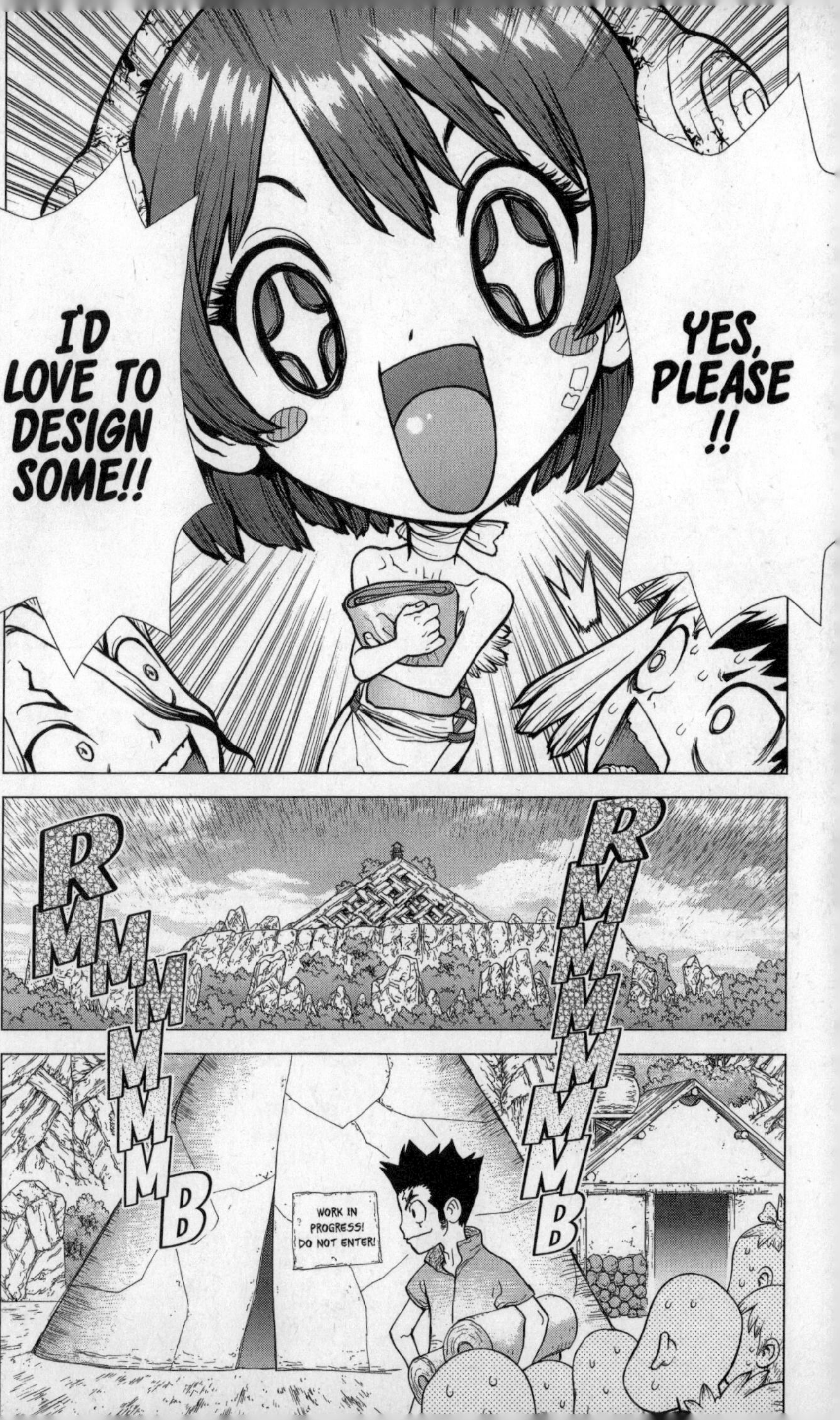
YES, PLEASE!!
I'D LOVE TO DESIGN SOME!!
RMMMMMMMMB
RMMMMMMMB
WORK IN PROGRESS! DO NOT ENTER!

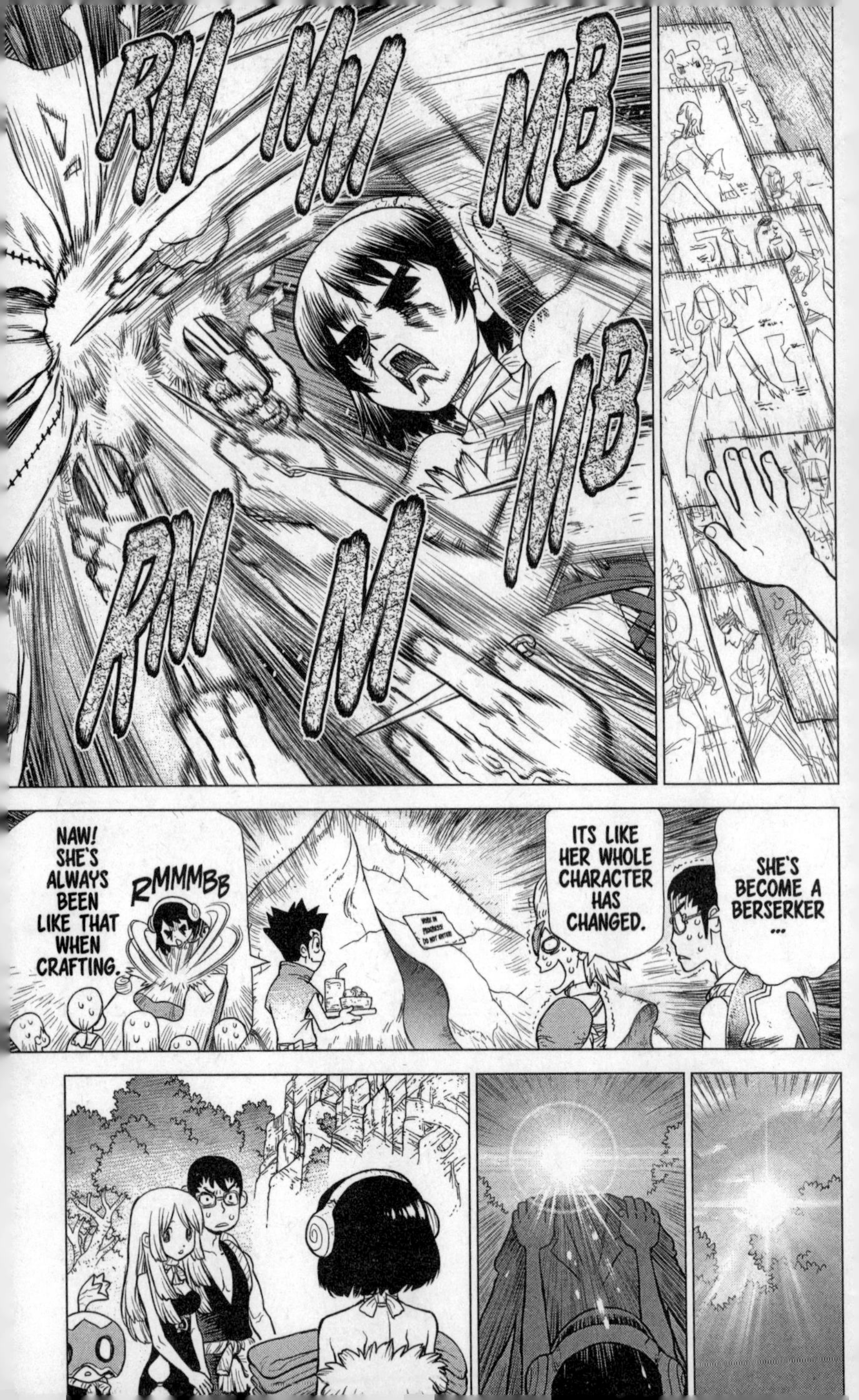
RMMMB
RMMMB
SHE'S BECOME A BERSERKER ...
ITS LIKE HER WHOLE CHARACTER HAS CHANGED.
RMMMBB
NAW! SHE'S ALWAYS BEEN LIKE THAT WHEN CRAFTING.

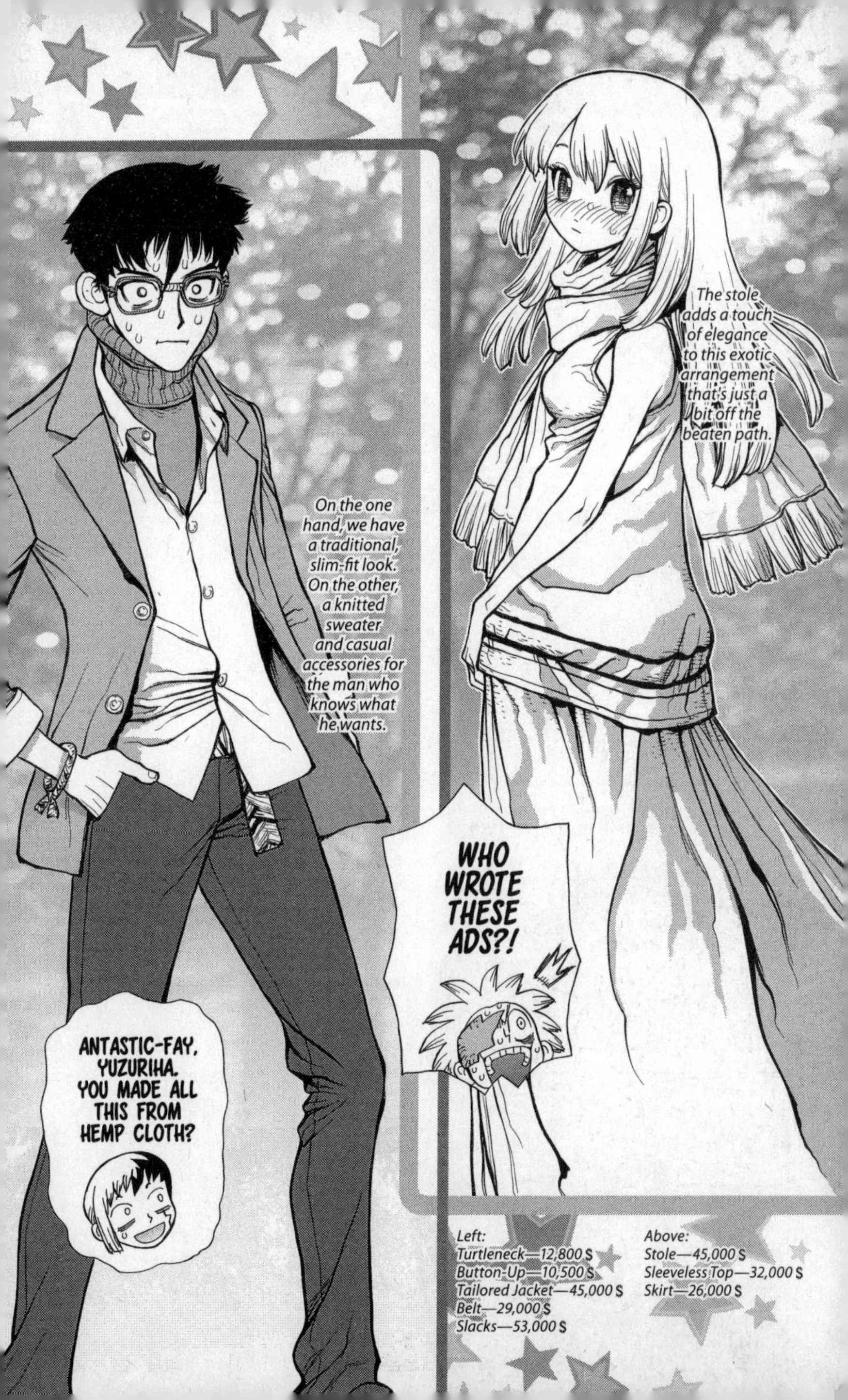
The stole adds a touch of elegance to this exotic arrangement that's just a bit off the beaten path.
WHO WROTE THESE ADS?!
Above:
Stole—45,000 $
Sleeveless Top—32,000 $
Skirt—26,000 $
On the one hand, we have a traditional, slim-fit look. On the other, a knitted sweater and casual accessories for the man who knows what he wants.
ANTASTIC-FAY, YUZURIHA. YOU MADE ALL THIS FROM HEMP CLOTH?
Left:
Turtleneck—12,800 $
Button-Up—10,500 $
Tailored Jacket—45,000 $
Belt—29,000 $
Slacks—53,000 $

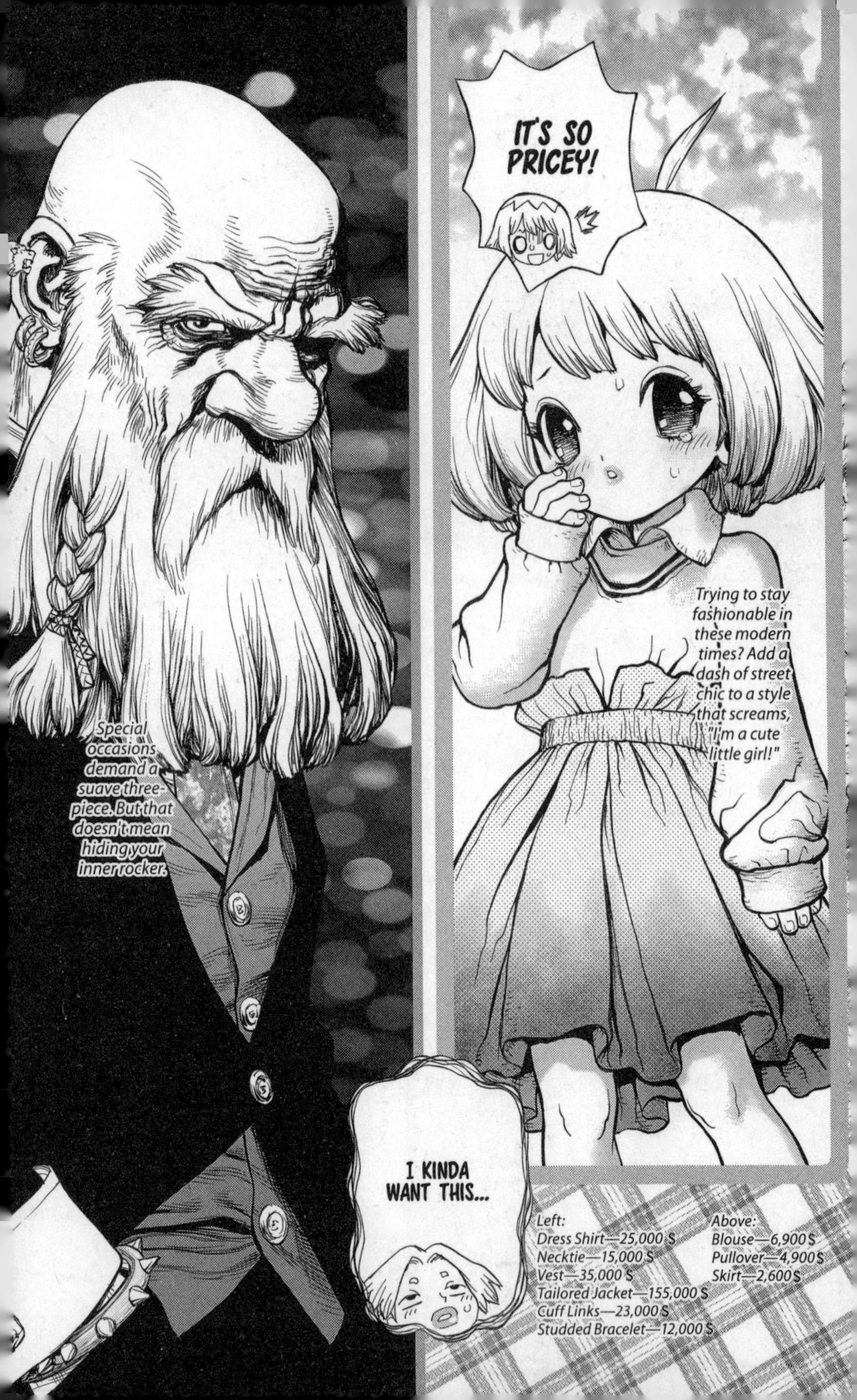
IT'S SO PRICEY!
Trying to stay fashionable in these modern times? Add a dash of street chic to a style that screams, "I'm a cute little girl!"
Left:
Dress Shirt—25,000 $
Necktie—15,000 $
Vest—35,000 $
Tailored Jacket—155,000 $
Cuff Links—23,000 $
Studded Bracelet—12,000 $
Above:
Blouse—6,900 $
Pullover—4,900 $
Skirt—2,600 $
I KINDA WANT THIS...
Special occasions demand a suave three-piece. But that doesn't mean hiding your inner rocker.

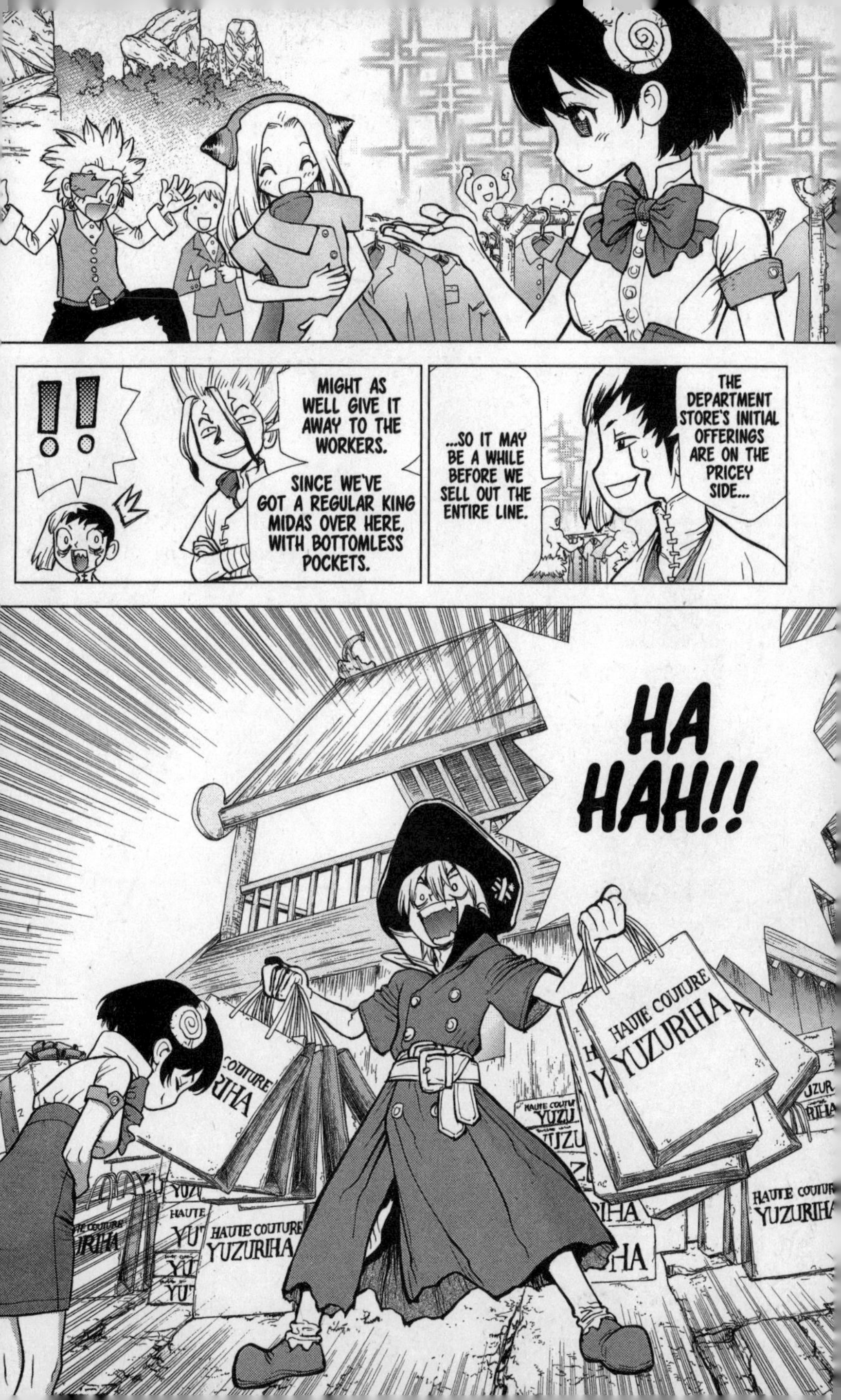
THE DEPARTMENT STORE'S INITIAL OFFERINGS ARE ON THE PRICEY SIDE...
...SO IT MAY BE A WHILE BEFORE WE SELL OUT THE ENTIRE LINE.
MIGHT AS WELL GIVE IT AWAY TO THE WORKERS.
SINCE WE'VE GOT A REGULAR KING MIDAS OVER HERE, WITH BOTTOMLESS POCKETS.
!!
HA HAH!!
HAUTE COUTURE YUZURIHA
HAUTE COUTURE YUZURIHA
HAUTE COUTURE YUZURIHA

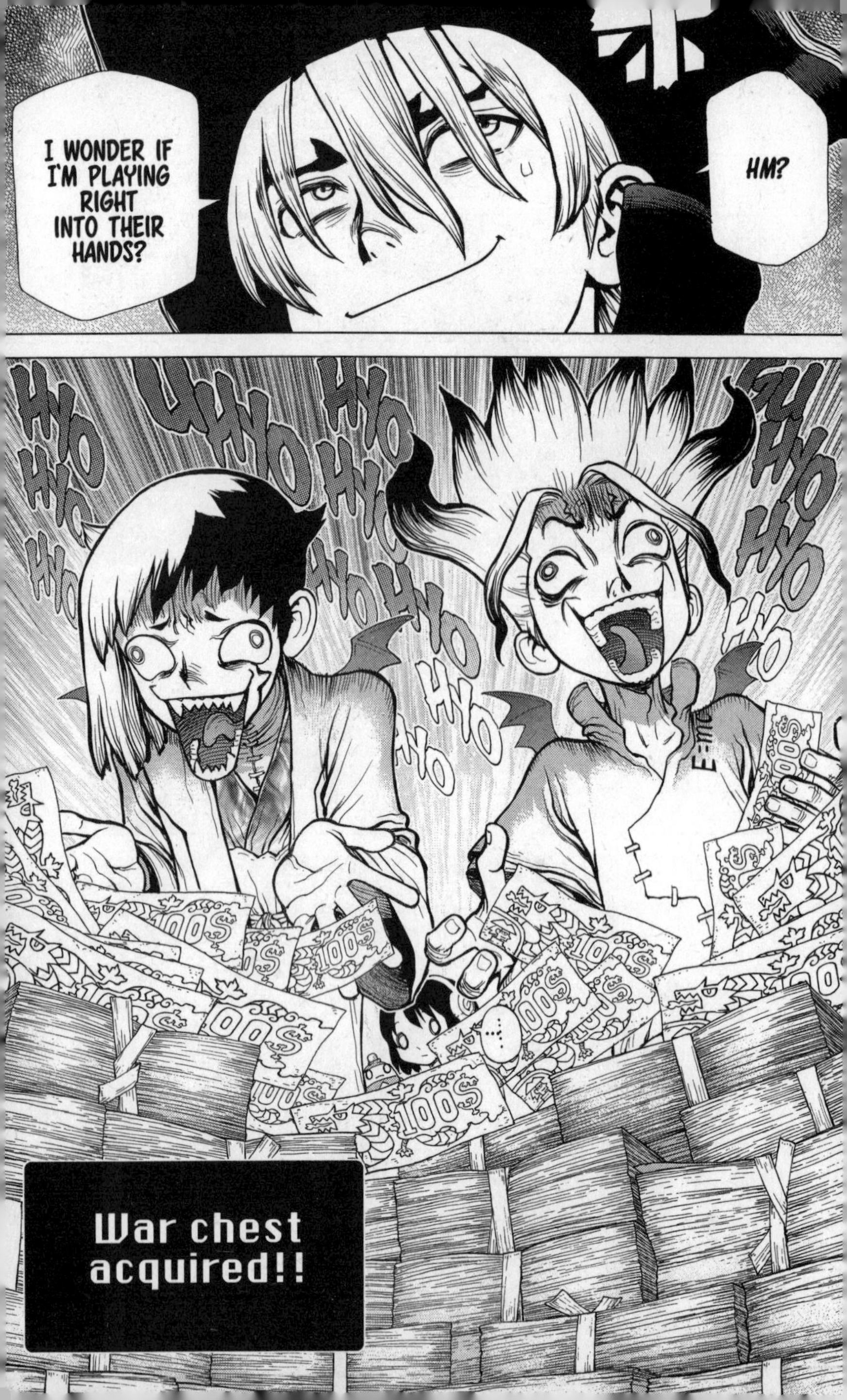
HM?
I WONDER IF I'M PLAYING RIGHT INTO THEIR HANDS?
UHYO HYO HYO
HYO HYO HYO
HYO HYO HYO
HYO HYO HYO
...
War chest acquired!!

Side Story

On Japanese New Year's

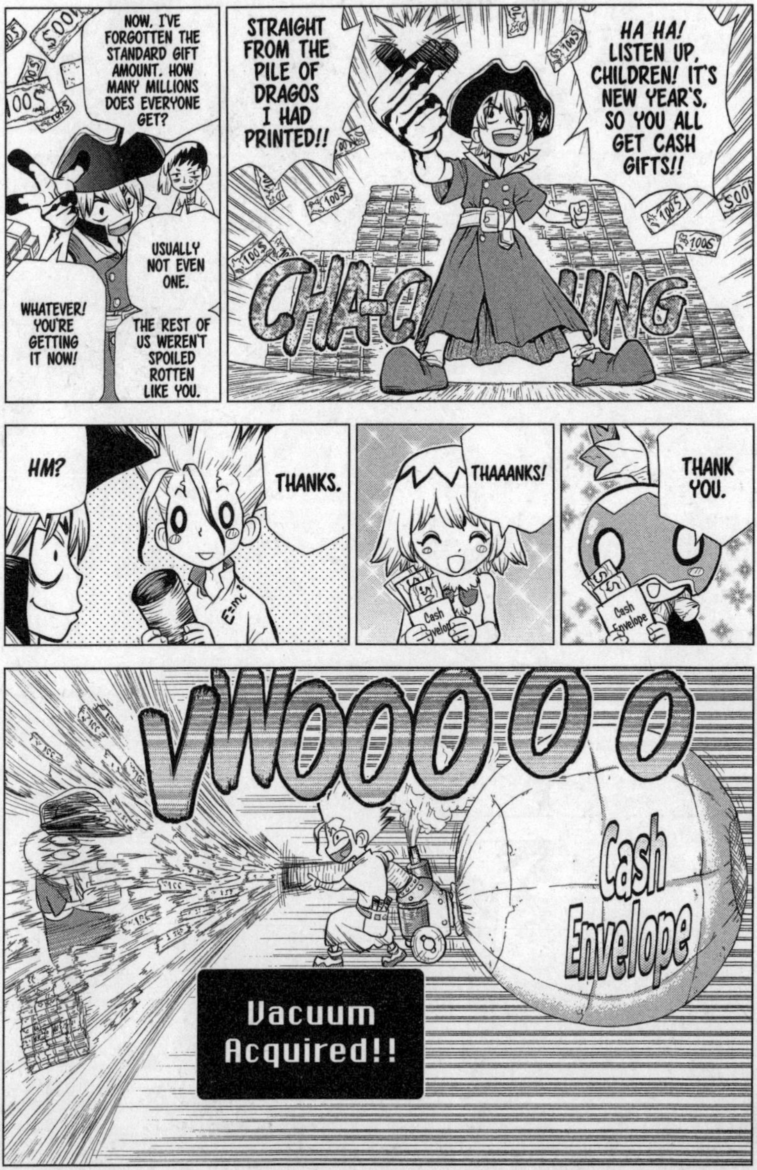
HA HA! LISTEN UP, CHILDREN! IT'S NEW YEAR'S, SO YOU ALL GET CASH GIFTS!!
STRAIGHT FROM THE PILE OF DRAGOS I HAD PRINTED!!
NOW, I'VE FORGOTTEN THE STANDARD GIFT AMOUNT. HOW MANY MILLIONS DOES EVERYONE GET?
USUALLY NOT EVEN ONE.
THE REST OF US WEREN'T SPOILED ROTTEN LIKE YOU.
WHATEVER! YOU'RE GETTING IT NOW!
THANK YOU.
THAAANKS!
THANKS.
HM?
VWOOOOOO
Cash Envelope
Vacuum Acquired!!

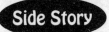

Z=88: Wings of Humanity

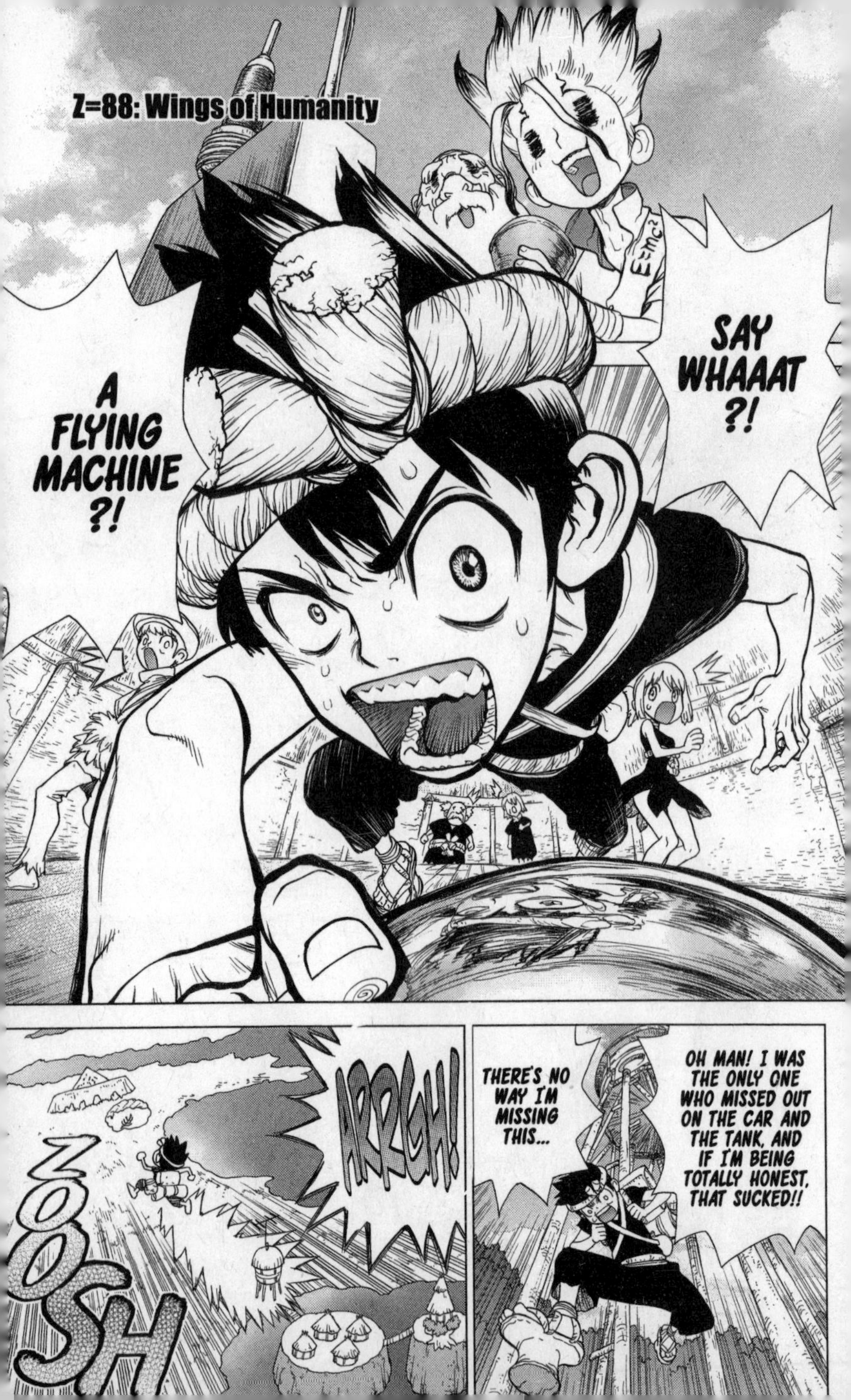
SAY WHAAAT?!
A FLYING MACHINE?!
OH MAN! I WAS THE ONLY ONE WHO MISSED OUT ON THE CAR AND THE TANK, AND IF I'M BEING TOTALLY HONEST, THAT SUCKED!!
THERE'S NO WAY I'M MISSING THIS...
ARRGH!
ZOOOSH

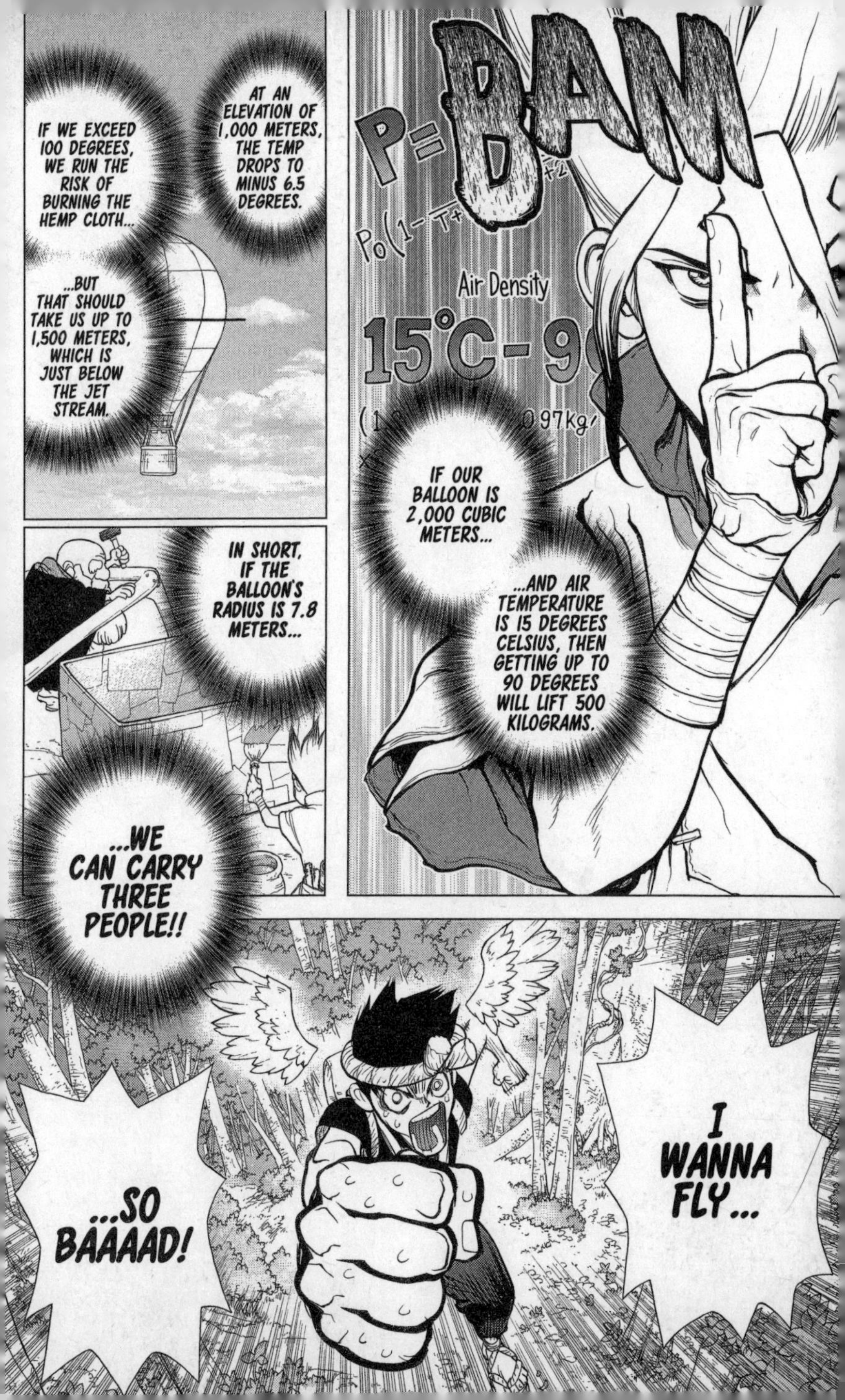
P=BAM
Air Density
IF OUR BALLOON IS 2,000 CUBIC METERS...
...AND AIR TEMPERATURE IS 15 DEGREES CELSIUS, THEN GETTING UP TO 90 DEGREES WILL LIFT 500 KILOGRAMS.
AT AN ELEVATION OF 1,000 METERS, THE TEMP DROPS TO MINUS 6.5 DEGREES.
IF WE EXCEED 100 DEGREES, WE RUN THE RISK OF BURNING THE HEMP CLOTH...
...BUT THAT SHOULD TAKE US UP TO 1,500 METERS, WHICH IS JUST BELOW THE JET STREAM.
IN SHORT, IF THE BALLOON'S RADIUS IS 7.8 METERS...
...WE CAN CARRY THREE PEOPLE!!
I WANNA FLY...
...SO BAAAAD!

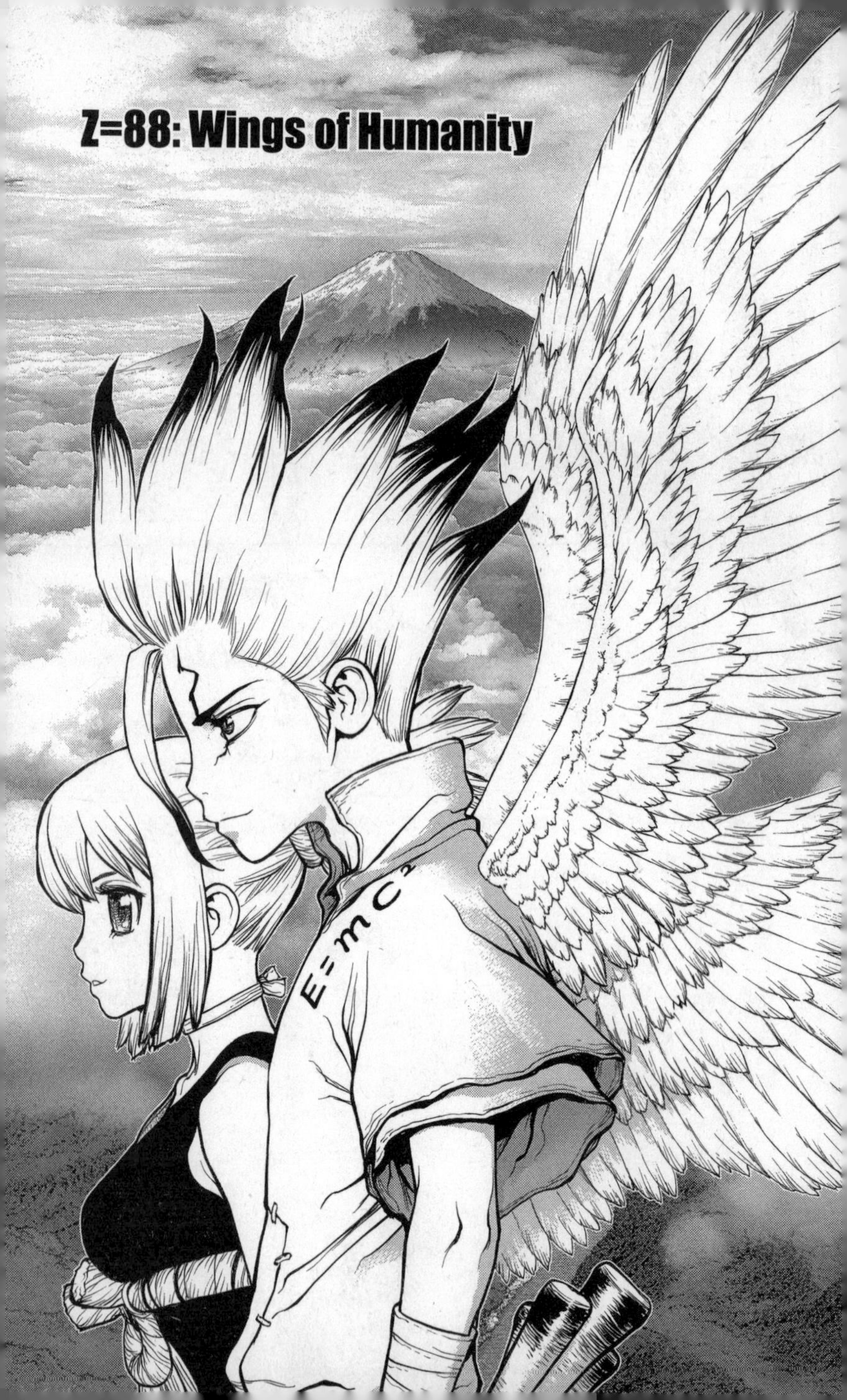
Z=88: Wings of Humanity
E=mc²

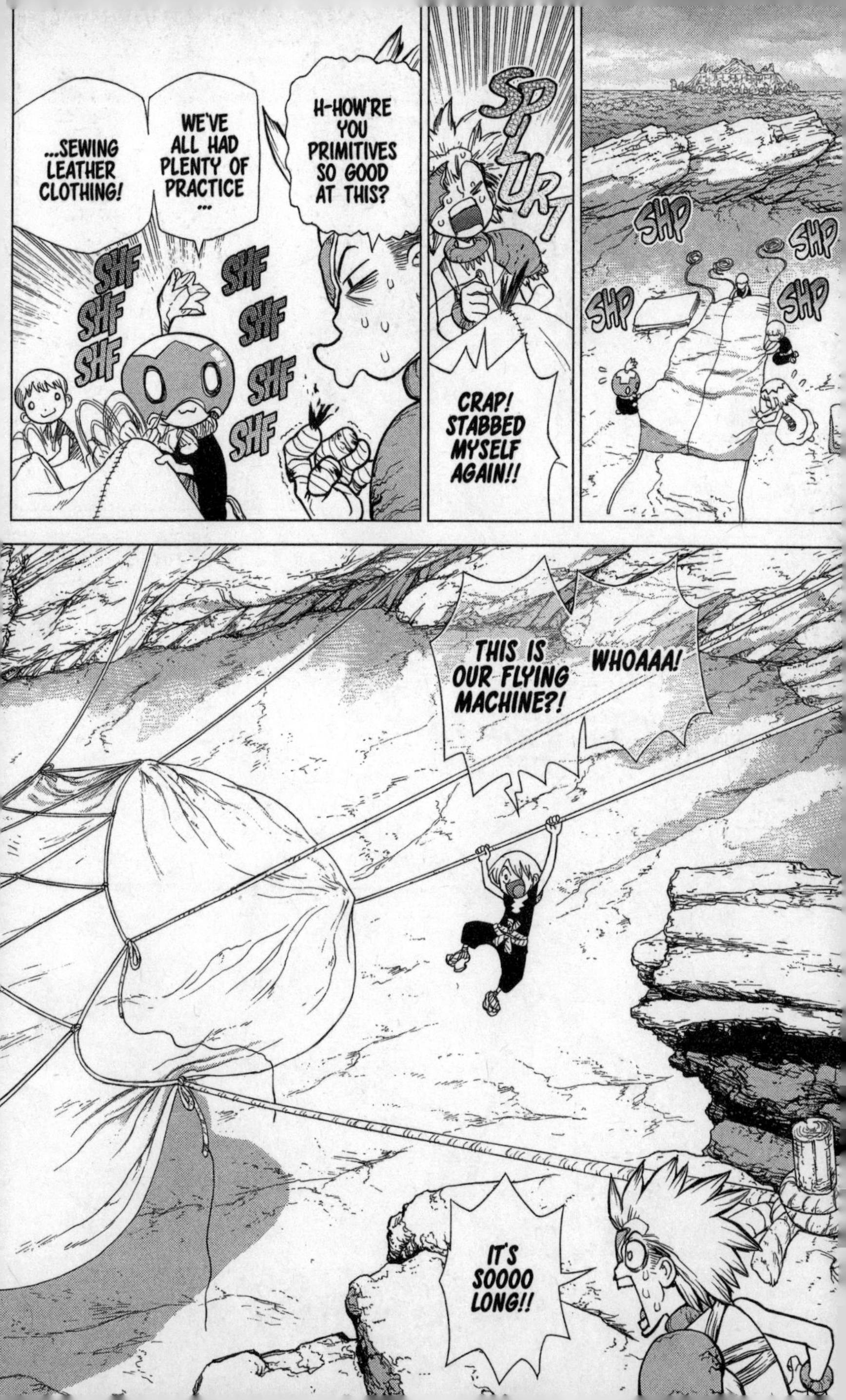
SHP
SHP
SHP
SHP
SPLURT
CRAP! STABBED MYSELF AGAIN!!
H-HOW'RE YOU PRIMITIVES SO GOOD AT THIS?
WE'VE ALL HAD PLENTY OF PRACTICE ...
...SEWING LEATHER CLOTHING!
SHF
SHF
SHF
SHF
SHF
SHF
SHF
WHOAAA!
THIS IS OUR FLYING MACHINE?!
IT'S SOOOO LONG!!

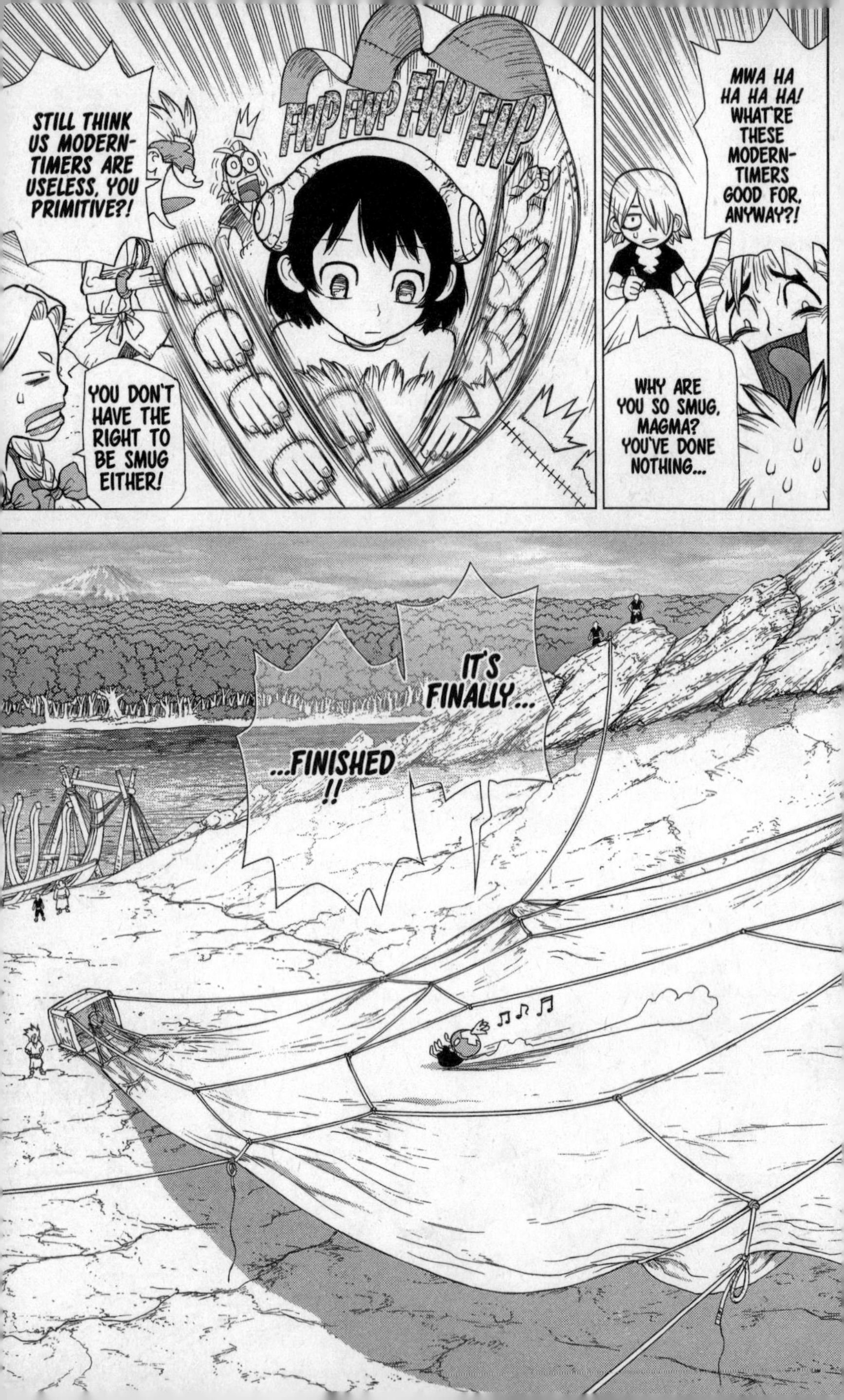
MWA HA HA HA HA! WHAT'RE THESE MODERN-TIMERS GOOD FOR, ANYWAY?!
WHY ARE YOU SO SMUG, MAGMA? YOU'VE DONE NOTHING...
FWP FWP FWP FWP
STILL THINK US MODERN-TIMERS ARE USELESS, YOU PRIMITIVE?!
YOU DON'T HAVE THE RIGHT TO BE SMUG EITHER!
IT'S FINALLY...
...FINISHED!!

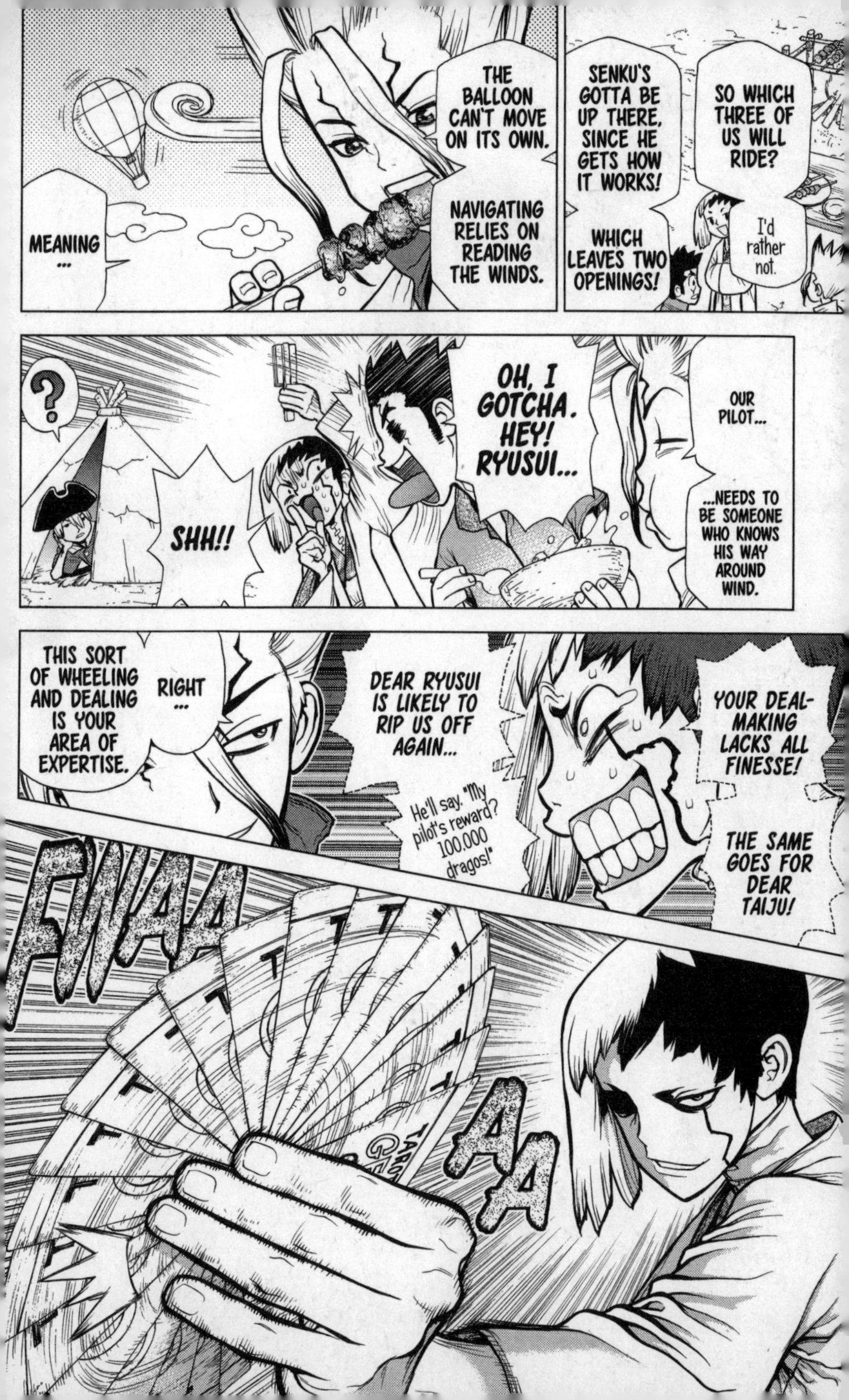
SO WHICH THREE OF US WILL RIDE?
I'd rather not.
SENKU'S GOTTA BE UP THERE, SINCE HE GETS HOW IT WORKS!
WHICH LEAVES TWO OPENINGS!
THE BALLOON CAN'T MOVE ON ITS OWN.
NAVIGATING RELIES ON READING THE WINDS.
MEANING ...
OUR PILOT...
...NEEDS TO BE SOMEONE WHO KNOWS HIS WAY AROUND WIND.
OH, I GOTCHA. HEY! RYUSUI...
SHH!!
?
YOUR DEAL-MAKING LACKS ALL FINESSE!
THE SAME GOES FOR DEAR TAIJU!
DEAR RYUSUI IS LIKELY TO RIP US OFF AGAIN...
He'll say, "My pilot's reward? 100,000 dragos!"
RIGHT ...
THIS SORT OF WHEELING AND DEALING IS YOUR AREA OF EXPERTISE.
FWAAAAA

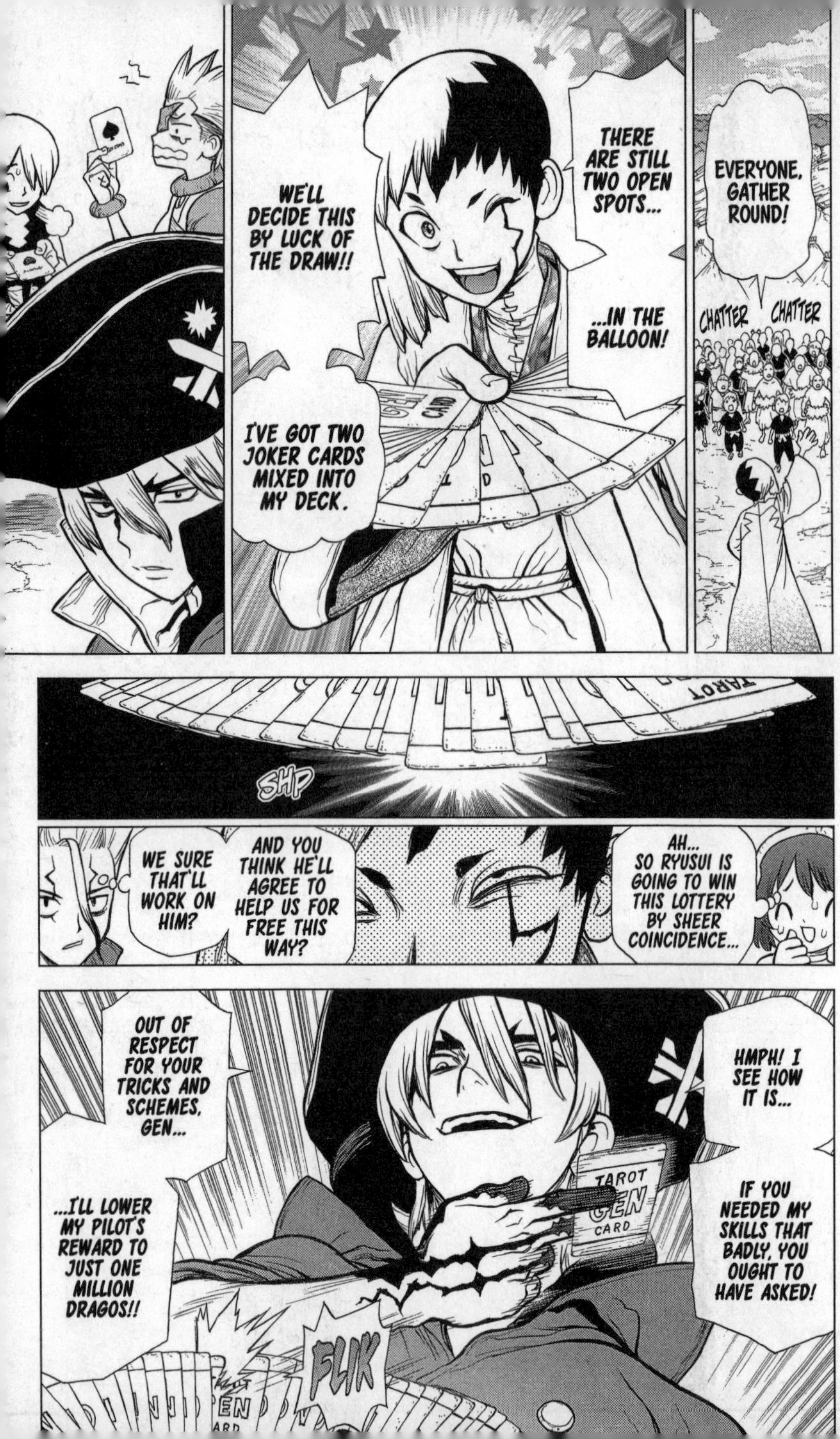
EVERYONE, GATHER ROUND!
CHATTER
CHATTER
THERE ARE STILL TWO OPEN SPOTS...
...IN THE BALLOON!
WE'LL DECIDE THIS BY LUCK OF THE DRAW!!
I'VE GOT TWO JOKER CARDS MIXED INTO MY DECK.
TAROT
SHP
AH... SO RYUSUI IS GOING TO WIN THIS LOTTERY BY SHEER COINCIDENCE...
AND YOU THINK HE'LL AGREE TO HELP US FOR FREE THIS WAY?
WE SURE THAT'LL WORK ON HIM?
HMPH! I SEE HOW IT IS...
IF YOU NEEDED MY SKILLS THAT BADLY, YOU OUGHT TO HAVE ASKED!
TAROT GEN CARD
OUT OF RESPECT FOR YOUR TRICKS AND SCHEMES, GEN...
...I'LL LOWER MY PILOT'S REWARD TO JUST ONE MILLION DRAGOS!!
FLIK

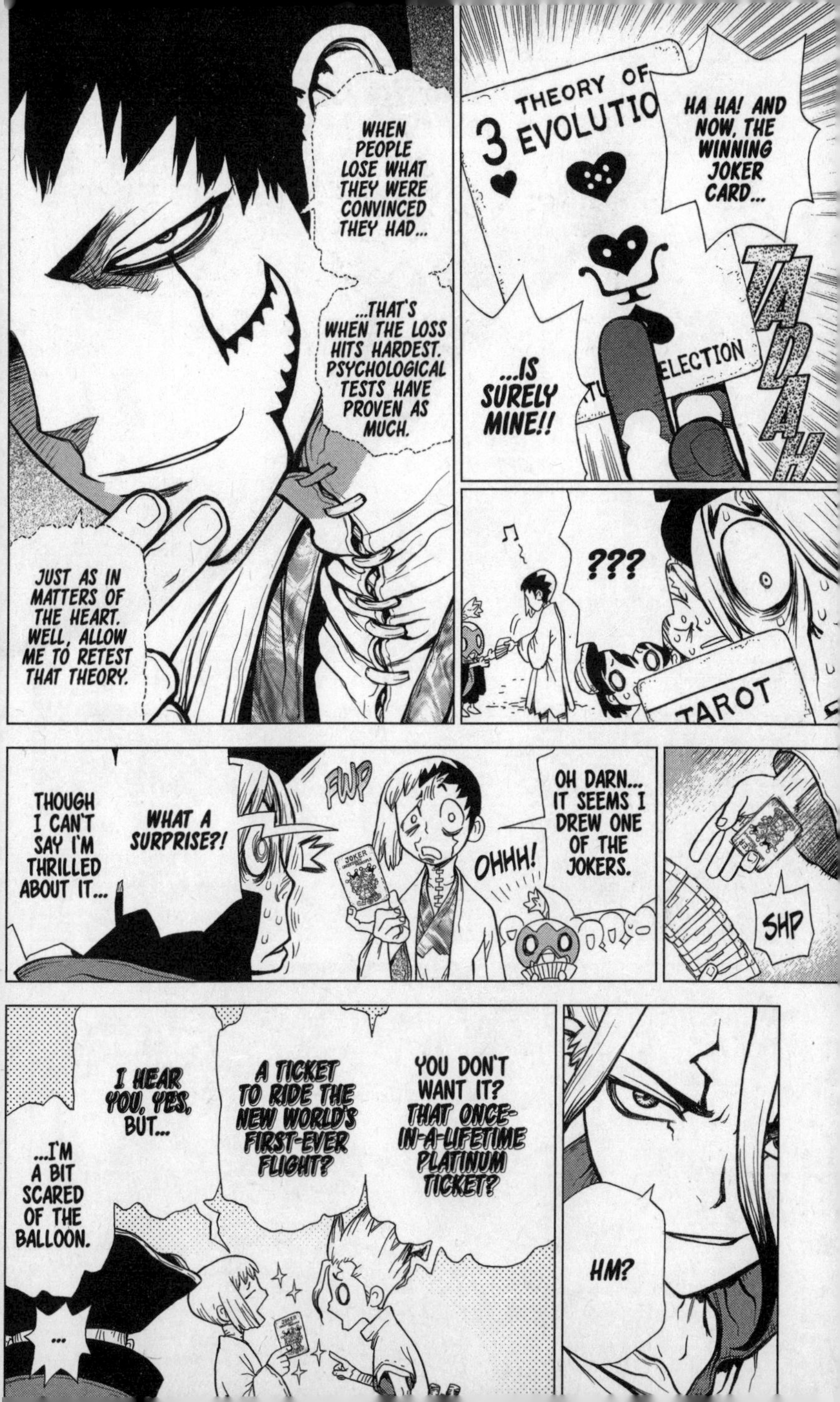
THEORY OF
3 EVOLUTIO
HA HA! AND NOW, THE WINNING JOKER CARD...
...IS SURELY MINE!!
ELECTION
TADAH
???
TAROT
WHEN PEOPLE LOSE WHAT THEY WERE CONVINCED THEY HAD...
...THAT'S WHEN THE LOSS HITS HARDEST. PSYCHOLOGICAL TESTS HAVE PROVEN AS MUCH.
JUST AS IN MATTERS OF THE HEART. WELL, ALLOW ME TO RETEST THAT THEORY.
SHP
OH DARN... IT SEEMS I DREW ONE OF THE JOKERS.
OHHH!
FWP
JOKER
WHAT A SURPRISE?!
THOUGH I CAN'T SAY I'M THRILLED ABOUT IT...
HM?
YOU DON'T WANT IT? THAT ONCE-IN-A-LIFETIME PLATINUM TICKET?
A TICKET TO RIDE THE NEW WORLD'S FIRST-EVER FLIGHT?
I HEAR YOU, YES, BUT...
...I'M A BIT SCARED OF THE BALLOON.
...

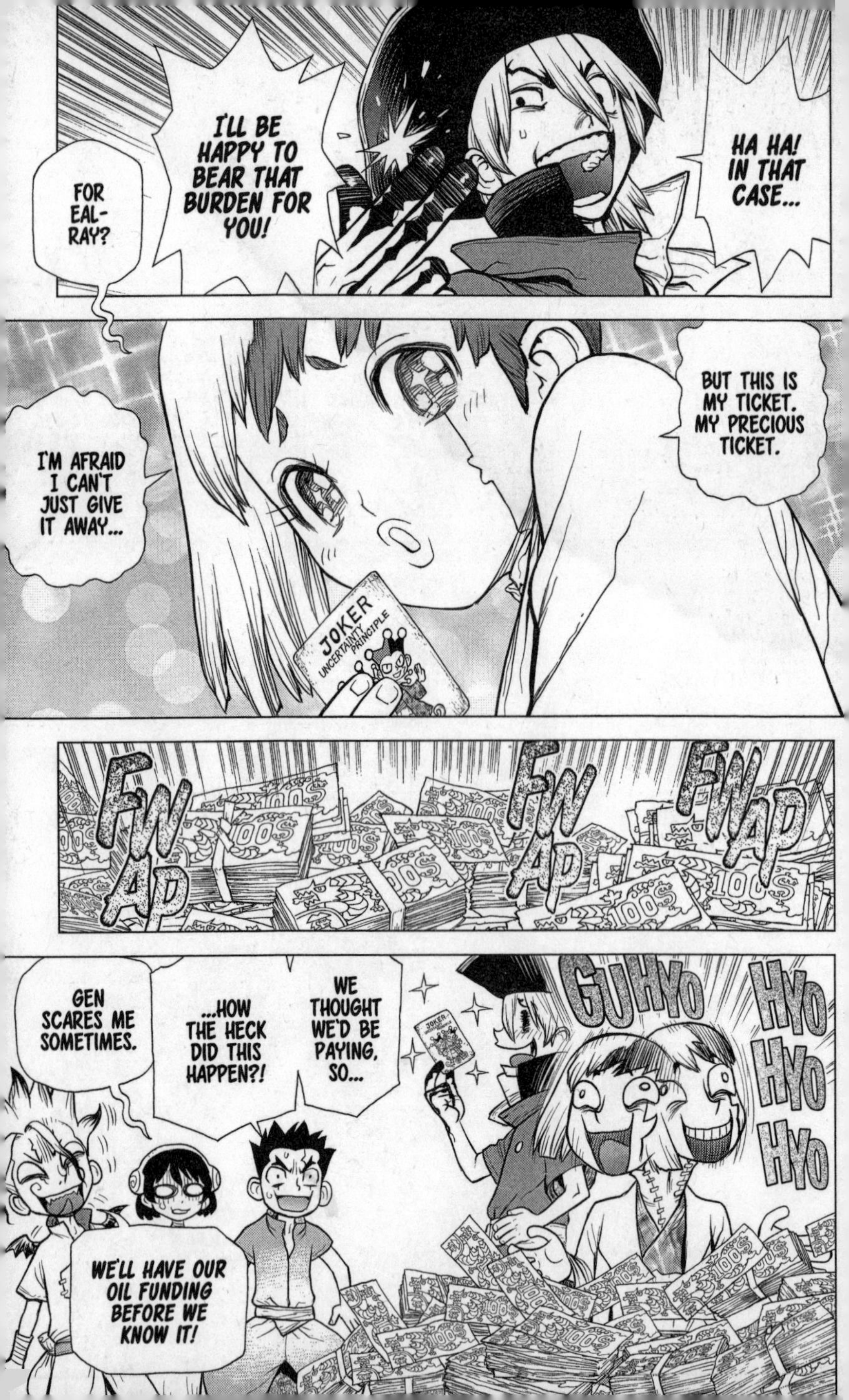
HA HA! IN THAT CASE...
I'LL BE HAPPY TO BEAR THAT BURDEN FOR YOU!
FOR EAL-RAY?
BUT THIS IS MY TICKET. MY PRECIOUS TICKET.
I'M AFRAID I CAN'T JUST GIVE IT AWAY...
JOKER
UNCERTAINTY PRINCIPLE
FWAP
FWAP
FWAP
100$
GUHYO
HYO HYO HYO
WE THOUGHT WE'D BE PAYING, SO...
...HOW THE HECK DID THIS HAPPEN?!
GEN SCARES ME SOMETIMES.
WE'LL HAVE OUR OIL FUNDING BEFORE WE KNOW IT!

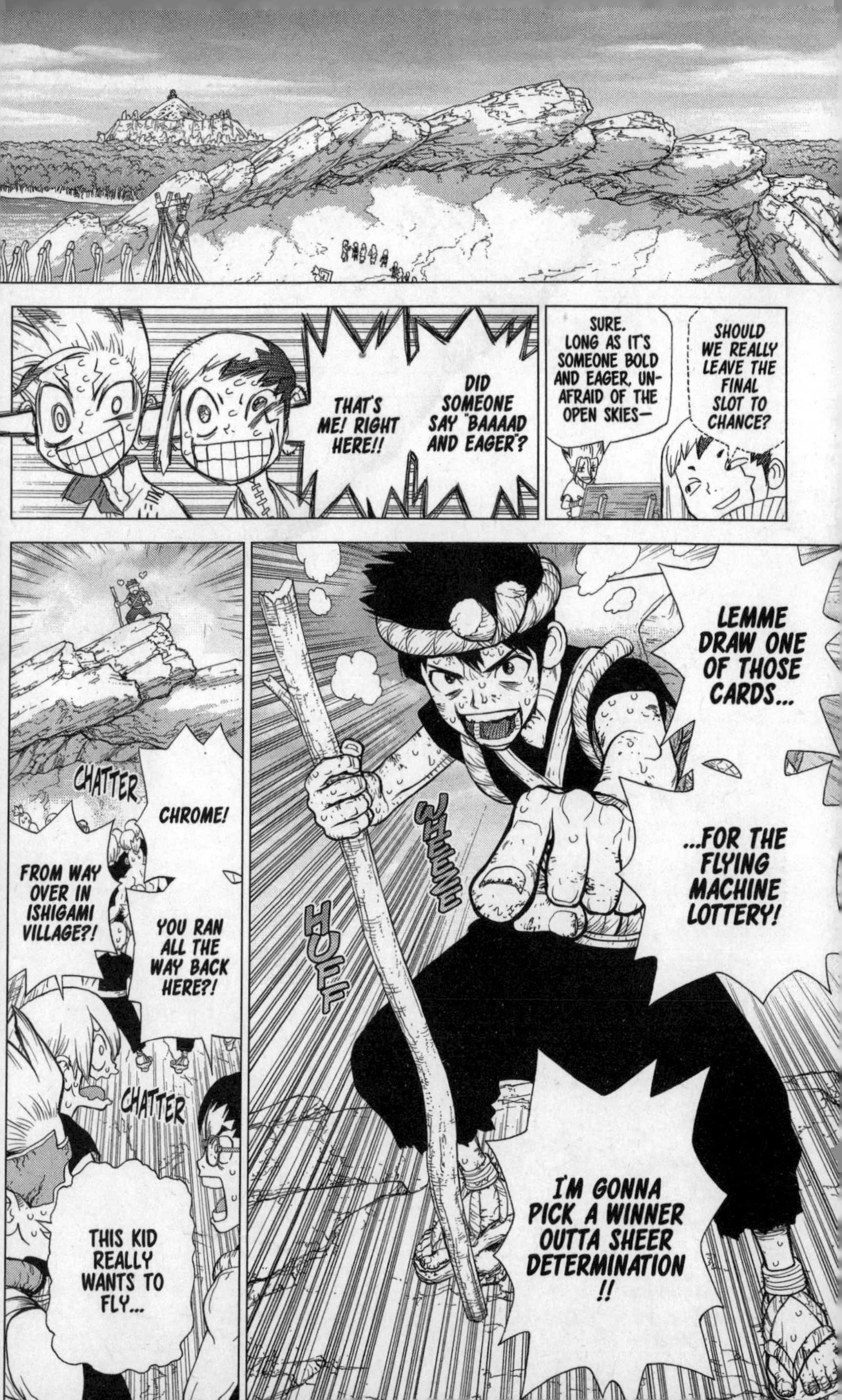
SHOULD WE REALLY LEAVE THE FINAL SLOT TO CHANCE?
SURE. LONG AS IT'S SOMEONE BOLD AND EAGER, UN-AFRAID OF THE OPEN SKIES—
DID SOMEONE SAY "BAAAAD AND EAGER"?
THAT'S ME! RIGHT HERE!!
LEMME DRAW ONE OF THOSE CARDS...
...FOR THE FLYING MACHINE LOTTERY!
WHEEZE
HUFF
I'M GONNA PICK A WINNER OUTTA SHEER DETERMINATION !!
CHATTER
CHROME!
FROM WAY OVER IN ISHIGAMI VILLAGE?!
YOU RAN ALL THE WAY BACK HERE?!
CHATTER
THIS KID REALLY WANTS TO FLY...

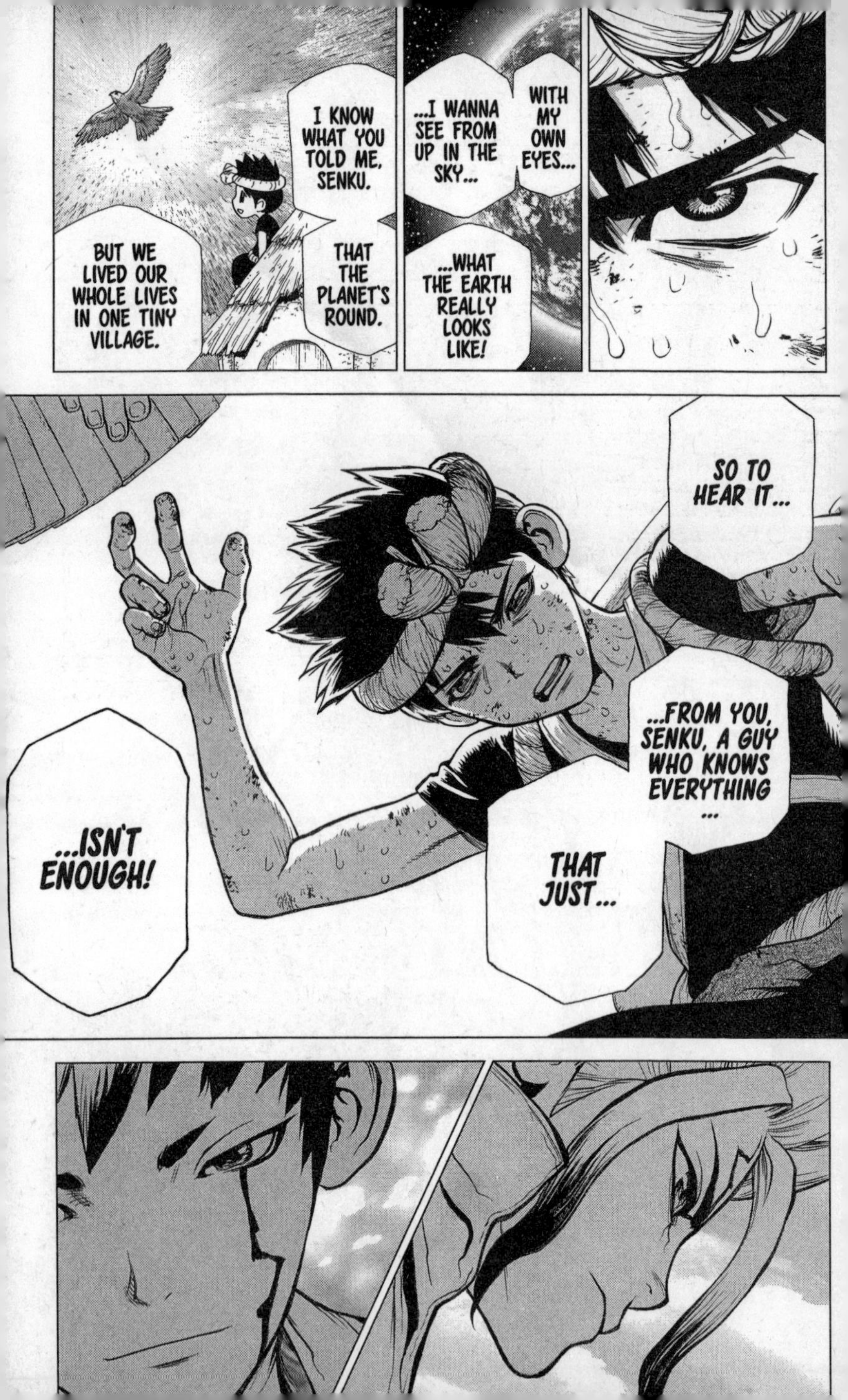
WITH MY OWN EYES...
...I WANNA SEE FROM UP IN THE SKY...
...WHAT THE EARTH REALLY LOOKS LIKE!
I KNOW WHAT YOU TOLD ME, SENKU.
THAT THE PLANET'S ROUND.
BUT WE LIVED OUR WHOLE LIVES IN ONE TINY VILLAGE.
SO TO HEAR IT...
...FROM YOU, SENKU, A GUY WHO KNOWS EVERYTHING...
THAT JUST...
...ISN'T ENOUGH!

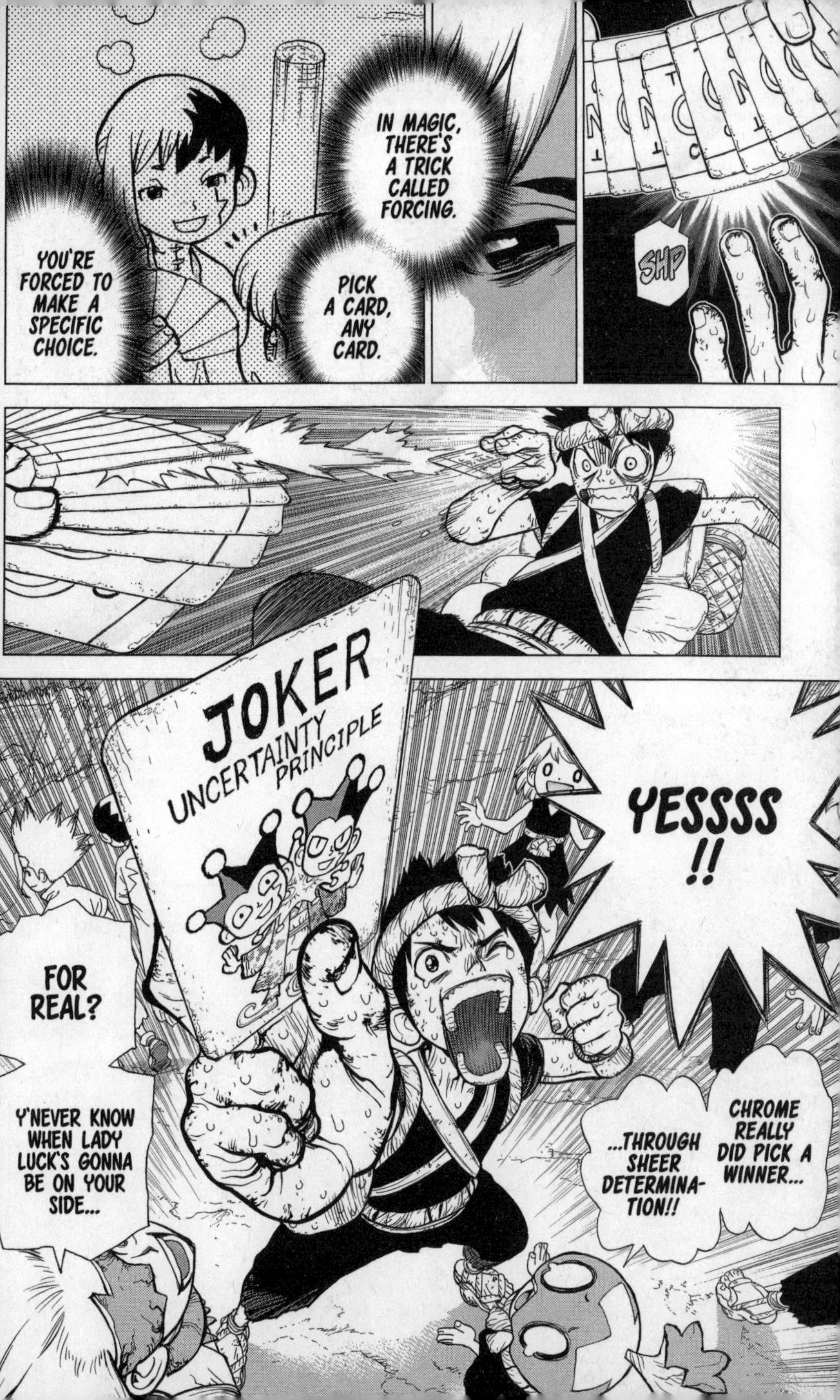
SHP
IN MAGIC, THERE'S A TRICK CALLED FORCING.
PICK A CARD, ANY CARD.
YOU'RE FORCED TO MAKE A SPECIFIC CHOICE.
YESSSS!!
JOKER
UNCERTAINTY PRINCIPLE
FOR REAL?
CHROME REALLY DID PICK A WINNER...
...THROUGH SHEER DETERMINATION!!
Y'NEVER KNOW WHEN LADY LUCK'S GONNA BE ON YOUR SIDE...

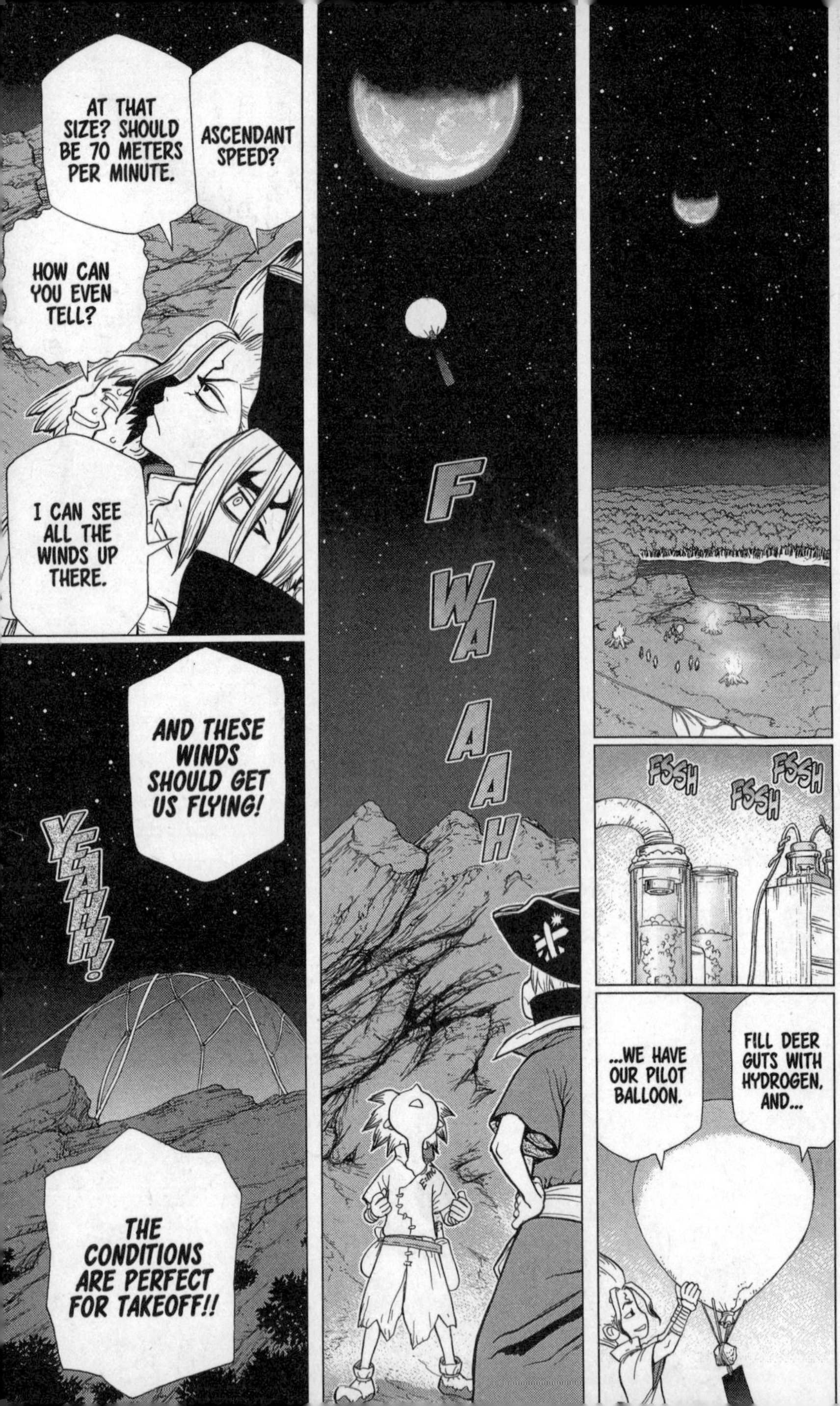
FSSH
FSSH
FSSH
FILL DEER GUTS WITH HYDROGEN, AND...
...WE HAVE OUR PILOT BALLOON.
FWAAAAH
ASCENDANT SPEED?
AT THAT SIZE? SHOULD BE 70 METERS PER MINUTE.
HOW CAN YOU EVEN TELL?
I CAN SEE ALL THE WINDS UP THERE.
AND THESE WINDS SHOULD GET US FLYING!
YEAHH!
THE CONDITIONS ARE PERFECT FOR TAKEOFF!!

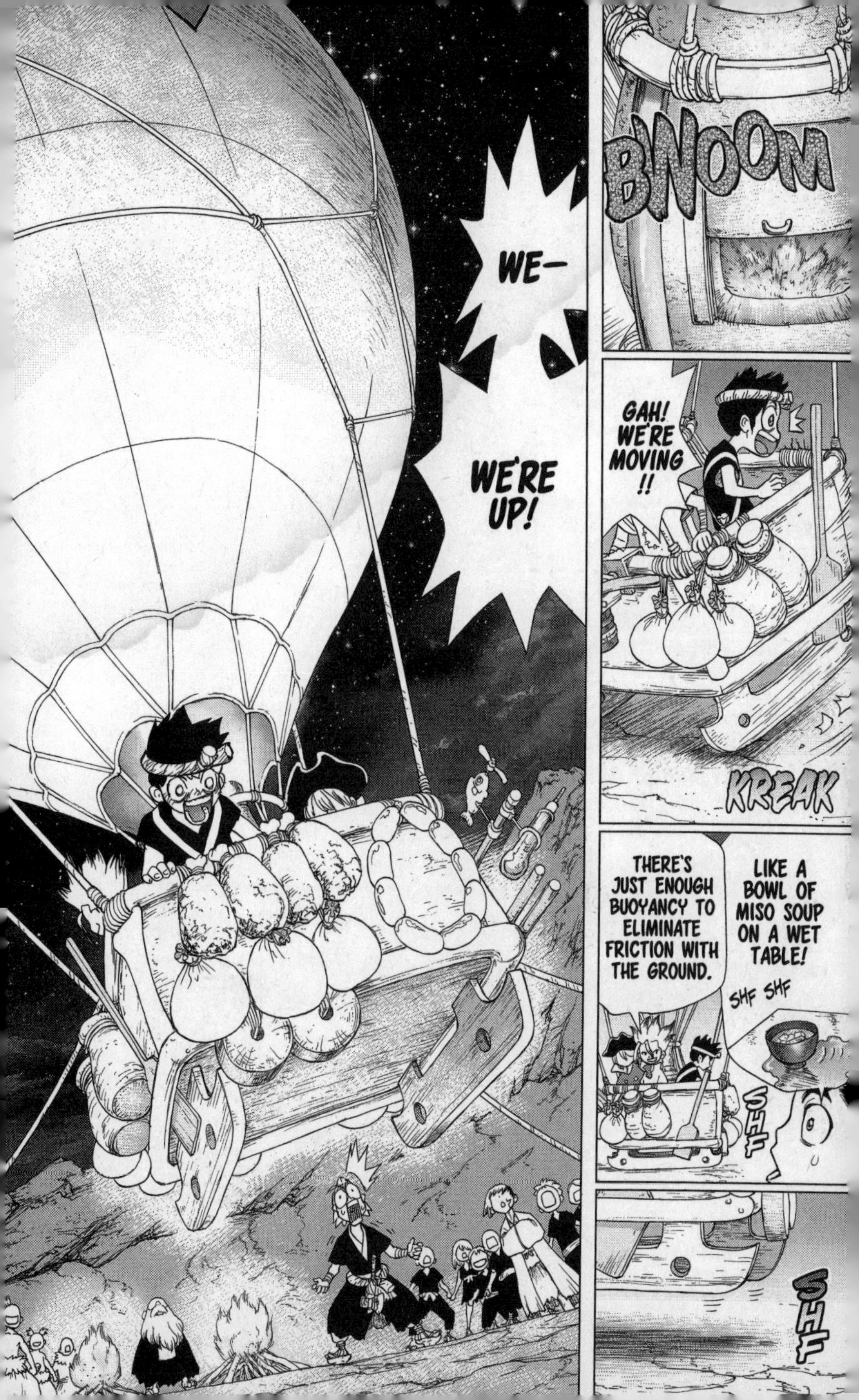
BNOOM
GAH! WE'RE MOVING!!
KREAK
THERE'S JUST ENOUGH BUOYANCY TO ELIMINATE FRICTION WITH THE GROUND.
LIKE A BOWL OF MISO SOUP ON A WET TABLE!
SHF SHF
SHF
SHF
WE—
WE'RE UP!

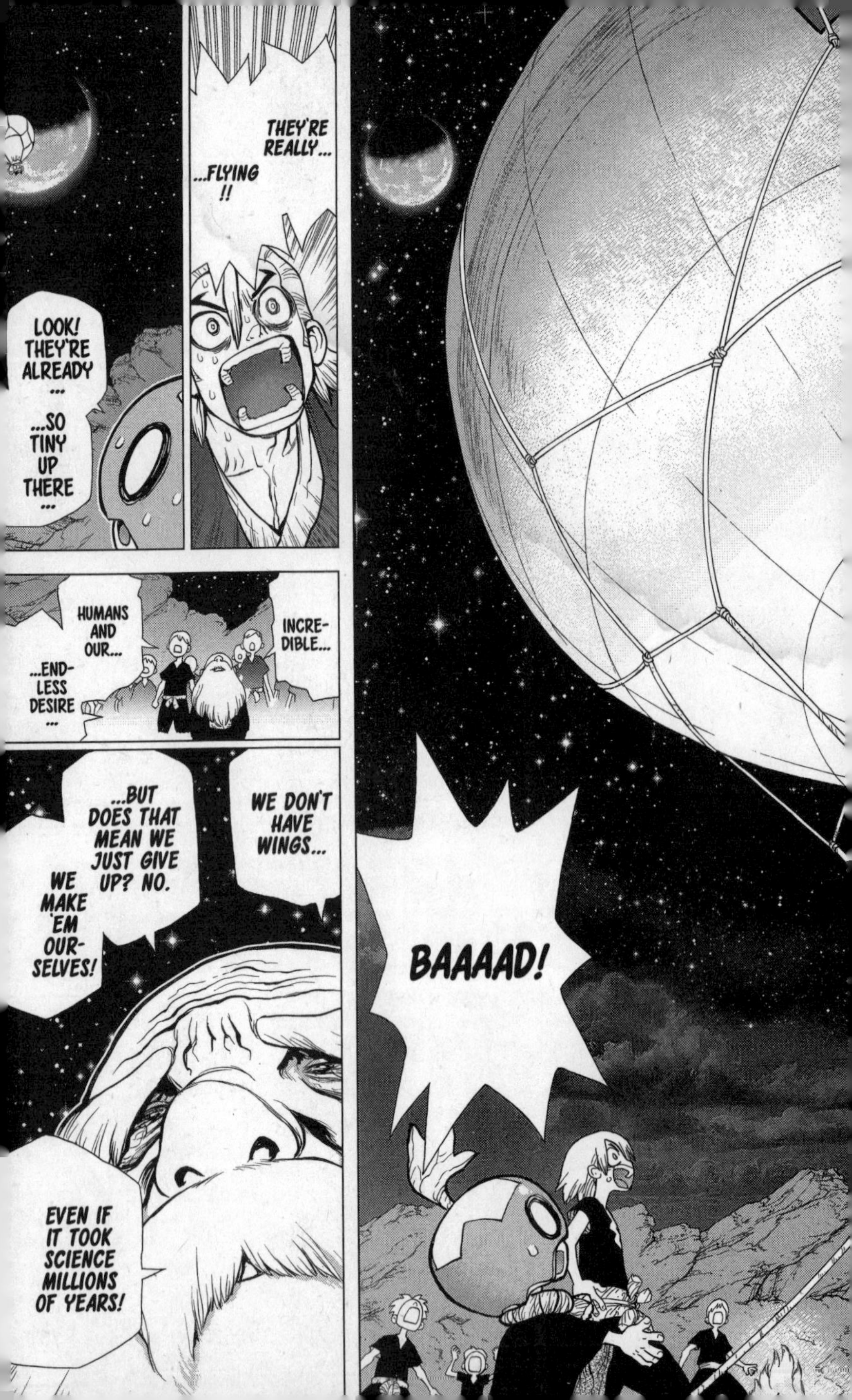
BAAAAD!
THEY'RE REALLY...
...FLYING !!
LOOK! THEY'RE ALREADY...
...SO TINY UP THERE...
INCREDIBLE...
HUMANS AND OUR...
...ENDLESS DESIRE...
WE DON'T HAVE WINGS...
...BUT DOES THAT MEAN WE JUST GIVE UP? NO.
WE MAKE 'EM OURSELVES!
EVEN IF IT TOOK SCIENCE MILLIONS OF YEARS!

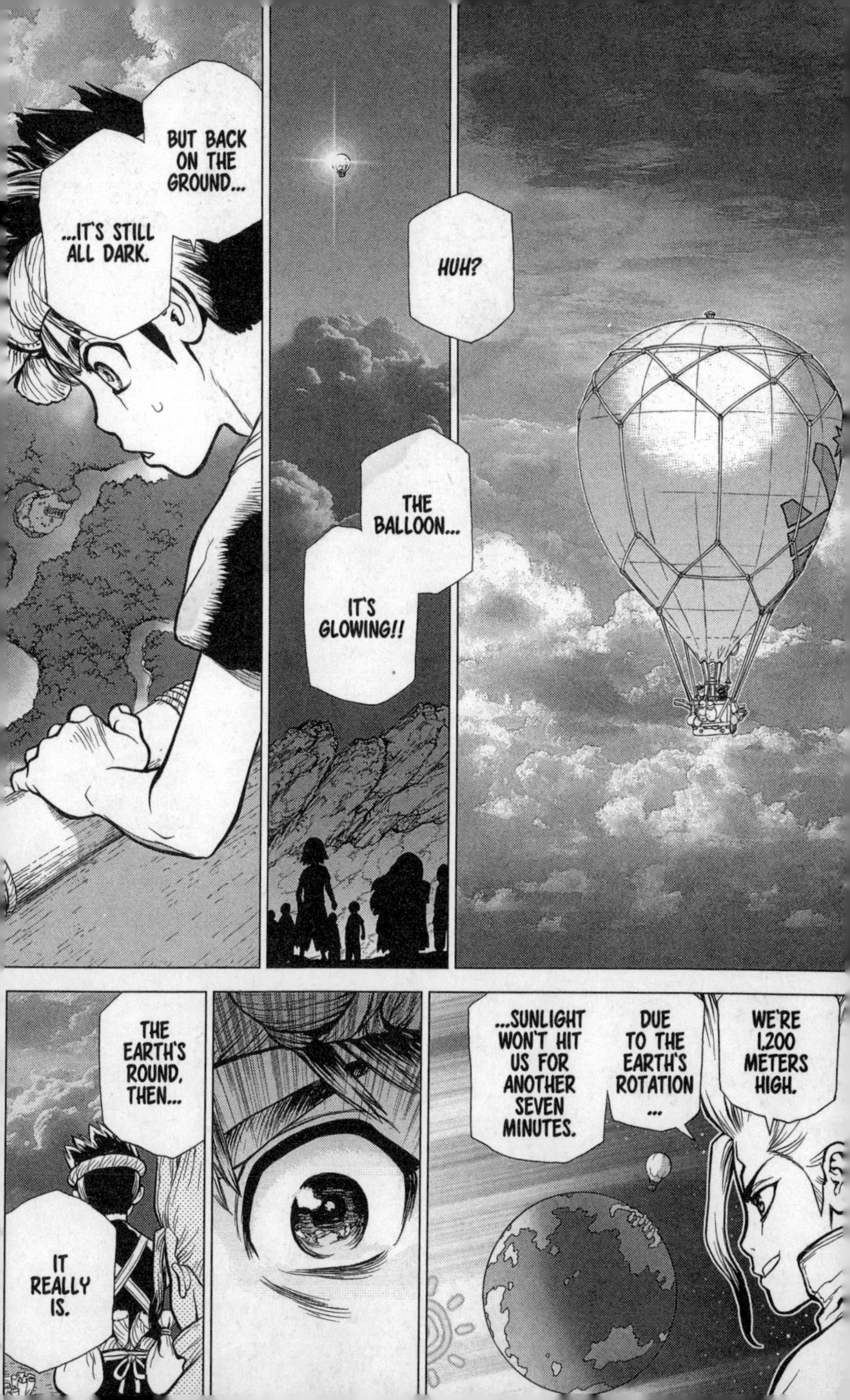
HUH?
THE BALLOON...
IT'S GLOWING!!
BUT BACK ON THE GROUND...
...IT'S STILL ALL DARK.
WE'RE 1,200 METERS HIGH.
DUE TO THE EARTH'S ROTATION...
...SUNLIGHT WON'T HIT US FOR ANOTHER SEVEN MINUTES.
THE EARTH'S ROUND, THEN...
IT REALLY IS.

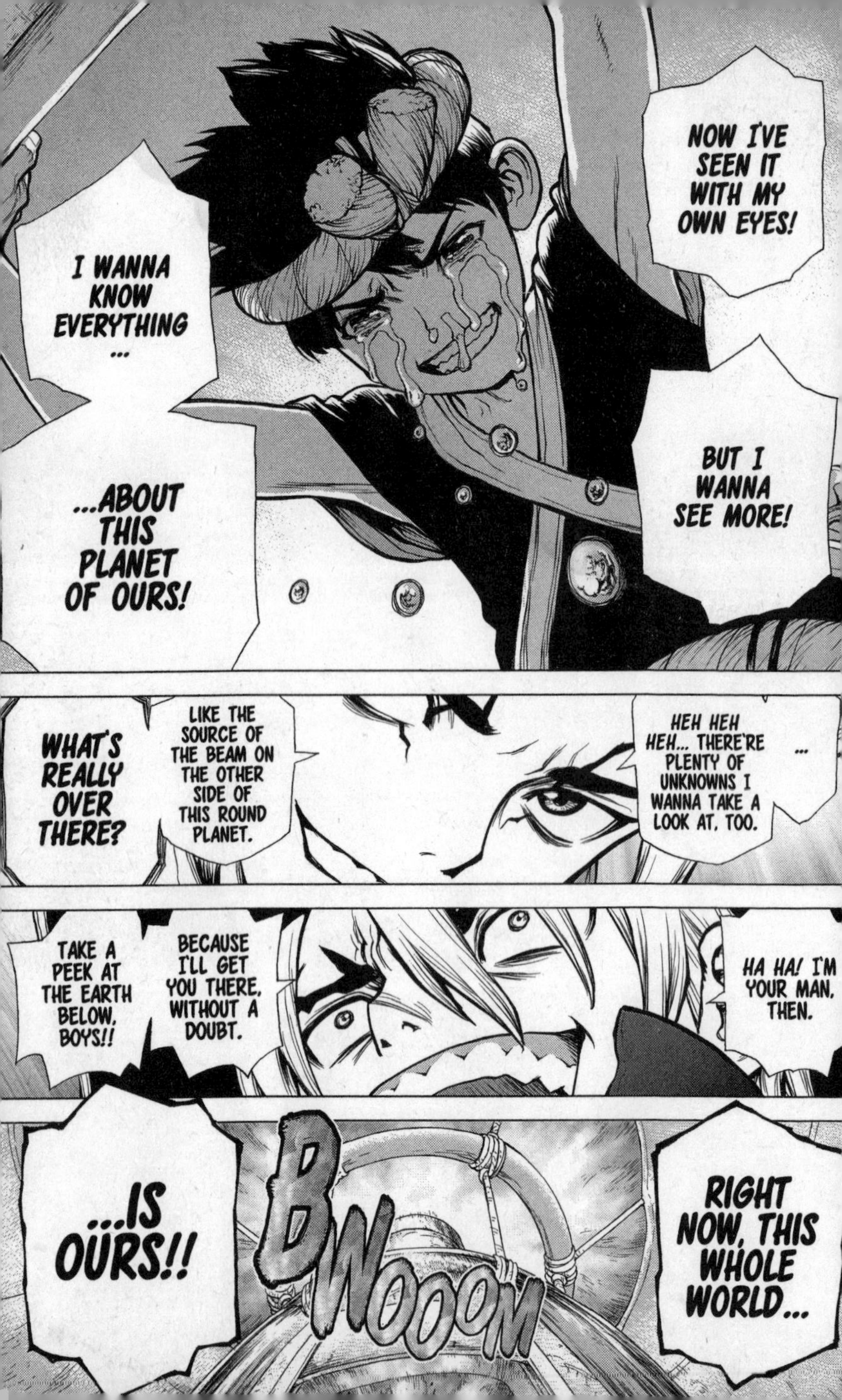
NOW I'VE SEEN IT WITH MY OWN EYES!
BUT I WANNA SEE MORE!
I WANNA KNOW EVERYTHING ...
...ABOUT THIS PLANET OF OURS!
HEH HEH HEH... THERE'RE PLENTY OF UNKNOWNS I WANNA TAKE A LOOK AT, TOO.
...
LIKE THE SOURCE OF THE BEAM ON THE OTHER SIDE OF THIS ROUND PLANET.
WHAT'S REALLY OVER THERE?
HA HA! I'M YOUR MAN, THEN.
BECAUSE I'LL GET YOU THERE, WITHOUT A DOUBT.
TAKE A PEEK AT THE EARTH BELOW, BOYS!!
RIGHT NOW, THIS WHOLE WORLD...
BWOOOM
...IS OURS!!

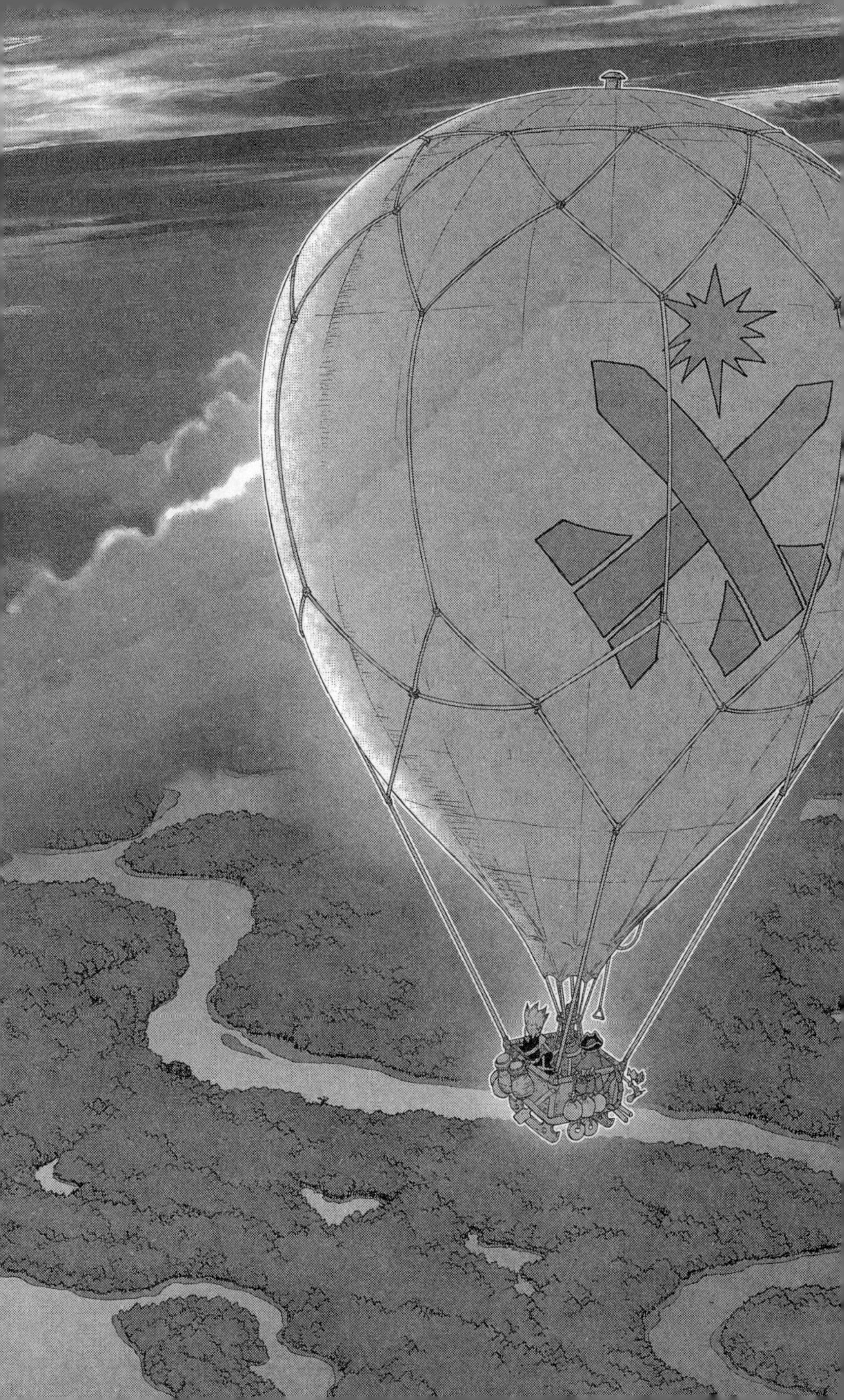

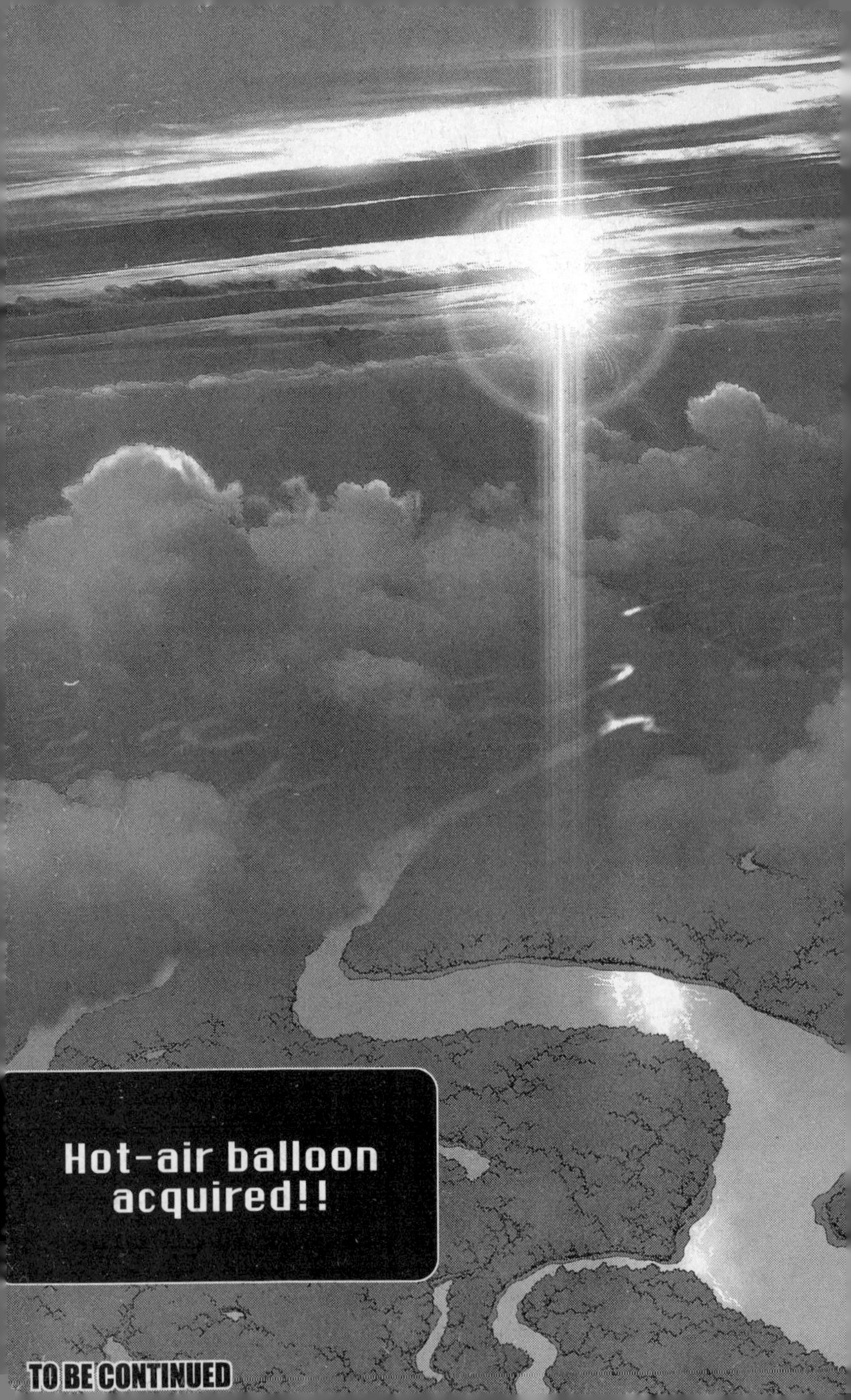
Hot-air balloon acquired!!
TO BE CONTINUED

DEMON SLAYER

KIMETSU NO YAIBA

Story and Art by
KOYOHARU GOTOUGE

In Taisho-era Japan, kindhearted Tanjiro Kamado makes a living selling charcoal. But his peaceful life is shattered when a demon slaughters his entire family. His little sister Nezuko is the only survivor, but she has been transformed into a demon herself! Tanjiro sets out on a dangerous journey to find a way to return his sister to normal and destroy the demon who ruined his life.

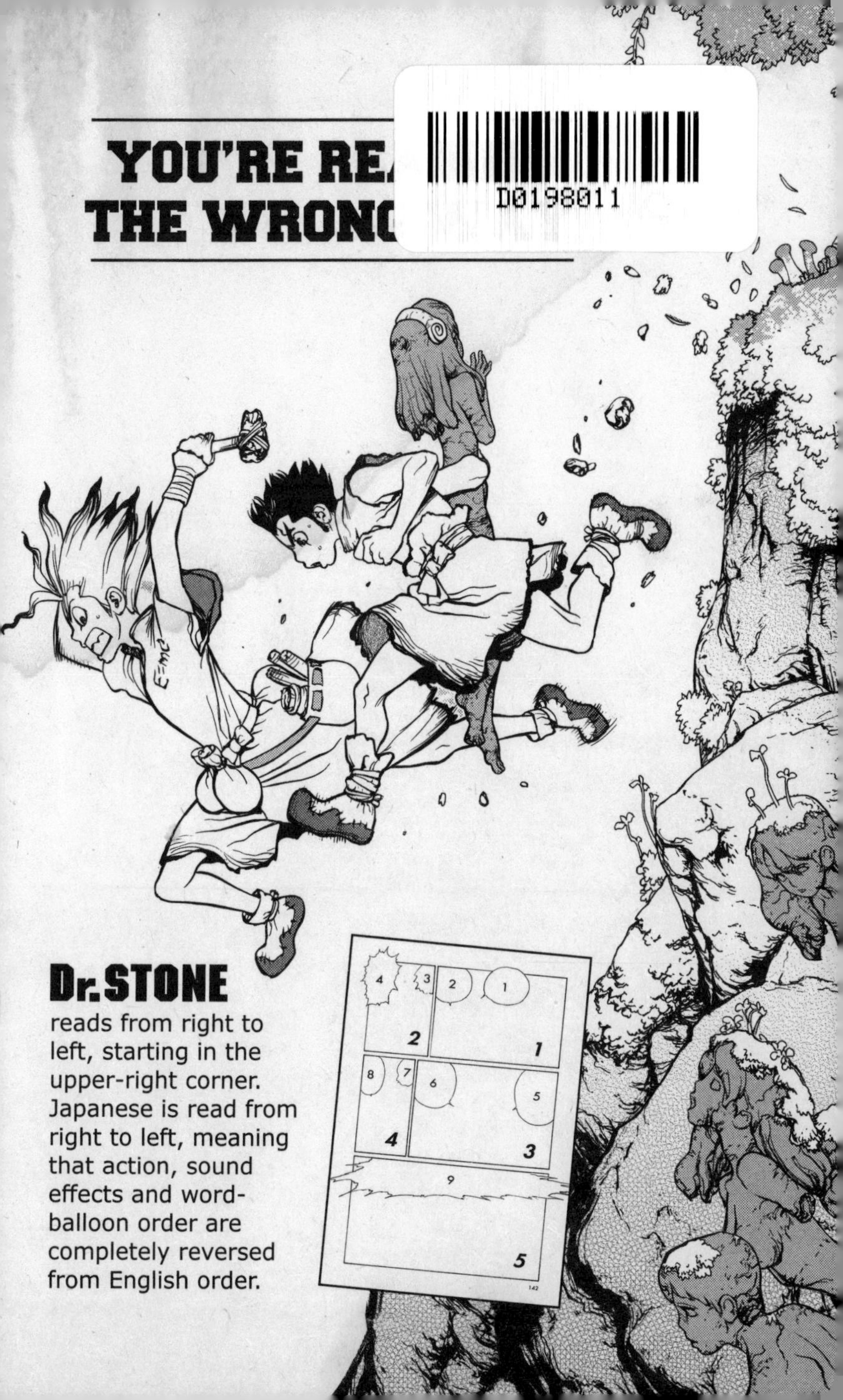

YOU'RE REA
THE WRONG

Dr.STONE

reads from right to left, starting in the upper-right corner. Japanese is read from right to left, meaning that action, sound effects and word-balloon order are completely reversed from English order.